A HISTORY BOOK FOR SCOTS

The selections in this book are taken from

SCOTICHRONICON
by
WALTER BOWER

New edition in Latin and English
with notes and indexes

General Editor: D E R WATT

Vol 1	Books I - II (1993)
Vol 2	Books III - IV (1989)
Vol 3	Books V - VI (1995)
Vol 4	Books VII - VIII (1994)
Vol 5	Books IX - X (1990)
Vol 6	Books XI - XII (1991)
Vol 7	Books XIII - XIV (1996)
Vol 8	Books XV - XVI (1987)
Vol 9	Critical Studies and General Indexes (1998)

(The publisher's imprint throughout is Aberdeen University Press, though since the collapse of that firm in 1992 the volumes have been issued by Mercat Press of Edinburgh.)

A HISTORY BOOK FOR SCOTS

SELECTIONS FROM

SCOTICHRONICON

Walter Bower

EDITED BY D E R WATT

MERCAT PRESS
EDINBURGH

This selection from *Scotichronicon*
first published in 1998 by Mercat Press
53 South Bridge, Edinburgh EH1 1YS

British Library Cataloguing in Publication Data
A catalogue record for this book is available from the British Library

ISBN 1873644 841

Typeset in Times New Roman 10.5 point at Mercat Press
Printed and bound in Great Britain by
Athenæum Press Ltd., Gateshead, Tyne & Wear

Contents

Preface x
Introduction xi

Prologue 1
The beginning of the book called *Scotichronicon* 1
Preface to the work 3

Book I
The legend of Gaythelos and Scota 5
The islands north-west of Europe 7
Simon Brecc and the Stone of Destiny 8
The origins of the Picts 9
The arrival of the Scots in Albion 10
King Fergus I of the Scots 11

Book II
War between the Britons and the Scots and Picts 12
'Fulgentius', the Emperor Severus and the Wall 13
A quarrel over a dog 16
St Regulus and the relics of St Andrew 16

Book III
King Fergus son of Erc 21
St Columba and St Kentigern 22
Why the English have tails 23
The proper cure of souls 24
The murder of King Fergus by his wife 25
Charlemagne 26
St Bridget's rules about fighting pagans 29
The Pictish royal succession 31

Book IV
The Scottish royal succession 33
The stratagem of King Kenneth son of Alpin 34
The church at Abernethy 37
King Hungus and the battle at Athelstaneford 37
King Indulf and the Danes and Norwegians 39
King Kenneth II and the succession 40
The assassination of Kenneth II by Finuele 40

A satire on the dress of the English 42
Kingly right 44
The vice of treachery 46
The prodigality of King Malcolm II 47
The life and death of King Duncan I 48
The duties of a king 50
The rule of Macbeth and the exile of Malcolm 51
The exile of MacDuff 52

Book V

Malcolm III defeats Macbeth 55
The marriage of Malcolm and Margaret 57
The virtuous works of Malcolm and Margaret 58
A judicial duel involving Edgar the Ætheling 60
King Alexander I and Alexander Scrimgeour 62
Alexander I and Scone 63
The last days of King David I 64
The saintly King David I 66

Book VI

The young St Waltheof 69
St Waltheof's vision of a baby 70
Fordun's address to the Scottish kings 71
Maurice bishop of Le Mans 73
St Waltheof at Melrose 75
Bower's abhorrence of perjury 76
The division of the see of Dunkeld 78
Bishop Walter Trayl of St Andrews 80
Prior Robert de Montrose of St Andrews 81
Prior James Biset of St Andrews 83

Book VII

The vision of Dryhthelm of Melrose 87
The vision of the Emperor Charles the Fat 89
Two beggars and the body of St Martin 92
William Rufus and new shoes 93
King William's dream and death 94
The conversion of a Cistercian monk 95
How parents should be honoured 96
Thunder at Dunfermline 97

Book VIII

Malcolm IV and Henry II 99
Pope Adrian IV on the misery of power 100

Epitaph on Malcolm IV 101
The sin of pluralism 102
The captivity of King William I 105
The council at Northampton 1176 107
King William and Donald MacWilliam 111
Philip II and the Jews 112
Philip II and the abbacy of St Denis 113
More examples of simony 114
Fighting in Galloway 116
Peace in England and Scotland 1193-99 117
Philip II and a vineyard 118
A bishop of Paris and his mother 118
William I and Harald earl of Caithness 119
Diplomatic relations with England 1209 121
Flooding at Perth in 1209 124
William I and Guthred MacWilliam 125
King William's problems with King John 126

Book IX

King William's death; inauguration of King Alexander II 128
King Philip II and virtuous recreation 129
Scottish churchmen and legates 1217-18 131
Cistercian monks and the eating of meat 134
The murder of Adam bishop of Caithness 135
More stories about King Philip II 137
King Alexander II attacks Galloway 138
King Louis IX and the Jews 139
The Bissets 140
Epitaph on Alexander II 143

Book X

Inauguration of King Alexander III 145
The translation of the mortal remains of St Margaret 147
Good and bad counsellors 149
The Comyns seize Alexander III 150
The battle of Largs 152
End of Norse rule in the Western Isles 155
Robin Hood and Little John 156
The right regard of prelates for royal authority 157
Gamelin and William Wischard bishops of St Andrews 159
Wischard and the canonical offence of pluralism 160
The Bruces earls of Carrick 164
Bagimond the papal collector, and stories about papal legates 165

Second marriage and death of Alexander III 167
The merits of Alexander III: the prophecy of Thomas the Rhymer 168

Book XI

The Interregnum and Great Cause 173
The humiliation of John Balliol 180
The Siege of Berwick 182
Battle of Dunbar; Balliol and Bruce; King John's abdication 183
William Wallace 185

Book XII

More on William Wallace 194
Stirrings of Bruce 195
Bruce and Comyn 196
Bruce's inauguration and desperate deeds 198
Reflections on Bruce's hardships 200
The ups and downs of worldly honour 201
The capture of Perth 203
The Battle of Bannockburn 204
James de Douglas and William de Sinclair 207
Edward de Bruce; Celebrations at St Andrews 208

Book XIII

Tit for tat 1322 210
Death of Robert I 211
The Guardian Thomas Randolph 212
James de Douglas and King Robert's heart 216
The perfidious English 216
Siege of Loch Leven castle 218
Inchcolm and English raiders 220
Black Agnes of Dunbar 222
Robert Prenderguest and sanctuary at Holyrood 223
Alan Steersman and Guardian Andrew de Moray 225
William de Douglas and William Bullock 226
A Bruce imposter and a Seton heiress 227

Book XIV

The battle of Neville's Cross 229
The Black Death: first and second occurrences 230
A papal appointment to Dunfermline Abbey 232
The battle of the Thirty 233
The Burnt Candlemas 234
Sons of Lindsay and Kirkpatrick 235
Floods at Haddington 236

A revolt against David II; plans for his succession 237
Choice of a wife 239
Good wives 243
Queen Margaret Logie 246
Robert II and his family 246
The Peasants' Revolt in England 247
An English invasion 1384 250
Invasion of Scotland by Richard II 1385 253
The prowess of William Douglas 254
The battle of Otterburn 255

Book XV

Aftermath of the coronation at Scone 1390 257
Clan fight at Perth 258
The pseudo-Richard II 259
Death of the duke of Rothesay 260
The character of Robert III 262
Founding of the University of St Andrews 263
Storks at St Giles in Edinburgh 265
Scottish forces in France 265
'Le qwhew' 266
The battle of Verneuil 267
Joan of Arc 268
Robert duke of Albany 270
The merits of the mass 270

Book XVI

Address to King James II 273
The marriage of Princess Margaret 274
Reflections on taxation 276
Reflections on legislation 278
Reflections on a battle in Strathnaver 279
The burning of Paul Kravar 280
A debate over foreign policy 280
The assassination of James I 282
The merits of James I 284
A poetic epitaph on King James I 287
Epilogue 288

Index 291

Preface

The very extensive literary work in Latin called *Scotichronicon* compiled in Scotland by Walter Bower in the 1440s has rightly been described as one of the country's national treasures. It was designed for reading by Scots—in those days Latin was not for educated people the barrier to understanding that it has become in recent times—but it contains not just a history of Scotland. The author ranges widely back in time to the days of the ancient Roman Empire, and to later developments on the Continent that had their effects on thinking and action in Scotland. And he offers reflections on the implications of these developments for the Scotland of his day. Hence the whole work adds up to 'A History Book for Scots', which is the title chosen for this book of extracts, through which modern Scots in their turn may hope to enlarge their understanding of their nation's characteristics.

The translated passages selected here from the full work provide a taster of the variety of the whole. Their presentation is enhanced by the design of the book's cover, which is based on aspects of an illustration of the departure of the mythical Scota and Gaythelos from Egypt which was inserted in the manuscript that was Bower's own working copy of the book. This is now MS 171 in the library of Corpus Christi College, Cambridge, and the illustration is used here by kind permission of the Master and Fellows of that College. More information about this and the other illustrations in this manuscript is to be found in the volumes of the full edition of the *Scotichronicon* published between 1987 and 1998 (see details opposite the title-page above).

Introduction

Walter Bower (1385-1449) was born and brought up at Haddington in East Lothian. About 1400 he joined the community of Augustinian canons who served the cathedral at St Andrews. He was one of the first students of the university there after its foundation in 1410, gaining degrees in both canon law and theology. Then in 1417 he secured a papal appointment as abbot of the small Augustinian monastery on the island of Inchcolm near the north shore of the Firth of Forth opposite Aberdour in West Fife. As holder of this office for thirty years until his death, he was one of the magnates of Scotland who attended the king's councils and parliaments, and was employed by King James I from 1424 onwards on financial and judicial business of the government. The assassination of the king in 1437 led to much confusion in public affairs during the long minority of the young heir James II. Though Bower still went out and about in the years that followed until his death, he must have devoted most of his time to literary work, whether on Inchcolm or using the monastic libraries that were available in such places as nearby Dunfermline Abbey and his old community at St Andrews Cathedral. This was the period when with the help of at least one of the canons of Inchcolm as his scribe he compiled the massive historical work which he called the *Scotichronicon*.

We do not know why he adopted this ambiguous title for the very extensive composition which he produced in two versions—a full version running to sixteen sections called 'books', and an abridged and re-arranged version divided into forty shorter 'books'. But the whole work does not add up to just a history of Scotland, even if that is certainly part of its characteristics. Bower was concerned also to inform his fellow-Scots about aspects of European history from the time of the late Roman Empire onwards which he thought they should know about, so that more familiar developments in Scotland should be appreciated in context. He does sometimes refer to people and events in England; but his focus is much more on the Continent and beyond—even as far away as Palestine in the days of the Crusades. Some space is allocated to critical stages in the history of the medieval Empire and of the Western Church as a whole under the Papacy; but Bower's main Continental emphasis is on developments in France. This can reasonably be explained as a cultural offshoot of the Franco-Scottish Alliance that was a central feature of Scottish policy from the end of the thirteenth century onwards, and was no doubt a consequence of the fact that most of the university teachers at St Andrews in Bower's time as a student were graduates of the University of Paris. This aim of putting Scottish history into a meaningful context, which characterises Bower's whole approach, justifies the choice here of an interpretative title for this collection of extracts from his curiously-named composition. These extracts are intended not just to illustrate Bower's narrative style or analytical skill, but also his thoughts about the past in terms of lessons to be learned for his own day. Modern readers can regard this collection as a trailer for dipping into the complete *Scotichronicon*, or as an illuminating work in its own right. Certainly Bower hoped that readers of any period would learn things to their advantage from his writing, whilst at the same time deriving pleasure from it. Non-Scots are of course welcome to share in this benefit!

How does this work by Bower fit into the Scottish historiographical tradition? We know that he incorporated with additions an earlier chronicle put together in the 1360s by John de Fordun, a supposed chaplain of Aberdeen cathedral. This covered in finished form the story of the Scottish nation from its mythical origins down to the death of King David I in 1153, and Fordun collected also some more scrappy annals covering the further two hundred years to his own time. His work remains of fundamental importance for study of the early centuries of Scottish history; but he did not include all the information that was available in his day, for Bower was able to find and incorporate materials (not least official documents) supplementary to Fordun's annals from 1153 onwards which provide a story down to the death of King James I in 1437 on a much more substantial scale than Fordun was able to offer.

It is characteristic of both writers that they sought to develop the literary effect of their chronicles by offering quotations from the Bible and the works of both classical and medieval authors, which were intended to broaden the reader's appreciation of the significance of the historical information that was being provided. Fordun is not known to have had a university education; but Bower's much wider literary range is first-hand evidence for the wide scope of the intellectual training offered from its beginning by Scotland's first university. Scottish readers were through his work introduced to an impressive range of helpful allusions and parallels, however it was that Bower had come across them. He was also a practised preacher who had collections of telling anecdotes to hand (especially those put together in France in the mid-thirteenth century by Vincent of Beauvais and Thomas of Cantimpré), from which he selected vivid illustrations of points that he wished to make. These anecdotes certainly help to make the *Scotichronicon* a good read.

Bower's work was compiled a few decades before the invention and spread of printing. We are fortunate in the survival of his manuscript working copy (kept since the Reformation in Corpus Christi College, Cambridge), for it helps us to understand how this vast work was put together. Manuscript copies of both this full version and the abridged version (especially the copy made originally for Coupar Angus Abbey before 1480) were commissioned by various individuals and religious institutions between Bower's death in 1449 and 1510. The work appears to have then fallen out of fashion, for no more manuscript copies are known to have been made, and it was only in the 1750s that the first full printed edition of the Latin text (without a translation) was published in Edinburgh in two folio volumes. That edition has served academic Scottish historians well for more than two hundred years. But then about twenty-five years ago a move was made by a group of some dozen scholars to share in the production of a fully modern edition of the Latin text with an English translation and a wealth of explanatory notes, so that now readers both in Scotland and the world over can sample the five thousand pages of this new edition in nine volumes which were published between 1987 and 1998.

The interest of each item in this collection of extracts from this new English translation is explained in the introductory notes. The choice of items is entirely subjective. Some deal with vital personalities or stages in the history of Scotland, from the telling of which the reader can form a view of Bower's interests and attitudes—his hostility to the English reflects the outlook of educated Scots who took part in public affairs in the fifteenth century. Then writing as a holy abbot he reveals his own priorities as a leading churchman, probably quite typical of his time with his views and prejudices. He is also a man who, though he is not known ever to have travelled outside Scotland, demonstrates a broad appreciation of matters of the intellect that must surely have been typical also of the interests of those who took part in the great experiment of founding the first university in their native country. His literary standards in so vast a Latin work are being studied seriously now that a modern edition is available: they should not be harshly judged on the basis alone of the translation made available here, for the aim of the editors of the new edition has simply been to reproduce the meaning and style of the Latin as accurately as possible, even if the English is sometimes ponderous and complex. The text follows closely the corrections made by Bower himself in his Latin working copy; where he introduced further revisions for his abridged version, or where the editors have used their discretion to clarify puzzling passages, such variations from the norm are marked by inclusion within square brackets.

St Andrews
September 1998.

Prologue and Preface

Prologue

Bower announces right away that he intends to incorporate in his book called Scotichronicon *the materials collected in the 1360s by John de Fordun, whose work in fact has no title in the surviving manuscripts, but is known to historians today in two sections usually called his* Chronicle *and his* Annals. *Bower incorporated his own additions from the beginning, so that in the end by far the bulk of the work is his. It is notable that the work was commissioned by the presumably literate layman Sir David Stewart, the laird of Rosyth in West Fife and so a neighbour of Bower at Inchcolm. (The Piso family in classical times were patrons of the poet Horace.) Any presentation copy for Sir David may or may not have been ready before his death early in 1444; certainly it does not exist now; but we do have the working copy that was kept in the library in Inchcolm Abbey with many marginal additions made after that date. In this copy he takes the trouble as described here in the first five books to distinguish passages from Fordun's* Chronicle *from his own additions; but he drops this practice when he comes to incorporating the* Annals.

The beginning of the book called Scotichronicon

Lest I write what is worthless, guide, Holy Virgin, my hand.
Guide my hand, direct my heart, Virgin Mary, I pray.

Here begins the book called *Scotichronicon*, begun by sir John de Fordun, chaplain of the church of Aberdeen, of worthy memory, and also continued, compiled and completed by the venerable father in Christ Walter Bower, abbot of the monastery of Inchcolm, also of worthy memory etc.

I am, I confess, a debtor, not through necessity but compelled by love. The debt-collector ought not to be harsh in compulsion, when the debtor is ready and willing to pay. So I must pay what I promised, and I have agreed to satisfy the urgent requests of the noble knight Sir David Stewart of Rosyth, that is to transcribe the following famous historical work recently and excellently begun by the venerable orator sir John Fordun, priest, clearly and elegantly written as a chronicle in five books. And not only, as I said before, to transcribe but also to continue the work right up to the present day, particularly since after completing his fifth book he left a great deal of written material, which had however not yet been everywhere arranged, but by means of which a careful investigator could easily continue the work to the aforementioned time. To him therefore after God will be ascribed the glory of the work, the elegant style of which I would judge to deserve not only the praise but also the admiration of the wisest men. Accordingly I shall insert at this point the following story. On a certain occasion when some men knowledgeable in scholarly matters met together, and were discussing the merits of the compiler of this book, there was among them a certain venerable scholar who said: 'I was well acquainted with the man whom you are rating so highly, the author of the book about which you are talking and almost boasting. He was an undistinguished man, and not a graduate of any of the schools.' He was given the following answer in my presence by one of those listening: 'This work of which he was the author is sufficient proof of the quality of his scholarship. In this work he puts into practice what Seneca says in an epistle. It is not the education of the schools but incessant reading that he calls learning. He would say that the man who expresses the most meaning in a few words is the best orator. This in my opinion at any rate is what the author of the work has done.' And this is how that book won the approval of all educated men, gaining for him the title of scholar and the name of orator, although he was not looking for it. 'I am a liar,' says Jerome, 'if Horace does not also feel the same as I do for instructing those Pisos and for restraining us.' That is to say that some people are always learners and never attain knowledge. While they criticise the judgment of others, they are happy with their own, and think that they know something. But just as teachers listen only to themselves, and boastfully rely on their own feeble intellects, so they set no value or very little on the writings or speeches of other people, but value their own very highly. Yet on the contrary it is the mark of the wise and well-educated man to compare his own writings with those of a master, and to derive form and method in them and with them and from them, and to imitate the arrangement both of the ideas and of the actual words, and to follow the construction. And so in my own case I feel that I am [following] far behind in a very different landscape; yet I am imitating the style of those I wish to emulate in the zeal of God, but especially imitating the style of the author of this book; and if I have not been able to achieve such great scholarship as he or those [other authors] either in this work or in other exercises, I have nevertheless wished to follow [in his footsteps], and I shall go on following him. But in the material which I add, may my patron forgive me if it should happen while I am transcribing this historical work that I insert here and there what occurs to me while I am writing. Since this task has been undertaken for myself and for the place in which by the will of

God I serve, I intend that it should be deposited with the librarian, especially since I am not intending (Heaven forbid!) to disparage even in the slightest such an excellent work, executed with such careful attention and such eloquent style, because when I insert something of my own in his work as it now stands, I shall preface it with the attribution 'WRITER', since not I but another is the 'AUTHOR'. Also whatever of my own I have interposed, I shall distinguish with a different style of handwriting, <or I shall mark with a line whatever I put in of my own up to the point where I affix the note 'AUTHOR' or 'WRITER',> so that in this way my patron the knight or anyone else whosoever who wishes to copy the present manuscript will easily be able both to omit my insertions, and bring the work begun by the master to completion on its own.

Preface to the work

Bower presents his readers with his literary creed and his ambitions as an historian. (Ennodius was a sixth-century writer in Italy.) The book is designed as a useful guide for leaders of society in general, but also as a good read for anyone.

As Ennodius bishop of Pavia writes: 'To write more than one needs to is vanity; to suppress what is necessary shows disdain.' So that I may avoid the infamy of the first fault, and not neglect criticism arising from the second fault, and trusting in God's help, I set my hand joyfully to valiant deeds in accordance with my promises, so that I may be able to complete this work successfully, since I consider that, as someone says: 'Joy gives eloquence which is denied by cleverness', and that application is the mother of arts, but carelessness is the stepmother of learning. Therefore to the honour of God, to the comfort of the king and the kingdom, and also to satisfy the request of the renowned knight who urges me on to attack a work to which I am so unaccustomed, and also to refresh myself in clear intervals, worn out and beset as I may be at times by various cares, and as a warning to and for the edification of future readers I attack this work. To begin with:

I beg the reader to ask Christ with faithful lips
that He may give the writer after death the joys of Heaven.
Let each pray that the writer may be given for his reward,
may be given sound faith, a good conscience and grace.

In particular I shall not aim in my writings at beauty of style with brilliant diction, but I shall try to devote my attention to the true riches of different historians and to events known to me otherwise. Indeed the chronicles by themselves are so brilliant, vouched for by the names of the writers, that they do not need the lustre of an elaborate style to delight the hearts of readers. In addition to this the artlessness of an uncultivated style has usually removed all suspicion of falsification. For how could anyone who is quite unable to produce a polished style know how to fabricate fiction? In this volume, I believe, rulers will find how to avoid the dangers of war and uncertain issues, religious will learn the rudiments of the monastic life, laymen will learn fruitful lessons, preachers will find tales with a moral. By force of its example kings will become more cautious, religious will be instructed more in accordance with their rule, and all those who are depressed will be given over to joy by reading it.

Book I

The legend of Gaythelos and Scota

Bower (following Fordun) cites many variants of the foundation legend of the Scottish kingdom. The following selection of extracts threads its way through the main story. Pharaoh Chencres cannot now be identified. Brigantia is the modern Corunna in north-west Spain (i.e. not in fact on the river Ebro, but looking north to Ireland). The explanation of the division between Gaels and Scots comes from Gerald of Wales, Topographia Hibernica.

From various writings of ancient chroniclers we deduce that the nation of the Scots is of ancient stock, taking its first beginning from the Greeks and those of the Egyptians who were left after the rest of them had been drowned in the Red Sea along with their king.

In the third age in the time of Moses there was a certain king of one of the kingdoms of Greece called Neolus or Eolaus. He had a son who was good looking but mentally unstable, Gaythelos by name. Since he had not been permitted to hold any position of power in the kingdom, he was provoked to anger, and with the support of a large company of young men he inflicted many disasters on his father's kingdom with frightful cruelty. He greatly outraged both his father and the inhabitants [of the country] with his violent behaviour. So he was driven out of his native land and sailed off to Egypt; and there, since he was outstandingly brave and daring and also of royal descent, he was united in marriage with Scota the daughter of the Pharaoh Chencres.

The aforesaid Pharaoh was drowned with his armies including 600 chariots, 50,000 cavalry and 200,000 infantry. Now those who survived by staying at home, hoping to be freed from the servitude of the corn-tax formerly imposed by Joseph in time of famine, unexpectedly drove the king's son-in-law Gaythelos Glas (who wished to pursue the innocent Hebrews) right out of the kingdom along with his followers for fear that he might establish dominion over them. So all the nobles both Greek and Egyptian alike whom the voracious sea had failed to devour were cruelly driven away by peasants enrolled in a servile uprising.

So Gaythelos gathered together all his followers and left Egypt with his wife Scota. Because he was afraid to return to the regions from which he had come to Egypt because of old feuds, he directed his course westwards, where he knew there were fewer and less warlike peoples with whom he would have to fight, since the men there were untrained in fighting.

The legend of St Brendan: 'Now Gaythelos was driven from Egypt and after sailing in this way over the Mediterranean Sea he landed in Spain. He built a tower on the River Ebro, having seized by force from the inhabitants a place for his settlement called Brigantia. There his descendants multiplied greatly...He summoned his sailors and ordered them to take arms, to provision small ships with all speed and to explore the boundless Ocean in search of uninhabited lands. They went off to their ships, unfurled their sails and left the Spanish shore. Leaving behind the known, they made for unknown regions over the sea. After sailing with good speed and guided by the favour of the gods they saw an island rising up in the distance surrounded on all sides by salt sea. They put into a nearby harbour on this island and after beaching their ships went all round exploring the island. After seeing as much of the island as they could they sailed quickly back to Brigantia, reporting to their king Gaythelos on the very beautiful tract of land that they had found in Ocean.'

But Gaythelos was overtaken by sudden death. Before this he urged his sons to invade the aforesaid land with armed force, accusing them of laziness and cowardice if they gave up such a notable kingdom which they could enter without fighting or any danger.

The legend of Brendan says: 'One of the sons of Gaythelos called Hiber, young in years but strong of purpose, was roused to war and took up arms. He got ready an expedition as best he could and approached the aforesaid island. He killed some of the few inhabitants whom he found and enslaved the rest, but he claimed the whole land as a possession for himself and his brothers, calling it Scotia after his mother's name.'

In the book of the miracles of Ireland I have found it written as follows—that the Hibernians are also called Gaitheli and Scoti.

> As ancient histories record, after the confusion of languages in Nimrod's tower [Babel] Gaythelos the grandson of Phenius became highly skilled in a variety of languages. Because of his skill the king Pharaoh gave him his daughter and heir Scota as his wife. So since the Hibernians are originally descended from Gaythelos and Scota, they are named Gaitheli [Gaels] and Scoti [Scots] according to their birth. Gaythelos, so they say, invented the Hibernian language which is also called Gaelic, that is to say compiled from all languages.

The reason for what was once upon a time called Albany now being called Scotia is found in the same passage: 'The northern part of the island of Britain is called Scotia because that land is known to have been inhabited by a people originally descended from the Scoti. This is demonstrated by the affinity of both language and culture, of arms and customs right up to the present day.' (c.1, ll.1-4; c.9, ll.1-12; c.11, ll.4-13; c.12, ll.20-24; c.15, ll.17-21; c.16, ll.21-32; c.17, ll.9-13; c.18, ll.21-27, 47-62)

The islands north-west of Europe

Bower is careful to avoid any suggestion that Scotland had ever been dominated by Britain or formed part of England. Thule has been variously identified. Kilrymont is the old name for St Andrews in Fife. Bower himself presided over the Augustinian canons of Inchcolm.

Europe also has many large islands, the largest of which is Albion situated in Ocean in the north-west. Its southern and larger part was once inhabited by Britons and called Britannia, but its name now is England. The northern part was inhabited from antiquity by the Scots and was called Scotland, which at the present time also is a kingdom ruled by its own prince under the protection of God. The Scots also have many islands to the number of one hundred or more in their possession from ancient times. Beyond their shores in the north-west there is no land to be found except for a certain island, so men say, called Thule seven days' sailing time away from them. One day's sailing time beyond that, they say, the sea is motionless and solid.

Of these islands the following are said to be and are royal islands namely Iona or I or I Colmekill, on which St Columba built a monastery, and which was the burial place and royal seat of the kings of Pictavia and Scotland right up to the time of King Malcolm the husband of St Margaret. Also the island of Bute on which there is a royal castle. Also the Isle of Man on which there is a royal castle and monastery. Also the Great and Little Cumbrae islands, Inchmarnock, the island of St Blaise of Pladda and Ailsa Craig. Besides the royal islands the larger islands are these—Islay, Tiree, Lewis, Skye, Oronsay, where there is a monastery of the Black Canons which St Columba founded, Jura, Gigha and St Kilda, which is known to be to the west-north-west on the very edge of the world, beyond which no land is to be found in these regions.

There are also other islands in an arm of a sea of Ocean which is called the Firth of Forth, namely Bass, Fidra, May, where the priory is a cell of the canons of St Andrew of Kilrymont, and where St Adrian is buried with his companions the hundred holy martyrs. There is another island twelve miles from there which is called Inchkeith, on which St Adomnan formerly ruled as abbot. He received St Servanus and his companions with honour on that island at his first arrival in Scotland. There is a third island as well towards the west six miles distant from Inchkeith, which is called Emonia, between Edinburgh and Inverkeithing, commonly called Inchcolm, on which there is a monastery of Black Canons of the order of St Augustine. There are also very many more islands scattered over Ocean, all of which I need not enumerate.

Also beyond Britain in Ocean between Britain and the west lies the island of Ireland where the Scots established their first settlement. (c.6, ll.9-45, 47-48)

Simon Brecc and the Stone of Destiny

Many supposed generations later comes a version of the story of Simon Brecc and the Stone of Destiny. The simile of an anchor is a variant of the classical metaphor of the ship of state. The particular place called Tara that is mentioned is uncertain. The prophecy about the influence of the whereabouts of the Stone in the future relates to the situation after 1296 when Edward I of England removed it from Scone to Westminster. But neither Fordun nor Bower could have imagined the Union of the Crowns of 1603—nor the return of the Stone to Scotland in 1996!

Now there was a king of the Scots in Spain called Milo who had several sons. Yet he loved one of them whose name was Simon Brecc more than all the others, although he was not the oldest nor the heir. So his father sent him to Ireland with an army, and presented him with a marble throne of very ancient workmanship, carved by a careful craftsman, on which the kings of the Scottish people in Spain used to sit. So it was kept carefully in its own particular place to be as it were an anchor. Now this Simon Brecc set out for the aforesaid island accompanied by a great crowd of people, and after subduing it under his rule he reigned there for many years. He placed the aforesaid stone, that is the throne, in a place in his kingdom of some height which was called Tara. For the future this was to be his royal seat and the chief place in his kingdom, and there the kings descended from his line used to have their seat throughout many ages, adorned with the insignia of royalty.

One story is that Gaythelos took this seat with him from Egypt to Spain together with the other royal appurtenances; but others say that Simon Brecc let down anchors from his ship and secured them in the sea near the Irish coast. When he was forced by adverse winds to pull them up again from the stormy waves, he only just managed to do so with the utmost possible effort, and along with the anchors he raised from the depths of the sea and pulled into the ship a block of marble cut in the shape of a chair. So he accepted this stone as a precious gift bestowed on him by the gods and as a sure omen that he would be king, and beside himself with excessive joy he gave solemn thanks to his gods with such great fervour, as if they had absolutely handed both the kingdom and the crown over to him. He also received there a prophecy about it from his gods, as is affirmed in writings, that in future in whatsoever kingdom or lordship they found the stone after it had been forcibly removed from them through the power of their enemies, the prophets bade them regard it as certain that they and their descendants would reign thereafter in that same place. This has been expressed in prophetic verse as follows:

> If destiny deceives not, the Scots will reign 'tis said
> in that same place where the stone has been laid.

And this according to the claims of popular opinion up to the present day is shown to have been true on many occasions in the early wanderings of the Scots. (c.28, ll.1-38)

The origins of the Picts

The version of the origin-legend of the Picts given here associates them with south-west France (and later specifically with the province of Poitou), and suggests that they moved from there via Ireland (already occupied by the Scots) to mainland Britain (called Albion here). Alternatively the Picts were thought to have originated in Scythia (i.e. the Ukraine).

After a long time had passed in which the Scots lived in peaceful and quiet prosperity, a certain unknown people, afterwards called the Picts, appeared from the lands of Aquitania and landed on the Irish shores from their ships. They humbly asked the elders for permission either to live by themselves in an uninhabited region or to live side by side with the Scots all over the island. For they said that they had recently been driven out of their own country by the strong hand of their enemies, although they had done nothing to deserve it, and they had been up to then afflicted by great and fearful dangers from storms at sea. The Scots would not however allow them to remain among them on the same island; but after admitting them to friendship and the protection of their peace they sent them across to the northern limits of Albion, hitherto uninhabited, along with some men given to them as companions. So, as the Picts began to inhabit the lands there and since they did not have any women of their own race with them, the Scots gave them their daughters as wives under a pact of eternal alliance and a special agreement about dowry. (c.30, ll.1-17)

The arrival of the Scots in Albion

The Scots crossed over from Ireland at first as wives of the Picts, but then in ever-increasing numbers of both sexes. This led the Picts to fear for their predominance and to attempt to drive the Scots out. A thousand years later they were themselves to be destroyed by the Scots under Kenneth son of Alpin in the mid-ninth century.

The daughters and other female relatives of the Scots whom the Picts took as their wives were gradually brought by their husbands to their own land. They were followed by countless numbers of their kinsfolk, fathers and mothers, brothers and sisters, nieces and nephews, and also many others who were not only motivated by love for a daughter or sister, but rather they were very strongly attracted by the grassy fertility and abundant pasture for their herds in the land of Albion for which they were heading. The number of people of both sexes following them and taking their cattle with them who went off in a short space of time to live with the Picts was larger than has ever been recorded as having left their own land without a leader. But their number was also increased by an endless succession of criminals, because anyone who was in fear of incurring the penalty of the law went off to live with the Picts scot-free. Then they sent for their wives and children and remained there peacefully never again to return. Meanwhile the Picts bitterly resenting the arrival of such large numbers (for they were gripped by fear of the Scots) ordered it to be proclaimed that in future no foreigner was ever to obtain permanent settlement in their land. And to those who had previously agreed to stay with them of their own accord, they gave every opportunity to depart. For when they first came into the island, they understood from oracular responses made by their gods (or rather demons) to whom they sacrificed before engaging in any kind of action, that if they did not succeed in overcoming the Scots, they would be utterly destroyed by them. And so observing that the number of Scots in their midst was increasing, they began to be more and more afraid and drove them out of their land with violence. This [prophecy] was proved true, not immediately but a thousand years later, when their race together with their language was then utterly destroyed by the Scots. (c.32)

King Fergus I of the Scots

It was to provide assistance to the Scots who were being persecuted by the Picts in Albion that Fergus came over from Ireland to well-wooded Argyll to establish himself as first king of the Scots there.

Moreover while the Picts were inflicting injuries and hardships of this kind on the Scots colonists, news was secretly brought to the chiefs of their nation concerning the nature and extent of the misery the Scots were living through because of the Picts. And also at the same time certain people arrived who described to them the beauty of a region so extensive and of such great fertility in which there were only birds, wild beasts and animals, and which could easily be brought into cultivation. So when a certain nobleman Fergus son of Feraghad or Ferard who was descended from the line of ancient kings heard that a tribe of his own nation without anyone to lead or govern them were spending their time wandering through the desert wildernesses of Albion, after having been thrown out by the Picts, he began to blaze with anger in his heart. He had in addition been greatly attracted by the good report concerning that region in which he had perhaps the intention to rule, which was pronounced to be very fertile by those who had seen it, except for the fact that all the ground at that time was covered with very dense forests. We have clear proof of this right up to the present day whenever huge tree roots and trunks happen to be found underground, often even in the most level places, where the earth has been dug out or excavated by chance and that too where you would say that there is not a sign that forests had ever grown before. So inspired by these encouragements and by the ambition to rule he gathered to his side a great company of young men and proceeded immediately to Albion. There he separated out the Scots already living there from among the Picts and settled them along with those he had brought with him in the western territory of the island and set himself up as the first king over them in that place. (c.36)

Book II

War between the Britons and the Scots and Picts

Bower follows Fordun's account of a long period of strife (vaguely dated 53-208 A.D.) between the Britons under Roman occupation and the Scots and Picts. In fact the Romans never invaded Ireland—the suggestion here that they did is an example of sources being misunderstood at some stage.

Around about this time, that is in the twelfth year of Claudius's reign, the war of the Britons against the Scots and Picts is said to have arisen. It continued for one hundred and fifty-four years right up to the fifteenth year of Severus's reign without any intervening interval of stable peace. At any rate it began in this way as follows: Vespasian was sent across to Britain with various legions by the emperor Claudius. After all rebellion had been stamped out, he reimposed the annual payment of tribute on the Britons, and returned to Rome. He left part of his army there to defend the country, with instructions to force subservience on the Irish people with the help of the Britons, and likewise on the Scots and Picts, or else to destroy them. Finally the Britons in company with the Romans advanced on Ireland, where various defeats were inflicted and suffered on both sides, but they achieved little or no success. From there they returned to the neighbouring regions of the kingdom of the Scots and the Picts, and because these peoples refused to submit to the Romans, they spread destruction everywhere with fires, slaughter and rapine. Meanwhile as the wars waged by the Romans and the Britons intensified, the fierce nations of the Irish, Picts and Scots, who were driven by the same need to act together, united in a very strong alliance against the Romans, since a three-ply rope is difficult to break, and began to devastate the whole of Britain. For with the Irish bursting in from the west, the Scots from the west-north-west, and the Picts from the north, they divided the various parts of the kingdom amongst themselves, and destroyed the people with pitiable slaughter. They spared neither women nor the tender age of children, but consumed everything that they laid hands on either with the edge of the sword or with fire. Not unnaturally the Romans in their turn did all they could to inflict a comparable disaster on them, and burnt to the ground everything in sight except for earth and stones, or slew everyone everywhere with the sword.

Then there was a most savage war between them, the like of which had never been heard of before, nor has anything as cruel as or more cruel than it ever been recorded in the histories of the whole world. The ordinary people of both nations, whose proper pursuit was just agriculture, not killings and wars, were absolutely exposed on all sides to plundering and pillage. These wretches, the scum of the common herd, who did not know how to be of use to the city dwellers or to do any harm to the enemy, were slain without mercy. The remnant of the people, who were able by any means to escape the sharp edge of the sword, deprived as they were of any protection, lurked silently in mountains, caves and remote corners. They supported life miserably, well content with grass roots, fruit, the leaves and bark of trees, with acorns and wild honey, which was found in tree trunks or among reeds, or with the milk of any animal they might happen to have. And so it happened that, once the tillers of the fields had been cut down by the sword, as described above, or had run away, the citizens, shut in behind the strongest city walls, and the guardians of the towns were reduced to such great deprivation of famine and hunger that with no thought of their homes and all their wealth and possessions, but wishing to save themselves, their wives and their children from this disaster, they took them off to remote regions far away. Meanwhile the cities, having been quite often stripped of their defenders in this way and abandoned except for a few simpletons who were devoid of all skill in defence, were surrounded by the enemy. Their ferocity did not give the cities peace for very long. They united their forces and easily climbed the walls, which were immediately utterly destroyed. They scattered the stones in the ditches, and levelled the walls with the ground. And the witnesses for this disaster are the strongest cities of the Britons, namely Agned, which was restored by Aed king of the Scots, and was later called Aedinburgh or Edinburgh, Carlisle also and Aluclud or Aldclide, which is now called Dumbarton, and very many towns which they levelled with the ground, and which have not yet been rebuilt by anyone. (c.28 - c.29, ll.1-34)

'Fulgentius', the Emperor Severus and the Wall

Bower takes over Fordun's development of the story (dated 180-211) of 'Fulgentius', a supposed leader of discontented Britons against their Roman masters (in fact a character invented by Geoffrey of Monmouth), who allied with the Scots and Picts. The Emperor Severus restored the defences of the wall erected by Hadrian in 122-8 in an attempt to defend the province of Britain from attacks from the north. This did not prevent an invasion by boats across the river Tyne and the death of Severus at York in 211.

In the time of the preceding emperor Commodus civil dissension began to arise in Britain among the Britons because of the payment of tribute. For after the death or disappearance, as we find elsewhere, of their own king Lucius, after whom their royal line ceased to reign in Britain, tribunes were appointed there by the Romans instead of kings. Meanwhile the consul or duke of the Britons of Albany, Fulgentius, who was descended from the lineage of their ancient kings, refused under any circumstances to pay tribute to the Romans, and denied that he had any obligation to do so, since he had never sworn any submission or allegiance to them. This made him unpopular with his fellow-citizens, and they determined to force him to pay his share of the tribute by seizing his lands. But he repaid them with interest, by not only repossessing his own land but also by plundering theirs in frenzied attacks upon them. Afterwards as a result of this there followed fierce pillages, seditions and arson with no mercy shown on either side, and they everywhere devoured everything and everyone in turn, and the Britons of the south were completely divided from the Britons of the north. The Scots together with the Picts in their usual way laid waste and devastated the territories of Fulgentius that were nearest to them with frequent incursions, carrying off countless plunder. Fulgentius could not endure this, since he was being assailed with wars on all sides, and so he entered upon an agreement with the Scots for the time being. And when peace had been established by this pact, he concentrated all his efforts on attacking the patricians of the Romans, who were ruling the country at that time, and their British allies. While these troubles arising out of civil dissension were taking place in Britain, the customary payment of the tribute, that was usually sent to the Romans each year, remained completely unpaid. Many of the Britons gave up their allegiance to Rome, following the example of Fulgentius and hoping in this way to be freed from subjection to the tributes.

When Severus succeeded to the imperial throne, as has been said, he found the state in complete confusion everywhere, and endeavoured with great exertions to restore order. So after he had put Pescennius Niger to death, as he was attempting to rebel in the regions of Egypt and Syria, he defeated and pacified the Parthians, Arabs and Adiabeni. He also crushed the Jews and Samaritans, while they were planning another rebellion; and, after putting down many rebellions throughout the whole of the Roman world, he defeated and killed Clodius Albinus, who had appointed himself emperor of the Gauls, in the city of Lyons. So civil wars were stamped out everywhere with the greatest diligence, while Britain alone remained out of control because of Fulgentius's revolt. The emperor summoned his council, and asked who among the generals of all the armed forces would consent to take command of the legions and go with him to Britain. When he failed to hear anyone saying that he was ready to go, he took up his sword and said:

'I am ready. Everyone of you make your preparations, and follow me. You will go with me.' And so he immediately set out for Britain. The reason for his coming did not however escape Fulgentius, but he was given advance warning by friends through messengers sent secretly ahead that he had no hope at all of standing up to the attack of such large numbers of combatants. Therefore he hurried off into Scotland, and entered upon a firm agreement of perpetual peace with the kings of the Scots and the Picts and of eternal fellowship with their nations, leaving behind his two sons as hostages meanwhile. Then, supported by a very large army, he returned to Britain to join battle with all speed. He went back and forth frequently on this kind of expedition, until he was prevented by the fortification of a very broad vallum built by Severus across the island, and then at first for a short time he ceased activity.

The emperor Severus at that time, after he had defeated Fulgentius and forced him to flee to Scotland, had built a vallum across the island between the two rivers the Tyne and Esk at either end, to prevent the appearance in future of an open area for his unrelenting enemies the Scots and the Picts or even the Britons of Albany to launch an attack upon his allies, as they had been accustomed to do. So Fulgentius, realising that his route overland to York had been cut off by the vallum, quickly got ready small boats laden with food, instruments of war and cavalry. The infantry and the rest of the commanders of the land army went with Fulgentius to the river, and constructed for their present purpose coracles, that is portable skiffs with frames made by weaving together rods and withies, which were then covered all round with tightly sewn skins. Each one of them was able to take across two men or at any rate one armed man and an oarsman. They successfully crossed the river before daylight, either rowing in these coracles or swimming in the darkness of night. Then when all the units had been marshalled, Fulgentius laid strong siege to the city of York, which he had previously lost, when it was attacked by Severus, and received back certain of his nobles who had previously deserted him, and now returned to their former allegiance to him. Encouraged by the great numbers of fighting men who accompanied him, they preferred to be on his side rather than that of the Romans. So a few days later while Fulgentius was intensifying the siege, and was diligently mounting an assault with large numbers of siege engines that had been previously prepared for scaling or breaching the walls of the city, the same Roman emperor, high-spirited as he was, rushed upon them with his men in a sudden attack, and was killed, after joining battle with Fulgentius.

Bede records that Severus died a natural death in the same city. But Geoffrey [of Monmouth] testifies in what follows that he was killed by Fulgentius, just as in the account given here. (cc.36-38)

A quarrel over a dog

This story of how a long peace, supposedly of five hundred years, between the Scots and Picts came to an end in the time of the Emperor Diocletian (284-305) with a quarrel over a hunting dog has not been traced further back than Fordun.

In the time of this Diocletian or a little before, while the nations of the Scots and Picts were living peacefully together in their two kingdoms, and protecting their regions on all sides with united strength, it happened by chance that on a pre-arranged day certain noblemen from both nations met together, as was their custom, on the borders of the [two] kingdoms for some hunting. While the dogs were unleashed and they were running about in all directions chasing wild beasts for about the length of a day, a certain hound, which used to follow the scent on the tracks of the beasts, was stolen away by the Picts, and was immediately discovered in their possession. When the Scots demanded it back, [the Picts] refused to return it. A dispute arose, and [the Scots] tried to snatch it from them by force. But the Picts for their part made no attempt to mitigate their wrong-doing by giving them satisfaction, but rather made matters worse by even greater savagery, and they lost no time in starting to fight. As a result many on both sides of those who had met together were slain by each other's swords. For this was the occasion and beginning of the first dispute between them, as we read, after they had lived together in unbroken peace for five hundred years, and had joined harmoniously together in resisting all other nations with their united power. But soon after this, just as formerly their friendship with each other was keenly fostered by frequent exchange of kind services, by the alliances between their children, by the strong bonds of matrimony and also by frequent reciprocal dinner parties, as if they were one people, so with all the more savagery their enmity increased from day to day with plunderings, arson, slaughter and ambushes, and various disturbances and eruptions. And although secure peace and terms of truces were frequently agreed between them, the situation deteriorated daily, so that the one people was exerting all its determination to destroy the other. (c.42, ll.17-46)

St Regulus and the relics of St Andrew

Bower elaborates Fordun's version of the Scottish legend of St Andrew, dating it in the mid-fourth century. The arrival of Andrew's relics in east Fife is made to precede both the establishment of the Scottish monarchy there and also the foundation of the other Scottish episcopal sees. Thus the see of St Andrews is awarded primacy. (Patras lay on the south shore of the Gulf of Corinth in Greece.) Regulus is not a historical figure: he is known only in this Scottish legend. Some link had to be established to explain why supposed relics of the apostle could have landed up in Scotland, for general belief in their authenticity made Kilrymont a place of international pilgrimage. (King Hurgust and King Hungus were probably originally one historical person in the sources behind the suggestion here that they were two kings who lived more than four hundred years apart.)

About the same time the emperor Constantius the son of Constantine the Great in the twentieth year of his reign, motivated by enthusiasm for the Christian religion, and inspired by a special devotion which he had conceived long before in his heart for the blessed apostle Andrew, longed to do something as final proof of his devotion. He went to the city of Patras in the district of Achaia, where the apostle was martyred and buried, and from there he stealthily removed by main force the saint's relics, translated them to Constantinople on 9 May, and amid great rejoicing and to the accompaniment of hymns and chants placed them in golden and silver reliquaries with great honour.

Achaia is one of the seven provinces of Greece, and almost an island, for it is surrounded by sea on all sides except for the north side, where it adjoins Macedonia.

Therefore when Christ had entrusted the world to his apostles and disciples to be steeped in the catholic faith by their preaching, he allotted to Andrew the area around the Caspian sea, Scythia, Macedonia and Achaia, and also, as some would have it, Scotland. Since, as was previously described, the Picts derived their origin from Scythia, Andrew wished even after his death to convert those whom he was not able to convert while he was alive. This Andrew was the apostle of the Lord, the brother of Simon Peter, older than Peter by birth and first to be called, but second in rank or at least third, Galilean by nationality, born in the city of Bethsaida, gentlest of all the disciples. He excelled almost everyone in justice, piety and sanctity. He was dark-complexioned, handsome of appearance, of medium height, with a luxuriant beard. The translation of certain of his bones from Patras to Scotland was as follows.

It happened that by divine will on the third night before the emperor entered the city, the angel of the Lord appeared to a certain holy, God-fearing man, an abbot Regulus by name, the guardian of the relics, saying: 'Take with you suitable brethren and proceed to the sarcophagus, in which the bones of blessed Andrew were deposited. You will take from there three fingers of the right hand and the arm-bone that hangs down from the shoulder, one tooth and a kneecap. Guard them carefully in a place which I shall show you, until I return.' He quickly summoned the chosen brethren, and carried off all the bones, just as he had been ordered to. He hid them in a very secret place indicated by the angel. So the emperor came two days later with quick-marching legions, and captured the city, emptying it of all its wealth. He received the reliquary in which the relics were stored, and ordered it to be taken back to Constantinople with suitable reverence, while he escorted it with the army.

Finally after several years had passed by, the celestial angel again came back to Abbot Regulus, and with an intimidating look on his face gave him the following command in the name of Almighty God and in these words: 'Take up again', he said, 'the relics of blessed Andrew beloved of God, which you recently preserved on my instructions. And take with you a praiseworthy escort of saints, and lose no time in going to the western regions under the west-north-west at the world's end; and wheresoever the ship that carries you by the will of God runs the risk of shipwreck, but with you and your companions remaining unharmed, know that there the course of your hardship, or at least of your prolonged voyage, has reached its successful conclusion. Moreover guard against being negligent or forgetful of this kind of instruction, namely that in that place you should firmly lay the foundations of a church to the honour of the divine name and the glory of his saint and apostle of everlasting veneration, because it will come to pass that, just as the east was for a long time adorned by the sound of his preaching, while he was alive, as you are aware, so know truly that the whole of the west will also be adorned for ever with the miracles worked by his relics. For since that place has been chosen by God, it will be an apostolic see for ever and a firm rock of the faith, and rightly so because of his brother blessed Peter to whom the Lord said: "You are Peter" etc. So the kingdom in which it is situated will be a steady, strong anchor, and it will be famous for its devotion to the apostle of all the faithful, especially the kings and other powers in the land, from whose estates and endowments it will be abundantly enriched. Therefore crowds of the faithful frequently coming there from abroad from the opposite ends of the world to receive bodily and spiritual health will miraculously receive what they have requested, and will return joyfully to their homes, praising God, who is always glorious in his saints, in his apostle with exultant voices.' And with these words the angel disappeared from his sight, and blessed Regulus addressed himself to carrying out his instructions. So wishing to obey the divine commands, he summoned to his side wise and religious men of preeminent learning and character, each of whom had been forewarned by angelic exhortation to take part in his pilgrimage and his merit. He carried the sacred relics with him to the ship, and put to sea, prepared to reach the regions of the west-north-west. The following are the sacred names of the company of saints: St Regulus, abbot, St Damian, priest, Gelasius and Chubaculus, deacons, Merniacus the brother of St Damian, Nerius and Elrisenius from Crete, Mirenus, Machabeus and Silvius his brother. There were eight hermits namely Felix, Sajanus, Matheus, Mauricius, Madianus, Philip, Luke and Eugenius, and three virgin saints from Colosia namely Triduana, Potencia and Emerea.

Those very saintly men together with the virgins went on board a ship laden with all necessary supplies, and sailed around the shores of Europe by way of the Mediterranean Sea, until they came, worn out by many hardships, to the islands situated in Ocean beneath the setting sun. And when they had been wandering for the space of almost two years over unknown seas, as the breeze chanced to take them, not knowing what was their goal, suddenly a fierce wind from the east rushed into their sails with unusual force. Under its violent impulse their boat was driven onto the kingdom of the Picts amid the rocks of the island of Albion, just as the angel had foretold, and was smashed to pieces. Given strength however by God, blessed Regulus reached land unharmed with his companions on 28 September in great joy, with the sign of the Lord's cross going on before. And there in a grove of pigs, which is called 'Mucross' in the native language, he later dedicated a church to the glory of the apostle. In this place there occurred many astounding miracles from touching the relics, such as had not been seen or heard of, since the adoption of the faith in these islands up to that time. For sight was given to those who were blind from birth, speech to the dumb, walking to the lame, and on all who piously sought the apostle's support, no matter with what infirmity they were afflicted, healing was immediately bestowed through the compassion of God. After frequent miracles of this kind occurred daily, people came from all the nations bearing gifts, clapping their hands, and as suppliants raising endless hymns of praise to God for such a patron.

For this reason the following lines are found to have been written in olden times at Rymont.

Here that bay of the sea was a barren shore,
which now surpasses the richest places of the world in fertility.
Here a region previously bare is now green. It was poor before
and is now rich. Long ago it was vile and is now beautiful.
Hither therefore come men who are lords of remote castles to pray,
a motley throng setting out from their native land.
The boastful Frank, the war-loving Norman,
the Flemish weaver and rough Teuton,
English, German, Dutch, the man from Poitou with no knowledge of
wool,

and the blood-thirsty man from Anjou,
those who drink the waters of Rhine and Rhone and the powerful Tiber
come here to lay their prayers before Andrew.
We too, provided we have a name among such great people,
come here carried along on prosperous wheel.

At that time Hurgust son of Fergoso king of that region was delighted with the sanctity of the place, and built his own palace there beside the church, and granted certain lands to blessed Regulus and his brethren for sowing corn, to be cultivated as alms for ever. Later kings followed his example, as the warmth of their devotion dictated, and their property increased, although modestly, until King Hungus, who ruled over the Picts after 800, handed over a tenth part of his kingdom to blessed Andrew, in return for the miraculous aid afforded to him in his expedition against the Saxons, as will appear below in Book 4, Chapter 13 and following. The blessed men founded a little cell in the form of a monastery, and appointed guardians of the relics. The blessed men went out preaching through the countryside, not on horseback but, just as long ago the apostles went, two by two to sow the word of God everywhere among the heathen, miraculously performing innumerable miracles. When therefore they had imbued these people with the faith, inspired by heavenly teaching, and confirmed their faith with various miracles, the most blessed Abbot Regulus died full of days and at a great age at Kilrymont (the name having been changed from Mucross by the king) thirty-two years after he had come shipwrecked to the island of Albion, during which he engaged in the work of the Gospel and wonderfully pleased God. (cc.58-60)

Book III

King Fergus son of Erc

The date 403 is too early by almost a century. Fergus son of Erc is a historical figure, who was the first DálRiatan king to rule from a Scottish rather than an Irish base. His brothers were the supposed founders of the tribes of Loarn and Angus in Argyll. His authority came to be extended eastwards over the lands of the Picts i.e. east of Drumalban, the mountain barrier stretching from Ben Lomond in Stirlingshire to Ben Hope in Sutherland.

Therefore in 403 in the sixth year of the emperors Arcadius and Honorius, which was also the 733rd year of the kingdom of the Scots in the island of Albion and the 1903rd year from their first beginning, that is from their setting out from Egypt, and the 5923rd year from the beginning of the world, Fergus son of Erc son of Echadius (who was the brother of the king Eochaid who was overthrown in battle by the tyrant Maximus) an energetic young man, excelling all others in valour, strong and mighty and daring as well as eager and successful in battle, came fearlessly with his two brothers Loarn and Angus and his fellow-countrymen from the islands both Irish and Norse to Scotland the kingdom that was his by right. He put to flight far from there his enemies who had long been living in the country.

Moreover as King Fergus advanced with his army through his ancestral territories, which little by little he brought into his peace along with their original inhabitants, he was met by the nation of the Picts in military order; and to allay suspicion that the smallest trace of hatred or treachery was to be found in them they opened to the Scots of their own accord the gates of all the castles and fortresses belonging to the Scots, which they had held up till then with Maximus's permission, and handed them back to them.

This same king reigned for sixteen years in Scotland, the last three of them beyond Drumalban, that is beyond the ridge of Albany, the first of the kings of Scottish race to reign in the land of the Picts from the mountains to the Firth of Forth. But whether it was by the sword or by any other right is not clear to me, since none of his predecessors had held sway there before. Certainly the Scots did join up with the Picts, as mentioned above, after they had driven out the Romans and Britons from their own abodes, and in close-packed array they often invaded their kingdom of Britain, which at that time was bereft of all warrior-strength, as is recorded in the chronicles of various authors, putting some of the wretched peasants to the sword, while the remainder who were left alive were carried off into slavery. (c.1, ll.18-29, 44-51; c.2, ll.28-39)

St Columba and St Kentigern

Bower as abbot of a monastery dedicated to St Columba (d.597) quotes probably from memory (i.e. with minor slips) two stanzas of the Office Hymn for Columba; but he does not correct Fordun's attribution of a story about the saint's distant knowledge of a battle (taken from Adomnan's Life of Columba*) to the wrong battle. St Kentigern (d.612) was Columba's contemporary, so that it is possible that the two men did meet. In his time his diocese of Glasgow stretched south to Stainmore on the Yorkshire/Westmorland border, as Bower thought it should by rights still do. The church at Ripon in Anglian Northumbria lay not very far away.*

In the eighth year of his reign and the ninth year of the reign of Brude son of Maelchon over the Picts, which was the year 565, there came from Ireland to Scotland the holy priest and abbot Columba a man whose life was as miraculous as it was holy, founder of monasteries and father and teacher of many monks, concerning whom it is thus said:

He was humble, kind, courteous,
a man of noble birth, upright of stature,
cheerful of countenance, venerable,
pure in mind and body.

No one knows how to describe in words or writing the sum total of Columba's marvellous deeds and signs taken one by one, his prophecies and his famous miracles.

Leaving his beloved native land Ireland,
he came by Christ's grace to Scotland.
Through him the king of the Pictish nation
took the first steps in amendment of life. (c.26, ll.24-39)

At the very time of the battle also the saint Columba while staying on the island of Iona, just as Adomnan mentions in his writings, suddenly summoned a servant and said: 'Ring the bell.' The brothers roused by its sound quickly ran to the church, led by the saintly abbot himself. To them on bended knee in the church he said: 'Now let us earnestly beseech God in prayer on behalf of King Aedan and his people. For they are entering upon battle at this hour.' And after a short interval he looked up to the sky and said: 'Now the barbarians are being turned to flight. No matter how unfortunate Aedan has been at other times, nevertheless God has granted him this victory.' The saint also told them prophetically and accurately about the number of three hundred and three slain in the army of Aedan.

Contemporaneously with St Columba there flourished blessed Kentigern bishop of Glasgow, a man of amazing sanctity and worker of many miracles. His venerable bones lie buried in the same place famous for many miracles performed to the glory of God. The furthest boundary of his bishopric at that time was at Rey Cross below Stainmore, as it ought by rights to be now.

In the *Life* of St Kentigern we read that St Columba came to Glasgow and that each saint comforted the other with mutual exchange of talk and that they also exchanged staffs. And now the crozier sheathed in golden ornamentation and studded all round with various kinds of pearls which blessed Kentigern had received from blessed Columba is still preserved to this day with great reverence in the church of St Wilfrid of Ripon. (c.29, ll.12-29; c.30, ll.1-7)

Why the English have tails

Bower adds to a brief mention by Fordun of the arrival of St Augustine of Canterbury in England in 597 several stories about him which he appears to have found at Dunfermline Abbey in the exemplar of a later manuscript that is now in the Royal Palace Library in Madrid and is still unpublished. The tradition mentioned in the first of these stories that at least some Englishmen had tails is one to which Bower refers again in other parts of his book. It was presumably generally believed in fifteenth-century Scotland. ('Muglington' has not been identified; 'mughel' or 'muggle' is a rare Kentish word for 'tail'; Tamworth is in Staffordshire and Rochester in Kent; 'blessed Thomas' is St Thomas Becket.)

When blessed Augustine was preaching the word of life to the heathen among the West Saxons in the county of Dorset, he came into a certain village where no one wished to receive him or to listen to his preaching. They rebelled against him in all respects and tried to contradict everything that he said and to obscure everything by taking a wrong meaning out of it, and, a thing which is wicked even to mention, they were so bold as to sew and hang fishtails on his clothing. But what they themselves believed they were doing to harm the holy father actually turned out to be to the eternal disgrace of themselves and their descendants and their innocent country. For God smote them in their hinder parts, giving them everlasting shame so that in the private parts both of themselves and their descendants all alike were born with a tail. Now a tail of this kind is called by the local inhabitants in their native language 'mughel' from which the village in which this kind of injury was inflicted on blessed Augustine got the name of Muglington (that is the town of the people with the mughels) which it has to the present day.

It is said also that, following their example, in the province of the Mercians in the village which is called Tamworth the inhabitants of the place offered a similar insult to the blessed man, but they did not go unpunished because both they themselves and their descendants, as everyone knows, suffered the shame of a like punishment and disgrace. A similar incident occurred in the time of the exile of blessed Thomas primate of England, because to insult him (as they believed, but their wickedness deceived them) the people of Rochester disfigured and cut off his horse's tail, which has led to their descendants in that place being found born with tails. (c.33, ll.1-27)

The proper cure of souls

As part of an assertion that popes of his time (compared with Pope Gregory the Great c.600) were allowing slackness in the parish cure of souls, Bower selects a story from the collection of exempla (i.e. improving tales) called On Bees *made by the thirteenth-century Thomas of Cantimpré (from Brabant in modern Belgium) about an uncle and nephew both called Bruno who were successively priests of a parish near Eisenach in Germany. The locale was irrelevant for Bower's purpose.*

For in his book on bees Barbason writes about a certain priest holding a cure called Bruno who lived in the region of Germany in the town of Wartburg. He was a good and upright man and had a relative also called Bruno who was a priest, a man highly regarded for his knowledge and character. His uncle Bruno the priest often used to ask him to undertake the charge of his parish, while he himself now that he was old would enter a monastery. After many entreaties he agreed although reluctantly, since he was apprehensive about being in charge of such a big parish. When he got his way the elder Bruno entered a monastery and soon afterwards departed this life, while the younger Bruno delayed taking on the cure of souls, because he already held another benefice (a chaplaincy in the castle worth twenty marks), and so put a priest as vicar in the parish instead of himself.

So one night when the younger Bruno was resting in his bed, the elder

Bruno who was now dead appeared to him in a black cape and said to him:

> You are behaving badly in the matter of the flock
> entrusted to you. Now you limp on cloven foot.
> See what your future punishment will be. Turn back.

And saying this he raised the cape in which he appeared to be clad and showed that he was seriously afflicted with burns. At this the younger Bruno woke up recollecting the vision and the lines of verse, then soon fell asleep again. The dead man appeared to him in the same form and said:

> You are the cause of my punishment.
> Rest is closed to me through you.
> See how I am burnt, fuel and food for the future flames.

And saying this he again showed him the tortures inflicted by fire. After he had gone to sleep for the third time, he appeared to him and said:

> Sometimes mingle serious matters with worldly pleasures.
> From these first-fruits reap the harvest or repent.

At his words Bruno arose and on bended knees he vowed to God that he would fulfil what he had promised to his uncle when he was alive. Immediately the dead man appeared clearly in great splendour and congratulated him on his vow and said: 'I rejoiced when they said to me: "We will go into the house of the Lord."' And saying this he ascended on high. See therefore how much danger is involved in taking on the cure of souls and then leaving it in the hands of a careless man, as you can observe in the case of the elder Bruno who carelessly abandoned his charge and in the case of the younger Bruno who entrusted to another priest without a cure the charge he had undertaken. So in the first lines of verse the elder conveyed allegorically that the younger was divided in his affection, which ought to be directed wholly towards the flock entrusted to him; and he demonstrated that he was lame when he devoted himself to the one benefice of a chaplaincy in the castle and carelessly deserted the charge of the parish entrusted to him. (c.37, ll.16-64)

The murder of King Fergus by his wife

The story of the poisoning of the Scottish King Fergus son of Aed Find (778-81) at the hands of his queen, as explained in her confession, has the appearance of an oral saga.

[Fergus] is said to have been poisoned by his wife the queen who was excessively jealous of him because of his affairs with other women. She afterwards openly admitted the deed, although she was suspected by no one of such a crime. When she looked upon the dead king's body, with mournful cries and tearing her hair, she burst out with these or similar words: 'Most wretched of women, more savage than any wild beast, basest betrayer, what have you done? Have you not wickedly killed with a most cruel kind of treachery, most like in this respect to the asp and urged on by wanton madness, your lord the king, most loving of all husbands and handsome beyond the love of women, whom alone you loved with the innermost love of your heart more than all men now living? But this wicked crime will not go unpunished. I shall be avenged upon myself. Accordingly do you, accursed hand, hasten to prepare and do not let pass this same cup with which you drank the health of your lord, not long ago your sweetest lover, or boldly prepare an even more bitter cup for my lips too!' Then after she had drained the lethal draught she immediately began: 'But that witch's potion ought not to suffice as full atonement for me who committed such a great crime. No! rather should I be tied to the tails of horses and dragged off to be hanged and this unspeakable body should be burnt to ashes in fires of thorns and the ashes scattered to the wind.' (c.55, ll.6-27)

Charlemagne

Bower devotes considerable space to information which he thinks should be available in Scotland about kings of the Franks, not least about Charlemagne, king c.742-814, and emperor from 800. (The feast of St James falls on 25 July each year. The pilgrimage church of St James of Compostella is in north-west Spain. The famous battle at Roncesvalles, a pass over the Pyrenees, was fought in 778. St Denis is near Paris.)

The name 'Charles' is interpreted as 'the light of the flesh' because he outstripped all fleshly kings since Christ by the light of every virtue and knowledge and valour. He had brown hair, his complexion was ruddy, his person was handsome and attractive but his glance was fierce. His height was eight times the length of one of his own feet, which were very long. His hips were broad with a stomach in proportion. His arms and legs were massive and he was very strong in all his limbs, most skilled in combat and a very spirited soldier. His face was one and a half hand's breadth in length and his beard one hand's breadth, his nose about a half hand's breadth and his brow was one foot. His eyes were leonine, sparkling like rubies. His eyebrows were half a hand's breadth. He caused immediate terror to anyone on whom his full gaze fell in anger. The belt with which he was girt extended to eight palms' breadth, not including the part which hung down. He ate little bread but would devour a quarter of a ram or two hens or a goose or a leg of pork or a peacock or a crane or a whole hare. He drank soberly a little wine and pure water. Such was his strength that he would cleave with his own sword an armed soldier sitting on a horse from the top of his head to the ground together with his horse with one stroke. He used easily to hold out four horseshoes at the same time in his hands. He would quickly lift up an armed soldier standing up straight in the palm of his hand from the ground as high as his head with his hand alone. He was very generous in gifts, very upright in judgments, very clear in his speeches.

In four festivals throughout the circuit of the year, that is Christmas Day, Easter, Pentecost and the Feast of St James, especially when he was holding court in Spain, he wore the royal crown and carried the royal sceptre. Before his judgment seat a naked sword was carried after the manner of the emperors. Around his bed every single night all through the night one hundred and twenty brave orthodox Christians were stationed to guard him. Forty of them kept the first watch of the night with ten of them at his head, ten at his feet, ten at his right hand and the same number at his left, holding in their right hands a drawn sword and in their left a burning candle. In the same way forty men kept the second and third watch of the night right until daybreak, alternating with each other while the others slept right till daybreak.

He freed the whole land of Spain and Galicia from the power of the Saracens, laying siege to Pamplona for three months. The walls collapsed and fell completely into ruins in answer to his prayers. The same thing happened in the case of the strongly fortified city which is called Lucerna in Valverde. He captured other strong cities and towns by great military might and consummate skill.

He enlarged the church of blessed James of Compostela and established canons in it according to the rule of blessed Isidore. He founded churches of the Blessed Virgin at Aachen and of St James in the same town, and of St James in the city of Béziers, and also at Toulouse, and that one which is in Gascony within the city commonly called Dax, and St John of Sorde in the rue St Jacques and the church of St James in Paris, and innumerable abbeys scattered throughout the world; and in Alemannia he founded as many abbeys as there are letters of the alphabet in alphabetical order and also archbishoprics at Trier, Cologne, Mainz and Salzburg.

He also killed Aigolandus and conquered Ferracutus the giant along with countless others. In answer to his prayers the sun stood still for the space of three days until the battle of Roncesvalles was finished and he wreaked vengeance on the pagans.

It was his custom at night when he lay down in bed to have pen and parchment near his head, so that if any useful action for the future occurred to his mind while he was in bed, he would write it down and authenticate it, in case it slipped his memory.

After the battle of Roncesvalles this Charlemagne summoned a council in St Denis and after bestowing many gifts decreed that each and every owner of each and every house in the whole of Gaul should give four pence annually for the building of the church [there], and to all serfs who freely gave these pence he gave their freedom. Then standing near the tomb of blessed Denis he begged him to pour forth prayers to the Lord for the salvation of those who freely gave those pence, and to pray for those Christians who likewise had given up everything for the love of God and had fallen in battles with the Saracens that they should receive the crown of martyrdom. On the following night the blessed Denis appeared to the king as he slept and awoke him saying: 'For all those who are going to be killed in battles with the Saracens, inspired by the example of your valour, I have obtained from God pardon for all their sins, and for those who are going to give money to build my church I have obtained from God healing of their serious wound.' When this was reported by the king, the people offered money very devotedly in return for the promise of salvation. And whoever gave liberally was everywhere called a freeman of St Denis, since he was free from all serfdom by order of the king. Hence arose the custom that that country which was previously called Gaul was then given the name of Francia and was freed from all servitude to other nations. Therefore a Frank is called free because glory and dominion over all other nations are due to him.

James of Vitry writing about Charlemagne says that one day he summoned his three sons, Gobard, Lothair and Louis wishing to test their obedience. Holding a small apple in his hand he said to Gobard: 'Open your mouth'. But he disdaining to open his mouth ordered the other two to do it, and they held their mouths wide open while Charlemagne placed apples in their mouths. 'Because,' he said 'you have obeyed my command, I give to you a kingdom and to you a dukedom.' When he saw this Gobard said: 'Look, father. I am opening my mouth.' He answered him: 'You will have neither an apple nor a country.' The same thing happens in a spiritual sense to those who postpone confession.

After his innumerable praiseworthy deeds and with his empire and kingdom at peace and their boundaries extended and with the state of the church ordered in a holy and religious manner, the glorious emperor and king Charlemagne died in the seventy-second year of his life and was buried at Aachen. His son Louis the Pious became Roman emperor after his death in 814 and he reigned for almost twenty-seven years. (c.61; c.62, ll.38-79)

St Bridget's rules about fighting pagans

When Bower was writing in the 1440s the writings of the visionary St Bridget of Sweden (c.1303-73) were just becoming available in Scotland. It was a time when the papal call to crusade against the Turks, who were then threatening Constantinople, was being preached urgently. Bower selects here Bridget's apparently divinely-inspired arguments in justification of killing pagans, whether by Swedes in the eastern Baltic region or by others in the eastern Mediterranean. Bridget's writings in her Celestial Book *were meant to be a guide to rulers everywhere, in the form of advice which she claimed to have received as the 'bride of Christ' from Christ himself.*

Because it was stated in the previous chapter that those who are going to be killed in battles with the Saracens will gain pardon for all their sins, I have accordingly taken the trouble to note down the following points in this chapter in order to make known the way in which pagans can be safely attacked. Just as it is written in the *Celestial Book for Emperors and Kings*, chapter 39:

> A certain king of Sweden asked the bride of Christ to enquire of the Lord if he approved of his going with his army against the pagans, since he had vowed to do so. As the bride was praying on his behalf Christ appeared to her saying: 'If the king wishes to go out against the pagans, I advise him rather than command him, because it is more meritorious to act according to advice than to carry out commands. Therefore I make two recommendations to him, first that his heart should be pure and his body fit—a pure heart, so that there is no other purpose for going forth except the love of God and the salvation of souls; fitness of body, so that it may be measurable in fasting and hardship. Secondly, let him ensure that he has vassals and soldiers who are willing and in a state of grace. So let him first of all go round his kingdom, examining how justice has been observed, in what manner and through whom the laws and government are administered, because the man who is trying to send other people to heaven must necessarily begin from himself, correcting his own errors and after this go on to admonish his subjects and to reprove them and to urge them on by examples of virtue.'

In the following chapter:

> Christ spoke to his bride saying: 'It is said that no one ought to be driven against his will to the kingdom of heaven. I reply that when

> good flowers are hampered by weeds, is it not always better that the weeds should be cut down to prevent the flowers being hampered as they grow up? Therefore let those who go to the lands of the infidels first offer them peace and good faith and liberty; and if the infidels do not accept their advice and admonitions, then zeal and force must be used. For with regard to all those who die for love of me, I God, Love personified, will repay them an hundred-fold. And furthermore the infidels themselves will suffer lesser punishments than if they were to live longer and die in peace, because if they lived longer, they would have more time to sin. For love is such a good thing that the least thought of it will have its reward. How much greater then is a good deed?'

In chapter 42 of the same book:

> The Son of God speaks to his bride saying: 'Let the king who seeks a harvest of souls and wishes to lead an expedition against the pagans have two banners. On the first let my passion be portrayed to illustrate mercy. On the second let the sword of my justice be shown. Therefore when the king comes to the pagans, let him first raise the first banner of mercy, offering them peace. If they refuse to accept it, let him thereafter raise the banner of justice and, trusting in my goodness, let him not fear the great numbers of the enemy and let him not retreat out of cowardice nor listen to the voice of those who say: "Go back home. What more hardship must we suffer?" For if the king is steadfastly afraid to proceed, let him not attempt or begin the good deed, because it would be better not to take up what is difficult than not to carry out with love what has been begun. Let the king also take with him clerics of approved life and religious of various orders who truly despise the world, because there are many in heathendom and among the gentiles who bring forward their own doctrines and they must be answered wisely. Let the clerics also instruct and influence the people not to run the risk of anathema because of their greed nor to die on account of rebelliousness and intemperate way of life.'

And in book 6, chapter 51 of the same work:

> The Son of God speaks: 'Every man who desires to visit the lands of the infidels ought to observe five rules:—
>
> 1. He ought to unburden his conscience by means of contrition and true confession, as if he were on the very point of death.
>
> 2. He ought to lay aside all frivolities in his behaviour and in his

dress, paying attention not to new fashions but to those praiseworthy customs instituted by his ancestors.

3. He ought to refuse to have any temporal possessions except for what is essential and what is to the honour of God. And if he knows of anything wrongfully acquired either through himself or his parents, he ought to wish to make restitution, whether it be large or small.

4. He ought to strive towards this goal, that the infidels should come to the true faith, but he should not covet their riches nor their oxen nor any other thing except only what is necessary for the body.

5. He ought to be willing to die for the honour of God and so to organise himself beforehand in a praiseworthy way of life that he may deserve to attain a precious death.' (c.63)

The Pictish royal succession

In the context of mentioning under the dates 824-31 the reign of Dungal son of Selbach as king of Scots (though in fact he reigned 723-6), Bower follows Fordun in describing the peculiarly Pictish custom of matrilinear succession. He is preparing the way for the mid-ninth century assimilation of the Pictish kingdom under the Scottish kings, without being able to suggest why a long peaceful relationship between the two peoples had led to the forcible destruction of the Pictish kingdom.

In the following year also the great question about the right to the kingdom of the Picts in the light of a claim that it ought to belong to the Scots began to arise and was often ventilated on the lips of everyone, both magnates and people. It was never however translated into action. Immediately after the completion of five years Conall died and Dungal son of Selbach began to reign in 824 in the eleventh year of the Emperor Louis and he reigned for seven years. He renewed the war against the Picts which had lain dormant for fifty years. He said that their kingdom was his according to the provisions of an ancient pact. For the ancient law about the succession of their kings and princes according to Bede and the chronicles is as follows: 'When the Picts first entered this island and had no wives of their own nation they asked the Scots for their daughters. They agreed to give them to the Picts only on this condition that when the matter (that is the succession to the kingship or lordship) was disputed, they should choose kings for themselves from the female rather than the male line. It is at any rate well known that this rule was always observed among the Picts.' And this perhaps could have been the cause of this strife or contention. Since it is true, as one infers from their chronicles and histories, that in the days of peace true friendship was cherished between them from the beginning to such an extent that their royal family continually married the sons and daughters of Scottish kings and princes, and conversely the Scottish royal family entered into marriages with the Picts. For He, to whom nothing is unknown, knows the cause of this final contest and through whose fault this savage war began, which had no end until, as He who is the ruler and destroyer at will of all kingdoms decreed, the Picts were completely overcome and the Scots finally won the palm of victory and their kingdom. (c.64, ll.29-57)

Book IV

The Scottish royal succession

Bower follows here Fordun's inadequate attempt to expound the Scottish system of royal succession down to the accession of Malcolm II son of Kenneth in 1005. In fact the succession of a brother was very exceptional, and it was normal for the kings to alternate between two segments of the dynasty, probably following a system of designated successors.

The dates of the true succession of the kings of Scots, reigning along with the Picts in the northern part of Albion after the time of Fergus son of Erc, have been given above. Now it is appropriate to proceed to the monarchs who secured complete sovereignty over the whole of Albion, after the nations of the Picts had been overthrown, and to reveal certain of their achievements and the dates of their reign, based on the information given in the books of the ancients.

We must first however speak of the rule of succession of these kings. For often the question arises, why sons did not normally succeed to rule over their fathers' kingdom, as the custom of the present day requires, rather than brothers succeeding brothers, as has been shown in the successions of previous kings. Now this was the practice in those days, since both Scots and Picts and also the majority of kings of kingdoms and certain rulers of the empire had the same law of succession, namely that if the brother of each deceased king or the son of his brother was superior to the king's son in years and ability to rule, he took precedence over the king's son on the throne, although he was more distant in degree. For it was not proximity of blood but the ability that comes with maturity that raised one or the other to reign on the throne of the kingdom. It was the tiny size of the population in early times, few in number as they were, that caused the custom of this kind of succeeding to the throne to prevail. It was in trying to acquire or preserve for themselves a settled abode in freedom that they established this aforementioned law. For since they were exposed to wars on all sides, they shrank from handing over to youths control not just over their kingdom but even over their lives.

This ancient custom of royal succession lasted without a break right to the time of Malcolm son of Kenneth and until he himself, in view of the threatened loss of the kingdom, which might have come about from following this custom, decreed by a general ordinance as a perpetual law that each king for the time being in turn should be succeeded in ruling over the kingdom after his death by his nearest offspring, that is his son or daughter, his grandson or granddaughter, whichever then surviving might be nearer, but failing these, the nearest heir descended either from the royal line or a collateral branch should possess the right of inheritance. (c.1)

The stratagem of King Kenneth son of Alpin

This Kenneth probably succeeded his father Alpin as king of the Scots in 840, became king of the Picts also in 840, and died in 858 leaving a united kingdom with a single patrilinear dynasty permanently thereafter. His stratagem for gaining the support of his magnates is part of an oral saga incorporating a traditional motif; it leads up to the story of the total annihilation of the Picts by Kenneth coming over the mountains from the west at a time when Danish raiders were attacking from the east. (The river Tyne mentioned as a boundary was perhaps the one in East Lothian rather than the one in Northumbria.)

Kenneth son of Alpin succeeded to his father's kingdom in 834 and to the kingdom of the Picts, after they had been overthrown, in 839 in the twenty-fifth year of the emperor Louis's reign and the eleven hundred and sixty-ninth year of the establishment of the kingdom of the Scots in the island of Albion. It was also the two thousand three hundred and forty-ninth year of their exodus from Egypt under their first king Gaythelos son of Neolus king of the Athenians and under Scota wife of Gaythelos. Kenneth reigned as sole ruler over these kingdoms of the Picts and Scots for about sixteen years.

The following lines of verse were written about him after the expulsion of the Picts:

First to reign in Albany, 'tis said,
was Kenneth son of Alpin, warrior bold.
He expelled the Picts, reigned twice eight years
and in Forteviot met his death.

He was a brave and prudent man, famous for his penetrating intellect and a very daring leader in battles. He used amazing cunning in leading the Scots against the kingdom of the Picts. The reason for this is as follows:

First because in the year of his coronation he summoned the magnates to a council and made it known that he wished to be avenged for the brutal killing of his father and of his kinsmen recently slain in battle, many of whom had been [wickedly] put to death, after they had surrendered.

Secondly because of the theft of one hunting-dog that was stolen from the Scots by the Picts, which was the occasion of the first hostility [between peoples] who had lived peacefully side by side for five hundred years before this.

Thirdly because after the treaty was broken the Picts allied themselves with the pagan Saxons for the purpose of exterminating the Scots.

Fourthly because the Scots said that the kingdom of Pictavia ought to be theirs according to the law laid down in an ancient covenant at the time the Picts asked the Scots to give them their daughters. They agreed to give them their daughters on condition that, when the succession to the kingdom was in doubt, they would choose kings from the female rather than the male line. This they had refused to do a little before the time of Alpin.

Therefore Kenneth earnestly urged the magnates to hurry on with this work and to make preparations for an expedition on the appointed day, laying aside all other concerns. But the magnates were not only terror-stricken beyond measure as a result of the battle in the recent past in which King Alpin fell along with many thousands of men, they were also in a panic at the din of that battle, and with their hearts utterly failing them, like idiots or weaklings they replied with one voice to the king, saying: 'Whatever, Lord King, you order us to do, either to defend your kingdom or any other task whatsoever, it is our wish and our duty to obey, with one exception. We utterly refuse to cross the borders of the kingdom of the Picts. For to be brief we do not dare to invade them, since we have become so fearful from the time of the battle to the present day that even if an angel sent down by God from heaven made this pronouncement to us, we should perhaps fear to consent. Long ago in the time of our grandfathers and recently also in our own time the courage of the Scots exceeded the valour of the lion or unicorn. It is the nature of the first of these to fear no attack; of the second never to fall alive into man's power. It can be killed but never subdued alive. And if ever by the exertion of hunters it happens to be taken alive, it immediately dies. But the die of our destiny rolls the opposite way, because now we are more fearful than women, or, if one may say so, than leverets.'

So the king, seeing that he was making no progress either by wheedling or harsh exhortations, decided to employ some cunning. For he remembered that they had not altogether declined the expedition but had shown some indecision when they said that, even if an angel ordered them to set out for the kingdom of the Picts, they would perhaps not obey. He immediately worked out a stratagem in his mind and revealed the answers of the magnates in secret to a certain skilled craftsman, who was a great favourite of his, and informed him how to carry out the whole scheme. Since the man was a clever craftsman he gladly supported the king's wishes, promising moreover that everything would be faithfully accomplished to the best of his ability. So he carefully took some scaly fish skins which shine with a kind of brilliance in the darkness of night and used them cunningly to adorn a cloak which sparkled as if with the shining feathers of angels. He put it on so that it completely covered the appearance of his whole body. Clad in this kind of garment, he secretly entered the magnates' bedrooms by night in the form of an angel and amazingly deluded their senses or rather their understanding, wide-awake as they were. Exhorting them in the name of the living God, he ordered them to obey all their king's commands and in particular not to quail at the prospect of destroying the kingdoms of the Picts. The magnates, taken in by such cunning ingenuity, hastily approached their lord the king and promised their obedience in all matters. 'For', they said, 'Your Majesty, we have seen beyond a shadow of a doubt an angel of God face to face, and he warned us to follow you wherever you offered to go.' Their chamberlains of their own accord swearing a great oath also bore witness to this. And the king on oath to them let it be known that he himself had heard and seen the same thing through that angel.

Now after these matters had been settled in this way according to his wishes and brought to the desired goal in all respects, by universal and voluntary decision war was declared upon the Picts and, after his armies were assembled, Kenneth invaded their kingdoms. So great was the fury with which he raged not only against men but also against women and small children that he spared neither sex nor any holy orders, but every living thing which he had not carried off with him he destroyed by sword or fire. Then in the sixth year of his reign when Danish pirates had occupied the shores of the Picts and crushed them with very great slaughter as they were attempting to defend their seaboard from plundering, so Kenneth himself crossed the mountainous region of their territory (that is the backbone of Albany, which in Scots is called Drumalban) and turned his arms against the remaining boundaries of the Picts. After many Picts were slain, he forced the rest to flee and acquired sole rule over both kingdoms. The Picts recovered their strength to some extent with English help and kept up the attack on Kenneth for four years; but after a while he weakened them with unexpected raids and various slayings. At last in the twelfth year of his reign he joined battle seven times in one day and, after overthrowing innumerable nations of the Picts, he confirmed and ratified his possession of the whole kingdom from the River Tyne next to Northumbria to the Orkney Islands, as formerly St Adomnan the abbot of Iona prophesied.

It was not only the kings and leaders of that people that were destroyed in this way but its whole stock and race also is said to have been lost together with its own distinctive language, so that whatever is found attributed to them in the works of old writers is believed by most people to be fictitious or apocryphal. To those however who are in the habit of reading histories it seems not at all amazing if God, the omnipotent ruler of all kings and kingdoms and the wonderful preserver in the case of good deeds but terrifying destroyer in the case of bad deeds, has often permitted mighty peoples and kingdoms to perish, as their sins demanded, and will often permit it in the future. (c.3-c.4, l.34)

The church at Abernethy

Bower associates the founding of a religious community at Abernethy in south-east Perthshire with the Pictish king Garnard (c.586-597). In his own day it had become a secular collegiate church under a prior. It seems to have kept a record of its own traditions of links with the Irish saints Patrick and Bridget (presumably in the later fifth century), though they are not otherwise known to have visited Pictavia as suggested here. The church at Dunkeld in Perthshire is said to have been founded by the Pictish king Constantine son of Fergusa (789-820) as part of the Columban cult. It is quite possible that a series of bishops (otherwise unknown) held office at Abernethy while it was the Pictish capital.

That King Brude also was succeeded by Garnard son of Domnach or MakDomnach, who founded and built the collegiate church of Abernethy, after blessed Patrick brought blessed Bridget into Scotland together with her nine virgins, just as we find in a certain chronicle of the church of Abernethy, and offered to God and blessed Mary and blessed Bridget and her virgins all the lands and teinds which the prior and canons [now] hold from ancient times. Those nine virgins died within five years and were buried in the north part of the said church. There were three elections held in that church during the time when there was only one bishop in Scotland. In those days it was the principal royal and episcopal seat of the whole kingdom of the Picts and continued so for some length of time. The church itself was founded two hundred and twenty-six years, nine months and six days before the church at Dunkeld. In another chronicle I have found that it was founded two hundred and forty-four years before the church at Dunkeld. (c.12, ll.30-45)

King Hungus and the battle at Athelstaneford

The dates of the principal participants in the legendary story here of the battle of Athelstaneford do not fit. Hungus was king of the Picts

820-834, while Athelstan was under-king in south-east England only for his father Æthelwulf between 839 and 856. It is Bower with his local knowledge of East Lothian that identifies the battle-site as Athelstaneford. The story became part of the Scottish legend of St Andrew (see above).

For in those regions which Athelstan's father had bestowed upon him during his own reign, Hungus king of the Picts led a great army to lay waste the nations of the Angles nearest to him, the Northumbrians, causing immense devastation as he passed through their country. After various days' marches he came at last for rest to a pleasant plain in Lothian not far from the River Tyne, two miles from Haddington, at a place which is now called Athelstaneford, where he gave orders for his camp to be pitched in order to refresh his army with suitable food, worn out as it was by the length of the journey. And since the plain itself was rich in corn and grass and woodland shrubs and well-watered with springs and rivers, he decided to spend some days there, as if he had nothing to fear.

When Athelstan heard this, he brought together the might of the whole race of the Angles both north and south and with his battalions arranged in separate companies, he came unexpectedly upon the place where Hungus was encamped and so successfully surrounded him on all sides with his divisions that no way of escape was left open to him. The terrified king and his panic-stricken magnates were very apprehensive, for they had no expectation at all that they could be saved, at least by human intervention. Therefore they had recourse to divine guidance which never fails those who ask for it in sincerity, and vows were humbly made by individuals, both high and low, to God and his saints and especially to St Andrew the Apostle. So the king promised in a solemn vow that he would give to blessed Andrew a tenth part of his kingdom to the honour of God and the Blessed Virgin Mary, on condition that the saint would restore him and his army safely to his own land and rescue him unharmed from the power of a people so innumerable and so proud.

Now on the following night blessed Andrew appeared to the king saying: 'God the ruler of all kings, with whom the prayer of the humble always finds favour, has hearkened to your prayer through my intercession and tomorrow he will give you a joyful victory and will lay your enemies low before you, nor will they prevail in battle against you, because an angel bearing the standard of our Lord's Cross will go in front of you in the sight of many. Therefore when you return triumphantly into your own kingdom, do not be unmindful of your vow but beware of putting off the fulfillment of what you promised of your own accord by a decision of your free will.'

The king awoke from sleep and revealed to his companions and people all that he had heard in the vision, how the Lord had granted him through the prayers of his apostle Andrew certain victory over his enemies. Therefore all of them were gladdened beyond belief from confidence in that vision and they were no longer the cowards of the day before and the day before that, but they had become brave and much bolder than usual. Although they were far fewer in number, they rushed against the enemy with shouts and bugles blaring. Immediately such panic seized their enemies' hearts that they all broke rank and turned away to flee, except for a few around the king who held their ground, but they were likewise overcome and killed at the first clash. King Athelstan's head was cut off from his body as a reminder of such a miraculous slaughter and the king took it with him and ordered that it should be attached to the highest point of a certain rock in the middle of the Firth of Forth on a certain island near Queensferry which is called Inchgarvie, to be seen by all those who made the crossing throughout several years. (c.13, l.59 - c.14, l.43)

King Indulf and the Danes and Norwegians

King Indulf reigned 954-962. He was troubled by Danish and Norse attacks on both the east and west coasts of the country. His death came in a fight either at Cullen in Banffshire or near Stonehave in Kincardineshire near the mouth of the river Cowie. He was buried on Iona.

A rumour spread about at that time of the return of the Danes and Norwegians put all the islanders into a state of great panic, for they hated the Scots as much as the English. Very soon what was feared actually happened in the spring of the following year. Sailing in a fleet of fifty ships, with piratical savagery they repeatedly devastated, now the southern regions of the kingdom, now the northern, just as they happened to be driven by the onslaught of the winds. While the king was striving to confront them in the north, the outcry of the people proclaimed that they were laying waste the south. At last one day when, as it happened, the raiders were spread out in detachments laying waste the countryside near a place which is called Cullen, the king set up an ambush in a hiding-place not far from the shore, for he happened to be there with a few men at that time; but would that he had not been there! While the raiders had dispersed and scattered themselves in companies over the fields and villages, he rushed at speed against them with loud shouts and, after most of them had been killed, he forced the rest to seek a remedy in flight. Finally, great-spirited as he was, he threw away his armour (more's the pity) so that he could with greater speed pursue his fleeing foe and, after being hit on the head by a dart from one of the ships, he died the same night. His body was taken to Columba's Isle with fitting honours and he was buried along with his ancestors in the customary royal tomb. (c.27, ll.35-57)

King Kenneth II and the succession

Kenneth II reigned 971-995. In the context of a description of the way that the Holy Roman Emperor was chosen by seven electoral princes, Bower copies a proposal for simplifying the Scottish law of the succession suggested by the king (cf. above c.1). In the event he was immediately succeeded by several more distant relations before his son Malcolm II took the throne in 1005.

Hearing these rumours about a change in the law of succession, King Kenneth wished to abolish the custom of succession observed by the ancient kings of his kingdom, who up to this time had reigned in complicated succession, and he wished that after any king his offspring of legitimate birth should be adorned with the diadem of the kingdom in preference to all others. He himself had a distinguished son Malcolm, to whom he was absolutely determined that the kingdom should be assigned. Therefore he decreed with the consent of all the nobles apart from a few supporters of the ancient custom of succession that every king on his death should in future be succeeded by his son or daughter, his grandson or granddaughter, or his brother or sister in the collateral line or, failing these, any other survivor of the late king who was nearest to him in blood, even if he was an infant one day old, since it is said: 'The age of the king rests with the loyalty of his subjects.' And henceforth no law to the opposite effect was to prevail. (c.32, ll.19-34)

The assassination of Kenneth II by Finuele

This story about the murder of King Kenneth in 995 is probably based on an oral tale. (Dunsinane was a hill-top castle in Perthshire; Fettercairn is in Kincardineshire.)

The princes of the other line of succession hated King Kenneth and his son, claiming that they were now deprived of the right of succession, which had been customary since ancient times. The chief among them Constantine the Bald son of King Culen and Grim son of Kenneth son of King Duf endlessly plotted their death and at last found accomplices for perpetrating the crime. Implicated in their activities and counsels was Finuele daughter of Cunchar or in other accounts daughter of Cruchne mormaer of Angus. The king before this had ordered her only son to be put to death at Dunsinane, whether by the severity of the law or because of some crime or for any other cause I do not know. This cunning woman, eagerly desiring the death of the king, caused a certain kind of trap never before seen to be set up in a secluded cottage. The trap had firing devices fitted on all sides of it, always at tension with separate strings for each and equipped with very sharp darts, and in the centre of them there was skilfully attached to the firing devices a statue standing in the form of a boy. If anyone touched the statue and moved it in any way whatsoever, the bowstrings of the firing devices would be promptly released on all sides and he would be pierced by the darts which would instantly have been shot. When the machinery for accomplishing this crime had been completed, the aforesaid wicked woman always had a smile for the king on her face and at last tricked him by flattering him with cunning words.

Now the king one day set out with a few followers to hunt in the woods not far from his own palace, chasing beasts in various directions with hounds. By chance in the course of hunting he happened to stop near the township of Fettercairn where the traitress lived. When she saw him she urgently begged him on bended knees to come to her house. 'Otherwise', she said, 'I consider that I am undoubtedly held suspect in your majesty's favour. But God knows and you, Your Majesty, will soon discover that, although the wagging tongues of the ill-disposed utter many kinds of lies about me, I have always been loyal to you and always will be as long as I live. For no matter what you have recently done to my most wicked son, I am well aware that it was done not undeservedly but rightly.' And running up she whispered in the king's ear: 'I shall reveal to you, my lord, the accomplices of my accursed son who are traitors to you and the manner of their treachery, if you come with me. They hoped indeed to implicate me in the conspiracy with them in order to deceive you, but I immediately refused to consent to their unspeakable treacheries. However they compelled me to take an oath with my hand on the gospels that I would never betray their secrets. And, although I promised them this on oath, nevertheless I would have been a most false traitress to you, my lord and king, to whom beyond all others unshakeable and loyal allegiance is due, if I had kept hidden the danger to your person. For who does not know that no conspiracy against the safety of the king's majesty can be binding?'

In this way the crafty woman cunningly misleading the king's mind drew him (alas! over-trustful of her) with her into the house with every circumstance supporting her. Why prolong the story? Why spend time over grievous events? After the king dismounted, she quickly guided him on his own without anyone attending him, taking him by the hand into her house where the trap was lurking and, as if intending to reveal the traitors' secrets, just as she had promised, she shut the door behind him and showed him the statue, which was the lever for the whole trap. When the king enquired of her what the purpose of this statue was, the traitress smiled and replied: 'This statue, my lord and king, which you see, if anyone were to touch and set in motion the top of its head, amazing and amusing sport would arise from it.' He, completely unaware of the hidden trickery, easily drew the head of the device towards himself with his hand and so released the bolts and handles of the crossbows. The darts were suddenly shot from all sides, he was transfixed and died without uttering another word. Hastily the traitress left by the back door and for the time being hid in the cover of the woods, but shortly afterwards she reached her fellow conspirators without being caught.

The king's attendants for a long time awaited his return from the house, wondering why he was spending so much time inside. Finally they stood before the gate and beat persistently on the door. When they heard no reply, they broke it down in a frenzy. Presently when the king's death was discovered, a great hue and cry arose, as they sought the wicked woman in all directions. But they ran about to no avail because they could not find her anywhere. Not knowing what to do, they burned down the town and reduced it to ashes. They carried the king's blood-stained body with them and shortly afterwards buried him on Iona with his forebears in the royal fashion. (c.35 - c.36, l.29)

A satire on the dress of the English

In the context of a series of remarks about the characteristics of the English, Bower quotes the view that such is the variety of dress adopted by them that 'almost anyone at all is now considered to belong to neither sex'. He then includes the following poem which has not been found anywhere else.

The variety of their garments is a source of amazement to me.
Some of them are short—they could not be shorter,
scarcely touching the wrists—not to be raised by the hand.
Why are the clothes so short? Times change and clothes change with them.

These short clothes are more abbreviated than they were designed to be
by the skill of the tailors, and the limbs are exposed.

Such clothes are worn in England
by noblemen at home.
It is clothes and not their wearers that everyone respects.

Overcoats have sleeves reaching down to the heels
which you could easily wind three times round your arms.
You could wipe your bottom with them instead of rags
in the privy without doubt.
Alas! the leather skins would be badly worn away by their backsides.

There are wide windows cut out of the clothes,
gaping from the armpit, slit right down to the shin.
The chasuble and the long vestment is given
to the celebrant priest.
A prince would stain it purple in order to endure it.

Long points of hoods reign in this region,
hanging down to the belt as a sign of their devotion
Newfangled bells shine from the padded chest
not known of old.
If your foot goes to sleep in the street, do not let your enemy know.

His beard hangs from his chin like long goats' whiskers
and like pigs' bristles is tended with a comb.
For this reason he loves his hair, if he would be bold.
Hence the belief—
in the whole wide world there is none bolder than a he-goat.

A dagger fitted with an ancestral handle
hangs from his pouch, by which he swears when offended.
Throats will be cut, unless by money
wrongs are redeemed.
Not everyone they lie in wait for meets his death.

A cap like an earthenware pot covers each head.
It is secured with a red cord.
Tubes form the clasp of its band. Every servant
that lives and serves
has a head the same as a gentleman.

If you see any lady fully dressed,
you will perceive her trailing behind her a dress with a tail

two ells long, like the wild beasts.
Flee from her as from death.
Thus she bears an acceptable gift to her lord.

The English race is like some kind of monkey.
It apes all the others daily, as it sees them.
Idleness produces more and more frivolity and worldliness
in their licentious minds
May the king of all grant to *us* the kingdom of heaven.
(c.39, ll.34-83)

Kingly right

Malcolm son of Kenneth took the throne in 1005. (The 'Plain of Bards' has been identified with Monzievaird in Perthshire.) Bower takes the opportunity to explain the four attributes of kingship which were recognized in his own day, and develops his argument in typical fashion with parallels derived from the thirteenth-century encyclopaedist Vincent of Beauvais and from the Bible. (For Nimrod the 'mighty hunter', who was the first after the Flood to impose his rule over the Assyrian Empire, see Genesis 10:8.)

King Grim reigned for the space of eight years,
the son of Kenneth who was the son of Duf.
He was killed on the Plain of Bards
by Kenneth's son named Malcolm.

One need have no doubts about the right of this Malcolm because he was permitted to acquire by battle the kingdom that was also due to him by right of succession, since certainly a king is the legitimate ruler of any kingdom by fourfold right or at least by one or other of this sort of right. Malcolm was the legitimate ruler of that kingdom by three of the aforesaid rights. For every king claims legitimacy for himself through blood descent or by right of election or through achieving power by conquest or through the gift of a higher prince. Kings nowadays claim their rights through descent and proximity of blood and that is considered the height of justice. Malcolm had similar justice on his side, as is shown in chapter 32 above in this same book.

Secondly, some kings are appointed by election and those who are duly chosen according to rule have a clear right as long as they live. Thus the doge of Venice and present day Roman emperors are chosen by election. Vincent [of Beauvais], *Speculum Historiale* Book 2, Chapter 6 says:

> The Thracians choose a king for themselves, in whose election it is not nobility of family that is important but general consent. For the people choose a king who is outstanding in character, experienced in mercy, well on in years and who has no children—for no man who is a father is allowed to rule—and if he does produce offspring he is divested of royal power to prevent the kingship becoming hereditary. He has with him forty counsellors to prevent him being sole judge and they examine everything with him. If he is detected in any crime, he is given the death penalty, without however anyone laying a hand upon him—contacts are forbidden him, even the opportunity for conversation. We read that when the Romans wished to elect Hadrian's son as emperor, his father opposed them to their face, saying: 'Before my very eyes you are doing what you ought not to do. For the principate should not go by descent but by good deeds, and he who is born king but is undeserving will prove a worthless ruler.'

Thirdly, some become kings through conquest and that was the first form and method by which men began to reign over the earth and to become kings, first of whom was Nimrod...

Fourthly, someone becomes king through the gift of a more powerful ruler, just as Herod was king of Judea, the kingdom conferred on him by Caesar. Saul, David and Solomon were kings of Israel through the gift of God, since Solomon was the youngest of all his brothers, just as David was among his; nevertheless by order of the Lord Solomon became king, while the other brothers were ignored. You have a similar situation in the previous account of Kings Aedan and Eochaid Buide, who were chosen by the Lord and whose older brothers were rejected in accordance with instructions given to St Columba by an angel to adopt them as kings... Therefore if an earthly emperor can bestow a kingdom, how much more can God who is the highest emperor of all! In this connection it is written in Daniel, Chapter 4: 'The Highest holds sway in the kingdom of men and He will give the kingdom to whomsoever He wishes.'

We have inserted this here in order that you may know that up to this time, thank God, the posterity of this unconquered king have happily reigned in succession [in Scotland], except that during certain corrupt periods Macbeth and the idiot Lulach, Donald Ban and Duncan in turn usurped the kingdom for short periods of time. (c.41, l.43 - c.42, l.56)

The vice of treachery

Following after details of the assassination of Malcolm II in 1034, Bower abbreviates a reflective passage with literary and biblical allusions composed by Fordun on treachery as the worst of vices. Unlike Bower, Fordun did not have a university education; but he apparently could range quite far for his material. (Not all the quotations here have been identified. 'The Philosopher' is probably Aristotle; Peter of Blois was a twelfth-century writer; the story about Fabricius comes from the fourth-century Roman historian Eutropius.)

Even a king of such prowess and excellence, a prince of such invincible courage, a soldier of such valour and daring could not escape death at the savage hands of wicked traitors. How unspeakable is the frenzy of traitors, the accursed nature of secret treachery which deceives only those who put their trust in it and especially those to whom it is bound by fealty. Evil incomparably foulest of all evil and detestable to all men. In truth a traitor is not a human being because he has broken faith and deserves no other name than that of traitor, acquired by renouncing his good faith. 'Good faith', says the Philosopher, 'is the strongest virtue of the human heart, it is not compelled by any need to deceive, it is not corrupted by any bribe.' The man who is faithless is void of all true goodness. That is the sin which one ought to hate of all the sins that can be hated. How much worse in this respect than demons are those who are enmeshed in this sin.

St Augustine says: 'The man who is openly hostile could easily be avoided by taking care. This hidden and intimate evil crushes before it can be foreseen.'

Jerome says: 'Good faith should be observed towards kings and princes. The man who has not shown it cannot find rewards with God.' Because as [Peter of] Blois says: 'Nothing is more hateful in a soldier than the vice of treachery. Although Joab had acted courageously in all respects, he is not however included in the catalogue of heroes of David, because his treachery against Abner and Amasa blackened his courage [...] It is only faithfulness which enlarges the glory of princes and people, which strengthens peace and strikes terror into the enemy.' At any rate God the Just Judge took vengeance on the treacherous murder of the pagan Julius Caesar. Suetonius tells us: 'Virtually none of the assassins of Caesar survived him by more than three years nor did any die a natural death. All were condemned and met their deaths by different chances, some in shipwreck, some in battle, not a few savagely killed themselves with the same daggers with which they had stabbed Caesar.' Therefore let traitors beware lest they betray any Christian prince or any other person who reposes trust in them for fear of the Just

Judge who wreaked such vengeance on traitors for a pagan.

There follows an example of how beautiful faithfulness is in man and how vile treachery. Once upon a time Fabricius was sent to Pyrrhus king of Epirus to ransom some Roman prisoners of war. When the king learned that he was a poor man, he promised him a fourth part of his kingdom, and invited him to give up his own country and come over to his side. Fabricius would have nothing to do with this. After a year had elapsed the same Fabricius was instructed to lead an army to fight against Pyrrhus and, at a time when his camp and that of Fabricius were close together, Pyrrhus's doctor came to Fabricius by night, offering to kill Pyrrhus with poison, if Fabricius gave him certain guarantees. Fabricius ordered him to be taken back to his master in chains and for Pyrrhus to be told what he had proposed against his life. Then the king in amazement is reported to have said: 'Fabricius is a man whom it is more difficult to turn aside from honesty than the sun from its own course. Here were two completely dissimilar men, one of whom could not be bribed by any munificence, not even a quarter of my kingdom, although he is a poor man, to side with an enemy against his own country, and who was not willing to conquer his enemy through treachery. The other of his own accord offered his lord the king for sale at a meagre price.'

Therefore as Ambrose advises: 'Let us beware of the traitor lest we who are many are led astray by one man.' (c.47)

The prodigality of King Malcolm II

Bower copies from Fordun an explanation of how various types of land-holding had come about. The language certainly does not match the customs that were current in the time of Malcolm II, and relate more to the situation from the twelfth century onwards. (The royal seat on the moothill at Scone is the Stone of Destiny.) The explanation of how the king came to require unprecedented taxation from time to time relates to Fordun's own day in the 1360s, when money had to be found to pay David II's ransom on his release from imprisonment in England.

The histories record that the aforesaid Malcolm was also so lavish or rather prodigal in gifts that, although he had held all the lands, regions and provinces of the whole kingdom in his own possession in the ancient manner, he kept hold of none of it for himself apart from the moothill on which stood the royal seat at Scone where the kings sitting on the throne in royal attire are accustomed to proclaim judgments, laws and statutes to their subjects.

From ancient times indeed kings had been in the habit of giving to their knights greater or smaller tracts from their own lands in feu-ferme, a portion of some province or a thanage. For at that time almost the whole kingdom was divided up into thanages. He apportioned these lands to each man as he thought fit either for one year at a time for ferme, as in the case of tenant farmers, or for a term of ten or twenty years or life with at least one or two heirs permitted, as in the case of certain freemen and gentlemen, and to some likewise (but these only a few) in perpetuity, as in the case of knights, thanes and magnates, with the restriction however that any of them should make a fixed annual payment to the lord king.

Since Malcolm had kept back nothing for himself, as has been said, from all those lands and annual revenues, at last at a general assembly he was compelled by necessity to ask them that a definite income in keeping with his position as king should be provided, either in the form of lands or revenues or at least a sufficient annual subsidy with which the dignity of his majesty might be supported in all respects, without however crushing the poor people with the heavy burden of annual taxation. This was gladly approved and granted by everyone, both commons and nobles. Moreover all the nobles of every rank agreed that the wardship of all their lands and their heirs should remain with the lord king for a period of twenty years together with reliefs and marriages after the death of each magnate or freeholder.

So it seems that King Malcolm although great-hearted both in peace and war distributed his possessions recklessly, not because he had freely given suitable gifts to those who served him well in military campaigns and to the deserving, but because he squandered extravagantly without setting any limit to his generosity not just a part of his possessions but rather the whole of them, keeping nothing for himself. Generosity is rather thoughtlessly employed where it entails the inevitable asking back of the gifts. (c.48, ll.1-39)

The life and death of King Duncan I

Bower here added literary touches to Fordun's account of the reign of Duncan I (1034-40). His father (Abthane Crinan) was a married abbot. Malcolm III Canmore and Donald Ban came to be kings 1058-93 and 1093-4 respectively. Cumbria was then a province of Scotland usually held by the king's heir. Duncan's reign is portrayed in idyllic terms before it was cut short by Macbeth as a member of the alternative segment of the royal family. (Pitgaveny is near Elgin in Moray.)

After the burial of Malcolm with his forefathers on the island of Iona he was succeeded by his grandson Duncan, son of Abthane Crinan and Malcolm's daughter Bethoc. His reign began in 1034, the tenth year of the emperor Conrad II and he reigned for six years.

While his grandfather was still alive, Duncan had two sons called Malcolm Canmore (meaning 'big head') and Donald Ban by a relative of Siward earl of Northumbria. His father immediately after his coronation gave Malcolm the province of Cumbria. Nothing worthy of mention happened in the kingdom during this short time of Duncan's reign, because he enjoyed secure peace with everyone both foreigners and dwellers in the kingdom except for the fact that certain members of an ancient family of conspirators were accused by a widespread rumour of having conspired to kill the king just as they had conspired to kill his grandfather, his predecessor. And although this had often been made known to him by those loyal to him, he nevertheless refused to give credence to them, saying that it was incredible that they would dare to have the presumption to carry out such a crime. And so it happened that the man who previously refused to give heed to the warnings of those loyal to him, because he did not believe them, afterwards fell suddenly and unexpectedly into the snares of traitors.

For he observed the praiseworthy custom of traversing all the provinces of his kingdom once a year to comfort graciously with his presence his own peaceful people. We can appropriately compare him to the king of the Indians about whom Aristotle says in *De Regimine Principum* that there was among the Indians a custom that the king should exhibit himself openly to the whole people once a year clad in royal armour and explain to them what he had done during that year for the country. Then any poor person whatsoever was permitted to air any grievance and obtain redress for it.

When therefore King Duncan was making his annual progress through the kingdom in this way, it was his practice to correct abuses unlawfully inflicted on the lower classes by the more powerful, to prevent unjust and irregular imposts on the part of his officials, to crush the wickedness of brigands and other criminals, who raged violently among the people, with a kind of judicious severity, and to calm down the internal disputes of his subjects. This good quality in particular was inborn in him that he never allowed any discord to arise among the nobles in the kingdom either in his own time or his grandfather's; but immediately on hearing of it he prudently restored harmony.

Should not such a king be greatly revered, should he not be loved and honoured by all the inhabitants of the kingdom? Alas for the wicked arts of treachery, alas for the accursed arts of betrayal! Confidence is publicly broken with impunity; 'a stepson can scarcely trust his stepfather, a father his son, a sick man his doctor, when the reign of the Lord's Anointed hangs in the balance.'

He was killed through the wickedness of the family of the murderers of both his grandfather and great-grandfather, chief among whom was Macbeth son of Findlaech, by whom he was fatally wounded in secret at [Pitgaveny]. He was carried off to Elgin and died there. He was buried on the island of Iona. (c.49, ll.1-4, 12-59)

The duties of a king

In his next chapter Bower reflects on the threefold functions of a king. Besides biblical allusions he includes parallels from the first-century A.D. Latin writings of Valerius Maximus and Seneca, and from the Greek writer Plutarch of the same period. The two lines of verse are adapted from Virgil.

Just as antiquity tells us, kings ought to observe three functions, namely that they establish reasonable laws by their wisdom, secondly that they bring malefactors to justice by means of their power, thirdly that they grant mercy to those who need it freely and compassionately. And in response to these three functions their subjects ought to show three qualities, honour, fear and love. For a king who establishes rational laws wisely deserves to be held in honour; a king who punishes rebels through his power ought to be feared; but above all he who rules mercifully ought to be loved.

In addition to the fact that a king establishes reasonable laws by wisdom, it is requisite that the laws are established harmoniously, observed habitually and confirmed through reason firmly based on natural law. To begin with no law can be established except by the unanimous will of some nation, because a nation which is on the one hand impious in itself and on the other hand mixed (that is derived from different and diverse kinds) will never agree in establishing law, because, just as they are by nature composed of different varieties, so also they will be diverse in their wishes. And on that account it is very difficult for a very mixed nation of different blood (say composed of Scots and English or of country and town Scots) to agree on establishing anything or observing it in practice, because in such a community a man loves himself and no-one loves his country, just as is clear enough the other way round. For example some six or seven legitimate brothers, who are devoted to some state or community, will be more useful to that state than twenty men of mixed origin, as is made clear in the case of the Maccabees, sons of Mattathias.

Secondly it is necessary that the laws are well thought out through long familiarity and firmly rooted in good custom.

Thirdly that the laws themselves, well thought out in this way, must be firmly established through valid reasoning.

Hence Moses is honoured among the Jews because of his law-giving, Mahomet among the Saracens, Lycurgus among the Spartans, Phoroneus among the Greeks because of laws of this sort. 'Honour the king' (I Peter 2).

Secondly the duty of a king is chiefly to bring malefactors and rebels to justice through his power. Valerius [Maximus] records an example of this in his fifth book concerning Brutus the consul of the Romans. Sitting on the judgment seat he ordered his sons who had been arrested first to be beaten with rods, then to be tied to the stake and beheaded, because they wished to restore the tyranny of Tarquin which he himself had driven out. For he put off the father in order to act the consul. Concerning him the poet says:

> This Brutus summoned his sons, who were stirring up renewed wars,
> to punishment in the name of fair freedom.

The service of fear is deservedly due to a king because of this kind of rigorous justice. There is the example of King Solomon who, when two prostitutes were in dispute before him, one of whom had overlain her son in her sleep and then had placed him in the arms of the other woman and had taken her living son from her, said: 'Fetch me a sword and cut the living child in two' etc. There follows at the end: 'All Israel heard the judgment which the king had given and they feared the king' etc.

Thirdly the duty of a king is to forgive mercifully, because according to Seneca *De Clemencia* Book 1, Chapter 2: 'Mercy befits no man at all more than a king...it is a baleful force to be strong only for wrong-doing;' and in Chapter 3: 'War is the savagery of princes...no matter what house Mercy enters, she will make it happy and peaceful.' For the king, as Plutarch says, ought to be among his people like a minstrel, who controls wayward strings and reduces them to sweet harmony by loosening those that are taut and tightening those that are slack. For it is safer to loosen strings rather than to cut them. For the loose string is corrected by skill and gives out the sound it should, but the string once broken no skill can repair. (c.50)

The rule of Macbeth and the exile of Malcolm

When persecuted by King Macbeth, young Malcolm fled to the court of Edward the Confessor, who was king of England from 1042, while his brother Donald went to the Western Isles (which were then part of the Norwegian kingdom). The story here of Macbeth's cruelties has been seen as having more a literary purpose in introducing what is going to follow regarding MacDuff rather than any necessary basis in history.

Then Macbee or Macbeth, supported by swarms of malcontents and with very powerful resources, attained the dignity of king in 1040 and reigned for seventeen years. In the same year the emperor Conrad died and he was succeeded by Henry III or II...surnamed 'the Pious', who also reigned for seventeen years. After the death of King Duncan King Macbeth hunted down with all his might Duncan's sons, Malcolm Canmore (who should have succeeded Duncan) and his brother Donald, striving to kill them; but they resisted as best they could and remained in the kingdom for almost two years hoping for victory, while few of the people gave assistance openly either to Macbeth or to them. When therefore they did not dare to continue the struggle any longer, Donald went to the Western Isles and Malcolm to Cumbria, since it was abundantly clear that death rather than life awaited them, if they had remained. Then Malcolm, wishing to follow the advice of Earl Siward in all his actions there, made his way to him, and acting immediately on his advice and under his escort he sought an audience with King Edward who was reigning at that time in England, and was gladly admitted to his friendship and the assistance he had promised, very merciful and kind as he was. For he too like Malcolm had recently lived in exile.

While Malcolm remained in England for about fourteen years, both his enemies and his friends often advised him to return, his enemies anxious to destroy him and his friends striving to promote him to the kingship. Certain of the magnates of the kingdom often at that time spoke together in whispers about recalling Malcolm on the grounds that he was the true heir to the kingdom; but they did it too openly and for that reason they had no success at all. For what was sometimes spoken in the ear of certain people was openly declared to the king, as one person betrayed another. So he condemned to various punishments many of the magnates who were bound by a vow of conspiracy and especially those whom he knew were close friends of Malcolm. Some of them he consigned to execution, some he thrust into squalid prison, others he reduced to extreme poverty by confiscating all their goods. Several also fearing the ferocious sentence of the king fled from the kingdom, hoping however to return some day, leaving behind their lands and their children and their wives as well. (c.51, ll.1-38)

The exile of MacDuff

The story of MacDuff as Bower copied it here from Fordun is the earliest known version of it: it is probably based on an oral saga. The MacDuff family probably enjoyed already the special status held by later earls of Fife in the inauguration ceremonies of the Scottish kings at Scone. (Their castle of Kennoway is in central Fife.)

Edward king of the English reigned for twenty-four years, showing great kindness to Malcolm Canmore. The chief and most prominent of all those who were striving to raise Malcolm to the kingship of the Scots was the excellent, noble and loyal thane of Fife, MacDuff by name, who concealed the undivulged purpose of his heart more carefully and for a longer time than all the others. He was however regularly denounced before King Macbeth and finally came under suspicion. On a certain day as time went by the king seized an opportunity—what the occasion for it was I know not —first more savagely than usual perhaps accusing him of crimes arising from disloyalty, then openly adding that he would crush his neck under the yoke like an ox's in a wagon, and he swore moreover that this would not be long delayed. But MacDuff wisely, as required by the sudden crisis befalling him, although a great fear had seized hold of him, presented to Macbeth the cheerful and good-humoured face of innocence and mollified his ferocity for that occasion with the clever wheedling of his words. And so cautiously withdrawing from his presence and secretly leaving the court, he hastily departed for his castle of Kennoway, took up provisions and hurriedly made for the sea. Since the favourable wind was not expected to last much longer, he boarded a small boat that was filled with meagre supplies, and after suffering many dangers at sea through fierce storms, he put into harbour in England, scarcely alive but safe. There thanks to Malcolm he was received into favour.

When his clandestine departure was discovered by the king, he summoned in a fury all his horses and horsemen and hastily pursued the fugitive, until he saw for certain that the small boat on which Malcolm had set sail had left the land and was now under way and there was no hope that he could catch up with it. Hastily returning and laying siege to all MacDuff's castles and forts, he captured lands and estates. Whatever was valuable or seemed desirable he commanded its confiscation and, carrying off all MacDuff's property, he ordered it to be placed forthwith in his own treasury.

Moreover he caused him to be publicly proclaimed by the herald's voice an exile for ever, stripped of all his estates and all the rest of his possessions. So throughout the whole kingdom a great howl of protest arose especially among the nobles, since the thane was held in warm affection by all. Because the king, guided by anger rather than reason, had too precipitately made a man of such energy and power an exile or disinherited without a decree of the general council and nobles, they said that it was completely unjust that any noble or commoner should be condemned by a summary sentence of exile or disinheritance, before he was called to court on a lawful day at the statutory time. And possibly, they said, when he came at that time he would clear himself according to the laws and go free. But if he failed in court, he should put his body at the disposal of the king or otherwise give satisfaction, or, if he failed to come when convened, then he ought first of all to be proscribed as an exile or, if his fault demanded it, disinherited. (c.54)

Book V

Malcolm III defeats Macbeth

After making sure of MacDuff's loyalty to him, Malcolm sent him on ahead back to Scotland to prepare the way for his own return. In 1054 he was established in southern Scotland by Siward, the Danish earl of Northumbria (died 1055). Macbeth then moved north and was eventually killed at or after a battle at Lumphanan in Aberdeenshire in August 1057 (wrongly dated here). Bower adds a sour paragraph about English unwillingness to credit Scots with laudable exploits; then he takes over from Fordun a sympathetic attitude to those of Macbeth's subjects who deserted him as a tyrant.

Once the investigations into these dilemmas were completed, and all doubts and ambiguity removed, Malcolm sent Macduff back to Scotland secretly to tell his friends to make their preparations stealthily in expectation of Malcolm's definite return shortly. After Macduff had departed, Malcolm went into the presence of King Edward at the earliest opportunity, humbly petitioning him that he would graciously deign to permit certain of the nobles of England, who were willing of their own accord to set out with him for Scotland to win back his kingdom. The king kindly gave his immediate assent to his request and granted full licence to anyone who wished. Moreover he graciously promised that he himself would come to his aid with his military might, if it were necessary. Then Malcolm withdrew from his presence, expressing his boundless gratitude to the saintly and kind-hearted king who was merciful to all who consulted him, and ready to help those who were unjustly afflicted. As soon as he was ready, Malcolm set out to win Scotland for himself, taking with him as his companion Siward earl of Northumbria alone of all the English nobles. He had not yet crossed the border of the kingdom, when he heard that the whole population of the kingdom was in turmoil, and divided into factions between Macbeth and Macduff. Macduff as he was going ahead had spread the news [of his coming], rashly failing to keep to the agreed procedure. So Malcolm with his soldiers increased his speed, and did not rest until he had assembled a strong army with contingents joining in from all sides. Many of those who had previously followed Macbeth, immediately defected from him, and went over to Malcolm with all their strength. Thereafter Macbeth, perceiving that his might was diminishing daily, while Malcolm's was increasing, suddenly left the southern regions and made for the north, where he thought he could defend himself more securely in the narrow defiles and hidden depths of the forests. However Malcolm by a quick march unexpectedly pursued him over the mountains and as far as Lumphanan, and there suddenly intercepted him in a light skirmish, and killed him along with the few who resisted on 5 December 1056. For all the people that Macbeth led out to battle knew full well that Malcolm was their true lord; therefore they refused to fight a battle against him, and fled away and deserted the field of battle at the first sound of trumpets. William [of Malmesbury] writing as follows about the aforesaid battle says: 'Siward earl of Northumbria joined battle with Macbeth king of Scots by order of King Edward, and deprived him of his life and his kingdom. And he installed Malcolm son of the king of the Cumbrians as king in that same place.' See how William ascribes everything to Siward, depriving Malcolm of all glory in the victory, when in actual fact Malcolm alone with his own men and standard-bearer was responsible for the whole victory. This at any rate we must suppose that Macbeth's people would not have fled from the battle, if Malcolm had not been there, even if King Edward had been present with his forces along with Siward.

See also how, or rather, it is somehow instinctive with the English to be very sparing with their praises, when they ought to praise warmly some laudable achievements of the Scots. I am afraid that the historians of the all-too envious English are fatally infatuated in considering another nation's success as an adversity, and another's adversity as a success. They are sad when others rejoice, they rejoice when others are sad. It follows from this that when they are about to give a description of some brilliant Scottish exploit, they either try to obscure it with their exquisite style of writing or steal the Scots' glory merely by passing over it in silence.

That loyal people cannot be blamed for their flight, since they were oppressed under a tyrannous regime, neither able nor daring to rise in revolt, but always brooding over the cruel death of their king in their hearts and the unjust banishment of his heir over such a long period of time. And so refusing to submit any longer to their distressful subjection under a man of no higher rank than themselves, they seized the opportunity, and by their flight gave [Malcolm] the chance of definitely recovering the kingdom. For it seems, and it is true in my opinion, that the loyal indigenous people of any kingdom, when its head, that is its king, has been forcibly removed, or has suffered any kind of insult, certainly suffers along with him, and mourns for the taunt he has suffered, as if they were lamenting a reproach to themselves, since it says in the proverb: 'If the head aches, the rest of the body is sick.' And this is true of a healthy body which suffers along with the headache, not of decayed or cancerous bodies which do not feel the sickness of their aching head. For it often happens from contact with such diseased parts of the body that certain parts fall into incurable diseases, and sometimes their head is also infected by them with this kind of disease to such an extent that the whole body can be rendered monstrous. Surely any body whatsoever can rightly be called a monstrosity, whose foot, that is its lowest part, wasted away by a feverish illness that has not been assuaged in good time with cautery at the hands of physicians, invades worthier parts, and infecting its head with poison removes it, placing itself upon the neck and shoulders in place of the head contrary to nature? (c.7, ll.1-58; c.8, ll.1-25)

The marriage of Malcolm and Margaret

For the story of how St Margaret came to Scotland with others of her family including Edgar the Ætheling (i.e. 'royal prince') and was married c.1070 to King Malcolm Canmore, Fordun (followed by Bower) takes over the version that was recorded soon after Margaret's death in 1093 by Turgot prior of Durham (later bishop of St Andrews). These members of the Anglo-Saxon royal family were trying to return to Hungary where Margaret had been born. (St Margaret's Hope is a bay in the Firth of Forth now occupied by Rosyth in Fife.)

When Edgar the Ætheling perceived that the affairs of the English were everywhere in turmoil, he took ship and attempted to return to the land in which he was born along with his mother and sisters. But the Supreme Ruler who rules the winds and the sea stirred up the sea, and its waves rose high with the blast of the winds. As the storm raged, all were put in despair of their lives, they commended themselves to God, and entrusted their ship to the sea. So after very many dangers and immense hardships the Lord took pity on His desolate family, since when human aid is seen to fail, one inevitably turns to the Lord. At last battered by countless perils on the sea, they were forced to land in Scotland. So that saintly family landed at a certain place which since that time has been called St Margaret's Bay by the local inhabitants. And we believe that this did not happen accidentally, but that she came to that place by the providence of the most high God. So while the aforesaid family lingered on the said beach, and were all fearfully awaiting the outcome of the affair, their arrival was reported to King Malcolm, who was at that time staying with his people not far from that place. He dispatched messengers to the ship to find out the true state of affairs there. The messengers went to that place, were amazed at the unusual size of the ship, and hurried as quickly as possible to tell the king what they had seen. When he heard this, the king dispatched a larger number of envoys to that place, more intelligent than the previous ones and drawn from the ranks of his greatest nobles. They were made welcome as envoys of the king's majesty, and having carefully assessed with no small admiration the nobility of the men, the beauty of the women and the earnestness of the whole family, they held a pleasant conversation with each other thereafter. To cut a long story short, the envoys appointed for this purpose inquired into the final outcome, the sequence of events and the reason [for their coming], with sweet eloquence and eloquent sweetness. They for their part, as being strangers and incomers newly arrived, explained to them humbly and eloquently the cause and manner of their landing in words without guile. The envoys went back and reported to their king the courtesy shown by the older men, the good sense of the younger men, the wisdom of the matrons and the loveliness of the young girls, and one of them added the words: 'We saw there a certain lady, who, I tell you, Your Majesty, I suspect and judge is the mistress of the family on account of her incomparable beauty of person and wealth of pleasing eloquence as well as abundance of other good qualities. Her wonderful charm and character I consider easier to admire than to describe.' And no wonder they believed her to be the mistress, who was the mistress not only of that family but also heiress to the whole of England after her brother, and indeed predestined by providence to be the consort and future queen of Malcolm's kingdom. Now the king when he heard that they were English and were at that place, visited them and spoke to them in his own person, and inquired more fully where they came from and where they were going. For he was as fluent in the English and also the French language as in his own, since after the death of his father he had stayed in England for fourteen years, where, as it happened, he had heard something to acquaint him with this saintly family, so that for this reason he dealt with them more gently and behaved more kindly towards them.

As soon as the king saw Margaret, and learned that she was of royal and also imperial descent, he sought to have her as his wife, and succeeded, with Edgar the Ætheling her brother giving her away, more in accordance with the wishes of her people than her own desire, or rather at God's command. (c.16 - c.17, 1.5)

The virtuous works of Malcolm and Margaret

Bower improves on the accounts of both Turgot and Fordun to produce his own version of the saintly ways of Malcolm and Margaret.

I shall at this point deal briefly with some of the virtuous works and almsgiving of that magnificent king Malcolm and his queen, as Turgot testifies in the Legend of the life of the blessed queen. For just as the prophet

David sang in the Psalm: 'In the company of the holy, you will be holy,' so the king himself learned from the saintly queen to enjoy saintly works, and with her encouragement to refrain from wickedness, to confirm the truth of what St Paul said: 'Through his Christian wife a heathen man is sanctified.' Not surprisingly he was afraid to offend in any way the queen herself, whose manner of life was so much to be revered, since he had observed that Christ dwelt in her heart, or rather he was eager to obey her requests and wise counsels promptly in all respects. What she rejected, he also rejected; and what she loved, he loved from love of her love.

So although he was illiterate, he often used to handle and examine the books from which she was accustomed to pray or read. And when he heard from her which of them was particularly dear to her, he also began to regard it as particularly dear, and to kiss and caress it often. Sometimes also he would summon a goldsmith and give orders that the book was to be embellished with gold and precious gems, and when it had been embellished, the king himself would take it to the queen as a mark of his devotion.

And he learned from her example frequently to prolong the watches of the night in praying, and to pray to God devoutly with heart-felt groans and tears. 'I confess,' says Turgot, 'I confess that I marvelled at the great miracle of God's mercy, when at times I saw such great earnestness in prayer on the part of the king, such great remorse in the heart of a layman at prayer. During the period of Lent and the days of Advent before Christmas, unless he was prevented by important temporal business, after the completion of Mattins, and when the solemnities of the early morning Mass had been celebrated, the king would return to his chamber, and along with the queen would wash the feet of six poor people, and bestow on them something to alleviate their poverty. It was the chief duty of the chamberlain to bring in poor people every night before the entrance of the queen, so that on entering she would find them ready for her to serve, or rather for her to serve Christ in them. After this was done, she went off to rest and sleep. When it was morning she arose from her bed, and devoted much time to prayers and psalms, and while reciting the psalms she performed the work of mercy. For in the first hour of day she had nine orphan babies who had no means of support brought in to her to be fed. For she had ordered that mild food which is pleasing to infancy should be prepared for them daily. When it was brought in, she herself knelt to serve them, made little drinks for them, and was not too proud to spoon food into their mouths. So the queen, who was revered by all peoples, for Christ's sake performed the duty of a careful servant and the devotion of a very sweet mother. She could fittingly have employed that saying of blessed Job: "From my infancy my compassion has grown with me, and it emerged with me from my mother's womb."

Meanwhile the custom was for three hundred poor people to be brought into the royal court, and when they were seated all round in order, the king and queen entered, and the doors were shut by attendants. For except for the chaplains, some religious, and some attendants, no one was permitted to be present at their works of almsgiving. The king on one side and the queen on the other served Christ in the persons of the poor people, and offered food and drink specially prepared for this purpose with great devotion. For the king and queen were both equal in works of charity, both outstanding in the pursuit of holiness. After this the king would devote careful attention to temporal matters and the business of his kingdom, while the queen would go into the church, and there offer herself wholeheartedly as a sacrifice to God with prolonged prayers and tearful sobs.' (c.23 - c.24, l.14)

A judicial duel involving Edgar the Ætheling

Bower repeats here Fordun's unique account of a judicial trial by combat fought out by two Englishmen at the court of the Norman King William II Rufus in 1093. There are political overtones, for one of the contestants was acting as a champion for the English prince Edgar, who was being accused of treason against the Norman dynasty that had supplanted his family on the English throne. The story tells of an outstanding example of the new-fangled Norman practice of the knightly duel as a means to letting God reveal the truth.

At the same time during the reign of William II a certain degenerate English knight Orgar by name, wishing to ingratiate himself with the king, brought an action falsely accusing this Edgar the Ætheling (that is 'glorious by birth', for this was the title given to him) of treason against the aforesaid King William. The case on this charge was brought before the king's presence, because Edgar was descended from royal stock, and was next in line to the kingship by English law. The king to safeguard himself declared the charge to be valid, and supported the plaintiff with his royal power of protection. And there could no longer be any doubt about the condemnation of Edgar, if the charge brought against him could have been proved. Edgar was troubled about this, and began to make careful enquiries as to whether anyone would dare to support his side of the case either by speaking or giving advice. But fear of the king frustrated his offers of rewards, because the magnates believed that they could not support him with impunity, since they would have incurred the hatred of the king if they defended him. So as he was at a loss and weighed down with excessive anxiety, a knight from Winchester, English by birth and nobly born, by name Godwine, mindful of Edgar's ancient lineage, promised that he would lend his aid in this difficult case. Now the day was at hand that had been arranged for the determination of this case. The supercilious person of the plaintiff promptly appeared. Since he was seen to excel in physical strength, and because of his skill in fighting at which he was adept, he considered that he had no equal in combat; and in addition to this estimation he had the support of the king. Puffed up by these considerations he believed that he could easily prove any accusation that he had brought against his opponent. So because of this man's false accusation Edgar was compelled to defend himself in a duel, or to substitute another man for himself in the fight. For by getting a decision in this way he hoped to establish the truth of the matter. So Godwine took Edgar's cause upon himself, and after the customary exchange of oaths on both sides he publicly declared that he would champion Edgar. Immediately there was a great preparation of arms on both sides. They came together to do battle. Orgar stepped forward elated by the support of the king, protected by the king's henchmen on both sides, and resplendent in his richly ornamented armour. Godwine on the other hand, although he did not have the same support from the nobles who supported the king, yet with no less self-confidence, entered the place for the contest. Although he feared the king's anger because of his championing of the opposing side, he still considered that he ought by rights to repay this natural debt to further the cause of him whom he knew ought with more justice to hold sway over himself and all the rest as their natural overlord. Hence also he rebuked the false accuser with just reproach, on the grounds that being English by birth he appeared as an opponent of the natural order. For he ought to have venerated Edgar as his lord, since he was by right of birth the man to whom he owed himself and all that he had. When silence had been imposed on all by the herald, and the pledges from both sides had been thrown into the place for the contest by the judge, who proclaimed that God who knows what is hidden would show the truth of this case, the affair was finally committed to arms and the cause to the Celestial Judge.

They lost no time, as the one rose up against the other, the plaintiff against the defendant. Soon strokes came thick and fast on this side and on that. Orgar made an attack, and while his opponent took the blow on his shield, he cut off a large part of the shield. Godwine was no less active, his temper roused by the heavy stroke, he rose up to strike, and while his opponent was rashly lowering his shield, with a forceful stroke between the head and the shoulder he broke that bone which joins the left shoulder to the neck together with the knots of his cuirass. But the hilt of his sword was loosened by this stroke and cheated the hand of the striker; his sword slipped from his grasp. His opponent noticed this, and although seriously wounded, and with his left hand damaged, nevertheless he rose up more violently against his adversary, thinking that he would all the more easily disable him, because he was deprived of the assistance of that with which he should particularly have fought. However this hope deceived its master. For although his adversary was opposing him with all his might and main, Godwine held out his shield, and amid the mighty blows of the striker raised from the ground the sword which had just fallen from his grasp. Since he was unable to hold it firmly because of the loss of the hilt, he grasped the edge of the sword with his first two fingers, and even though he could not do any harm to his adversary by striking without injury to himself, nevertheless by attacking and aiming deadly strokes, he appeared to be a match for his adversary. For he neither gave ground before the attack of the enemy, nor did he cease from strokes. With one stroke indeed he gouged out the eye of his adversary with damage to his head, and with repeated strokes he wounded and rendered the rest of his treacherous enemy's body so useless that Orgar no longer seemed able to keep his feet, but collapsed on the ground more dead than alive. And now as the enemy fell with a great clatter of arms, his opponent was not slow to place his foot upon him, and immediately the deceit and cunning of his enemy was now openly revealed, and he was publicly proved guilty of perjury. For he drew out a knife which lay hidden in his boot, and tried to stab his opponent, although he had sworn before the beginning of the conflict that he would bear nothing in this duel but knightly weapons. Soon however he paid the price for his perjury. When the knife was snatched from him, and hope deserted the guilty man, he immediately confessed his crime. However this confession did nothing to prolong his life. As wound succeeded wound, he was pierced all over, until the violence of the pain and the extent of his wounds expelled his wicked soul. When this was concluded, everyone marvelled at the outcome of this duel, and praised the just judgment of God, because the false accuser had been beaten in the fight, and the man who was the champion of truth and innocence had not suffered even one wound from his attacker. Thereafter he found great favour with the king and the nobles because of this outstanding proof of his prowess, to such an extent that the king granted him the lands and possessions of his vanquished foe to be held with hereditary rights. (cc.27 - 28)

King Alexander I and Alexander Scrimgeour

There follows a version of the origin-legend of the Scrimgeour family, the head of which came to hold the appointments of hereditary royal Standard Bearer and Constable of the Castle of Dundee in Angus. King Alexander I (1107-24) seems likely himself (despite what is said here) to have held the earldom of Gowrie (west of Dundee and including Liff and Invergowrie) before succeeding his brother Edgar on the throne. The Augustinian house at Scone near Perth may not have been founded until c.1120; it was certainly endowed with the lands mentioned here. (The nickname 'Scrimgeour' means 'the fencer'.)

[King Edgar] was succeeded by his brother Alexander nicknamed 'the Fierce'. He is called 'the Fierce' because his uncle the earl of Gowrie gave him as a baptismal gift the lands of Liff and Invergowrie. When he became king, he began to build a royal palace at Liff, when behold certain ruffians of the Mearns and Moray made an attempt to capture the king by night within the precincts of the palace, and when they were trying to break down the doorposts, one of the king's chamberlains called Alexander Carron cunningly led the king out through a latrine. He went aboard a galley at Invergowrie, and made for the southern regions of Scotland, gathered together a large army, and hurried against the rebels. Because God had supported him in time of danger, he wished to show his gratitude to Him. So he founded a monastic church at Scone, and after he had given them the lands of Liff and Invergowrie as endowment and glebe, he quickly resumed his expedition along with his men. When they arrived at the Water of Spey, his enemies were massed together in a great army on the opposite bank; and as the water was rising excessively high, the king was advised not to ford the Water until it subsided. He was blazing with anger at the sight of his enemies threatening conspiracy, and not being able to contain himself, he handed over his banner to his chamberlain (the aforesaid Alexander) to carry; and these two were the first to attempt the ford; the army followed, and the enemy was turned to flight. From this time the said Alexander and his heirs were standard-bearers, and because of this they had lands conferred on them by the king in perpetuity. But because this Alexander cut off a hand in an English tournament, he left the surname *Scrimgeour* for himself and his successors right to this day. (c.36, ll.1-27)

Alexander I and Scone

Bower takes over Fordun's enthusiastic assessment of King Alexander. The Benedictine monastery at Dunfermline in west Fife had been founded (mainly at the instigation of Queen Margaret) as a daughter-house of Canterbury. (The Boar's Chase was an area surrounding St Andrews in east Fife; the island of Inchcolm in west Fife contained Bower's own Augustinian monastery; Nostell is near Pontefract in west Yorkshire—the first prior and canons at Scone came from there.)

King Alexander reigned for seventeen years. He was a well-educated and devout man, deferential and friendly to clerics and religious, but excessively terrifying to the rest of his subjects; he was a great-hearted man, extending himself in all directions beyond his strength. He was very enthusiastic in constructing churches, searching for relics of the saints, and in the manufacture and arrangement of priestly vestments and sacred books; he was also very generous beyond his means to all comers; so devout was he in respect of the poor that there was nothing that seemed to give him greater pleasure than receiving, washing, feeding and clothing them. Following in his mother's footsteps, he rivalled her in holy deeds to such an extent that he endowed three churches with many great gifts, that is to say the church of St Andrew at Kilrymont and the churches of Dunfermline and Scone, the one founded by his father and mother, the other founded by himself to the glory of the Holy Trinity and St Michael the archangel, which was founded and built at Scone the chief seat of the kingdom. It was he who conferred the Boar's Chase on blessed Andrew, and who also founded the monastery of canons of the island of Inchcolm near Inverkeithing, and who conferred so many great privileges on the aforesaid church of the Holy Trinity at Scone, which he founded and built in the place where both the Pictish and the Scottish kings from ancient times had established the chief seat of their kingdom; and he had it dedicated after it had been built of stone construction in the manner of that time. In response to the king's command almost the whole of the kingdom flocked to its dedication, which was performed by Turgot bishop of St Andrews. Under God's dispensation he unreservedly handed over the church with all its pertinents to be governed by canons regular who were summoned from the church of St Oswald of Nostell, and to all the others who would serve God after them until the end of the world. (c.36, ll.39-69)

The last days of King David I

Bower devotes surprisingly little space to the long reign of David I (1124-53), being content for the most part to copy much of the Lamentation *or* Eulogy *of David composed by Ailred of Rievaulx (died 1167). But he does have a chapter derived from Fordun about the king's last year (after the death of his heir Henry in 1152), when Henry's eldest son Malcolm was acknowledged as the new heir, and the next son William was established in Henry's earldom of Northumbria. It was a Celtic custom for an heir to make a circuit of the kingdom to establish his title. (The 'I' mentioned is Fordun, as taken over by Bower.) David's authority at his death extended southwards to include both Northumbria and Cumbria.*

Hiding his grief over the death of his only son, King David immediately took Malcolm the first-born of his aforesaid son, and, giving him Duncan earl of Fife as his guardian together with a large army, since he himself was an old man and could not travel around the kingdom without injury to his health, ordered that his young grandson should be taken around the provinces of Scotland, and proclaimed as heir to the kingdom. The king also took the younger brother William with him to Newcastle, and, having received hostages there from the chief men of Northumbria, he made them all subject to the boy's lordship. What was done concerning the third grandson David, or where he was, I have not found in the records. Returning [from there], the king, although advanced in years, left nothing in disarray or out of order in the whole extent of his kingdom. Then in the following year he went to Carlisle after Easter to put in order the affairs of the western part of his kingdom, just as he had done for the eastern part. Suddenly the pious and godly king was laid low with a serious illness, and, after he had gloriously ruled the kingdom for twenty-nine years and one month, met a happy death on the Sunday before the Ascension day on 24 May 1153, giving his body to the earth and his spirit to Heaven to consort with the angels. He was buried with great honour beneath the floor before the high altar in the church of the Holy Trinity of Dunfermline, which was founded first of all by his father and mother, enlarged by his brother Alexander with possessions and buildings, and by himself enriched with generous gifts and distinctions; and there in ripe old age he was placed beside his parents and brothers. His memory is blessed throughout all the generations, because no prince to equal him has arisen from time immemorial. In his devotion to divine worship he took care to say all the canonical hours each day including the vigils of the dead.

It was indeed praiseworthy in him that he wisely moderated the ferocity of his people in a spirit of wise counsel and resolution, and that he was very constant in washing the feet of the poor, and compassionate in feeding and clothing them. He also showed himself to be unassuming and meek in the presence of foreigners and pilgrims and regular and secular clergy, and lavishly gave them gifts from his munificence. For the king was glorious in his everyday temperance, the holiness of his way of life, his simplicity in dress, in his disciplined behaviour; and in the nobility of his character he showed himself to be a model even for men of religion. Assuredly his life deserving the praise or rather the admiration of all was followed by a precious death. Therefore whoever desires to die a happy death, let him learn to die from the example of his most happy death by reading the life of this king beloved of God and the *Lamentation* for his death that follows. (c.44, ll.1-29, 35-49)

The saintly King David I

Ailred of Rievaulx had personal acquaintance with King David from the 1130s onwards, and produced a tribute in an elaborate literary style for a man whom he much admired. Here three chapters have been selected out of fifteen included by Fordun and Bower as a sample of the flavour of the whole. David's endowment of church institutions was lavish, with his favour being spread over various religious orders. His social concern and humble demeanour were especially notable. The whole country flourished under his rule. (His only son Henry died before him in 1152, leaving David's three grandsons—the later Kings Malcolm IV and William I, and David earl of Huntingdon.)

He excelled in these matters, it seems to me, because he observed such moderation on each side that in the strictness of his justice he was loved by all, and in the leniency and mercy of his justice he was feared by all, although he always wished to be loved rather than feared. So deservedly he was seen as beloved by God and men. Clearly beloved of God, since immediately at the beginning of his reign he diligently practised the things that are of God in building churches, in founding monasteries, which he also endowed with properties and riches according to the needs of each. For although he found only three or four bishops in the whole kingdom of the Scots, while the rest of the churches were drifting aimlessly without a shepherd to the detriment of both morals and property, at his death he left nine bishoprics including both ancient ones that he had restored, and new ones that he erected. He also left monasteries of various orders, Cluniac, Cistercian, Tironensian, Arrouaisian, Premonstratensian, order of Beauvais, namely Kelso, Melrose, Jedburgh, Newbattle, Holm Cultram, Dundrennan, the monastery of Holyrood Crag near Edinburgh, Cambuskenneth, Kinloss and a monastery of nuns near Berwick, and, as some say, a monastery of nuns of St Bartholomew near Carlisle, and Premonstratensian canons of Newcastle and a monastery of Black Monks there, and another of nuns there, as appears in his prologue to the *Statutes of Burghs*, and he also introduced thirteen monks from Canterbury to Dunfermline, and left many other monasteries fully staffed with brothers. When he was with them, he was like one of themselves, praising good deeds, and, if there chanced to emerge deeds less worthy of praise, modestly shutting his eyes to them, making himself available to all, concerned about everyone, giving generously, and asking nothing for himself. Oh sweet soul, where have you gone to, where have you withdrawn to? Our eyes search for you, but will not be able to find you. Our ears are pricked up to hear the voice of your cheerfulness, the voice of humility, the voice of confession, the voice of consolation, and behold, silence! Where is that most pleasant face which showed itself so gentle to the poor, so humble to the holy, and so cheerful to its friends? Where are those eyes full of piety and grace with which you would rejoice along with the joyful, and weep along with those who wept? What are you doing, my eyes, what are you doing? Why do you hesitate to give birth to what you are labouring with, to bring forth what you are hiding within you? Let the tears fall by day and by night, do not be sparing of them, since these will be my delight in remembrance of my most sweet lord and friend. Nor do I grieve alone. I know that priests and clerics whom he revered as fathers grieve along with me; nuns and monks whom he embraced as brothers grieve; knights grieve, whose friend rather than lord he knew himself to be; the widows whom he protected grieve, as do the orphans whom he comforted, the poor whom he supported, the wretched whom he cherished.

For he was a comforter of those who mourned, a father of orphans, and a very ready judge of widows. For although he entrusted other business of the kingdom to other judges, he always reserved for himself the affairs of the poor, orphans and widows. He himself was auditor, advocate and judge in cases of this sort, and no poor person, widow or orphan, who intended to lodge some complaint, was ever forbidden access to him, but was immmediately brought in by the doorkeeper. Even if [the king] was engaged in the most important and pressing business and consultations even with important and select persons, it was all interrupted, and he or she was heard. I saw also with my own eyes, when sometimes he was ready to go hunting, and with his foot placed in the stirrup he was intending to mount his horse, that he withdrew his foot, left his horse and returned to his hall at the voice of a poor person demanding that audience be given to him, and he would not return to what he had planned on that day, but exceeding or at any rate imitating the judgments of the most civil and magnificent emperor Trajan, he heard the case for which he had been called kindly and patiently. It was his custom besides to sit at the door of the royal hall and to listen attentively to cases of poor people and old women, who were summoned on certain days from particular regions wherever they came from, and to strive hard to give satisfaction to each one. For often they argued with him and he with them, when he refused to accept the legal standing of a poor person contrary to justice, and when they refused to give assent to the reasoned argument which he demonstrated to them. I say nothing of the wonderful courtesy and pleasant manner with which he won the affection of all, or of how he adapted himself to everyone's disposition, so that he was not thought to be soft to harsh people, nor harsh to those who were soft. Finally if it happened that a priest or a knight or a monk, a rich man or poor man, citizen or foreigner, business man or countryman had conversation with him, he discoursed suitably and unassumingly with each concerning his business and duties in such a way that each one thought that he cared only for his affairs. And thus he sent them all away cheerful and edified. For thus he did his best to entice that rough and uncouth people to calm and civilised manners, so that he took care not only of the important matters of his kingdom, but also of the most trivial such as gardens, buildings and orchards so that he might encourage them to similar interests by his example.

You who were formerly a beggar among all other countries used to inflict famine on your inhabitants from your harsh soil; now softer and more fertile than the others, you have relieved the poverty of neighbouring regions from your abundance. King David adorned you with castles and cities, he raised you up with lofty towers, he enriched your ports with foreign merchandise, and added the riches of other kingdoms for your delight. He exchanged your rough cloaks for expensive garments, and covered your long-customary nakedness with fine linen and purple cloth. He calmed your savage behaviour by means of the Christian religion. He imposed upon you chastity in marriage of which you were for the most part ignorant, and gave your priests a more honourable way of life. He persuaded you to go regularly to church, and take part in the divine sacrifices both in word and deed; he showed that the due offerings and teinds should be paid to the priests. So what will you give him in return for all that he has given you? You have assuredly the means to repay the debt. You have those to whom you may give thanks for his benefits, those to whom you may repay the kindness which he earned. You have him in the persons of his grandsons, from whom it may be that Divine Providence removed the support of their grandfather so soon for no other reason than that your loyalty might be tested, and your gratitude tried. They are indeed under age, but the age of a king is reckoned according to the loyalty of his knights. Pay to the sons what you owed to the father; let them find you grateful for the benefits which you have received. (cc. 48, 49, 53)

Book VI

The young St Waltheof

Bower includes several extracts from the Life *of St Waltheof (latterly abbot of Melrose 1148-59) by Jocelin of Furness (written probably c.1207). Waltheof and his brother Simon were the sons of the Norman Simon de Senlis I earl of Huntingdon by Matilda heiress of the Anglo-Saxon earldom of Northumbria, whose second husband was to be King David I of Scotland. There follow two passages of the* Life *describing the saint's boyhood. Some of this is probably imaginative hagiography.*

The aforesaid Earl Simon the father of the boys loved the first-born more dearly, like another Isaac loving his Esau; but their mother, good woman, loved Waltheof with deeper affection, as Rebecca loved her Jacob. And when the brothers were children, they understood, behaved and played as children do. Simon the elder boy was in the habit of collecting little twigs and branches to build castles to his own little design, and mounting his horse or steed, and grasping and brandishing a little stick like a lance, he painstakingly engaged in pretend warfare with boys of his own age based on the guarding and defending of a make-believe and imaginary castle. But Waltheof as a small boy made buildings like churches out of small sticks and stones, and stretching out his hands played the part of a priest celebrating mass; and because he did not know how to pronounce the words, he used to utter sounds in imitation of the chant. The boys would often indulge in this kind of game, and they would cause many people to watch and laugh. On one occasion a certain wise monk who was standing and watching with the others said to the onlookers: 'What do you make of this children's game?' They declared that he was merely a simpleton, in that he was one of those who cannot tell their right hand from their left. He said: 'Not so, not so! For this game acts as a kind of prelude that foretells the life and end of each boy. For the first will entangle his life with warfare until his death, while the second will live as a monk and crown his days with good.' None of these words went unfulfilled; but what he predicted in conjecture or prophecy came about in each case. Simon indeed with great labour at length obtained his paternal earldom long after his father's death. And after becoming an active knight, in the reign of King Stephen he built new castles and took over others built by other people; he added earldoms and cities to his earldom, and ended his life in secular warfare, though in Christian fashion, while Waltheof, after leading a life celebrated for his virtues and also for his miracles, in the end fell asleep in the Lord, as the account in the book on his life makes clear at greater length.

Waltheof, a boy of innate good character, followed his mother (who loved him dearly), no longer a countess but now made queen, to the court of King David. There he was nurtured and brought up. He grew big and strong, and the grace of God was demonstrated in him by clear signs. For in the palace he conducted himself as a cleric, in the crowd as a monk, among the courtiers as a hermit. Among the other virtuous qualities which he possessed, one unique distinction, the shining glory of chastity, travelled with him from his mother's womb to Heaven. King David did not behave as a step-father, but as a father, and loved and reared him as his own son. He often invited Waltheof to come him with him when he went hunting, sometimes giving him his bow to carry. Waltheof, however, escaped from the king's sight as best he could, and entrusting the royal bow to someone else, he used to penetrate the shady parts of the wood; and seeking and finding some clearing among the bushy thickets, he would sit and read a book deliberately brought for the purpose and taken out from a fold in his clothes, or devote himself to prayer. When he had been doing this repeatedly, the king happened one day to find him following his usual practice, and on returning home he told the queen what he had seen, and speaking with great insight, he said: 'Your son, my queen, is not one of us. He has nothing to do with this world. Either yielding to fate he will soon depart from this life, or he will withdraw from secular affairs and take refuge in some form of the monastic life.' Whether these words were spoken by the most Christian king as a conjecture or a pronouncement at the prompting of the Holy Spirit, they were carried into effect not long afterwards. The queen as a wise and most excellent woman treasured up all these words and pondered over them, giving thanks and commending her son to her Maker who ordains everything. (c.5; c.6, ll.26-53)

St Waltheof's vision of a baby

This story of a vision by St Waltheof is inserted by Jocelin in the Life *at the stage when Waltheof was prior of the Augustinian house at Kirkham near Malton in East Yorkshire in the early 1140s. It is apparently a story told of many saints in support of belief in the mystery of the mass.*

One most sacred Christmas Day he was celebrating mass in a spirit of great devotion and with his usual shedding of tears. As he elevated the Host in the secret part of the canon and uttered the operative words of the sacrament when the substance of the bread is changed into the body and the substance of the wine into the blood of the Lord, he found a baby in his hands, surpassing all the sons of men in beauty, as if wearing a golden crown on his head which was glowing brightly with starry jewels. This little boy seemed whiter than any snow, with sweet-flowing laughter in his eyes and a serene expression. He caressed Waltheof's head and face by touching, stroking and smoothing them with a delightful movement of his hands; and when placing his head against Waltheof's head and, more precious than the whole world, his mouth against Waltheof's mouth, he imprinted kisses over and over again. Waltheof was indeed intoxicated by the torrent of pleasure in the house of the Lord, as if he had been brought into a wine-cellar, and planted innumerable kisses on the feet and hands and the various limbs of this little Jesus of ours: he felt that his beloved was wholly desirable for him, and delightful as he reflected on the happy experience. At length the beloved baby raised his hands and blessed him with the sign of the cross, and vanished from his sight; and he saw nothing in his hands except the usual Host.

Whenever the man of God inwardly recalled this divine vision, he was filled again with incalculable joy in his heart, and was drenched in a quiet flow of tears. The man of God concealed all this for a long time, but later spoke about it, revealing all the secrets of his soul to his confessor, and peremptorily bound him by virtue of his obedience not to divulge it to anyone while he was still alive. The confessor indeed complied with the other man's instructions, and so long as the man of God lived kept that story secret; but after his death the confessor revealed it to some monks. The same man of God also declared that he had felt no greater weight when actually lifting up the boy himself than when elevating the Host placed on the altar. From reflection on this wonderful vision then, not only does one acknowledge the sanctity of the man, but also the catholic faith in the life-giving sacraments of the altar is strengthened, the assertions of the orthodox fathers are confirmed, and the detestable error of heretics who deny the divine mystery of the body and blood of the Lord is confounded. (c.8)

Fordun's address to the Scottish kings

Bower includes Fordun's chapter of reflections on the duties of the kings of the Scots, heirs as they were through Malcolm III and St Margaret of two royal lines. Fordun is referring to Ailred's Genealogia Regum Anglorum *(composed 1153-4 for the young Henry II just before he became king of England), and seems to be accepting a mid-twelfth-*

century view that David I was the rightful heir to both kingdoms. Bower, the experienced if disillusioned royal councillor, adopts these words as his own.

Kings of the Scots! Since the royal lines of your own family as well as of the English combine and meet together in you, as is abundantly clear in what has been written above (and will also be clear in what follows below), where you have read about certain royal actions and virtues of your Scottish family, now as a consequence and here accordingly we want to write to you about some charitable works of the kings of your English family, and about some warlike activities briefly excerpted from the chronicles of Ailred the abbot of Rievaulx, so that by reading at leisure the histories first of one group of your old ancestors and then of the other, even if they are brief, you may praise God as with joyful hearts rejoicing exceedingly because you are descended from glorious roots that have been joined together. Indeed these two royal lines, for whom the size of the island was formerly insufficient for living in peace and harmony, are now joined together as one and are at peace in the person of one ruler by an ordinance of divine grace as no one doubts. Therefore as the offspring produced from these roots it is your duty to take care not to become degenerate (God forbid!), and produce bitter and useless fruits, but rather sweet and tasty ones, and to maintain the traditions of the brilliant fighting force of a victorious fighting island, that is of the Scots and the English. First also take care to love and fear God, the most invincible king of all kings, and by rendering devoted praise to him to serve him alone; and to defend the kingdom with a protective sword against external invaders; and to preserve the just and customary liberties of the church of God; and to govern with the laws by kindly cherishing with the sceptre of justice the people subject to you; and if there are any magnates at variance with each other, invite them humbly to be at peace. But at the same time rebels against the royal authority, and evil men among the people, should be compelled to submit to just judgment, or if they will not accept correction, they should (to use the words of the prophet) like potter's vessels be shattered with a rod of iron. At the same time let the rod that gives direction to your kingdom be that of equity. What is more contemptible, what is more shocking than for a knight to rebel against the king, that is a limb against the head? When a crisis for the whole body or kingdom appears to threaten, do both [body and kingdom] deserve mutilation, or a delicate and mild remedy for restoration to health? For an internal calamity, not only one affecting the king, but any kind of dissension, should be guarded against with attentive care. If nevertheless it comes about, it should by no means be brought to an end by a slow reconciliation, but by a quick one, just as in the case of the flesh a suppurating wound has to be healed to begin with by medical applications, or if the swelling has increased, then the infected matter should be extracted from it skilfully with a knife. But believe me, the best cure for all dissensions or illnesses, and the speediest, is to make a careful stand against them at the start. Now let us return to our main theme. (c.9)

Maurice bishop of Le Mans

Faced with the fact that in his old age St Waltheof in 1159 rejected an order from his monastic superior (the abbot of Rievaulx) to accept election as bishop of St Andrews, Bower introduces stories about various valid responses to such situations. One of these stories comes again from the collection of exempla compiled by Thomas of Cantimpré (see above III, c.37). It appears to relate to the Maurice who served as bishop of Le Mans in France 1216-31. ('Postulation' is a technical term under canon law for an appointment that is conditional on a dispensation from the strict letter of the law.)

We have similarly read that:

> at one time the church of Le Mans had languished for a long time without a pastor of integrity; and after the bishop's death the day for an election came round. But since scarcely any group of clergy is so short of persons that it does not have at least one man who out of filial piety grieves at the mother church's failure and rejoices at its success, one of the canons of this church indeed approached a certain recluse who was very famous for her sanctity to ask how a worthy bishop might be elected. Moved by his entreaties, turning from prayer she said: 'Dear brother, I was transported into Heaven and saw that the Blessed Virgin Mary, the protector of the church, when the subject was raised, advanced to the feet of her son to ask for an answer. The son, courteously rising to his feet, said to her: "It will be for you, my lady mother, to appoint whomsoever you wish." Christ's mother therefore withdrew along with some holy angels to discuss the business; and at length returned saying: "My son, on the advice of the blessed ones, it is my wish that Maurice formerly archdeacon of Troyes be appointed bishop of Le Mans." And the son said: "You have made a worthy choice; so be it."' And next the recluse said to the canon: 'See therefore, dear brother, that you keep what you have seen secret until it is achieved.'
>
> This Maurice as archdeacon used to go round the diocese on foot, and visited it as a preacher bearing just his staff. Later, after abandoning

the archdeaconry, he sought out a convent of black nuns (by whose charity he had been brought up while still a boy), so that he might admonish them in the direction of a more perfect life, and so that he might through his preaching teach the ignorant people of the district in accordance with the needs of the time. And the outcome did not disappoint him.

To be brief—the election came round at Le Mans. There was a double election, namely of the provost and the dean, of whom the first was intelligent and of noble birth, and the other was well-read and rich. When therefore neither was willing to give way to the other, the provost said to the dean: 'I appreciate that the bishopric is not useful for me, nor for you. I have honour enough, and you have wealth. I am unwilling to give way to you, and you to me, The only outcome therefore now in this matter is that an already partly devastated church is being completely weakened as a result of our dispute. I would prefer therefore, if you also were willing, that between us we would agree on postulating a man of good reputation and modest standing, who would be willing and able to restore our disastrous and confused situation. Such a man is the venerable Maurice, a man singularly honoured by every standard of holiness, who could rule even the whole world under divine providence. I am ready to postulate such a man with all my resources, and I certainly believe that anyone who objects will be acting contrary to God and his own salvation.' Then the dean smiled and said: 'So be it, but with this condition: if this man declines to accept the bishopric, he should make way for me.' Then the provost triumphantly shouted to him: 'Let this be ratified and carried out.' And soon the postulation was made and confirmed with everyone's consent. The dean assumed that Maurice would never accept the bishopric: the provost to be sure assumed more worthily that the saintly man, motivated by love of Christ for the salvation of many, would not dare to reject so great an office when it was offered.

Two canons therefore were sent and found him according to his habit walking on the road on his way to a preaching engagement. When he had been shown the letter containing his call, he replied: 'You will go to your lodging. I shall return this evening after my preaching, and in the morning I shall give the answer which the Lord has provided.' So it was done. They returned to their lodging; he went on his way; he preached; while still fasting he heard confessions until the evening; he returned home and greeted his guests; dinnerless he made for his oratory and spent the night alone at prayer; and in the morning he gave his answer to the canons: 'This is the advice of God and his mother: It is not becoming to decline what you offer.' Need more be said? He was received with appropriate honour, enthroned and consecrated; and was so famed for the conduct of his office that there is thought to have been no one like him in the last five hundred years. (c.26, l.66 - c.27)

St Waltheof at Melrose

Bower quotes again from Jocelin's Life, *illustrating with biblical allusions Waltheof's acts of mercy when abbot of Melrose in times of food scarcity. The foodstores on the abbey's farms at Eildon and Gattonside are said to have been miraculously replenished until the next harvest came round. The story is unique among the traditions of Scottish saints, and illustrates the inspiration aroused by the early Cistercian monks at Melrose from having such an abbot.*

Although the conjunction of the aforesaid and other virtues in this man of God had built a lasting dwelling-place for his abode, compassion for the poor and sick made its claim on his whole being as if he had been born for the service, exercise and practice of that alone. Accordingly the saying of the blessed Job when making a pithy statement about himself is deservedly appropriate for him: 'Mercy grew up with me, and it came out with me from my mother's womb.' It follows that the saintly man, not only when healthy, but also often when suffering from illness, sometimes leaning on a staff, sometimes supported by the arms of his sons, was in the habit of making daily visits to the infirmaries not only for the monks and lay-brothers, but also for the poor and guests; and after ascertaining from each of them what they would like, and what they lacked, he carefully arranged for each man in both directions to be given what were the needs of each. At all times, but especially when the land was stricken by a famine, when an innumerable crowd of the poor in order to preserve their lives gathered at Melrose to obtain the food necessary for life, this man of God did not spare their cattle, sheep and pigs, but regularly provided relief for everyone's needs so far as he could. In these circumstances when an adequate supply of the abbot's food for those in need ran short, the very Fountain of Mercy often miraculously provided supplies from the copious abundance of His overflowing bounty, as the following story will reveal.

On one occasion when the calamity of a deadly famine threatened, a vast crowd of destitute people reckoned to number four thousand gathered at Melrose, and erected huts and tents for themselves in the fields and woods around the monastery to a distance of two miles. The abbot in his usual way went out with some of the brothers and the cellarer (called Thomas, who in fact and nickname was Good), to survey this great multitude. As he saw it, he joyfully said: 'What an awesome place is this! Truly this is the camp of the Lord.' And next he said: 'My heart goes out to these people; but I do not have to hand anything to set before them. We must see to it that they have food until the autumn, lest (God forbid!) they succumb to starvation,' The Spirit filled the aforesaid cellarer since he was a man of compassion, and was for that reason very dear to the abbot, and he gave this answer to the saint: 'Dearest father, we have a great deal of livestock, cattle at pasture, sheep, wethers, and fat pigs, and no small amount of cheese and butter. We shall slaughter the animals, serve the rest of the products gladly, and dole it all out generously as food for them. Yet the shortage of bread touches and pains my heart, because with our corn nearly all exhausted, [only] a very small supply is still left in the barns of two of our granges, namely some wheat at Eildon kept for the use of the abbey community, and some rye at Gattonside reserved for the servants.' The good father was delighted at the cellarer's words; with bent head he gave him many thanks, and blessed him in the name of the Lord.

The abbot then made his way to the grange of Eildon along with the cellarer, and entering the barn he thrust the staff which he was carrying in his hand into a heap of sheaves; he genuflected, made the sign of the cross, blessed the crop there, and withdrew. Then he went away to Gattonside, and entered in the same way as he had done before, saying to the cellarer: 'Make a distribution now, and give both to us and to the poor with confidence, for God will make it grow, he will increase and multiply it to the extent necessary for our use and that of the poor.' What a remarkable event and a rare one! The corn which was stored in the corners of each barn and was thought to provide sufficient food for scarcely two weeks, stretched out for three months, as if it were inexhaustible. It remained at the same level (in imitation of the widow of Zarephath's handful of flour) until the gathering of the new harvest had been accomplished. From the time when the harvesting of the new corn produced enough for them, the depletion of the aforesaid corn became apparent. In the same way at a former time the manna, which sustained the Children of Israel in the desert for forty years, failed them after their entry into the Promised Land and the gathering of new crops. (c.33 - c.34, l.19)

Bower's abhorrence of perjury

In the context of a long discussion of a disputed election in 1178 to the see of St Andrews, when at one stage King William I swore an oath never to accept one of the candidates, and this royal oath came to stand in the way of papal efforts to have that candidate installed, Bower reflects first on the differing circumstances when oaths should or should not be kept. Then he inserts a chapter of comment on life in his own day, when perjury was all too common among members of juries or witnesses in trials. It is a sermon with biblical references against such sinful behaviour in general, and is a good example of Bower the preacher.

I hope that the reader will not be annoyed if I here make a little digression, for I see every day something that grieves me, that very many people both when serving on juries and when bearing witness take little or no care over making their oaths void. And for this reason, as a warning against perjury, some sort of account of this topic is included here. For every perjurer is a traitor by his disloyalty as far as God is concerned, causes harm by his deceit as regards his neighbour, and is destructive by his wickedness as regards himself.

As to the first point: it would be a great act of treason if a chancellor (or the person who had the custody of the king's seal) were to seal an agreement which the king particularly disliked. Even if he did this in accordance with the papal seal, he would be *ipso facto* excommunicated and would have to be handed over to the secular arm. God's name is a name entrusted to us as a particular seal for bearing witness and confirming the truth. Hence: 'You are to fear the Lord your God; and serve him alone, and take your oaths in his name' (Deuteronomy 6). This is why the apostle says that 'an oath provides a confirmation to end all dispute'. Deceit indeed is something that God dislikes intensely, as it is the opposite of him, because he himself is truth; and therefore whoever takes on himself God's name to confirm a piece of deceit is betraying God. This same point is clear secondly because if anyone was to hand over to enemies one of the lord king's castles that had been entrusted to his loyalty, he would be a traitor to the king. The Lord's name is a castle which we invoke and to which we flee at every time of need. Hence Solomon says in Proverbs: 'The Lord's name is a tower of great strength;' whoever flees to it will be saved. This castle is handed over to an enemy when it is entrusted to demons and deceitful men as support for deceit. This same point is clear thirdly because if anyone was to slander his lord maliciously and implicate him in a crime, he is a traitor to him; but anyone who brings God to bear as a witness to deceit, who endeavours to involve the Lord in a crime and to deprive him of the good name by which he is invoked and which is the supreme truth, he is a traitor to God. Hence so far as he is concerned, he is more insulting to Christ than were those who crucified Christ, for they did not inflict on Christ anything more than the evil of a punishment, but such a man is endeavouring to involve him in the evil of a sin. When the Devil has been required under oath in the Lord's name to tell the truth, he does not ordinarily lie, nor do we find that he adds an oath to his lies, even if he is untruthful and the father of all liars; and so it is no wonder if God promises them retribution, as he says in Malachi 3: 'I shall be quick to testify against sorcerers, adulterers and perjurers.'

Secondly, a perjurer causes harm by his deceit as far as his neighbour in concerned. For he deceives a judge and deprives a bona fide owner of his right, and on that account is bound to repay what has been kept back in full. If however one man pays by making complete restitution, the others are released from their obligation.

Thirdly, a perjurer is destructive by his wickedness as far as himself is concerned, because anyone who knowingly commits perjury when placing his hand on the book (by which means he touches the Gospel) is entrusting that hand to the Devil unless he speaks the truth. Hence that hand becomes the Devil's hand, and henceforth and thereafter he signs himself, eats and works with the Devil's hand. Hence by that hand the Devil holds on to him until he repents with good effect. In the missal indeed upon which a man swears are written four passages —that is the consecration of the body and blood of Christ, the intercession of the saints, the blessedness of the blest, and the damnation of the condemned. This then is the meaning of his oath, as if to say: 'If what I now swear is untrue, may the celebration of masses be of no help to me, nor the prayers of the saints; but deprived of all the blessedness of the saints, may the curse of the condemned come over me.' Similarly when a man knowingly rushes into perjury, he renounces all the good steps which he has taken when travelling on foot, or when at other times visiting the sick or going to church, unless he speaks the truth; also by placing his hands on the book, he renounces all good works of alms-giving, if he has done any. Similarly in kissing the book, he renounces all the praise and prayers which he has made to God. On this account Scripture has it: 'A man given to oaths will be wicked to the core; and the rod will never be far from his house.' (c.38)

The division of the see of Dunkeld

The separation of the see of Argyll from that of Dunkeld is likely to have been arranged in the later 1180s. A single bishop had served a mainland Scottish diocese stretching eastward from the original DálRiada once the Isles had been lost to Norway in 1098. Bower's explanation of the reasons for this split includes some comments on the geographical character of Argyll as he knew this region in his own day, though his implication that Gaelic was not then commonly spoken in Dunkeld as well as Argyll must surely be misleading. As a member of the regular clergy he sermonizes on how the leaders of the secular clergy of his day ought to behave—with improbable quotations from two works of the classical writer Horace to back up his argument. He particularly disliked the practice of 'commend', whereby some monasteries were beginning to be entrusted to the care (and profit) of bishops.

At that time the whole of Argyll was subject to the bishop of Dunkeld and his jurisdiction as it had been from long before. Argyll is an extensive and spacious region, and containing in many places many and various goods, but owned by a ferocious and savage people who were in fact untamed up to that time. Besides they knew only one mother tongue into which they had been born and brought up, that is Scottish or Irish Gaelic, and they understood no other except that. What therefore was the man of the Lord who did not know this language to do? Because it seemed to him dangerous to abandon his own sheep, whose care he had undertaken, without a shepherd, even less did he judge it safe for himself to answer to the Chief Shepherd at the Last Judgment on their reckonings, since one party did not reciprocally understand the language of the other; but in any account that was to be demanded or rendered the people thought the pastor savage, and the pastor the people. Considering the salvation of souls to be more profitable than the increase of possessions, the bishop sought as much as he could to relieve himself of a burden and give satisfaction to God and the people. In no way did he agree to have charge of those to whom he had no hopes of being of assistance, since they were like savages to him. Therefore he sent his chaplain called Harold, a discreet and honourable man who was knowledgeable and skilful in both languages, with his letter to the apostolic see, humbly requesting the lord pope to divide the bishopric of Dunkeld into two sees, namely Argyll and Dunkeld, and to consecrate his chaplain Harold as bishop of Argyll, with the bishopric of Dunkeld retained for his own service. For he confidently claimed that each bishopric would have sufficient resources to match the support needed for its bishop and his staff at a suitably honourable and affluent level, and to provide abundantly for all their needs without any shortage, provided they were the kind of men who were not extravagant, nor destroyers of with Christ's patrimony, and not too greedy, but following moderation and the middle way within due limits in all things, not inclining too much to right or left; hence:

> There is a measure in affairs; there are, in short, fixed bounds,
> beyond and short of which right can find no place.

Richer bishops should pay attention to this, those who with exceptionally fat benefices obtain churches and monasteries in commend, who busy themselves not only with avoiding decrease but with increase of

Their property, legally if they can, but if not, in any kind of way.

They should note what a poor bishop has done, following the example of the blessed Martin, who divided the only cloak he had with a poor man who was cold. (c.39, ll.24-67)

Bishop Walter Trayl of St Andrews

For his biographical notes on Walter Trayl, bishop of St Andrews 1386-1401, Bower is writing from personal knowledge of the man under whom he is likely to have served as a novice Augustinian canon at St Andrews cathedral priory. Trayl had been employed at the papal court when appointed a bishop back home in Scotland. He is notable for his legislative and judicial activities. The emphasis here on his attack on clerical concubinage is a guide to what Bower considered significant.

[After the death of Bishop Laundels] the said Walter Trayl succeeded to the bishopric. Although he belonged to a family of middling status, nevertheless by the nobility of his character he surpassed his lineage. Once he had been made bishop therefore, with his appointment graciously expedited and confirmed by bulls of the lord pope, he hurried to his native land and satisfied the demands of his office well enough; [as priest and bishop, and a good skilled master of the virtues, a good pastor among his people,] he had been given authority by the pope over peoples and kingdoms, that is those of good birth living in his diocese and the magnates of the kingdom, to eradicate deeply-rooted sins, and tear down the ramparts of heretics, and destroy the deliberations of the wicked, and build on the foundation of morals and plant on faith. For it was suitable for such a man to be put in charge of such a church, on whose judgment depended the government of almost the whole kingdom in matters of difficulty. He bestowed on everyone what was of advantage to them—advice to the king and court, cash payments to his church: and being thus involved in the concerns of the court, because he had concern for everything, he left room for neglect in neither of his administrative functions. By thus adorning himself everywhere with the embellishments of the virtues, he inculcated spiritual lessons in people all the more on that account. Thus he suppressed vices in himself, lest they held sway; he tamed the flesh, lest it be in control; he raised up the spirit to take the lead; not as it were lording it over the clergy, but having become a model for his flock, he presented himself as an example of good works towards everybody.

He reproached laymen who maligned the church with ecclesiastical censure; he curbed clerics from worldly affairs and commerce; and he restrained priests with concubines from all brothel-keeping throughout the whole of his diocese, and banished them [from vile filth of this kind], so that there was no cleric there at all among the men of holy church who obviously and openly kept a concubine without Walter either humbling him, however eminent he might be, with imprisonment, or depriving him of his benefice, or otherwise very shrewdly sanctioning a permanent separation.

This severe critic of morals therefore and corrector of faults, than whom no one was more severe in his rebukes, more gentle in his compassion, more lavish in his expenditure, more friendly in his conversation, more ready with his assistance, [had no fear of the threats of the magnates, nor was he a respecter of persons, nor was anyone found like him in maintaining the law of the Most High.] Broken by old age [when he was about seventy] he died in the castle at St Andrews which he had himself built from the foundation in 1401. He served as bishop for sixteen years, and was honourably buried in the burial place of the bishops next to the high altar in the church of St Andrew on the north side within the screen. There it was written of him:

> This man was an upright pillar of the church, a bright window,
> a scented censer, a resounding bell.
> (c.45, ll.41-90)

Prior Robert de Montrose of St Andrews

Bower must have spoken with many canons of the St Andrews monastery who had known Robert de Montrose as prior 1387-94, and about the shocking story of his murder. Robert had previously served in the Loch Leven priory , which was a cell belonging to St Andrews, and must have had legal training to qualify him to preside over the bishop's court as his official. Bower writes of him as a model religious superior. (The quotation from the Decretum *of the canon law is in fact also taken from the writings of St Augustine.)*

After him a very religious man was elected prior, namely sir Robert de Montrose a canon of the same house, prior of Loch Leven and official of the court of St Andrews. He was a very knowledgeable man, distinguished for his eloquence, warily circumspect, a ruler with foresight, and an outstanding preacher. Intent as he was on the observances of the rule, he became a model for his flock in the cloister, a good pastor among the people, and thus was pleasing to God. For he did not disdain the people, but was their teacher, and gave individual attention to each person. He did not flatter the rich, neither did he take fright at the threats of the magnates; he did not harass the poor, but cherished them; he did not turn a blind eye to the offences of those subject to him, but corrected them. In every situation and in everything he did he showed himself obedient to his elders, charming to his juniors, kindly to his brothers in religion, stern to the proud, generous to the humble, compassionate to the penitent and unbending to the incorrigible. All this being so, the prior could truthfully express and share the opinion of his father Augustine, who when writing a letter to Vincent the Donatist said this: 'I do not dare to claim for myself that my house is better than the ark of Noah, where among so many men one back-slider was nonetheless found; or better than the house of Abraham, to whom it was said: "Put away your slave-girl and her son"; or better than the house of Isaac, to whom it was said regarding his twin sons: "I have loved Jacob, but hated Esau."' 'I honestly acknowledge that from the time when I began to serve God, just as I have had difficulty in finding men better than those who have had success in monasteries, so I have not found men worse than those who have been failures in monasteries.' And so it is written with a transferred meaning in the *Decretum*, xlvii, 'Quantumlibet'.

Hence it happened that the same prior had in the cloister a certain brother called Thomas Platar, who was not fully responsive to discipline as he spurned with contempt the corrections of the subprior and the order. On this account, when the prior endeavoured in all suitable ways to direct him back to proper behaviour and to the rule, now with threats, now with blandishments, whatever effort he made to achieve improvement, this man hardened his heart and tended [all the more] to evil doing. At length the prior turned his thoughts to himself, noting the proverbial saying that: 'He who does not correct what ought to be curbed, commits an offence, and he who neglects what he is able to correct is as guilty as the one who commits the fault, for he knows without doubt that exemption from punishment is the offspring of indifference, the mother of insolence, the root of impudence, and the nurse of transgressions.' While the prior was considering how to win over the brother, the misguided man was plotting the death of his own father. For one evening when the prior by himself (as was his custom) was mounting the stairs to spend the night in the dormitory, at the prompting of an evil spirit the man seized the chance to approach his prelate, and taking an iron dagger from under his cloak wounded the prior mortally in the cloister. He survived for three days; then saying farewell to the brothers he fell asleep in the Lord, and was buried with his fathers in the new chapter-house. The parricide sought to flee after comitting this crime, but he was immediately seized, and after the two days of the prior's funeral, when wearing his vestments and a mitre, and after the customary sermon by sir Walter Trayl as bishop had been delivered to the clergy and people, he was hurriedly made over to perpetual imprisonment, where he feebly tasted the bread of sorrow and the water of affliction. He died shortly afterwards, and was buried in the midden.

This man restored his house in noble fashion as long as he lived, and built it up in notable fashion. He raised and completed new work in the main body of the great church up to the rafters and the roof covering at very great expense. And he ended his life here on 24 March 1393, after holding office as prior for thirteen years. (c.54 - c.55, l.5)

Prior James Biset of St Andrews

Bower writes with personal knowledge of Biset, who served 1394-1416 as head of the Augustinian cathedral monastery at St Andrews, and under whom Bower had lived as a novice and young canon whilst a student of canon law. Biset was himelf a canon law graduate of Paris, and as prior was one of the founders of the University of St Andrews in 1410 (see below XV c.22). Bower has much to say in his praise, not least regarding his building works following the disastrous fire at the cathedral church in 1386. The many and varied responsibilities of the head of a major religious corporation are illustrated here, covering not only the community and buildings at St Andrews, but also at the many parish churches throughout the diocese that were formally appropriated to the monastery, in whose welfare Biset took an active interest in return for the regular financial support they were bound to provide. (Monymusk was a subordinate house in Aberdeenshire.) The verses at the end may well have formed part of Biset's epitaph.

He was succeeded by that man of distinguished character and mirror of virtue sir James Biset, a canon of the same house and licentiate in decrees. Born into a quite notable family, which is usually a stimulus for good, by the nobility of his character he surpassed his family and his times. He was a nephew as sister's son to the most devout and pious father sir Thomas Biset [an earlier prior]. In his close copying of his uncle's religious practices, he is identified as second to none of his predecessors as prior in the kind of way in which he worked. Inasmuch as a branch of the true vine developed from a choice side-shoot into a special tree, and with a numerous progeny of fruits, the fine fragrance of Christ was found everywhere for God and men. He was also humble, friendly and kind beyond all others, sympathetic and sincere to his brothers and the needy, unique both in matters spiritual and temporal, surpassing practically all his other predecessors; he completed the nave of the great church properly, and likewise the cloister, in all respects with rafters and roof covering; he renewed the choir [enclosure] tastefully with stalls, and the cloister quadrangle with both roofing and paving. He also restored the whole monastery and each of its domestic buildings with alterations and new buildings, along with granaries, mills, malt-kilns, piggeries, barns and byres; some of these were new buildings, with others it was a matter of covering and roofing; likewise also the guest-hall, which he constructed in an appropriate style with columns and glazed windows with its two apartments. The courtyard also of the whole monastery, both at the lower level and outside, he quietly constructed and finished with stone paving. He refurbished at a good standard all the churches attached to his office, and whichever others were annexed to the monastery, as regards the buildings and the ecclesiastical vestments. For he expended on each church what was important to it, decorating the outside with material adornments, and establishing the conventual part with spiritual texts. He took very great care that the altars sparkled, the lamps shone, the clergy were suitable, the canons were adornments morally, the altar-vessels clean, the vestments laundered, and that the divine offices were celebrated in due order. For he knew that in [care for] these matters lay the honour of God, the seemliness of his house, many kinds of meaning in the sacraments, the performance of the clergy, the devotion of the people, and the instruction of all without distinction. But also when taking thought first for himself and then especially for the convent, from whatever he could raise from teinds, dues, rents or other annual payments, or other legitimate profits, he saved and gave the whole amount (save support for living expenses) towards the erection of ecclesiastical buildings, expenditure on guests, and the needs of the poor. In addition he withstood many assaults both from outside and of a civil and domestic nature, all of which he both endured in manly fashion and fended off with vigour for the common benefit of the brothers. Who adorned with so many signs of the virtues would not be swollen with pride? When pride is an adjunct to good qualities, it tends to detract from them, and kills the shoots of the virtue that they sprout. I believe, I say, and I know; and because of this I have spoken. But he was assuredly humbled, because always and everywhere he dug within himself a foundation of humility, by which he was brought to the heights of charity. Which of his brothers would fall ill and he would not himself lose his strength? Who would not experience scandal and he would not himself be painfully affected? To put it briefly: he became all things to all the brothers, so that he might help them all to salvation.

This prior was tall in stature, placid in character, and circumspect in all his actions. For he patiently withstood impending injustices with the eye of caution, and speedily wiped out attackers with the hand of prudence; and (not to mention his other virtues) he was humble at heart, thoughtful in what he had to say, judicious in his opinion, courteous in conversation, slow to take revenge, ready to forgive; he had a great love for humble people, he rebuked the conceited. He was not feeble in his gestures, careless in his gait, nor heedless in his speech; but the appearance of his body and bearing offered the onlooker a likeness of his mind, and an expression of his integrity. Why should I take time over the details? His deeds still proclaim how alert was his mind, how prudent his understanding, how responsive his temperament, how outstanding his knowledge of the church, how retentive his memory, how skilfully expressed his learning, how commendable his good works—these facts still resound even if our discourse falls silent. Also the extent of his character and ability, and of his life in religion, and of how he was endowed with finesse as an administrator—the reader may learn about these from the canons and other neighbours who knew him when he was alive.

But there is also no doubt that the sons of God who will arise in this monastery will give an account to their brothers so that a second generation may be informed, and they may place their hope in God, and not forget the prior's deeds, but also examine his ideals. For many of his novices, who had been instructed under his training and had attained to the pinnacles of the virtues, were soon after his death employed in other celebrated places as fathers and pastors. One of these was the bishop of Ross; another two were appointed as abbots at Scone and Inchcolm; and three were in succession appointed priors of Monymusk. This is not surprising because the prior arranged for two of his canons to become masters of theology, one of whom succeeded him as prior, the other was appointed at Scone; two also qualified as licentiates and five as bachelors of decrees. At that time, touched by the delightful mildness of a breeze from the south, the paradise of a cloister at St Andrews was experiencing spring with as many flowers as it abounded in distinguished men of virtue, when during the time of this prior the monastic company flourished in the sacred rites of the cloister. In the sphere of the preoccupations of Martha the scion of legal studies bloomed again, and the seraphic enclosure reached boiling point in the theological branches of knowledge. In the first place peace and harmony of conduct, secondly peace and a just proportion of studies, thirdly peace and progress in meritorious actions produced a man who was pleasing in the sight of God and a sweet melody in the ears of men. He did many other good things indeed during his lifetime, for he redeemed lands which had been mortgaged at the time of the accidental burning of the church, and he left the monastery free of debt with a stock of iron, lead, timber planks, wooden beams, pitch, salt and gold on deposit, and in peace with a numerous company of brothers. And he ended his life at a great age in the prior's apartment on the morrow of the feast of the Nativity of St John the Baptist 1416. He served as prior for twenty-three years, and was buried with his fathers in the new chapter-house. He will receive, it is hoped, his rewards as one of the righteous in the glory of the future resurrection, because it is not likely that the generosity of the Supreme Creator would not respond to his religious works with appropriate recompense. God in the abundance of his holiness exceeds the merits and prayers of those seeking mercy. Hence:

> This man called James, shining like a polished jewel,
> lived in the life of the cloister like a hermit.
> (c.55, l.6 - c.56)

Book VII

The vision of Dryhthelm of Melrose

Bower selects from Vincent of Beauvais a version of a story dated c.700 in Bede about a monk of the original monastery at Old Melrose in Roxburghshire called Dryhthelm, who was believed to have returned from the dead, and to have related then a vision of life after death. The story has an inner meaning which has been summarised as a warning to readers that 'salvation lies in present recognition of the reality of paradise and heaven, purgatory and hell.' (King Aldfrith of Northumbria reigned 686-705; Æthelwald was bishop of Lindisfarne in the early eighth century.)

There was a man, the father of a family in a district of Northumbria, who died in the early hours of the night, but came to life again at dawn, causing those who were watching to flee. His wife, however, although terrified beyond measure, remained. To her he said: 'Do not be afraid; I have risen from the death which held me in its bonds, and I have been permitted to live again amongst mankind; but I am to live in a very different manner from before.' He immediately rose and went to the oratory in the village and prayed till dawn. And then he divided his property into three parts, from which he gave one to his wife, another to his sons, and the third immediately to the poor. Not much later, with his wife's permission, he arrived at the monastery of Melrose, which is encircled by the river Tweed, and having received the tonsure, he accepted from the abbot a secret retreat. There he stayed until his death, leading an exemplary life.

He told the following story: 'I was guided by a man of shining countenance, who was wearing bright robes. We went in silence in the direction of the rising of the sun at the summer solstice. We came to a very wide, long and deep valley, which was on our left, and had one side which was exceedingly terrible with raging fire and another no less dreadful with frozen hail blowing over absolutely everything. Both sides were full of souls, which in turn were furiously tossed from this side and that. For when they could not endure one side, they leapt across to the other. I thought to myself that this was Hell. My guide, however, answered my thoughts: "This is not as you think Hell." And when we went further, I saw an area so full of murky darkness that I could make out nothing except the shape and garment of my guide. And there suddenly appeared masses of flame, constantly rising from and falling back again into a pit. And at once my guide disappeared and left me alone. The tips of the flames were full of human souls, which were like sparks flying upward with the smoke and dropping back. And an incomparable stench rose up with them. Meanwhile a shrieking and taunting crowd of evil spirits were taking five human souls away into the darkness. One of them was tonsured as a cleric, one was a layman, and one was a woman. And they took them down into the midst of the burning pit. Some of the spirits from that abyss, however, ascended the noisome flame with blazing eyes, noses and mouths, and with the fiery tongs which they were carrying threatened to seize me. But they could not touch me. And there suddenly appeared behind me something like a bright star glimmering in the darkness. Here was my guide, who soon put them to flight. Turning to the right he began to lead me in the direction of the rising of the winter sun, and soon, having been led into a serene light, I saw a very great wall which seemed to be endlessly long and broad. And at once, by what means I know not, we were on top of it, and there was below a very broad and pleasant plain, full of growing flowers and the sweetest scent, with a light brighter than that of the sun at noon, in which there were several bands of abbots and many companies of happy people. And when he led me through their midst, I thought that this was the kingdom of Heaven. But he answered: "This is not as you think the kingdom of Heaven." And going on from there, I saw a much more glorious light, I heard the sweetest sound of people singing, and I became aware of the most marvellous fragrance.'

'And when I was hoping that I might enter this place, my guide soon turned around back on to the road by which I had come. And while we were returning he said; "The valley that you saw is the place in which are tried and chastened the souls of the people who delayed to confess and make restitution for their sins until on the point of death, when they leave the body as penitents making confession. These people will nevertheless by God's mercy enter the kingdom of Heaven on the Day of Judgment. The alms, fasts and prayers of those who are still alive, and especially the celebration of masses, are responsible for freeing many of them before the Day of Judgment. But the pit which you saw is the mouth of Hell. Those who fall into it will never be released. The place of flowers is that in which are received the souls of those who die practising good works, but are not of such perfection that they deserve immediately to enter the kingdom of Heaven. They will all enter it on the Day of Judgment. But any who are perfect in word, thought and deed come as soon as they die to that kingdom in the vicinity of which lies the place in which you experienced the sound of sweet singing and the very delightful fragrance. I left you for a time in order to find out what your future ought to be." And while I was dreading the thought of resuming a corporeal existence, I suddenly found myself, by which means I know not, back living in your world.'

He used to tell these things not indiscriminately to everyone, but only to those who either feared everlasting torments or longed for eternal joys. In the vicinity of his cell lived a monk and holy priest, named Hæmgisl, who to this very day lives in solitude in Ireland, spending his last years on a diet of bread and water. It was through him that the content of the vision was made known. Also King Aldfrith, a most learned man in all respects, listened attentively to the man who eventually became a monk in the monastery mentioned above. The abbot of that monastery was at that time a holy man and priest, Æthelwald, who is now bishop of Lindisfarne. That brother who saw the vision was called Dryhthelm, and he used regularly to immerse himself in the adjoining river to control the heat of his body, even to the extent that broken pieces of ice fell down from his clothing around him. For he never took off the clothes which had become wet and cold in the river, until they were dried by the heat of his body. When he was asked why he exposed himself to such bitter cold, he replied: 'I have known it colder.' And when he was asked why he kept to such an austere and hard way of life, he responded: 'I have seen it harder.' (cc.7-8)

The vision of the Emperor Charles the Fat

This elaborate story of a vision experienced by Charles the Fat, Carolingian emperor 881-7, is taken by Bower from the version handed on by Vincent of Beauvais. It appears to have been preserved in France in support of the claims of Louis III the Blind (whom Charles had adopted) to be his legitimate successor (901-27). This is indicated at the end of the story by the passing on of a symbolic thread. Bower wallows in details of the supposed miseries of the after-life, which can, however, be ameliorated by 'masses, prayers, obligations, psalmody and alms' here on earth. (St Remigius was the sixth-century Apostle to the Franks, who baptised their early king Clovis I.) Bower explains clearly at the end his motives in introducing this material about Frankish kings; he hopes to have an effect on kingly behaviour in Scotland in future.

The vision of this Charles is reported thus: 'In the name of God the king of kings I the Emperor Charles by the gift of God king of the Germans and patrician of the Romans and emperor of the Franks [witness that] on the holy night of a Sunday after the celebration of the sacred night-office when I was going to lie down wanting to go to sleep, a voice came to me saying ominously: "Charles, your spirit will now leave you for no short time." And immediately I was carried off into the spirit, and was supported by a man of great radiance holding in his hand a ball of thread which was very bright and discharged rays of light, just as comets do when they appear. And he began to unwind it, saying to me: "Take the thread from this glowing ball, and fasten it firmly with knots to the thumb of your right hand, for you are to be led by that means to the labyrinthine torments of hell with their burning pitch, sulphur, lead, wax and fat." There I found my father's and uncles' bishops. When I fearfully asked them why they were undergoing such severe torments, they answered: "We were your father's and uncles' bishops, and when we ought to have been urging upon them and their people peace and harmony, we were to such an extent sowing the seeds of discord and inciting evil deeds that we now burn in the infernal tortures that you see along with other devotees of murder and plunder. And indeed those of your bishops and vassals who take pleasure in now doing the same things will come to this place." And while I was listening to these things with trepidation, behold the blackest demons flew towards me with fiery hooks wanting to take hold of the ball's thread which I was holding in my hand and to pull it towards them; but the rays of light from that ball repelled them, and they were unable to touch it. Then running up behind my back they wanted to hook me and hurl me down into those sulphureous pits. But my guide who was carrying the ball threw the thread over my shoulders, doubled it, and vigorously hauled me along after him. And thus we climbed very high mountains of fire from which arose swamps and and boiling-hot streams and all sorts of bubbling metals, where I met again countless souls of my father's and brothers' men and nobles all pitched in headfirst, some up to their hair, some up to their chins, and some up to their navels. And they wailed and cried out to me: "While alive we in the pursuit of earthly ambition delighted along with you, your father, your brothers and your uncles in making war, in murder and in plunder. Because of this we are tortured in the boiling streams that you see and in different kinds of metals."

'And when I was fearfully approaching this sight, I heard behind me souls cry out: "The powerful will be powerfully tormented." And I looked back and saw on the banks of the boiling river pitchy and sulphureous furnaces full of great dragons, scorpions and serpents of various kinds. I also saw there some of my father's, brothers' and uncles' leading subjects saying to me: "Woe is me, Charles! you see how severe are the torments we experience because of our ill-will and arrogance and the bad advice we gave to our kings and to you on account of our greed." And while I was sighing deeply because of my grief, dragons ran towards me with open jaws full of fire, sulphur and pitch wanting to gobble me up. But my guide trebled the thread over me, and by its rays of light their fiery mouths were subdued. And he pulled me along more forcefully, and we went down into one valley which was in one part dark and hot like a fiery furnace, and in the other part in truth so very pleasant and so very bright that I am unable in any way to describe it. I turned towards the part which was dark and vomiting flames, and I saw there some of the kings of my house in great torment. And then very much hemmed in, I thought that I was immediately to be overwhelmed in this defile by jet-black giants who set that valley on fire with kinds of torches. And while I was greatly trembling, the thread from the ball brightened my vision, and I saw on the side of the valley the smoke grow white for a short time, and there were two springs flowing. One was exceedingly hot, the other in truth clear and cool, and there were two large casks there. And when I went to that place with the thread from the ball directing my steps and leant over the top of one cask in which there was boiling-hot water, I saw my father Louis standing in it up to his thighs. And as I was oppressed by grief beyond measure and overwhelmed by anguish, he said: "Charles my lord, do not fear. I know that your spirit is to go back to your body again, and that God has allowed you to come here to see how on account of our sins I and all those whom you have seen undergo such torments. For on one day I bathe in this boiling-hot cask, and on the other I am moved across into that other very agreeable cask of water. And this happens through the prayers of St Peter and of St Remigius with whose protection our royal house has hitherto ruled. But if you along with my bishops, abbots and all the clergy through masses, prayers, obligations, psalmody and alms will soon help me, I shall be quickly freed from this cask of boiling water. For my brother Lothair and his son Louis, through the prayers of St Peter and St Remigius, are already delivered from these punishments, and have together flown to the joy of Paradise." And he said to me: "Charles, look back to the left." I looked back and saw two very tall boiling-hot casks. "Those," he said, "are prepared for you, unless you mend your ways and do penance for your impious transgressions." Then I began to be really afraid.'

'But when my guide saw me in such a state of fear, he said to me: "Follow me to the right-hand side of the most splendid valley of Paradise." And while we were walking, I observed in great splendour among the famous kings my uncle Lothair seated on a stone of topaz of wondrous size and crowned with a precious diadem, and next to him his son Louis similarly crowned. And when he saw me Lothair invited me to come near to him and in welcoming tones said: "Charles now the third to succeed me as head of the Roman Empire, come to me. I know that you have come through the place of punishment where your father my brother has been put for the term allotted to him, but he will very soon be freed from these punishments through the mercy of God, just as we were freed through the influence of St Peter and the prayers of St Remigius to whom God gave the great apostleship over the Frankish kings and peoples. Our house will now cease to rule as kings and emperors if you will not support the remnants of our line, because I know that quite soon the power of imperial authority will be taken from your hand and that you will live for a very short time afterwards." Then Louis his son turned to me and said: "By hereditary right Louis my daughter's son ought to assume the imperial authority which you have hitherto held." And when this had been said, the little infant Louis now seemed to me to be present. Then seeing him Lothair said to me: "This infant appears to be like that boy whom the Lord set in front of his disciples, saying: 'For the kingdom of heaven belongs to such as these. I tell you [this] because they have their guardian angels who look continually on the face of my heavenly father.' Be sure to return to him the power of imperial authority through the medium of the ball's thread which you hold in your hand." I therefore untied the thread from my right thumb and gave to him through the medium of the ball's thread absolute authority over the empire. And immediately that ball which shone like the rays of the sun totally rewound itself in his hand. And thus after this miracle my spirit, fatigued and exceedingly frightened, returned to my body.' He lived for hardly two years after this vision.

We have digressed into this long history of the Franks mainly because of this terrifying vision, so that if our book comes into the hands of our kings, they will be afraid on this account of arriving at this place of torment because of bad advice and their own transgressions. (cc.19 - c.21, ll.1-34, 51-55)

Two beggars and the body of St Martin

This is an amusing tale (dated c.877) about the frustration of two beggars at Tours in France, who were miraculously healed by the power of the body of St Martin (the long-dead local saint) against their wishes.

It is also reported that at this time there were two partners, one of whom was blind and the other crippled. But the blind man carried the cripple, and the cripple showed the blind man the way. And thus in such a way they for a long time did their begging and acquired a lot of money. But when they heard that many invalids were being cured at the body of St Martin, they began to fear lest while during the translation the body was being taken in procession outside the church, it would be brought past the house in which they were staying, and that they would by chance be healed; for they did not wish to obtain a cure lest the source of their income would be lost. On this account they fled from that quarter of the town and went to another, through which they thought the body would certainly not be brought. While they were therefore moving away, they unexpectedly encountered Martin's body directly, and because God bestows many benefits upon those reluctant to receive them, both men against their wishes were immediately healed, although they were extremely annoyed as a result. (c.24, ll.23-39)

William Rufus and new shoes

Bower copies Vincent of Beauvais' version of earlier accounts of King William II Rufus of England (1087-1100). Not only was this king prodigal in his expenditure, he accepted advice from Ranulf Flambard (bishop of Durham 1099-1128), who helped him to fleece the church in England of some of its revenues wherever the king's rights could be pressed, and to make unsuitable appointments to leading church posts.

In 1092 William the Bastard, a man of extraordinary strictness and sternness, died. His son William the Red succeeded him, while Henry IV was emperor. Archbishop Lanfranc educated this William the Red, made him a knight and on the day of SS Cosmas and Damian crowned him as king. He was so generous as to be prodigal, so high-minded as to be vain, so strict as to be cruel. He revered God too little, men not at all, although God should be respected at all times [and] man as suits the occasion. He wanted the price of his clothes to rise immeasurably, scorning anyone who had lowered it. One morning when he was having new shoes put on, he asked the chamberlain what was their cost. And when he had replied that they had cost three shillings, the king full of indignation raged saying: 'You son of a whore! Since when has the king had such low-priced shoes? Go and bring me some purchased for a mark of silver.' The man went and brought much cheaper ones, and lied saying that he had bought them for what he had been ordered to pay. The king said to him: 'These are appropriate to the royal dignity.' And thus it followed that the chamberlain set the price of the king's clothes at will, thereby purchasing much for his own use. Eventually impoverished by the expense, the king turned his mind to plunder, in which crime he was assisted by Ranulf a cleric raised to the heights from the lowest order of men through eloquence and cunning. It was on his advice that when pastors died, the sacred lordships held in free alms were farmed out. For when the death of any bishop or abbot became known, a royal clerk was hurriedly sent to the place to detail in writing everything he found and to pay all revenues in future into the royal treasury. And whoever had given the more evidence not of his character but of his cash was put in place of the dead man. A host of people followed the court and throngs of gluttons, so that a certain sage rightly said: 'The court of the king of England is not a hall of majesty, but a stall of minions.' (c.31, ll.23-53)

King William's dream and death

Another tale hostile to the same King William's reputation which Bower has found in some unidentified source, involving a disgusting vision that much upset the king, but did not persuade him to reform. The moralizing couplet at the end is adapted from the classical poet Ovid's Art of Love*! It is not particularly apt here.*

We may read in the chronicles that the king himself had dreamed that once he was exceedingly hungry and confined alone within a certain very large but empty church with no possible way out. Then looking here and there for something to satisfy his hunger, he was unable to discover anything edible. Climbing up the steps to the altar he saw a certain very beautiful naked man stretched out on his back on that altar, whose right hand was placed under his head as a pillow, whose whole body was wounded, who was drenched with fresh blood, and who was giving forth convulsive sighs and groans. The king showed no compassion whatsoever to him, but inflamed by his voracious appetite devoured half of the wounded body with gnashing teeth like a rabid dog. And when he was not satisfied by this, but was even more hungry and began to gnaw at the other part, the reclining man started to raise his head a little and with his right hand slapped the wretched king so hard that he immersed him in a deep well nearby. Awakened in alarm at this, the king roused the chamberlains with a dreadful cry. The servants came running and persistently sought the reason for the extraordinary cry, and the king soaked with sweat was hardly sane for two days. No notice was taken of others who interpreted the dream. There was among them a certain devout monk who openly advised the king not to delay in amending his way of life, to recognize the fact that he had pillaged half of the mystical body of Christ in [the persons] of the laymen and secular clergy of his kingdom through escheats, exactions and royal taxation, and, because he was then setting his hand to enfeebling the church and despoiling its servants, to be properly fearful of a fall. The king, inasmuch as he could respond, that is weakly and with difficulty, said to him: 'I am bound, brother, to live; and while I live, I shall be the last in the kingdom to allow any weakness.' Henceforth he kept to his bed and room for about a month; and while he was in some way recovering by the grace of the Comforter, he went hunting with some knights in the New Forest, where in a wood he was struck in the chest by an arrow which had been shot by Walter Tirel a French knight, who intended to hit a deer, but felled the king who fell to his death. A little earlier the king had unreasonably banned others from hunting, so that his case verifies the saying that:

In human affairs there is no juster law
than that the murderer perishes by violent death himself.
(c.34, ll.24-61)

The conversion of a Cistercian monk

Bower includes a story collected by Vincent of Beauvais that is connected with the early days of the new monastic order founded in 1098 at Cîteaux near Dijon in France. The dream provides an explanation of the great attraction of this new order devoted to the simple communal life, which under the influence of St Bernard was to spread with remarkable rapidity throughout Europe. By Bower's time it had eleven houses in Scotland.

In 1104 a certain cleric from Vendeuvre-sur-Barse while studying at the schools of Lyons saw in a dream a certain valley which lay under a certain mountain, upon which was sited a certain very beautiful city, whose appearance was so attractive to the onlooker that anyone who saw it could not see enough of it and strived in every way to find a means of succeeding in getting to it. Besides these things he saw a certain river at the foot of the mountain which in fact ran around the foot. While he was exploring this river looking for a way to cross, he saw on the bank twelve or fourteen poor men washing their garments in the river. Among them was one dressed in the whitest clothing, who was very different from the others and was helping them clean their garments. After he had helped one he went to help another. Then the cleric who saw this approached the one who was helping the others and said: 'Who are you people?' He said: 'These poor men are doing penance and washing away their sins. And I am the Son of God, Jesus Christ, without whose help neither they nor any others can succeed. This beautiful city which you see is Heaven where I reside, and when each has washed his garment, that is has done penance, he will enter it. You yourself have for long sought the way to it, but no way other than this leads to it.' When this had been said, the cleric woke from his sleep and began to wonder at his dream. But when not long afterwards he had returned from school to his own locality, he told the bishop of Chalon-sur-Saône, whose familiar he was, about this dream. When the bishop heard about it, he persuaded the man to leave the world and enter upon the religious life, recommending to him above all orders that new Cistercian Order. He came to Cîteaux and found an uncultivated and deserted place and the brothers living alongside the beasts. And at the wickerwork door of the monastery hung an iron knocker. By its sound the porter was summoned to the door by those wishing to enter. Called by this sound the porter came to the cleric when he was standing outside and greeted him with a bow. When the cleric saw him he immediately recognised the same man he had seen among those who were washing their garments in the river. And he asked him to bring the abbot to him. Thus Abbot Robert and the whole community came to him and the cleric recognised that he had seen all of them washing their garments in the river. And he immediately fell at the abbot's feet tearfully asking that he be received. Not long after he had been received he became prior. (c.50, ll.15-53)

How parents should be honoured

In the context of telling how the Emperor Henry IV had to face a rebellion by his son and heir just before his death in 1106, Bower takes the chance to reflect on the duty of honouring one's parents in general. It is a comment on his own experience, which he backs up with another exemplum from the collection of Thomas of Cantimpré (see above III, c.37).

In Normandy there was a certain man who was rich but of low birth, who had but one son whom he had indulgently brought to manhood. Thus a certain noble knight along with his followers met the father and said: 'We think that my daughter is clever and extremely beautiful. If you will accept her, your family will be able to have an exalted and gratifying future. We will give her to your son as his wife, but only on condition that you make over all your property to your son, who will provide most handsomely for you his father and his mother for as long as you live. For there are all sorts of situations in which your son could, if you remain in possession of the property, be disinherited.' The father listened to this and had his doubts about it, but was eventually compelled by his friends, despite his anxiety, to make over all his goods. Thus the marriage took place, and the son and his wife in the first year at least honoured his parents by keeping them well-supplied; but in the second year they supplied less, and in the third year gave more modest supplies than they should have done. In the fourth year, at his wife's suggestion, the son set up a little house for his parents opposite his, so that the unseemly condition of the old would be less irksome to the young, and there he supplied them less publicly with even less. Thus in that place the aged father along with his failing wife suffered extreme poverty to the extent that he scarcely dared to enter his son's house, but informed his son of his needs through one of the son's minions. But one day the old lady happened from opposite her son's house to catch the smell of a goose which had been roasted on the fire and said to her husband: 'It is alright for me as a woman to be content with little; but you must hurry to your son's house and at least on one occasion satisfy your feelings of hunger with the goose which I see has been prepared for eating.' When the old man heard this, supported by his stick he hurried to his son's house. But as soon as his son saw him he took the goose off the fire and hid it away; and immediately upon meeting his father asked him what he wanted. And soon the father saw what had happened, concealed his intentions, and sadly and tearfully returned home. But the son ordered a girl to replace the goose on the fire at once, and, as soon as she caught sight of the goose in the inner room, she discovered a most hideous toad clinging to its breast. 'Hey, master!' she exclaimed. At the girl's shout, the master came and made an effort to drive off the toad, violently attacking it in his rage. And the toad immediately sprung from the goose and attacked his face, so that it could be neither removed nor driven off by any skill or stratagem, but by sticking there punished the man's wickedness for many years. So, miraculously repentant and contrite, the man confessed to a bishop and received as penance orders to tour all the land of Normandy and the cities of France with his face on display and to tell the people everywhere of how it had happened, so that through this example sons would take it upon themselves to honour their parents and would learn how dangerous and harmful it is to wrong them and not return the service which parents give to their sons. (c.51, l.40 - c.52)

Thunder at Dunfermline

Bower offers a digression on the subject of thunder, first as a natural phenomenon explained by reference to biblical quotations from the Psalms, and then by telling a startling tale from his own times regarding a thunderstorm in the vicinity of Dunfermline in west Fife near his own monastery on Inchcolm. (Richard Mongal appears to have left Scotland on pilgrimage to the tomb of St James in north-west Spain in 1415.)

The chance now arises of saying a little about thunder, because we have often made mention of it in our book, and because it is a subtle matter in its motion, yet according to the philosophers is nothing other than the result of the force of the winds drawing into the sky waters which are thickened into clouds. Enclosed in these the winds try to break out, and with a great crash dash the clouds to pieces and throw out a great flame. Thus the noise of the clouds and winds is thunder. The flame sent forth is lightning. This is so penetrative when it touches anything because it is much more precise than the flame we know and because it is driven by the great force of the winds from the north, whence it at times immediately knocks down and kills what it touches by the force of nature, and sometimes knocks down and burns up things by the incomprehensible will of God for reasons known only to himself, so that howsoever it happens, God's judgment is to be feared. On this it is said: 'Thick clouds came out of the radiance before him, hailstones and glowing coals. The Lord thundered from the heavens and the voice of the Most High spoke out'. And this was not unreasonable, as you know, since he wants us to respect him as our Lord; but what is written is true of many people: 'There is no fear of God before their eyes.'

What I add to this I have learnt from various trustworthy men, especially from the venerable man sir Richard Mongal, prior of the monastery at Dunfermline, a man undoubtedly devoted to the religious life, who piously with the permission of his superior [sir William de St Andrews the abbot] ended his life while on pilgrimage to Santiago de Compostela. For he said that he knew personally those women who one summer, when there was a great dearth of food in the kingdom, got together in a group of three or four from the town of Dunfermline to go down to the shore at Limekilns to gather seaweed, shell-fish and small fish. I do not recall whether it was when they were going or coming back, but it happened that following the gloom caused by a particular cloud which had become very thick above them, a great rainstorm, driven by a certain wind, suddenly descended which immediately soaked them right through to the skin. Then there was a crash of thunder and a flash of lightning appeared at which the poor wretched girls, as if besides themselves, protected themselves by devoutly making the sign of the cross and saying the *Benedicite*. One of them who was more forward, as if she despised all feeling of fear, mocked her companions and with a raised voice said: 'Cristis croice epon my ender endis', which is to say: 'The cross of Christ on my buttocks!' Scarcely had she said it when she was immediately thrown to the ground and by the violence of the lightning, as if by a hammer, dashed to pieces, and nothing of her body remained unburned except her genitals at the front and on the other side the entrance to her anus, which were visibly intact. (c.59, ll.23-67)

Book VIII

Malcolm IV and Henry II

This extract follows the activities of King Malcolm IV from 1157 to 1160. He met King Henry II of England at Chester in 1157 and exchanged his rights over Northumberland and Cumberland for rights over Huntingdon. In 1159 he took a force to assist Henry in the siege of Toulouse in France. In 1160 he had to face a revolt by many of the Scottish earls, which was resolved without bloodshed and not repeated. Later in the same year he made a big impact on the peripheral lordship of Galloway, though troubles were to continue there for some years yet.

It was for reasons of this sort that very serious disputes arose between the kings. But through the good offices of the chief men of both kingdoms a temporary and feigned peace was made between them. During this period of peace, at whose suggestion it is not known, the young King Malcolm, being completely guileless and, innocent as he was, believing Henry's every word, came to King Henry at Chester and did him homage, in the same way in which his grandfather King David had been the liege-man of the old King Henry, called Beauclerc, the husband of King David's sister Matilda. Some assert that he hoped that by so doing he could more peacefully retain his possessions, yet without any deminution to his [royal] titles. At Chester certain of his advisers were influenced by motives of deplorable avarice, for as is commonly said, they were seduced by English money. Soon after that the king, led astray by their false advice, in that same year restored Northumberland [and that without the knowledge of his brother William] and Cumberland to the king of England, without consulting his chief men, save only a few. In return for this the king of England restored to him [after his own peculiar fashion] the earldom of Huntingdon, [which had belonged to his brother David]. Because of this the entire body of opinion in all Scotland was stirred to hatred of their lord the king and his biased and corrupt advisers, and murmured against them, albeit in secret. Meanwhile, in the following year, the same two kings met at Carlisle to discuss their common interests, but did not part on good terms, as several events subsequently revealed. However a few years later, in the seventh year of the reign of Malcolm king of Scots, King Henry brought a large army against the city of Toulouse. Louis, king of the French, who was guarding the city, frustrated

Henry's main purpose, and so he retreated, and out of the most stable peace there arose disagreement of a most extreme kind. King Malcolm took part in this expedition with Henry against the wishes of the majority of his chief men. While they were returning from Toulouse he was invested by Henry with the sword of knighthood at Tours.

At length, when the chief men among the Scots saw the excessively close friendship between their king and Henry king of England, they were much troubled and all Scotland with them. For they were afraid that his friendship would bring them into contempt and disrepute. Trying to avoid this by every means possible, they sent a delegation after the king, saying: 'We do not want this man to reign over us'. So, when he had returned from the army at Toulouse and arrived in Scotland, for various urgent reasons, acting on his royal authority he ordered the prelates and magnates of the kingdom to meet him at the royal burgh of Perth. Meanwhile, the chief men of the realm being stirred to anger, six earls, Ferteth earl of Strathearn and five others, acting against the king not from motives of personal gain or treacherous conspiracy, but rather out of a desire to protect the common weal, tried to seize his person. They besieged him in a tower of that same city. But by the divine judgment their attempt was foiled for the moment, and after a few days the king was reconciled to his nobles through the mediation of the clergy. Subsequently he got together an army on three occasions in that same year and marched into Galloway, otherwise known as Galwidia, against rebel forces. When they had finally been vanquished, brought into alliance and made subject to him, he returned in peace without any loss to his own forces. Subsequently he subdued them so effectively that their under-king, Fergus, renounced all warlike acts, sent his son and heir Uthred to the king as a hostage, and took on the habit of a canon at Holyrood in Edinburgh. (c.3, l.29 - c.4, l.25)

Pope Adrian IV on the misery of power

For reflections by the English pope Adrian IV (1154-9) on the misery of holding his high office, Bower quotes Vincent of Beauvais, who has little sympathy for the complaint. Then he develops this line of thought with a quotation from the first century A.D. writer Valerius Maximus.

He very frequently added this too that, though he had risen to ever higher rank in the church, through all the offices from simple cleric in a monastery up to supreme pontiff, his ascent added not a jot of happiness or tranquillity to that which he had enjoyed in his former life. If I may use his own words: 'The Lord has always enlarged me with the hammer on the anvil. But now, if it please him, let him place his right hand under the load which he has laid upon my weakness, for I cannot support it.' Surely he who fights to attain such misery deserves that misery. So that the man who is exceeding rich on the day he is elected will be poor on the following day, and will be under obligation to an infinite number of creditors. So to strive after the papacy, and to ascend the papal throne even if that means shedding the blood of a brother, is to succeed Romulus in his internecine murder, not St Peter in feeding his spiritual sheep. Thus it is aptly said: 'The supreme pontiff is the servant of servants, not just by a form of words, but in actual fact.' For he must serve the slaves of avarice, namely the citizens of Rome; so much so that, unless he does serve them, he becomes an ex-pope or an exile from Rome. Any king who is eager to rule will, if he examines his own thoughts on the matter, experience pretty well the same feeling of misery. As Valerius writes: 'A king indeed, when the time has come for him to be crowned with the diadem, usually holds the crown in his hand for a long time and says: "O crown that brings eminence rather than happiness!" If anyone at the beginning of his reign realized how many dangers, cares and miseries were attendant on wearing it, he would not want to lift it up, even if it was lying on the ground.' For remember that envy follows hard on the heels of renown, and the more exalted your rank so you are bound to be more anxious and harrassed. (c.5, ll.1-28)

Epitaph on Malcolm IV

The apparently extravagant praise heaped here on King Malcolm at his death in 1165 is partly derived through Fordun ultimately from the English chronicler William of Newburgh writing in the 1190s, and partly quoted directly from Reginald of Durham's Life of St Godric *(the hermit of Finchale near Durham) written in 1170. It is not a matter of hindsight by Bower. (Archbishop Thomas of Canterbury is St Thomas Becket [died 1170].)*

In this year King Malcolm, whose path was strewn by God with the blessing of a sweet fragrance, conceived the longing to be fired with the sublime love of God. Throughout his whole life he made himself so conspicuous by the unspotted whiteness of his chastity, his exemplary humility and innocence, by the purity of his conscience and by the holiness and seriousness of his disposition that among laymen he seemed like a monk, having only his layman's garb in common with them, and to those he ruled a veritable angel dwelling upon earth. After a reign of twelve years, seven months and three days, Christ called him home on Thursday 9 December, and casting aside his human form as one destined to join the company of the angels he not so much lost his kingdom as exchanged it for another. It was in his twenty-sixth year, in the prime of life, that the angels snatched from this world this man who lived a life of angelic holiness among men, of whom the world was not worthy. For St Godric the hermit correctly predicted this when he said: 'Assuredly of all the wealthy potentates who are to be found between the furthest Alps and the remotest reaches of the kingdom of the Scots, two, namely Archbishop Thomas of Canterbury and Malcolm king of Scots are most acceptable to God and will become even more gracious in his sight. But King Malcolm will receive his reward from the Lord sooner'. We read this in the *Life of [St] Godric*. (c.10, ll.32-53)

The sin of pluralism

After a brief quotation from Vincent of Beauvais about a case of the canon law offence of pluralism (i.e. the holding of two or more incompatible benefices in the same hands) in north-east France in 1173, Bower launches into a long scholastic study of the practice, probably thinking mainly of some of the notable pluralists in the Scotland of his day. It is an example of his ability as a man with a university degree in canon law to tease out a problem with the help of references to the letter of the canon law, to the Bible, to the classical writer Seneca and the twelfth-century Bernard of Clairvaux. (Polyphemus was a one-eyed giant blinded by Odysseus.)

In the aforementioned year Robert provost of Aire held two bishoprics, Arras and [Cambrai]. He was the son of a country tradesman of Chartres who, so they say, employed a familiar evil spirit. It was this evil spirit who gained him his advancement to these two charges of which the tenure was incompatible, and it was thanks to it that he had arrived at such an exalted position. In the fourth year after his promotion to such an exalted position he was killed by ruffians. I can recall having read only very occasionally of anyone who possessed several rich benefices dying a Christian death. For in the view of the holy [fathers of the church] it is a mortal and damnable sin to hold several benefices simultaneously in this way, provided that one is sufficient for one's needs. They try to prove this as follows, distinguishing the prime moving forces of our actions, namely nature, [divine] grace and vice. When therefore someone has or wishes to have several such benefices, then the prime moving force of this activity is nature, or grace, or vice. It is clearly not nature, which is content with little. Thus Seneca says: 'Nature requires very little.' Augustine's remarks tend to the same opinion, for he says: 'Human nature is content with a modest competence, but wilfulness and luxury have added much that is extra.' The apostle, writing to Timothy, confirms this: 'As long as we have food and clothing we ought to be content with these.' It is also quite clear that grace is not the prime moving force of this activity, for this is content with even fewer things than nature. For it is that water which quenches the thirst for earthly things of which the Lord says: 'He who drinks from the water which I shall give will not thirst ever again.' So the remaining possibility is that vice is the prime moving force of this activity. So it is clear that it is unlawful for one man to have several such benefices.

This can be shown quite clearly if we consider the reasons why some believe that they may lawfully do this. For some believe that this is permitted them because they spend [the revenues of] the benefices to good purpose, others because they are noble, others because they put in a vicar, others because they appear to themselves to be fulfilling a useful role by their administration of the temporalities, or because of worldly wisdom or power. Against the first group we say that it is not good enough for a doctor to spend the money given him by his sick patient to good purpose, and to have no thought for his sickness. So I say to the man who has benefices in the church: 'It is not enough for a man to spend the revenues of these to good purpose, unless he performs the duties which are attached to them.' Against the second group we say that by the same token a layman or laywoman could hold ten benefices in which they too could place vicars. Besides it is ridiculous to contract a marriage in the expectation of putting in a vicar, and the man who does this seems to fall under the curse of Deuteronomy, namely: 'He will take a wife, and another will sleep with her.' Against those who believe that they can hold several benefices simultaneously because they are noble, wise and powerful, Bernard speaks ironically of such people when he says: 'Those men are the best stewards who take the least care in the most important matters, and the greatest care in the most unimportant.' For in the court of a lay prince it is not permissible for a man who has but one horse to demand the amount of oats needed for two. Why then in God's court, that is the church, in which there are so many who cannot have enough of the oats of the church for their needs, should it be allowed for anyone to demand several prebends for himself alone? How can that which is clearly laid down among men-at-arms be a matter of doubt among educated men? Even granted that it were lawful for one man to have several benefices, it is not expedient. Hence St Paul says: 'All things are lawful for me, but not all things are expedient.' It was lawful for the apostle to take money from those placed under him, but it was not expedient, for that could have given false preachers an excuse for greed and making profits. So though it might be lawful for a discreet and honest man to have many such benefices, yet because those who love the things of this world might take from that a precedent for greed and avarice, it is not expedient. In the same way to eat food sacrificed to idols is in itself lawful for a discreet man who is not venerating the idol while he is eating it; yet it is a sin to eat food offered to idols in the presence of the [spiritually] weak and simple, for they, believing that eating it involves the worship of the idol, are scandalized thereby. So Bernard says: 'The spiritually-inclined man, who weighs up all things to avoid being judged by anyone, will always preface every action by consideration of three factors: first of all whether it is lawful, then whether it is appropriate, and finally whether it is expedient.'

Something is said to be lawful in relation to a prohibition laid down by God, appropriate in relation to the situation of the person concerned, expedient in relation to possible offence given to a neighbour. So the wise man ought to consider whether an intended action is lawful, that is not forbidden by God, then whether it is appropriate to his own personal position. For something could be appropriate in the case of one person, which is inappropriate in that of another. This is particularly so in the case of learned men, who ought, in spiritual terms, to be the eye of the church. Worldliness and the stain of greed and avarice is unbecoming in such men, and to them the apostle is an example when he says: 'Keep yourselves free from every sort of evil', and this: 'Taking thought for what is good not only in God's sight, but in the sight of all.'

Though in certain cases, as in that where one benefice is held by [regular] title and another in trust, as also in the case of those who are given special permission on grounds of necessity, either because of the large number of benefices and the scarcity of priests, or because of the poverty of one benefice, a dispensation is granted for holding two benefices—or because of the small number of parishioners, as for instance under ten persons—in these circumstances it is lawful for a priest to have several benefices, just as it is lawful for one wife to have several husbands.

And as the laws decree, a man who is beneficed in one benefice is bound to minister in it. It follows that a man cannot minister in two at one and the same time. Therefore it is illogical that when any one man cannot fulfil one office with the attention due to its importance, he should appear capable of fulfilling two (see the *Sext*, question 1, 'Presbyteros'). For this results in a monstrosity, since different churches would share the same eye. For it is something unheard of that different bodies share the same part, for from this it would follow that the same person would at one and the same time occupy different places, something which appears to be unnatural. As a result of this [pluralism] the eye of one church is the mouth of another church, because the archdeacon of one church is the precentor in another. It happens also that the eye of one church is the eye of another, for I know a nonentity who is archdeacon in each of two dioceses. And if the archdeacon is the bishop's eye, then one of the two bishops is one-eyed, or has impaired vision [like Polyphemus,] and the other is blind. If someone is regarded as blind, and if he has his eyes on his purse, surely such a church, from which its eyes are so far removed, is considered to be blind. Solomon says: 'A wise person has eyes in his head. But a fool walks in the dark.' (c.20 - c.21, l.42)

The captivity of King William I

King William decided to ally with the eldest son of Henry II, called here the young Henry, who in June 1170 had been crowned as an additional king beside his father, and who by 1173 was raising armed rebellion against him. Bower traces his raiding campaign in northern England in 1173, when his forces included 'caterans' (i.e. marauders, usually from the Highlands), and again in 1174, when he was captured at Alnwick in Northumberland. William was taken to Richmond in north Yorkshire, then to King Henry at Northampton, and then with that king to Falaise in Normandy. Bower adopts Fordun's reflection that William would have had a just cause if he had fought for his own right as a descendant of St Margaret against the Norman interlopers. Then he adds his own thinking that William had been let down by the young Henry. (St Thomas is Thomas Becket.)

William king of the Scots had trusted the new king who had promised him Northumberland together with Cumberland, and hoped to make good his former losses in a new conflict. He therefore renewed the savage fighting against the old king and encamped with a huge army before the castle called Wark. After spending some short time there he advanced into Northumberland, savagely spreading devastation with his highland Scots called caterans or ketherans, whom some call Britons or men of Galloway. They show no mercy to places or sex or individuals or the elderly. The land this side of the river Humber was cruelly ravaged and the Scots in true enemy style laid waste with fire the greater part of Northumberland and cruelly transfixed with the sword the common people of that region. Then they turned towards Carlegium, otherwise known as Carlisle, and attacked that city with all the strength they could muster.

Now it so happened that at that time Robert earl of Leicester was sent over to England to help King William and his supporters. With him came his wife, who also wore armour, a very considerable number of knights with which the young King Henry had supplied him, and no small number of Flemish foot-soldiers. Before he and his men could reach King William as agreed, the earl encountered an army of English supporters of the old king which he had not reckoned on, and which was hurrying to block his advance. Very many of his foot-soldiers were killed and the rest routed, and on 16 October he was captured on the lands of the abbey of [Bury] St Edmunds and imprisoned at Portchester.

When the king of the Scots who was tied down by the siege of Carlisle heard this, and the news struck fear deep into the hearts of his army, he abandoned the siege and for the moment led his troops back to his own kingdom. Just before this a sign was seen in the sky, very bright and flashing with amazing intensity in a very clear sky which was completely free of clouds. So bright was it that all who saw it were amazed and said that it foretold the shedding of blood.

In 1174 King William led an army into England, besieged Appleby and took it, and gained control of Westmorland. The Northumbrians also obtained peace from him until a week after Pentecost by the payment of money. So having successfully concluded the expedition, he returned home without having suffered any losses. He remained in Scotland for a short time, then once more collected an army, led it back into England, and took Brough-under-[Stain]more. So, having laid waste Cumberland, he returned by way of Northumberland, and was laying waste to it and plundering it. He came before Alnwick, and was keeping it under surveillance, having retained only a few knights with him, while his whole army was scattered, engaged in plundering the district all about. Suddenly the enemy, pretending that they were Scots and unfurling banners, came upon him when he was not expecting them and, on 13 July, in the tenth year of his reign, he was taken prisoner and led off, almost all his troops being unaware of his capture.

Immediately after his capture William was led in dejection to Richmond, repeatedly imploring the help of St Thomas, and for a time was kept there in honourable confinement. When the senior king of England learned of what had happened, on his orders William was brought to him, and immediately after taken across to Normandy and placed in the *donjon* at Falaise, to be kept there as a valuable prize. When Earl David, William's younger brother, learned of this, he quickly abandoned Leicester, which he was besieging, and removed to Scotland with his troops as best he could.

Also at that time after the capture of their king, the Scots together with the men of Galloway, in the mutual slaughter that took place, killed their English and French relatives without mercy or pity, making frequent attacks on them. At that time also there took place a most wretched and widespread persecution of the English both in Scotland and in Galloway. So intense was it that no consideration was shown to the sex of any [of the victims], but all were cruelly killed without thought of ransom, wherever they could be found.

But King William richly deserved this fate for having helped a wicked and inhuman son wage an unjust war against his father, a war motivated by no love of justice. William abandoned the most just reason for going to war. For the the kingship of all England along with the crown was his by right, and this was well known. If he had acted as he did on his own account, shrewdly weakening his enemies, he would have cleverly deceived his ally, thus waging a just war by unjust means. For it often happens that the man who unjustly wages a just war, not only by unjust actions and for an unjust reason, but with unjust intent, is conquered or killed. It was perhaps the result of some secret dispensation of God's providence that the son should rise in rebellion against his natural father, for the senior King Henry previously rebelled against his spiritual father, St Thomas. For it is a very true saying of Our Lord: 'It will be measured out to you by the same measure which you have used.' But why did the young Henry incur this taint of ingratitude? For his sake King William suffered to the extent that he was kept in prison, while the young Henry could just as well have helped him through the intervention of his father-in-law, the king of France, as he did the others who were granted their freedom. The answer is an easy one, for Cassiodorus says: 'How will the man who dares to deceive his parents behave towards others?' (c.21, ll.55-86; c.22, ll.1-16, 36-52; c.23, ll.32-52)

The council at Northampton 1176

By the treaty of Falaise of December 1174 King William and some of the leading Scottish clergy swore fealty to Henry II. Now at Northampton in January 1176 Henry sought to secure the submission of the Scottish church as a whole to the metropolitan authority of the archbishop of York. The Scots managed to leave the council with the matter still left open, and by July 1176 secured backing from Pope Alexander III for the independence of the Scottish church, with Rome as its metropolitan rather than York.

The speech attributed here to a cleric called 'Gilbert' is found in no contemporary source, Scottish or English, and appears to have been composed by Fordun and developed by Bower. Certainly the anti-English tone reflects Scottish thinking in the fourteenth and fifteenth centuries rather than the twelfth. The theme that the English owed their conversion to Christianity to the Scots (ultimately through Iona) was one which Fordun had elaborated before. Though Bower reports a suggestion that 'Gilbert' here was the later Gilbert de Moravia bishop of Caithness 1222-45, this is fabulous; and no king's chamberlain of this name is known. But the occasion was one that roused both Fordun and Bower to rhetoric as a reflection of Scottish national attitudes in their own times. (The reference to 'David' is to the biblical king of that name; St Thomas of Canterbury is Thomas Becket.)

Subsequently after the end of winter, the king of England held a general council at Northampton on 29 January. The king of Scotland was present at this, and all the bishops and prelates of the kingdom of the Scots had come there in obedience to an instruction issued by each of the kings. From the one quarter they were ordered under threat of exile to be subject to the [arch-] bishop of York as metropolitan, and from the other were urged [to follow this course] by perverted reasoning passing for good advice. The Scots with all their might avoided this threatening danger, and unanimously rejected it following wiser counsels, though to remedy their situation they did agree to a truce. Subsequently through their efforts the former status of the Scottish church was confirmed by apostolic authority, and its independence buttressed by Pope Alexander by a clearly worded privilege.

In the aforementioned council held at Northampton, in the presence of Richard archbishop of Canterbury and Roger archbishop of York together with the clergy of both realms, a certain Scots cleric named Gilbert perceived their attempt to make the Scottish church subordinate, and having heard the insulting words which they had hurled at the Scots, almost fell down in a fit of fury, blazing with anger like a sword heated in the fire. None of his own prelates and fellow-clerics wanted him to speak. But the archbishops advised him that he might speak out whatever he wished to say. At first they thought him a fool, and said among themselves: 'There is pepper in the Scotsman's nostrils. For he is crammed full of words, and the anger of his belly is choking him. Just see how his anger is like unfermented wine which bursts new wine-jars when there is no air hole.'

He for his part vehemently vented forth his words as follows: 'Nation of the English, you could have been noble, nay rather more noble than the peoples of pretty well all other parts of the world. But you should not have cunningly transformed your noble power and the steadfastness of your formidable strength into the insolence of tyranny, nor the wisdom grounded in liberal learning but now full of sophistry into obscure word-play. For you are presuming to guide your actions without regard to justice and without giving good reasons for them. Rather, made arrogant by the large numbers of your troops and trusting in your luxuriant abundance in terms of wealth and of all things, with a perverted lust, a desire to rule, you hasten to make subject to yourselves all adjacent provinces and peoples—peoples, I assert, far more noble than you are yourselves—not in terms of numbers or power, but of ancestry, and more worthy in respect of their antiquity. If you were to pay attention to the ancient writings, you really ought to be subject to these peoples in all humility, or at least, extinguishing the source of all this rancour, share power with them in perpetuity, thus preserving brotherly love for the future.

Now also, on top of all the wickedness you have perpetrated in your arrogant exercise of power, you are trying to suppress your own mother, namely the Scottish church, which has been from the outset catholic and free, not basing your action on any lawful reason, but on the premise of your power. When you were wandering through the trackless desert of paganism, this church set you up on the mare of faith, and led you back to Christ, the way of truth and life, the host who dispenses eternal rest. This church washed your kings and princes along with their peoples in the waters of holy baptism, taught you God's commandments, and instructed you in morals. It received most gladly many of your nobles and lesser people who joyfully devoted themselves to learning, and saw to it that they were given their daily bread free of charge, books to read, and free teaching. Likewise it consecrated your bishops and priests, appointed and ordained them. Moreover over a period of thirty years or more it held the primacy over all the area from the north bank of the river Thames [northward] and the highest episcopal office, as Bede bears witness. Pray tell me, what recompense are you making to the church which lavishes upon you such great benefits? Surely not subjection, or the kind of recompense with which the Jews repaid Christ, namely evil for good? But indeed I expect nothing else. How has the alien vine become bitter! "We expected you to produce grapes, and you have brought forth grapes of the wild vine. We expected you to do judgment, and behold there is iniquity. We expected justice, and behold there is shouting." But in truth, if your wishes were to become reality, you would reduce to the most utterly wretched enslavement the very church which you ought to treat with every possible respect and reverence.

Ah! What a crime! What state can be more wretched than that of the man whose mind tenaciously retains the memory of wrongs, but forgets acts of kindness? Even that poison which snakes bring forth to destroy others they retain concealed within their coils. But the vice of ingratitude is not contained within these bounds. The ungrateful person torments and tortures himself, and hates and makes little of benefits he has received and which he is bound to repay, while he enlarges and increases injustices suffered.

I believe that Seneca is right when he asserts that some people hate more according as they owe more, and a trivial debt turns the debtor into a deadly enemy. What do you say, David? I confess: "They repaid me with evil for kindly actions and with hatred for my love." Gregory says: "It is unjust to serve the kind of master whom no service placates." Gilbert says: "You, the

English church, strive after what is forbidden, thinking in this way to gain your objective", or rather to carry off what has not been given to you:

> Seek that which is just, if you wish to enjoy that for which you have sought.

Besides—without inflicting any further words on my hearers—although not weighed down [with office], nevertheless in defence of the liberty of my Scottish church, I dissent from its being subjugated by the English, even if the whole clergy of Scotland disagrees with me. Here and now I appeal to the apostolic lord to whom that Scottish church is directly subject, and if I should have to die for the same, here and now I submit my head to the sword. And I do not think that my lords the prelates should seek further advice on this matter, nor do I agree with that course. For it is more honourable to deny a foolish request, than to permit long postponements in reaching a decision. For the man whose request is refused promptly is under less of a delusion.'

When they heard these words, some of the English, both prelates and magnates, joined in high praise of this cleric because he had vented his feelings fearlessly, speaking out for his own country and flattering no man, undeterred by the stern demeanour of his hearers. Moreover they very much feared the pope because of his recent stern judgment upon those who had attacked the freedom of the church and [acted] against St Thomas of Canterbury. Some others, because he expressed a view contrary to their wishes, cried out that he was a smoke-belching Scot and naturally impetuous.

Now Roger archbishop of York, who was foremost in urging the subjection of the Scottish church to his own metropolitan see, drew a sigh from the very bottom of his heart and brought the council to an end. He rose, assumed a cheerful expression, and patting Gilbert's head with his right hand said in a joking tone to the bystanders:

> That arrow did not come from his own quiver,

as if to say: 'When you stand before kings and rulers to defend justice, do not think in advance what to say. For what you are to say will be given you in that hour.' From then on, as indeed formerly, King William felt such affection for this cleric that he made him his closest confidant in his more secret business. It is said that this is the Gilbert whom the king subsequently made chamberlain of the realm, and that from that he was promoted to the bishopric of Caithness. Now his miracles have won him fame as a saint. (c.25, ll.15-28; c.26; c.27, ll.1-14)

King William and Donald MacWilliam

William had to face a serious challenge to his authority in the north of his kingdom in Ross and Moray on both sides of the Moray Firth in two stages, first in 1179 and then again in 1187. In the end the leader of the rebellion, Donald MacWilliam, a grandson of King Duncan II (1094), was slain. (Dunskeath lies on the north shore of the entrance to the Cromarty Firth, and Etherdouer [or Redcastle] at the west end of the Black Isle; 'Mam Garvia' has not been satisfactorily identified, but was presumably not far from the town of Inverness.)

Also in this year William king of Scotland, together with his brother David earl of Huntingdon and a great army, advanced into Ross against MacWilliam, whose real name was Donald *Ban*. There he fortified two castles, Dunskeath and Etherdouer. Having fortified these, he returned to the southern parts of his realm. But seven years after that, since Donald *Ban* continued in his customary wickedness, the king advanced into Moray with a large army, a very strong force, against this same adversary Donald *Ban*. Donald [boasted] that he was of royal descent, the son of William, the son of Duncan the Bastard, who was the son of the great king Malcolm, the husband of St Margaret. Relying on the treachery of some disloyal subjects, he had first of all by insolent usurpation forcibly removed from his king the whole earldom of Ross. He subsequently held the whole of Moray for a considerable time, and by employing fire and slaughter had seized the greater part of the kingdom, moving about all of it, and aspiring to have it under his control.

While the king with his army was staying in the town of Inverness, and had been harrying Donald *Ban* and his supporters with daily raids for booty and plunder, it chanced one day that when he had sent out his men as usual, up to two thousand strong, to reconnoitre and take booty across the moors and the countryside, some of those who were serving with the king's army suddenly and unexpectedly came upon MacWilliam as he was resting with his [exhausted] troops on a moor near Moray called 'Mam Garvia'. When MacWilliam saw that the king's troops were few in comparison with his own, he hurriedly joined battle with them, and charged the royal forces. They bravely resisted all his efforts, and because they trusted in the righteousness of their cause, continued to resist courageously. With God's help they cut down MacWilliam and five hundred of his men, and put the rest to flight, on Friday 31 July, thus repaying him with a just reward for his evil deeds. They sent his head to the king to be displayed to the whole army. (c.28, ll.38-70)

Philip II and the Jews

Bower selects from Vincent of Beauvais two passages datable 1180-2 and 1192 regarding the attitude of King Philip II Augustus of France (1180-1223) to the Jews in his kingdom. Bower clearly accepts such traditional horror stories about Jewish practices, and relates the persecution of Jews with satisfaction. (The countess of Champagne who held the town of Bray near Paris was an elder half-sister of King Philip.)

So at the very beginning of his reign, fired by his love of God, King Philip commenced upon the course of action which he had long kept hidden in his mind while his father was still alive, and had hesitated to put into effect out of respect for his father. For on his orders Jews throughout the whole of France were arrested in their synagogues on the sabbath. First of all they were stripped of their clothing, gold and silver.

Indeed at that time a very large number of Jews were living in Paris, having flocked there from different parts of the world on account of the long period of peace they had enjoyed there. For they had heard of the vigour which the kings of the French had shown in dealing with their enemies and the compassion they had displayed towards their subjects. During their long stay they had become so wealthy that they had made almost half the city their own. But contrary to the law of God and of the church, they kept male and female Christian servants in their houses, who actually joined with the Jews in observing Jewish rites. They also afflicted citizens, knights and peasants from the suburbs, towns and villages with usury beyond all bounds. They even detained some who were bound by their pledged oath in their own houses, as if in a prison.

Moreover they treated the sacred vessels which, because of the pressing needs of churches, had been deposited with them as a so-called 'pledge' so disrespectfully that their young children used to eat morsels of bread dipped in wine in chalices. So, since the Jews feared that their houses might be searched by royal officials, one of them set aside a gold cross and a gospel book decorated with gold and precious gems with some other sacred objects, and most shamefully threw them down into a deep pit where he was accustomed to relieve himself. What a shameful act! All the objects were subsequently found through divine revelation.

So an instruction was given by the king to the effect that all Jews should depart from his realm. Some were converted to the Christian faith. In consideration of their Christian religion he granted them all their possessions intact. But others began to entice the barons and the prelates of the church with gifts and promises, in order that through their persuasion and the promise of unlimited money they might deflect the king from his purpose. But the king could not be softened by entreaties or by promises of temporal possessions. So they were expelled and all their immovable goods passed to the royal treasury. The king ordered all their synagogues, which they called 'schools', to be cleaned out and, against the wishes of all his chief men, to be dedicated to God as churches; and he had altars consecrated in them so that Christ might be praised by the clergy in the very place where previously he was blasphemed after the manner of the Jews.

After his return to France [in 1192], and while he was staying at St Germain-en-Laye, King Philip heard of the ignominious death of a certain Christian, a deed perpetrated by the Jews themselves. Filled with compassion for the Christian religion he suddenly set out without his household knowing his destination. He came very swiftly to Bray and there, having set guards on all the town gates and seized more than eighty Jews, he had them [all] burned. The countess of that town, corrupted by their gifts, had handed over to them a Christian whom they had falsely accused of theft and murder. Inflamed by long-standing hatred they led him through the length of the town, with his hands tied behind him and his head crowned with thorns, flogging him, and afterwards hanged him on a gibbet. (c.30, l.39 - c.31; c.53, ll.26-37)

Philip II and the abbacy of St Denis

Bower produces an account of his own about the appointment of an abbot for the monastery of St Denis near Paris (which was under the particular protection of the French kings) by blending earlier accounts by Vincent of Beauvais and Caesarius of Heisterbach (see below VIII, c.35). It is an improving story which portrays the king in a good light, rather than a truthful account of what happened. 'Simony' was the sin of deliberately selling or buying spiritual authority. Bower relates several other examples of it, and concludes here with a comment on conditions in the Scotland of his own day, and a biblical quotation from the Psalms.

In the following year Abbot William was proving languid and careless in his administration of the [monastic] church of the blessed Denis. This displeased the king, and he set about looking for someone else to govern that church. Accordingly one day while the king was passing through the village of St Denis, he had come down to the abbey. When the abbot learned of this he was terrified, and immediately calling together the brothers to a chapter, he had himself deposed. When the king had given the monks permission to elect [a new abbot], a day was assigned for the election. According to Caesarius the provost of the monastery, who aspired to be elected, offered King Philip five hundred pounds that he might see fit to support his cause. The king made him no promises, but encouraged him to hope by accepting the gift, and caused the money to be handed over to his chamberlain. The cellarer, knowing nothing of this, did likewise, as did the treasurer.

So on the day appointed for holding the election the king sat in the chapter, while each of the three aforesaid simoniacal monks confidently expected and yearned after preferment. Meanwhile the king saw [sitting] in a corner a certain simple monk, and acting in obedience to his conscience called him over and urged the monks to choose him. All of them recognized him as being religious and devout, and so acceded to the king's request. The monk for his part strenuously excused himself from taking on the post, and gave many reasons why he should not, alleging among other things that the abbey was encumbered by debts, and he had no money of his own. The king replied with a smile: 'I am lending you 1,500 pounds, and if you need it, I will give it to you, since it happens to be owed to you. I will also give you counsel and help, providing that as a father in religion you perform your spiritual duties scrupulously and your other duties, taking into account the following stipulation and royal prohibition—that at this time immediately after your preferment you should not be willing to give or promise any gift to anyone from your own family or from the royal court, either cleric or layman. This was agreed, and he administered the abbey very well, always finding the king's favour very close to him.

How different are our present-day princes and prelates. They ought to keep their hands well away from every gift. They seek to deceive God by committing simony in an indirect and subtle manner, rather than openly and directly. But 'their iniquity has lied to itself'. (c.34, ll.16-54)

More examples of simony

Among a number of other examples of the subtlety of the sin of simony, Bower includes another from Caesarius of Heisterbach, (whose Dialogus Miraculorum *dates from the 1220s) and also one from the collection of exempla compiled by the Dominican Humbert de Romans (died 1277). Then he offers his own reflections on the dangers of this hidden sin called after 'Simon the Magician', who is mentioned only briefly in the Bible (Acts 8:9-24).*

Thus Caesarius writes that a certain holy anchoress gave the following reply to a Cistercian abbot—a man in other respects of good repute and exceptional wisdom—who wanted to know whether it was expedient for the salvation of his soul that he should be an abbot. She, advised and enlightened by the Holy Spirit as the occasion demanded, replied in the negative. 'For', she said, 'you entered office by an act of simony.' He was amazed and asked: 'What are you saying, good lady? May God forgive you, for I detest this sin above all others. I have never committed simony.' The anchoress replied: 'You are deceived, for when that election was imminent, because you aspired to be abbot, you did not walk in the ways of simplicity as formerly, but said to the simple monks: "It is detrimental to our honour if we choose someone from outside the abbey." It was obvious to you that there was no other suitable candidate for this post inside the abbey except yourself. In this way you became abbot, having deceived your brother monks.' Embarrassed because the truth had come out in this way, he resigned his office.

Because, as has been written, simony is committed not only by rendering a service or giving a present, but also by the tongue, that is by entreaty, consider the danger inherent in it as described by Humbert in *On the Gift of Fear*:

> A certain abbot on his deathbed asked his monks to choose as abbot after his death a monk of that monastery who was his nephew, [a monk who was indeed distinguished by his learning and moral qualities]. This was done. While the new abbot was walking in his garden by a stream that ran through the garden, he heard a mournful voice groaning. When he bade it speak, it said that it was the soul of the abbot his uncle, which had suffered immeasurable torment on account of his carnal affection and the simoniacal request which he had poured out to the assembled monks on his [i.e. the nephew's] behalf in order to have him elected abbot. The nephew wondered how he was being tortured so severely in tepid water since it was summer time. The voice said: 'Bring the copper candlestick which stands beside you at the window of your cell.' This was on his orders hurled into the stream and immediately melted like wax. When the abbot saw this he immediately shuddered with fear, renounced his charge, and there were no further occurrences of the voice.

Both these abbots who made this act of renunciation acted in the light of their own wisdom. For according to the decree of the canons simoniacs will be for ever damned unless they renounce their office and repent...

No other sin involves a crime against God as does the heresy of simony. And so among other sins He has punished it with greater severity, as we find in [*Decretum*] 1, Question 1, 'Quibusdam'. I hope that no one will be angry with me for saying something about it for the benefit of my readers, in order that the very great danger that it represents may be understood. Because, where the danger is greater, there one must exercise all the greater care in avoiding that danger. For it is quite clear how much that hidden sin, that poisoned honey and sweet poison offends Christ from the fact that at the time of his coming into this wicked world clothed in human flesh, even though he came to be judged and not to judge, to do away with sins, not to punish them, to show mercy rather than exact revenge, he was nonetheless so stern, severe and powerful in expressing his rage at the sin of simony that, as it were forgetting his innate mercy, he immediately devoted all his efforts to exacting punishment, without even judging the case.

So it is written in the gospel that having made a sort of whip from cords, he drove from the temple those who bought and sold, and upset the tables and money of the moneychangers. He also overturned the chairs of those who sold doves. These became an allegory for simoniacs when he said to them: 'My house is a house of prayer, but you have made it a cave full of thieves.' No wonder that he showed such passionate anger towards people of this sort, for simoniacs in so far as is in their power drive him from his office. For Christ has made himself the doorkeeper of the church, not wishing that anyone should enter into the church, that is enter upon any office in the church, except through him. Thus [he himself says]: 'I am the door. He who does not enter into the sheepfold through the door, but climbs in by some other way, is a thief and a robber.' And so those princes, prelates, patrons or protectors of churches who sinfully sell the church of Christ are driving Christ from his office, since they make money the doorway into the church, not Christ. Just so did Simon the Magician, to whom Peter said: 'May your money go with you to perdition. For you thought that the gift of God can be acquired with money.'

Many are deceived by the subtle nature of simony, as indeed are [simple] religious communities, who these days have the corrupt custom of admitting no one into the religious life unless they bring with them specified jewels, [chalices] or silver cups, spoons or other similar [gifts]. This custom is found in abbeys which are rich with great abundance of possessions, whereas it is forbidden even among poor nuns in the decrees [of canon law]. Thus simony occurs when nuns, however poor, admit others in return for a sum of money. (c.35, ll.29-70; c.36, ll.1-43)

Fighting in Galloway

Bower relates from Fordun the major advance of royal authority in the outlying lordship of Galloway in 1185. (Uthred had been killed in 1174.) Roland established himself with the help of King William as lord of a united Galloway 1185-1200. The various men (including Gillecolm) mentioned here as challenging his authority have not been identified; but their troublesome threat to the peace of neighbouring parts of Scotland south of the Firth of Forth was satisfactorily removed.

Also at that time Gilbert son of Fergus lord of Galloway died, who had favoured and prosecuted the civil wars, and who, as I mentioned above, had shamefully killed his own brother Uthred, after cutting out his tongue and blinding him. Clearly this [the death of Gilbert] occurred by the will of God, who mercifully heard the constant cries of the poor and needy, and rescued them from the power of stronger men.

On Gilbert's death Roland son of Uthred with the help of the king gathered together his army, and on Thursday 4 July engaged in battle Gilpatrick, and Henry Kennedy and Samuel, and their supporters from Galloway in very large numbers. They had been the ringleaders in all the fighting and warfare in the time of the aforesaid Gilbert. In this battle these most evil commanders perished together along with their accomplices, slain by an avenging sword. For the Lord inflicted well-deserved retribution on them.

In that year the same Roland on the king's orders hunted down Gillecolm, the chief usurper and ringleader of the brigands, and joined battle with him on 30 September. This Gillecolm was a threat to all Lothian, for he made frequent raids for booty, perpetrated robberies on the population, and had deprived a number of noblemen of their lives and property. But finally Gillecolm advanced under arms into Galloway, the territory of the said Gilbert, and unjustly took over part of it as a lordship of Galloway for himself. But after engaging Roland in battle, his usurpation eventually ended ignominiously, for Gillecolm perished aong with a great number of his accomplices. Roland's brother also fell in this conflict: a few of his supporters were also killed. (c.39, ll.13-40)

Peace in England and Scotland 1193-99

Bower copies from Fordun information about money sent in 1193 to England as a voluntary contribution towards King Richard I's ransom, and then includes Fordun's description of what has been called a 'golden episode' in Anglo-Scottish relations from the time of Richard's return in March 1194 until his death in April 1199. Perhaps this picture was influenced by hindsight in the light of how relations were to be troubled between King William and King John after 1200.

King William felt compassion for the distress of his kinsman King Richard and as an act of pure goodwill spontaneously sent down from Scotland two thousand marks from the royal treasury for this very purpose. From then for the rest of King Richard's lifetime, there was such great unity and concord between the two kingdoms, and such friendship based on true affection linked the two kings like David and Jonathan, that the one fully and faithfully fulfilled the other's wish, and each of the two peoples was thought of as part of one and the same people. Whenever it pleased them, Englishmen on foot or on horseback were able to pass unharmed right across Scotland, both on this side of the mountains and beyond, laden with gold or any other sort of merchandise, and in like manner Scots [could pass] through England. (c.55, ll.1-13)

Philip II and a vineyard

Bower offers again a tale taken from the Dialogus *of Caesarius of Heisterbach about the admirable qualities of King Philip Augustus. The story is probably mythical; but the medieval reader would recall the similar biblical story of the behaviour of Daniel as an examining judge. The moral is a general one.*

About the same time King Philip of France had a provost at Paris who desired his neighbour's vineyard and wanted to buy it. But the other party was unwilling. Eventually he died and the provost thought up a ruse. He bribed two town officials and took them by night to the dead man's tomb. He then dug up the tomb, placed in the corpse's hand the bag of money which he had offered to the man when he was alive, and closed up the hole. Next day he seized the vineyard. The dead man's widow objected, and came before the king, who appointed judges; but her case was rejected because of the testimony of the officials. The woman did not accept this and assailed the king with bitter words of complaint. He called in each of the witnesses separately and examined each of them individually. He made the first of them whisper the 'Our Father' in his ear. The king had him removed and placed under guard, and then spoke to the other official about telling the truth under pain of death, adding: 'Your colleague has told me the truth [as surely] as the 'Our Father' etc. is sacred.' The official then became frightened and revealed the whole sequence of events. The king restored the vineyard to the widow, had the officials beheaded and the provost buried alive. (c.55, ll.37-55)

A bishop of Paris and his mother

This story about Maurice de Sully bishop of Paris 1160-96 is one that was included in several collections of exempla. This bishop was responsible for building much of the present cathedral of Notre Dame in Paris. For Bower it was a good story with a moral.

That same year Maurice bishop of Paris of revered memory, a father to the poor and to orphans, passed over joyfully to the Lord. His industry and learning ensured that he rose from the very lowest rank in society and very great poverty to the honour of a bishopric. For when he was a young [scholar], poor and needy, he refused to accept the expected alms so that he would never be a bishop in this manner. Among all his other outstanding achievements he built the church over which he presided from the foundations up. When he was bishop his mother came to see him. She was an old woman, poor and clothed in rags. She took lodgings in a suburb and sent the landlord to her son the bishop, furnished with unambiguous tokens of recognition so that she might gain access to him and speak with him. This was gladly granted and the landlord borrowed more elegant clothes from neighbours and presented the bishop's mother to him next day. But when the bishop saw her decked out like this, not only did he not allow her into his presence, but he refused even to exchange words with her. So the old lady departed troubled and sad. But the landlord approached the bishop and as far as he dared accused him of being an ungrateful son. The bishop replied: '[I acted like this] for she is not my mother. For she was not accustomed to come clothed in such noble garments. Let her come to me with the appearance and clothes in which she first appeared before you, and if she is my mother, then perhaps I shall recognize her.' Next day she was presented to the bishop with pouch and staff, barefooted and dishevelled with an old pair of shoes slung about her neck. He acknowledged her most courteously and they rushed to embrace to the amazement of all the bystanders. From then on he treated her properly as a son should. Everyone commended him for this and he gained a great reputation as a result. (c.57, ll.20-48)

William I and Harald earl of Caithness

Bower takes from Fordun two stages dated 1196-7 and 1201-2 of the story of the troubled relationship of King William and Harald earl of Caithness 1139-1206 (who was also earl of Orkney in the Norwegian kingdom). Malcolm MacHeth, possibly an illegitimate son of King Alexander I, had been a rebel against King David I. John was bishop of Caithness probably 1185-1213; he and the earl quarrelled over financial levies for the benefit of the church. The bishop's mutilation in 1201 led to similar retribution against the earl's son Thorfinn in the same year.

In the preceding year there was such a severe famine in Scotland that people died in every part of the country. That year King William led an army into Caithness. He crossed the river Oykell, and after killing certain men who were disturbing the peace made both the provinces belonging to the men of Caithness subject to his will. He also forced Harald earl of Caithness to flee. Until then he had been a good and loyal vassal, but at that time he had risen against his lord the king at the instigation of his wife, a daughter of MacHeth and a base deceiver. The king then left men to guard the country and returned to Scotland. As well as all this in the next year, that is 1197, there was a battle in Moray near the castle of Inverness fought between the king's men and Roderic and Thorfinn Haraldsson. There the king's enemies were routed, and Roderic and many others slain.

All this made the king very displeased with Harald. He led his army back into Moray, and ranging over all those highland areas (namely Sutherland, Caithness and Ross), eventually captured Harald, and lodged him in Roxburgh castle, where he remained under guard until he had placated the king. At last he was reconciled with the king and left his son Thorfinn as a hostage for himself. A little later, because his father had broken his word, Thorfinn's eyes were put out and his genitals cut off, and he ended his life in prison.

During all this time there were incessant civil wars which, as usually happened, were waged in the most remote parts of Scotland. For Harald earl of Orkney sailed secretly across to Caithness. As he blamed John the bishop of that province for encouraging discord and opening up a breach between himself and the lord king by making accusations against him, he had him blinded and had his tongue cut out, or so he thought, for it turned out otherwise. For John retained the use of his tongue and one of his eyes to some degree. When the king learned of this, he did not delay, but before that Christmas sent an army to Caithness to attack the earl. But it returned without accomplishing anything, for Harald retreated to the most remote parts of his territory, but came back immediately once the army had returned home. So in the following spring, that is in 1202, as the lord king was preparing a naval expedition to Orkney against the said Harald, he came to meet the king at Perth under the safe conduct of Roger bishop of St Andrews. There through the intercession of the bishop and other men of standing he reached an agreement with the king, swearing that in all matters he would abide by the judgment of the church. So was he restored to his earldom on payment of two thousand pounds of silver to the lord king. (c.59, ll.14-34; c.62, ll.3-23)

Diplomatic relations with England 1209

Quite exceptionally Bower goes far beyond Fordun in providing details of negotiations between King William and a hostile King John of England April-August 1209. There were threats of force on both sides before a treaty was achieved that was backed up in the way that was then customary by an agreement for royal marriage alliances between two daughters of William and two sons of John. The text of this treaty has not survived; but Bower has clearly had access to a contemporary record of the negotiations which has been compared with a 'diary' of the different stages. This may have been compiled by either William Malveisin bishop of St Andrews, or Walter de St Albans bishop of Glasgow, or the royal clerk and chancellor William del Bois. Many details about the persons and places involved can be checked as accurate. The elderly and invalid William did well to resist pressure by John, even if it was at considerable cost. In the event, though William's daughters were handed over to John in August 1209, they were pawns in the diplomatic game who were never to secure the royal marriages they had been promised.

Because Scotland was the nearest country to the kingdom of England and shared a border with it, [King John] began to assemble his military might and vent his poison on that country. For ever since the destruction of the fabric of the castle at Tweedmouth by King William, he was fired with anger against the king of the Scots. With a large number of men, a strong force, he established himself about the river Tweed near Norham with a view to attacking the aforesaid King William. But King William gathered his army together and with an equally powerful force advanced as far as Roxburgh.

As emissaries from each side mediated between the two parties, many unheard of demands and requirements were made of the king of the Scots by the king of England, demands which were not consistent with the liberties of William's kingdom or [the welfare of] its people. The complete rejection of all of these by the Scots inflamed the dislike felt for them by the English still further. Eventually after a meeting of peace-loving nobles from both kingdoms, the king of England departed for Newcastle. Once both armies had returned home, William king of Scotland came to meet the king in person, after first receiving hostages together with a safe-conduct [guaranteed by] the magnates and nobles of England. Earl David his brother and a great number of the Scots magnates had accompanied King William. After they had held some sort of discussion there, the king of Scotland was suddenly taken ill. After the conference he was given leave to go there and then, and King John returned to England; and after he had recovered, the king of the Scots returned to his own territory. The entourages of the two kings were of the impression that a firm peace had been made between them on that occasion. But the outcome was quite otherwise, as will be clear from what follows. For when King William began to feel unwell, he accepted a pause for his own person until he could return home and recover. This he did at the insistence of the king of England, who urged it upon him.

So after the king had fully recovered he convened a great council at Stirling on the Octave of Pentecost. There he and his noble brother Earl David and pretty well all the bishops, prelates and noblemen of all his kingdom seriously discussed the reply which was to be sent to the king of England. Acting on a plan which had been worked out there, King William sent William and Walter the bishops of St Andrews and Glasgow, also William Comyn the justiciar of Scotia and Philip de Valognes the chamberlain, and through them communicated his response to the king of England. But when the emissaries delivered themselves of the response, they found the king of England more displeased than they had believed and much provoked by their answers, thundering out threats against the kings of Scotland and their country. So they cautiously deflected [the anger of] the king of England and hurried back to their native Scotland. They related the unexpected news to their king at Forfar and threw not just the king but the whole kingdom into a considerable panic.

So the king of Scotland ordered his army to be made ready and his castles to be reinforced with arms, soldiers and provisions, and set off in the direction of Lothian, going as quickly as he could to defend his borders, and as far as his strength allowed to counter any of his enemies who might rise against him. Meanwhile the lord king of Scotland sent back to the king of England that same bishop of St Andrews and the abbot of Melrose and certain others, and through them relayed a friendlier message than the previous one. For if possible he wanted to put together a treaty bringing peace and concord. While they journeyed to the king of England to fulfil the mission laid upon them, Saer de Quincy earl of Winchester and Robert de Ros came to Edinburgh on behalf of the king of England to talk with the king of Scotland.

Shortly before this the king of England had set out on an expedition into Wales. Now he led with him against the Scots two petty kings from there with about 13,000 of their men, together with 1,500 knights from England, about seven thousand crossbowmen and Brabançons, and a large army. So the king of Scotland after consultation with the aforesaid English emissaries, and without waiting for the return of his own previous emissaries, sent to the king of England Roger de Mortimer sheriff of Perth and a certain Templar who was his personal almoner, giving them a message that was even friendlier and more agreeable in its wording than the last. While they were hurrying off without delay, the bishop of St Andrews returned and, his business concluded, came to the court at Traquair with the news that the king of the English with his army had almost reached the Scottish border. He was under the impression that the army of Scotland was all ready and prepared for war. So the lord king of Scotland quickly caused his whole army to be summoned, and sent the same bishop to the king of England for a third time with all speed, to delay him with talking until he could assemble all his army again. But when the king of England with his army had got as far as Bamburgh and the king of Scotland was in the neighbourhood of Melrose, and had passed some days in the monastery itself awaiting the arrival of his troops who were streaming in to join him from every quarter much to his satisfaction, it was suggested to him by his followers that he should forestall war by making peace. He fell in with their advice and endeavoured to satisfy the demands and wishes of the king of England.

As a result of the efforts at mediation between the two kings made by the magnates and nobles of both kingdoms who had flocked there from both sides to do battle, both were eventually united and bound by a peace treaty which took the following form. The said king of Scotland was to give his two daughters Margaret and Isabella into the charge of the king of England with a view to their being married, the eldest to Henry the said King John's son when he should come to manhood, and the other to one of the English nobility or (as some would have it) to Richard the younger brother of the said Henry, or else to an English nobleman of such a rank as was fitting for a king's daughter to marry. There was however the proviso that if one of the king of England's sons should die before he had married, then the remaining son should marry the king of Scotland's eldest daughter. Likewise as regards the daughters it was stipulated that if one of them should die before she reached marriageable age, the other would marry the eldest son of the king of the English, or at any rate that one of the girls should be espoused to the one of the boys who would fall heir to England.

At last, after the intermediaries had held a preliminary discussion about the peace treaty which was to remain in force in perpetuity, the kings in person with supporters chosen from their councils met at Norham. There they reached agreement about the marriages as stated above, and it was also agreed that the castle which the king of England had tried to build at Tweedmouth should never be built in the future, and as compensation for the dishonour done to the king of England by its destruction by the king of Scotland, the king of Scotland should pay him 4,000 pounds. It was also stipulated that the merchants of Scotland should freely and in the customary manner enter England for the purpose of carrying on their trade, and that the king of the Scots should retain all his ancient honours intact. In return for the said marriages and for his observing all the other articles fully and completely 15,000 marks should be paid to King John of England (as well as the aforesaid 4,000 pounds) within a period of two years and in four equal instalments due on four fixed term dates.

To encourage greater stability in observing the pact William Comyn the justiciar of Scotia on behalf of his lord and Robert de Vieuxpont, a knight who was on close terms with the king of England and was a member of the English council, were chosen from each side and took an oath on the gospels in the name of the kings that they would observe the peace in perpetuity. Then all the nobility of England and Scotland who were present made the same promise under oath that to the best of their ability that agreement would be kept unbroken by both sides. And to remove any suspicion that the peace and the agreement might be broken by the king of the Scots, the lord king of Scotland voluntarily gave the king of England thirteen hostages for his maintaining the peace. And since that same king, being in some degree tired by reason of old age, had in mind to end his life in [an atmosphere of] genuine love and peace, he sent his daughters along with the hostages to the justiciar and the emissaries of the king of England at Carlisle, and handed them over on the Sunday which was the day after the Assumption of Our Lady. And the two kings' armies returned home with the utmost joy. (c.69, l.37 - c.71)

Flooding at Perth in 1209

This story of a great flood at Perth probably dates from September 1209, and is uniquely reported by Bower, who is also the first writer to suggest that 'Bertha' was an old name of Perth. The mound which fell into the river must have been the motte on top of which a royal castle stood until then, but was never rebuilt. The river Tay is tidal up to Perth, which must have meant that the flood waters coming down the river were particularly devastating there.

This year, or as some would have it around Michaelmas, there was such a downpour of rain that the torrents and rivers burst beyond their former channels and swept the crops out of the fields. The waters of Tay and Almond flowed right through the greater part of the town which used to be called Bertha and is now called Perth in Scotland. A mound which fell into the river not only destroyed several houses, but also completely swept away its bridge with the old chapel on it. The lord king William, his noble son Alexander and his brother the earl of Huntingdon left the same town in a very small boat and looked for dry land, accompanied by a very few of the magnates who happened to be there at that time. Some others among the nobility of

Scotland who had likewise been in the same town only just escaped, saving themselves as best they could in small boats or in upper rooms. For the level of the sea had suddenly risen, swollen by a high tide and the great increase of excess rain water, so that not only cobles and skiffs but even huge ships were able to pass freely through the royal town without encountering any obstacle, at any rate through the streets and open spaces, owing to the high level of the water. (c.72, ll.39-57)

William I and Guthred MacWilliam

Bower preserves the fullest known account of royal expeditions against Guthred MacWilliam (son of Donald MacWilliam—see above) in the north of Scotland 1211-12. (The island occupied by this rebel has not been identified.) Prince Alexander, King William's heir, had just been knighted by King John of England in March 1212: this was his first military expedition. (Kincardine was the royal manor and castle of this name [now scarcely traceable] after which Kincardineshire was called; the 'thanes of Ross' were probably local lords in Ross rather than the more technical managers of royal estates.)

In 1211 William king of Scotland sent a huge army together with all the nobles of his kingdom into Ross against Guthred MacWilliam. The king himself followed when he was able some time between the Nativity of St John and the autumn. On his way he built two castles, laid waste pretty well all of Ross, and took or killed as many of the said Guthred's supporters as he could find. But Guthred himself always avoided the king's army, meanwhile laying ambushes for it whenever he could by night or day, and driving off booty from the lord king's land.

At last the lord king sent 4,000 men picked from his army to seek out Guthred in the area where they thought he was hiding. He put in command of them four military men: the earls of Atholl and of Buchan, Malcolm Morgrund and his doorward Thomas de Lundie. They came to an island on which Guthred himself had gathered together provisions, and from which he had carried off his treasure, and there they engaged Guthred's men. Many were killed on both sides, but more from among the rebels. Those of them who remained retreated for the moment to the nearest forest and to safer places. About Michaelmas the lord king returned from there with a strong force and left Malcolm earl of Fife as guardian of Moray. But no sooner had the king departed than the said Guthred besieged one of the castles built by the king in Ross just a little earlier. He had made ready his siege engines and was just on the point of capturing it, when the garrison within lost their nerve and surrendered it of their own accord to save their lives, if nothing else. This Guthred granted them, and setting fire to the castle burned it down. The king was enraged on hearing this, but put off making any expedition because of the severe winter weather. But next summer Sir Alexander the lord king's son on his father's orders set out from Lothian for Ross with a large army a little before the Nativity of St John. The king intended to follow him after a short interval with another army drawn from his territory.

Meanwhile Guthred MacWilliam was betrayed by his own followers, captured, put in chains and taken to Moray to William Comyn earl of Buchan, the lord king's justiciar, for he was guardian of Moray at that time, since Malcolm earl of Fife had not long since gone to the king to discuss matters with him. The justiciar, who wanted Guthred brought before the king alive, got as far as Kincardine. There when he learned the king's will, which was that he did not want to see him alive, they beheaded Guthred, dragged him along by the feet and hung him up. He was already very close to death, for he had refused food ever since his capture. This Guthred had come to those parts from Ireland in the previous year around Epiphany, as part of a plot (as is commonly said) [hatched by] the thanes of Ross. He trod underfoot everything he encountered and plagued many parts of the kingdom of Scotland. (c.76)

King William's problems with King John

William in his old age had in 1213 to deal with an attempt by John at Norham on the river Tweed to secure the person of his heir Prince Alexander. William's advisers were divided, while he stayed away from Norham as an invalid at Newbattle Abbey in Midlothian and Haddington in East Lothian. And John was frustrated in his aims: he did not even succeed in forcing the Scots to hand over the English rebel baron Eustace de Vescy who had fled to Scotland the previous year; and until May 1213 at any rate he was the object of papal excommunication, and vulnerable to magnate disaffection at home.

Meanwhile King William, broken down as he was by old age and his exertions, began to lose his strength and to see that these were critical times for him because of the ill health arising from his infirmity. Consequently, since he desired above all else peace and tranquillity in his kingdom, he laboured anxiously far beyond his capacity to settle quarrels and maintain justice among his subjects, making no concession whatsoever to his advanced age. King John of England was aware of this, and notwithstanding the various peace treaties arrived at in the past, treacherously planned to bring the kingdom of Scotland under his rule as he had lately conquered the kingdoms of Ireland and Wales, and to subject it to perpetual domination. Clear evidence of this appeared subsequently.

For next year, as had been decided by the kings and their emissaries, [King John] came for a third time to Norham, suggesting to the king of Scotland a ratification in perpetuity of a more stable peace treaty (or so he alleged) as a pretext for his initiative. Prior to this William had been confined to his sick bed at Newbattle; but when coming at the sugestion of the king of the English as far as Haddington, he was unable to go any further. So when he had excused himself on the grounds of his illness, the king of England in reply demanded that William send him his only son and heir Alexander. He made a great many promises, among them that he would give him even better [inducements] in accordance with their long-standing threefold alliance.

The king was indeed disposed to do this, following the advice of some who supported the interest of the king of England. But he was dissuaded by others who gave him better counsel. For they recognized from experience a preconceived trick when it was on the point of success, and when a secret guarantee [*fides*] was detected, it furnished proof of this. So while the king [of the Scots] put up a sort of resistance, there was an absolute refusal to allow the prince to cross over to the king of England. For he was young and would not know how to deal with difficult matters of state or how to make an adequate response to the king of England if he raised further questions. Also they feared the evil intentions of King John. If he had control over the person of the son and heir of the king of Scotland, and consequently of the king—for as the laws bear witness a king's son should be called 'king', even though he may not possess the kingdom—they suspected that it would not be easy for Alexander to return, even if there were no other obstacle, until Eustace de Vescy the king of Scotland's son-in-law was handed back to the king of England...So the king of England was frustrated in his heart, and pretending to be angry, hastily returned to England, not daring to make any move against Scotland. For he feared the valour of the Scots and invasions by the Welsh and by foreigners. He also feared the disaffection of his own magnates and lay nobles who, if the king were engaged in fighting anywhere, would avenge injustices done to them, having as a ready excuse his rebellion against the Apostolic See. (c.78, ll.1-49)

Book IX

King William's death; inauguration of King Alexander II

No explanation is offered for the extraordinary haste in securing the new young king's inauguration at Scone the very day after the death of his father at Stirling, and before the late king's funeral. Perhaps there was fear of a rebellion in the north. Furthermore seizure of the throne by William's brother David earl of Huntingdon at the expense of the legitimate heir who was still a minor (as had happened in England in 1199) may have been feared as a possibility that did not eventuate if David was ill as stated here. At any rate there must have been careful planning as the old king was nearing his end.

After [the lion of justice] the splendid prince King William had died in the town of Stirling, early the next morning, on the advice of the prelates and nobles, they decided that the lady queen, who was in a state of extreme mourning and worn out with grief, should supervise the burial and press on with the funeral ceremony, along with Walter bishop of Glasgow, Robert bishop-elect of Ross, as well as William del Bois the chancellor and other faithful servants. Try as they might they could not bring the queen out of her grief. Meanwhile [the earls] of Strathearn, Atholl, Angus, Menteith and Buchan, along with William Malveisin bishop of St Andrews and other members of the three estates, hurriedly gathered in large numbers on the passing away of the king, and a select number of them were enlisted to get hold of the sixteen-and-a-half year old Alexander the king's son (a noble youth of good natural abilities) and bring him with them to Scone. There he was crowned on the Friday with more pomp and ceremony than anyone before him, amidst great joy mixed with sadness on account of the death of his father, so that you might say that it was right to rejoice for Alexander and right to weep for William. And on the following Saturday, that is the feast of St Nicholas, as well as on the following Sunday, he held his feast at Scone not simply in state but with regal lavishness, as was fitting; and early the following Monday Alexander, along with all the prelates and commanders [of the realm], as well as with that well-respected prince, his paternal uncle David earl of Huntingdon, very weak and ill as he was, met the body of his father [the king] at the bridge of Perth with a distinguished procession on its way to be buried. The body was being respectfully taken from Stirling to the monastery of 'Bayeux', that is Arbroath, which he himself built from scratch and royally endowed. There he was honourably buried—may God have mercy on his soul, Amen. (c.1, ll.1-30)

King Philip II and virtuous recreation

Bower takes the opportunity to insert a vaguely-dated reference to the puritanical practices of the French king whom he much admired, and to build on this a sermon on the characteristics of honest recreation as a guide to virtue. Displaying quite a range of reading to back up his argument, he offers a general guide to appropriate behaviour that will smooth social intercourse.

In the same year Philip the most Christian king of the French, now very old and ill, desiring to please the King of Kings as much as he could and knowing that wars were closing in on him from all sides, took sound counsel and drove from his court all parasites, imposters, jesters, magicians, gamesters, sycophants, swordsmen and other suchlike sons of iniquity given to sports and too much merriment, considering that every immoderate jest kindles lust. This is why Venus is called merry, regarding whom her servant says in jest:

> It is not her custom to visit the beds of mourners.

And lest anyone think that this most Christian of kings was wanting to condemn all relaxation, it should be noted that a perfect man also amuses himself the more freely for an hour so that afterwards he may devote himself more diligently to his work or his contemplation, as is clearly stated by John the Evangelist and the Blessed Anthony, because we rest to work, we do not work to rest. Indeed according to Cicero in the first book of *De Officiis*: 'Nature has not brought us into the world to act as if we were created for amusement or jest, but rather for earnestness and for some more serious pursuits.' Now he happens to say this because, although amusement does not in itself bring satisfaction in a person's life, it is nevertheless one appropriate virtue, because just as a man sometimes needs to rest from physical hardships, so the exercise of his mind requires relaxation from studies and serious matters and rest from the worry of his responsibilities. This is best achieved by honest recreation which consists of appropriate talk and discussion arranged between men. Therefore it is important to know that relaxation which is to become as virtuous as possible needs three things: seemly suitability, empathy, and a degree of moderation.

So the first thing to be borne in mind by those who are relaxing virtuously is seemly suitability, namely that the leisure activity is one that is becoming for the person involved and the people with him. Thus one sort of amusement suits a prelate or cleric or monk, another sort suits a soldier, man-at-arms or serf; and yet another sort suits an old person, and another a young person, because not everything suits everyone. Aesop wrote the fable of the ass and the young dog, in which the ass, observing that the idle dog was amazingly accepted and loved by their master, wondered what could be the reason why their master was so fond of the dog although it did no work at all. He noticed that every time their master returned home the dog ran to meet him and always welcomed him with his voice, his tail and in every way he could. So it seemed to the ass a good idea to copy the dog and so to win the favour of his master. So when his master returned home from the fields, the ass ran to meet him and violently putting his front legs round his master's shoulders started to bray loudly. His master was shocked and injured, and called for the help of his serfs, who soundly beat the ass and drove him away from his master. Likewise there are many who think that all sorts of amusement suit them, when in fact people find them disagreeable just when they think they are winning affection.

Legend has it that after Minerva had found some pipes she started to play them; but when she sat down beside a spring still playing them, she saw her swollen cheeks and her ugly face, and indignantly threw the pipes away never to play again.

The first thing therefore that a person who is relaxing should bear in mind is whether his activity is appropriate for his person and decent; and he is not to try to do anything that is unsuitable for himself or his status. And above all he is to beware of offensive conduct which might in any way lead to sin. This is why it is written [by Seneca] in *De quatuor virtutibus*:

> Believe that everything is tolerable except a shameful reputation. Also abstain from bad language, because lack of control in such matters encourages shamelessness. Have regard for useful expressions rather than witty ones that trip off the tongue. You will sometimes introduce jokes into serious matters, but they are to be restrained and not detrimental to dignity or truth. For laughter is reprehensible if it is excessive, or extravagant like a boy's or feeble like a woman's. Also laughter makes a man hated if it is proud or haughty or malevolent or furtive or elicited by another's misfortunes.

The second thing that virtuous recreation requires is empathy, so that the person who is relaxing always makes sure that his amusement is simple, innocent and harmless, lest anyone is hurt by it. Thus those who think about what they say only in terms of whether they will raise a laugh, and who do not care whom they hurt by their words, are scoffers and buffoons and are not persons of wit, according to Aristotle in Book VIII of his *Ethics*. Solomon says of this: 'It is a deceitful man who harms his friend and when he is caught says: "I was only joking."' But is it possible for someone who is amusing himself virtuously to mock someone else? Aristotle gives a sufficient answer to this question in Book IV of his *Ethics* when he says that some mockery is abusive and some is not. Now to give someone abuse is to dishonour him, and so the person who is amusing himself virtuously cannot say mocking things to anyone. For this was also prohibited in the laws of the gentiles. But there are some other mocking remarks about unimportant things that the virtuous man can suitably make either for entertainment or aiming at an improvement in behaviour, as St Thomas states.

The third thing that virtuous recreation requires is a degree of moderation, so that it is not repeated too often and does not go on too long. Now [St] Thomas makes the following point in his commentary on the fourth book of the *Sentences*, Distinction 16, last Question, first Article: 'It is a shameful and improper amusement that carries within it its own ugliness. The gentiles did such things in front of their gods in their theatres and temples.' And it is quite simply forbidden for all Christians, as is stated in [the *Decretum*], 'De Penitencia', Distinction 5, first Paragraph at the end.

A different kind of recreation is that of devotion and spiritual joy, the kind which Christians find in the celebration of the body of Christ, and also which David found in the presence of the ark of the Lord.

A third kind of recreation is that of [offering] human consolation, the centre of which is called quick-wittedness; and a person strong in that virtue is called by Aristotle a witty person. This virtue is so necessary an element in human social intercourse that according to him it is the special characteristic of a witty person to be tactful. This word [in Greek] is derived from 'epi', which means 'above' and 'dixios', which means 'suitable', and implies that such a man is extremely well suited to human social intercourse. And in Zechariah 8 we can read about such recreation: 'The streets of the city shall be full of boys and girls, playing.'

I have inserted this here so that kings and prelates may know which entertainers or imposters to allow into their courts and which to expel, just as this King Philip did, thus setting an example for other princes. (cc.14-15)

Scottish churchmen and legates 1217-18

The young King Alexander's policy of supporting the invasion of England in 1216 by Prince Louis of France against first King John and then the young boy Henry III led to a penalty suffered by the Scottish clergy. They were worsted in 1217-18 by the papal legate Guala, who had been sent from Rome to defend the rights of John and his son. As a punishment for their support of their king the Scottish clergy found themselves disciplined and having to accept financial penalties imposed by the legate, whose activities are here scornfully described in terms that are less than respectful for the papal office when its representatives were supporting the English side.

That year a great crisis arose in the Scottish church, for Alexander king of Scotland, as well as all the earls, barons, magnates and knights, bishops and prelates and indeed the whole kingdom were excommunicated and placed under an interdict. For when [the legate] Guala heard of the troubles, oppression and unbearable evils which were perpetrated in England by the king of Scotland, he [for he had come to see everything from an English viewpoint] laid an interdict on the king himself, along with his army and the whole kingdom of the Scots. Moreover at the request of Guala a rescript was sent by Pope Honorius to the priors of Durham, Guisborough and Tynemouth, who declared excommunicate the king of Scotland and as many others with him as had associated with King John of England when his kingdom lay under an interdict. Then the prelates of Scotland also [were excommunicated] inasmuch as they had associated with the king of Scotland and his army, because they had fallen under the ban pronounced by the Lateran Council, at which all those who fought against King John of England were excommunicated—for King John had by then been reconciled with the Roman church as its vassal: also because of the support which the king of Scotland offered Louis, eldest son of the king of the French; as well as because the king of Scotland had destroyed the castle of Tweedmouth opposite Berwick, in spite of its having been rebuilt contrary to an oath of the said John; and last but not least because he did not agree to return Carlisle to King Henry when requested and ordered to do so by Guala the legate. Then Guala the legate sent messengers to the king of Scotland with the promise of absolution, while negotiating and securing a perpetual peace, the surrender of Carlisle and reparations for losses sustained. And although Master Walter de Wisbech arrived in Scotland on the authority of the lord pope to lift the interdict, nevertheless Guala in his wily way craftily made him delay the absolution until a firm peace might be secured between the kings—or, according to some, until in the meantime he might slake the thirst of his moneybag with draughts of money and cups of gold. However the lord king and all the laypeople who were in his train were absolved at Tweedmouth by the archbishop of York and the bishop of Durham. And then he [Alexander] proceeded under safe conduct issued by the king and barons of England to Northampton, where he did due homage to the king of England for his honours and lands situated there. He also surrendered Carlisle, which he had captured, and confirmed the peace agreement. Then he returned home with the blessing of the king and the legate. But he was unable to get the prelates and clerics of his country included in the terms of this peace; for on the advice of certain men, guided by I know not what spirit, a general interdict was pronounced throughout the whole of Scotland around the feast of St Nicholas, and the church stopped celebrating the divine office, except for the white monks whose special privileges allowed them to celebrate it. All the other clerics, regular as well as secular, behaved as under suspension and excommunication. An exception was William Malveisin bishop of St Andrews, who had recently returned from France, where he had been staying during the hostilities. Not without difficulty he obtained the favour of absolution from the legate, having first sworn upon the host that he had not lent advice, help or favour to the adversaries of John king of England.

About the time of the Purification of the Blessed Mary the prior of Durham and an archdeacon of York came to Scotland, sent by the legate to England, and absolved the clergy of Scotland in the following way: they had both regular and secular clerics of the whole neighbourhood come together from the surrounding area to some burgh or city, and took a sworn pledge from them to the effect that they would abide by the legate's commands and would make a true and pure confession on the matters under investigation; then they absolved these men as they stood barefoot in front of the doors of the abbeys or churches at which they had gathered. And in this way they travelled through Scotland from Berwick to Aberdeen, moving from place to place as they pleased, and, on the advice of some who wished to please them, receiving everywhere costly procurations along with endless supplies of money and many gifts. They postponed, however, the absolution of the bishops of the kingdom, the household clergy of the king and clerics with rich benefices who either had taken part in the war or had in some way ministered to the combatants, while the abbots and certain other prelates whom they had absolved they kept suspended from office until they had more fully earned pardon from the legate himself. Therefore about the following Easter almost all the prelates of Scotland hurried to meet the legate to England at Northallerton; some of them he sent to Rome to be absolved; others he absolved there and then after being bribed with large sums of money; and several he either completely deprived of their benefices or suspended until the demands of his greed might be agreeably satisfied. Now it happened by God's righteous judgment that because they had neglected to develop the privileges granted them a short while before by the court of Rome and had refused to follow sound advice in such dire straits, they could be too intimidated by the false stories of the eminent legate Guala, since they had not experienced anything similar before. And it was just as Aesop in his fables tells us happened to a certain city—that a great mountain which towered above the city was in labour like the pangs of a pregnant woman, and was emitting great groans. When the whole city heard this it was afraid, and in the general commotion everyone was beside himself. At length the mountain brought forth a mouse. In this way rumour flies and the thing which everyone in the grip of fear was regarding as a great evil came to nothing. That is why the poet says:

> When the hill was in labour out came a silly little mouse.

And so our clergy, fearing more for their cassocks than for their consciences, accepted as their judge one who was not their judge. But once they had experienced his tyranny they learnt from that time on to struggle with a will to guard their privileges and the liberties of the kingdom. In the story in question it appears that our prelates and bishops were at that time too weak or too ignorant since, by not understanding their privileges and not appealing to the papal curia about such wrongs, they suffered loss beyond measure; and where they might have perhaps spent one thousand marks on expenses they ignominiously spent ten thousand pounds. (c.31, l.9 - c.32, l.50)

Cistercian monks and the eating of meat

A cautionary tale suggesting the devilish fate awaiting any Cistercians monks who transgressed the statute of their order against eating meat. The Scottish abbots of this order had to attend meetings at the headquarters of their order in France every fourth year.

In 1214 it happened that it was the turn of sir Radulf abbot of Kinloss to go to the general Cistercian chapter with certain fellow abbots of the Cistercian order according to the statutes of that order. And so with them he crossed the sea. One day one of the lay brothers, a cook, who usually looked after the abbots, taking pity on their exhausting hardships, and having more zeal than sense, bought for their meal such fish as he was able to find, as well as procuring a great deal of meat for the servants. Without the others knowing this same lay brother secretly collected not a little of the fat of this meat, which because of the heat of the fire was swimming on the top of the oil; he then secretly poured it on the abbots' dish in such a way that if any of them questioned him about the fat in their dish, he would reply that he had put butter into it. And so when the abbots ate what was put down in front of them in the usual way, their consciences did not prompt them to ask any questions. On the contrary they did not suspect that anything was amiss. Then after their meal they lay down for a rest, as was their custom. All the others, weary with toil, immediately fell into a deep sleep; but the said abbot of Kinloss, while meditating on I know not what psalm or customary prayer, observed entering through a window which was high above the ground but which remained intact a pitch-black Ethiopian with a horrible appearance. On seeing this figure he made the sign of the cross and silently waited to see what would happen. The sinister guest examined each one of the beds of the sleepers, and as if smelling something delightful and satisfying he lingered for a little by each one, chuckling; then with a big smile he moved on. But when he came to the bed of the above-mentioned lay brother, he kept applauding him above the rest for a long time and as it were giving him kiss after kiss, and embracing him in his arms, and bending down and thanking him as if for a blessing he had bestowed upon him. Then the Ethiopian went past the said abbot, glaring at him fiercely but not daring to come any closer. And he slipped away from the abbot's sight through the closed window like smoke. Then the abbot, [wondering] what this vision could mean and why the vile visitor had gloated beside the bed of the lay brother more than beside all the rest, started to wonder whether this lay brother might have done something which had either offended the Holy Spirit or pleased the Evil One. And so when they had finished their afternoon nap, the abbot summoned the lay brother and met with him secretly to describe to him in detail what he had seen while the others slept, saying: 'I am certain that unless you have given offence in some way more than the others, the Evil One, who is always saddened by our good works and delighted by our excesses, would never have applauded you above the rest.' The lay brother, immediately conscious of his sin and prostrating himself at the father's feet, revealed to him the chain of events in the order in which they had happened. And having made his confession and received his penance he never presumed to do the like again nor acted in any way with such presumption against the statutes of the order. And so you can see how the Deadly One will be delighted when brothers presume to eat meat contrary to the statutes of their order. (c.35)

The murder of Adam bishop of Caithness

Bishop Adam, who had attended the Fourth Lateran Council of the western church in 1215, was murdered at Halkirk south of Thurso in 1222 while trying with royal support to enforce in his diocese the same rights which the church enjoyed elsewhere in Scotland. The earl of

Caithness who, though living nearby, failed to save him, was at the same time earl of Orkney in the kingdom of Norway. King Alexander saw the need to avenge Adam's sufferings with an uprecedented extension of Scottish royal authority in this border region, to the extent that in late 1223 Earl John had to journey all the way to Forfar in Angus to make his peace with the Scottish king.

This year that illustrious pastor Adam bishop of Caithness, formerly abbot of Melrose, along with Serlo his monk earned the fellowship of the saints after much suffering. For after the savage threats of impious men, after the bruising of injuries and bloody wounds, after the clubs of James and the stones of Stephen, at length he suffered the fire of Laurence by being burnt in his own house called Halkirk. His body scorched by the fire and bruised by the stoning was found whole beneath a heap of stones after the fire, and was given an honourable burial in the church. All this happened because he demanded teinds and other ecclesiastical rights from those in his jurisdiction. They became inflamed with rage, and more than 300 men assembled in one place on the Sunday within the week after the [feast of the] Nativity of the Blessed Mary. And he was stoned by them, seized, beaten, bound, wounded, stripped and thrown into his own kitchen, which had been set on fire, and there he was burnt to death. Before this they killed the monk who was his companion, as well as one of his servants. But Earl John of Caithness, although he stayed nearby and had seen the people in arms converging from all sides, when asked by some of the bishop's servants to come and help, ignored what was going on, saying: 'If the bishop is afraid, let him come to me.' And it was because of this that many believed him to be party to this crime.

But our lord king Alexander, as he was on the point of setting out for England and had halted at Jedburgh to settle some business of his realm, was brought the news of this crime by trustworthy messengers. So he put that business aside and, raising an army as became a catholic man and a prince ordained by God, he set out for Caithness. Though the aforesaid earl proved on the testimony of good men that he was innocent and had offered no support or advice to those ruffians, yet because he had not immediately sought to take appropriate vengeance on them, had to give up a great part of his lands and [pay] a large sum of money to the king in order to win his favour. He likewise handed over for punishment many of those who had done this deed; and the king had their limbs cut off and subjected them to various tortures.

While the lord king celebrated Christmas at Forfar, the earl of Caithness came to meet him, and there after handing over money recovered from the king the land which he had made over the year before [as reparation] for the death and burning of the bishop already mentioned. However the earl did not escape punishment for that crime, for when seven years had elapsed that same earl was hemmed in by his foes in his own house, killed and burnt. Which only goes to show the truth of the following lines:

There is no juster law in human affairs
than that the murderer perishes by violent death himself.
(c.37, ll.7-41; c.38, ll.29-38)

More stories about King Philip II

After recording the death of King Philip Augustus of France in 1223, Bower assembles from different books a group of eleven exemplary anecdotes about him (cf above VIII cc.34, 55). He regarded Philip as an ideal king, a model for every Christian king. It was therefore in harmony with his intention that his book should offer guidance to the young James II that he collected these tales. Four of them follow here as samples from the whole series.

As the hour of his death drew near he said to his prelates and nobles who were present: 'How many keen and bold servants have I had at my court, who obeyed my every nod and ran as quickly as they could wherever I directed them! Now I do not have one who is eager to go this day and prepare a lodging for me. So farewell, my friends, and pray for me! For I am going on my last journey along a road I have never travelled, and to a far off land which I have never seen, and to the other world of souls whence no one returns. I am going to a fearful dwelling place and no one will accompany me there; I am going to the terrible judge and I do not know what will happen to me. See how I ask for someone to help me, and there is no one who can save me! I ask for someone to go with me, and there is no one who can come forward. Therefore have pity on me, at least have pity on me, you my friends, because the hand of God has touched me.' And after speaking these words and having first received the church sacraments he moved those present to tears and rendered his spirit to its Maker in the forty-third year of his reign.

While this king was staying in Paris a certain man-at-arms once approached him and brought a charge against his inn-keeper, who was a citizen of Paris. He said that when he had come to Paris to pay his lord's debts, and had given the bag of money to the inn-keeper for safe-keeping, the latter adamantly denied [he knew anything about it]. When the king heard this, since it could not be proved by the testimony of witnesses that the money had been handed over, and since both men appeared to be telling the truth, the king as if in jest took the gold ring which the citizen was wearing on his finger. Then he sent it secretly to the citizen's wife as a sign that she should send to her husband the bag which the man-at-arms had left with them. This she did, and he had the citizen immediately hanged, seeing that he had done many things of this kind before.

Once this king had poor clerks at his table, for it was always his custom at Paris to have a table in front of him full in this way. At length he saw at the far end of the table one of the clerks putting away a fine capon. So as a joke the king asked him privately which subject he was studying. 'Theology', said the clerk. The king replied: 'Surely you have read: "Do not worry about tomorrow?" So why did you put away the capon?' 'Because', said the other, 'I wanted to follow the gospel's injunction to put aside all care so that I should have not a scrap of worry about tomorrow.' The king was pleased with this reply and jokingly told it in public.

Also once the king, tired out by too many worries and pleas brought to his parliament by nobles and people of middle station, was wanting to find some rest; for this purpose he managed to get away from the crowd for a little while. And so taking some officials with him he got into an ornate little boat and began to row back and forward on the Seine, when who should come running up excitedly to the river bank but a friar, shouting that he wanted to have a word with the king. The king, somewhat annoyed that he was being disturbed in this way, replied to the friar: 'You ask to have only one word with me: speak boldly. But if you say more than one word, your cause is lost.' The friar was dismayed at this, but after a little thought stretched out his hand and said: 'Charity.' On hearing this the king put his hand in his purse and filled the friar's palm with gold pennies, and gave satisfaction for the one little word of the friar who asked for charity. (c.39, ll.32-48; c.40, ll.18-30; c.41, ll.13-22, 45-59)

King Alexander II attacks Galloway

Alan lord of Galloway died in 1233, leaving only daughters as his legitimate heirs. This provided the opportunity for armed intervention by King Alexander in 1235 to reduce this long semi-independent region to his rule. Bower reflects on this as the advantageous consequence of the king's mercy, though Alexander allowed the Scots (i.e. those from north of the Forth) their violent way with the Galwegians, and in fact Thomas of Galloway was not released from imprisonment soon (as suggested here), but kept in confinement for some sixty years! It was peace at a price.

In the year 1235 Alexander king of Scotland collected an army and entered Galloway to pacify the land and take revenge on the rebels. When the inhabitants learned of this, they emerged from the hills and woods to rush unexpectedly on the king while he was resting with his army in their tents. The place indeed gave them no little confidence, being swampy and beautiful with grass as far as the eye could see. [But] Thomas MacTaggart of Ross vented his fury on them forcefully from the rear, cutting many down and compelling many to flee. But Thomas the natural son of Alan lord of Galloway, who had previously while his father was alive been betrothed to a daughter of the under-king of Man, as the leader of this criminal affair returned to Ireland with Gilroth his accomplice. Also the next day all the Galwegians with ropes round their necks begged for grace and peace from the king. The king was kind enough to admit them to his peace because although (as we have said) he was always just in his actions, he nonetheless tempered his severity with mercy from time to time, because as Cassiodorus says in a letter: 'A liberal prince should ignore the bounds of equity in the interest of leniency, for it is to mercy alone that all the virtues are not unwilling to yield with honour.' Thomas the bastard son of mighty Alan (as above) came back once again from Ireland to Galloway with a certain son of an Irish king and many others, and as soon as he arrived there he broke up his ships to prevent the Irish thinking of flight. As soon as he saw that his men could not resist the king's majesty, on the advice of the bishop of Whithorn, Patrick earl of Dunbar and the abbot of Melrose he humbly sought the king's peace. The king detained him in Edinburgh Castle and then let him go. The rest of the Irish who wanted to flee the country were killed in one attack by the citizens of Glasgow; but the king ordered two of the more important by birth to be torn apart by horses at Edinburgh. The Scots themselves also who were then in the king's army ravaged the lands and churches of Galloway after his return with unheard-of cruelty, to the extent that they left a monk who was at the point of death at Glenluce naked except for his hair-shirt. And at Tongland they killed the prior and sacrist in the church. (c.49, ll.12-45)

King Louis IX and the Jews

Bower introduces two stories about St Louis IX king of France, both taken from the collection of 317 moral tales made by the Dominican friar Thomas de Cantimpré. This story dates from 1239-40, and illustrates both Bower's admiration for St Louis and his anti-Semitism. The Talmud was a compilation of the fifth century A.D. that reduced to writing various items of Jewish teaching that had previously been handed down orally. Louis ordered the burning of such books in 1242 and again in 1254. Bower has no sympathy for a Christian archbishop who had not done his duty in suppressing them.

This King Louis that same year at the urging of the excellent preacher Friar Henry of Cologne ordered under pain of death the collection at Paris of [copies of] that most abominable Jewish book, the Talmud, in which unheard of heresies and blasphemies against Christ and his mother are written in many places. Various copies of this book were brought to Paris for burning. In tears therefore the Jews approached the archbishop who was the king's chief councillor, and offered a countless sum of money for the preservation of the books. Corrupted by this, he went to the king and soon bent that young man's mind to his wishes. When the books had been returned, the Jews instituted the holding of a day of celebration every year; but in vain, for the Spirit of God ordained otherwise. For when a year had passed, on a certain day and at the place where the detestable books had been returned to the Jews—that is Vincennes near Paris—the said archbishop on coming to counsel the king was seized with a terrible pain in his bowels, and on the same day his life came to an end with a great deal of wailing. But the king fled from the place with his household, presumably fearing lest he be struck down by divine agency along with the archbishop. And not much later, at the instigation of the said Master Henry as before, the Jews' books were collected under pain of death and burnt in very large quantities.

It is common knowledge that all Eastern Jews reckon as heretics and excommunicates these Jews who against Mosaic law and the prophets acquire and copy this book called the Talmud. But then the extent to which an archbishop as defender of the law of Christ should be punished is suggested in these verses:

He offends against authority; he subverts justice; the peace and state of the church are afflicted;
for [all] this let this guilty person be struck down.
(c.54, l.41 - c.55, l.8)

The Bissets

This famous story of the murder of Patrick of Galloway, who in 1242 was probably still the heir to the earldom of Atholl through his mother, shows the country split in a way that the king found it hard to control. It is not now clear who in the Bisset family was immediately responsible, and Bower is wrong to identify the man who came to bear most of the blame as William Bisset, for this is clearly an error (corrected here) for Walter Bisset. The accusers among the baronial class were stirred up by members of the Comyn family, who seem to have had a marriage link with the family of the murdered man. They attempted to force the king's hand by their lawless attacks on the Bissets' lands, and won enough support to persuade an assize of the nobles (apparently against the king's wishes) to exile the leading Bissets for some years. It is no wonder that in 1243-4 the king felt the need to replace his justiciars for the north of the country by Alan Durward, in the hope that he would deal more firmly with the Comyns. In doing this, however, Alexander II paved the way for the split of the country between the Comynites and the Durwardites in the 1250s during the minority of his son Alexander III.

In 1242 while King Alexander was visiting Moray with the queen, news came of the arrival home of the king of England from overseas, and they hurried in the direction of that king. On meeting King Alexander that noble officer [Walter] Bisset put extreme pressure on him to spend two nights with him at his castle of Aboyne. The king stayed with him for only one night; but the same [Walter] with the lord king's permission remained in the company of the lady queen for four nights. At that time nearly all the nobles, magnates and knights of the kingdom gathered at the royal burgh of Haddington for a certain tournament, which in the end was turned into a killing-game. For that same night when the tournament was over some traitors said to belong to the Bisset following killed Patrick earl of Atholl, son of Thomas of Galloway, an outstanding young man, in his estimable lodging at the side and at the western end of the same king's highway to the north-west. It happened while he was asleep with two of his companions, in a villainous and heinous manner, as a result of long-standing hostility between their predecessors. And in order to hide this great crime they burnt down the fine manor, princely residence and house in which they lay dead, so that it might appear that they had not been killed by human hands, but had perished in an accidentally kindled fire. After Patrick's death David de Hastings acquired his earldom, which descended to him by right of his wife, who was a maternal aunt of the dead Earl Patrick.

Many blamed [Walter] Bisset for this crime. But how could he be involved in that crime on that night when he had to look after the queen at his castle of Aboyne? Since many people say many things, some say that he was not there in his own person, but his equipment and knights and all his armed strength were there with his knowledge. But the queen was ready to take an oath that the said Sir [Walter] was never inclined to attempt such a horrific act. 'Rare therefore is the trust which should be invoked' etc. The same [Walter] Bisset had all those who took part in and were responsible for this conflagration excommunicated in his own chapel and in all the churches of Scotland with the lighting and extinguishing of candles. In addition he asked the lord bishop of Aberdeen to publish the said sentence in [all] the churches located in his diocese, and that on the same day the bishop would confirm it. And this was done. At that time all the bishops of Scotland were attending a clerical council at Perth, when the king was present with all the earls and barons of his whole country. He had been called at the instance of the clergy, who were complaining of fighting men who were harassing them over teinds and the privileges of the church. The lord king in fact came to the council of bishops and laid it down that no knight or baron was to inflict any injury, annoyance or burden on them against the custom of Holy Church, with retributive penalties decreed in this connection. When the king had withdrawn with his barons [from the clergy's meeting place] to his own separate quarters at that council, all the earls complained about the burning of the earl of Atholl. And the king took advice, and wishing to do nothing about the growing difficulties without mature deliberation and discussion of the evidence, assigned them a day and place at Forfar when [Walter] Bisset would answer them.

In revenge for such a savage crime the relatives of the earl of Atholl took speedy action, namely [Alexander] the heir to Buchan and John the Red his nephew, who was a keen fighter and a most outstanding participant in all knightly encounters. They plundered and pillaged all the oxen, sheep and cattle and everything else that belonged to anyone of [Walter] Bisset's party or to those who were connected with him by any kind of kinship or legal title. [Walter] Bisset himself remained inside his castle there, burning all his barns and all his houses which lay outside the castle. When the king heard this, he was very annoyed; and sending instructions by his own knights he strictly ordered those of the Comyn party under every kind of pressing penalty not to rampage in his kingdom any more, but to restrain themselves peacefully until he pronounced judgment on the aforesaid crime. And when the common report rang in everyone's ears that the kingdom was being undermined by the Comyns' reign of tyranny, the king is said to have replied: 'It is a shame that the wretched people of this country think that every fly is an eagle, fearful at the sight of mice (that is brigands) as if at an invasion of lions.' By this means therefore the king at length made them desist from harassing innocent people. Then as the day approached for the Bissets to give their reply, the army of Mar and the knights living in the vicinity were called out to escort [Walter] Bisset from his castle at Aboyne to the king's meeting at Forfar. There they attacked him amid a mighty clamour over the burning of the earl of Atholl and his companions. This he firmly denied, offering to prove this in single combat with any knight at all, or to demonstrate his innocence by the oaths of as many long-serving knights as they wished. But the earls rejected whatever was offered, asking nevertheless if he was willing to entrust himself to the oaths of his fellow-countrymen and put himself to the judgment of the neighbourhood. But he, giving more weight to the malice of peasants and the inexorable hostility of his opponents, chose to submit to the reliable judgment of the lord king, entrusting his possessions, lands held in feu, and all his [goods] movable and immovable to the king's free disposal rather than face a jury with an unpredictable outcome. The lord king refused to dispossess him at once, but put off [consideration of] those vexatious proceedings. Therefore Bisset was given as a date for defending himself without appeal and bringing forward all pleas for delay the day after [the feast of] the blessed virgin Catherine at Edinburgh.

Meanwhile the king of Scotland visited the king of England at York on his return from overseas. [The same year] Andrew bishop of Moray died.

[Walter] Bisset and his knights appeared at Edinburgh on the appointed day. And the earls were there with a very large crowd as their adversaries, condemning him and all his supporters to death. There were negotiations on both sides for a settlement, and what a disturbance it was! At length William, John and Walter Bisset the uncle and their associates were outlawed from Scotland by the judgment and advice of all the nobles, with their lands, wives and children at the king's disposal. And touching holy objects they took an oath before the king and vowed to set out for the Holy Land without delay, and to remain there as pilgrims for all the days of their lives for the soul of the said earl. Thus they left, with permission to remain in the country for [only] forty days. Their descendants live in Ireland at the present day.

When the lord king saw that the justiciars whom he appointed to curb the attacks which Alexander de Buchan and John the Red and their accomplices were making on [Walter] Bisset's land had done nothing, and that they were not willing to restrain offenders nor to report them to the lord king, he removed them and appointed Sir Alan Durward as justiciar, who handled the affairs of the kingdom and of the king with diligence and moderation. (c.59 - c.61, l.13; c.61, ll.61-67)

Epitaph on Alexander II

Bower develops earlier thinking about the merits of Alexander II to illustrate his own ideals of kingship. Kerrera is the island that encloses Oban Bay in Argyll. It is likely that this account is confused in giving 8 July 1249 as the king's date of burial, for the Melrose Chronicle *reports this as the date of the king's death. As in 1214 it is likely that the funeral was held after the new king's inauguration (in this case on 13 July 1249). Bower is anachronistic in stating that Alexander II had in 1214 been 'anointed as king'. In fact it was only in 1329 that the pope authorised anointing as part of the ceremonial inauguration of Scottish kings. The quotation is from the biblical book Ecclesiasticus.*

In the same year that renowned king of the Scots, Alexander II, who always hated wrong-doing and loved equity and justice, while setting out to pacify the Argyll region was overcome by a serious malady and taken to the island called Kerrera, where after receiving the sacraments of eternal life his blessed spirit was plucked from the light of this world and (as it is right to believe) rests in heaven with all the saints. His body however was conveyed to the church of Melrose, as he had instructed during his lifetime, and there when due funeral ceremonies had been solemnly celebrated in royal fashion it was commended to the bosom of the earth on Thursday 8 July about 3 p.m. in the fifty-first year of his life and the thirty-fifth year of his reign (for he was sixteen and a half years old when anointed as king). Like the morning star he grew into the light and sunshine until the fulness of day. As a follower of this way of life he proved to be a source of strength to his fellow-soldiers, appreciative to religious, humble before priests, modest to his people, compassionate to the unfortunate, generous to those in need, lenient to the just, but strict towards the arrogant, alarming to malefactors and merciful towards the defeated. There was in him a wonderful zeal for the increase of religion, seen especially in his concern with building churches for the Friars Preacher. There was with him no regard for persons, but he judged the poor justly and brought forward arguments in equity on behalf of the meek of the land. This prince was a most upright character and the boldest of knights, who knew how to weep with those who were weeping and to rejoice with those rejoicing; he was nevertheless a comforter of those who were mourning, a supporter of orphans, protector of young men in wardship, most conscientious in hearing complaints personally, especially those of widows and the poor, and very fair in disposing of them, so that one can apply to him this quotation: 'Because he stood under the judgment and in fear of God, the Lord has made his people respect him, and he pleases the God of Israel in his goodness and his enthusiasm of spirit. Therefore He made a peace covenant with him to be the prince of his people, so that the dignity of king might be his for ever.' (c.63, ll.6-39)

Book X

Inauguration of King Alexander III

Bower again introduces a quotation from Ecclesiasticus, and refers also to the Canon Law and to lines by the Classical writers Lucan and Ovid. His account of the inauguration of the boy-king Alexander III introduces anachronistic references to a 'coronation', while 'consecration' would be more in harmony with thirteenth-century ideas. Every detail of this story has been much debated by historians, including the ambiguous mention of a 'royal seat of stone'. The part played by the 'wild highlander' in reciting in Gaelic the royal genealogy back to Gaythelos and Scota fits in with the early chapters of Bower's story, though here he ends with an original imaginative link between the Scots of his day and the culture of ancient Greece. Of more immediate import is the account of the different views on procedure adopted by the Comyn earl of Menteith and Alan Durward. As they fenced over these details, opposing positions were being established which were to split the magnates during the following years of the young king's minority.

As has been written: 'His father has died, and yet in a sense is not dead, for he has left a copy of himself behind. While still alive he saw and rejoiced in his son, and at his death he was not saddened or confused in the presence of his enemies. For he has left behind him a defender of his house against his enemies who will repay the kindness of his friends.' After the death of his devoted father, the boy Alexander, being eight years of age, came with a large number of bishops, prelates, earls, barons and knights to Scone on the following Tuesday, 13 July. There were present among the others David de Bernham bishop of St Andrews and Geoffrey bishop of Dunkeld, who was then still alive, a man beloved by clergy and people, careful in his administration of matters temporal and spiritual.

Immediately they had assembled, dissension broke out among the magnates. For some of them wished to make the king a knight rather than king on that day, with the explanation that it was an unlucky day. They said this not really because it was a day of ill omen, but because Sir Alan Durward, justiciar of the kingdom, who was regarded as the flower of the knightly order, wished to invest the king with the knight's sword on that day. So, since a great dispute was arising among the magnates on all sides, and there was beginning to be a quarrelsome separation into two parties, the knight Walter Comyn, a man far-seeing in his counsel and steadfast in spirit, wisely set about urging the two sides towards an agreement.

He said that he ought to have a voice in their deliberations because he himself as earl of Menteith had learned a great deal from experience. He roundly asserted that he had seen a king consecrated even though he was as yet not a knight, and he had often heard, and knew for a fact, that kings had been consecrated who were never invested ceremonially with the order of knighthood. He added this also, that inasmuch as a crowned king is adorned with golden knightly insignia (which crown and sceptre are said to signify)—comparing the position to that stated in the *Decrees* that the son of a king ought to be called a king even though he may not possess a kingdom—so all the more a king should be considered a knight. He added an illustration, saying that, just as a boat is tossed about among the waves without an oarsman, so a kingdom without a king or ruler is left in the lurch. He had beyond all measure loved as king the father who was now dead; he loved the son also, not just because of the father, but also out of a natural affection towards his proper lord. Therefore he proposed to elevate the boy to the throne as quickly as possible, considering the danger alluded to in the words of the poet:

> Delay is harmful, and always has been, for those who are prepared;

and:

> He who is not ready today will be less ready tomorrow.

He wisely applied himself to bringing the two parties together lest, if the quarrel were not quickly laid to rest, anger would grow into hatred, and would convert a mote into a beam, put a murderous spirit into men's minds and turn the magnates into parricides.

He persuaded each side that the king should be invested as a knight by the bishop of St Andrews, who filled the office of king, in the same way as William Rufus had been invested with the knightly insignia by Lanfranc archbishop of Canterbury who had also crowned him—for this see above Book VII, Chapter 31…This was done. For when David bishop of St Andrews girded the king with the belt of knighthood in the presence of the magnates of the land, and set out the rights and promises which pertain to a king, first in Latin and then in French, the king graciously conceded and accepted all of this, and readily underwent and permitted his blessing and ordination at the hands of the same bishop.

In accordance with the custom which had grown up in the kingdom from antiquity right up to that time, after the solemn ceremony of the king's coronation, the bishops with the earls brought the king to the cross which stands in the cemetery on the east side of the church. With due reverence they installed him there on the royal seat which had been bedecked with silk cloths embroidered with gold. So when the king was solemnly seated on this royal seat of stone, with his crown on his head and his sceptre in his hand, and clothed in royal purple, and at his feet the earls and other nobles were setting down their stools to listen to a sermon, there suddenly appeared a venerable, grey-haired figure, an elderly Scot. Though a wild highlander he was honourably attired after his own fashion, clad in a scarlet robe. Bending his knee in a scrupulously correct manner and inclining his head, he greeted the king in his mother tongue, saying courteously: 'God bless the king of Albany, Alexander mac Alexander, mac William, mac Henry, mac David...'

Then this same Scot read right through the aforesaid genealogy, linking up each person with the next, until he came to the first Scot, that is Hiber the Scot. This Iber was the son of Gaythelos, the son of Neolus formerly king of the Athenians by Scota daughter of the king of Egypt, the Pharaoh Chencres.

So the Scots gain additional lustre from the fact that they are sprung from the stock of the kings of Athens, the chief city and capital of the Greeks. It was from there, as our sources tell us, that Greece with its provinces became an imperial power, a nursery of great soldiers and mother of philosophy, and invented and fostered all the beneficial branches of learning. Its people are a most warlike race, well endowed with the gift of wisdom and knowledge, most eloquent in speech, obedient to the laws, pious, peaceable towards other nations, tranquil in its dealings with its own citizens, but implacable and belligerent in the face of injuries inflicted by its enemies. Its speech is clearer and more sonorous than that of any other nation. (c.1 - c.2, ll.1-16, 37-54)

The translation of the mortal remains of St Margaret

Bower presumably derived this story of how a great public event in Dunfermline Abbey was mysteriously interrupted in startling fashion from his neighbourly contacts with that abbey. The coffin of the newly-proclaimed saint was being moved (technically 'translated') to a position of greater honour to mark the papal recognition of her as a saint of the universal church. This had been negotiated at Rome by several of the Scottish bishops between 1245 and 1249. At the Reformation some of these relics of Margaret and her husband were moved again to the Spanish royal palace at Escorial near Madrid.

Next year, that is 1250, the king and the queen his mother along with the bishops and abbots and other magnates of the realm assembled at Dunfermline. There they raised the bones and earthly remains of the glorious Queen Margaret his great-great-great-grandmother from the stone sepulchre in which they had rested for many years, and with the utmost reverence raised them in a casket of firwood entwined with gold and precious stones. When the grave had been opened up by digging, such an intense and sweet-smelling fragrance poured from it that men thought that the entire sanctuary had been sprinkled with the fragrance of spices and the scents of flowers in full bloom. And a miracle, sent by God, was forthcoming there and then. When that famous treasure had been placed in the outer church preparatory to re-burial in the choir beyond the high altar, a move intended as a mark of honour, it was raised without difficulty by the holy hands of the bishops and abbots, and was being carried in procession, with instruments playing and the choir singing harmoniously. They got as far as the chancel door just opposite the body of Margaret's husband, King Malcolm, which lay under an arched roof on the north side of the nave, when all at once the arms of the bearers became paralyzed, and because of the great weight they were no longer able to move the shrine which held the remains. Whether they liked it or not they were forced to halt and quickly lay their load on the ground. After some delay more helpers were added, perhaps stronger than the first, to help carry the shrine, but failed all the more feebly the more they tried to lift it. At last, as they were all marvelling one to another, and saying that they were not worthy to touch such a precious relic, they heard a voice coming from one of the bystanders, but as is believed divinely inspired, which loudly proclaimed that it was perhaps not God's will that the bones of the holy queen be translated before her husband's tomb had been opened, and his body raised and honoured in the same way. These words met with general approval, and following the advice which they conveyed, King Alexander, [Malcolm's great-] great-great-grandson, with companions chosen for this purpose, lifted up the casket containing the bones of the king along with that, now raised, which held the remains of the queen, without expending any effort or encountering any obstacle. They solemnly placed both reliquaries in tombs which had been decked out elegantly for that purpose, as the congregation sang and a choir of prelates followed in solemn procession, on 19 June. There God in his mercy has often worked all manner of miracles through [the merits of] that holy queen. (c.3, ll.1-41)

Good and bad counsellors

After copying Fordun's account of the seizure of power in 1252 by the Comyn faction during the minority of King Alexander III, which ends with a despairing quotation from the biblical book Ecclesiastes, Bower launches into a discussion of his own about the qualities required in royal counsellors, quoting besides the Bible the classical writers Cicero and Plutarch, and the eleventh-century Arabic philosopher Avicenna. He goes on to fill two and a half more chapters with lengthy quotations (not copied here) from the fourteenth-century St Bridget of Sweden on the kinds of advice which counsellors should give to their king. As a royal counsellor of lengthy experience himself he knew what he was writing about.

Meanwhile all the original counsellors of the king were removed and new ones appointed, namely Walter Comyn earl of Menteith, Alexander earl of Buchan, William earl of Mar, Robert de Ros a blood relative of the king, and certain others. But there were as many kings as there were counsellors. For in those days you could see examples of oppression of the poor, disinheriting of nobles, exactions laid upon the inhabitants, pillage of the common people, sacrilegious thefts of teinds and the violations of churches, so that it could rightly be said: 'Woe to the land whose king is a boy.'

In exercising government nothing is more advantageous for a king than to have good counsellors. For if his counsellors should be false, then his own chief men are a king's enemies, for they give him advice that is not expedient for one in his position. These [evil counsellors] are particularly dangerous in any community because, just as the honour, well-being and success of a king and of the state of which the king is a head depend most of all on good counsellors, so confusion and the overthrow of the state arise especially from the presence of evil counsellors. For Cicero in his *De Senectute* says that a counsellor in the state is like a helmsman in a ship. In a ship some bale out the water, others pull on the ropes, while yet others climb the mast. But the helmsman sits quietly in the stern, and yet does far more than the others. And Avicenna says that the counsellor's function is to lay down the blueprint according to which everyone else has to work and be guided. He distinguishes four functions of the counsellor: giving counsel, helping, planning and making headway [with the project]. Consequently counsellors of the king and of the state ought to have these four qualities:

in their life holiness;
in their words truth;
in their zeal a sense of fairness;
in trying out what is new wisdom.

In the Roman state men such as these were called senators, and according to Plutarch the role they play in the community is that of the heart in the body. Hence Romulus, when he had founded the city which he called Rome after himself, chose thirty men from among the elders, so that in everything he did he might act on their advice. These, because of their age [*senectutem*] were called by everybody 'senators', and because of their careful forethought 'fathers'. For they were chosen after they had served their term in various positions and offices, as being more suited to matters which demanded wisdom in proportion as they were less able in terms of physical effort. These men were held in such high esteem among the Greeks that their rulers never went in procession to any solemn occasion without them.

Thus, just as those senators or counsellors are most beneficial to the state when they are good and virtuous, so they are harmful to a king, and most damaging to a prelate or judge, when they are evil. Thus when they are zealous only for their own personal and private gain, and not for the common good, when they have been corrupted by avarice and receiving gifts, when they have been frightened by threats and they forbear to speak the truth, when their judgment is ruled by love or hate, then by their counsel they destroy the prince whom they ought to guide and direct, and become the worst of enemies to the king and to the state as a whole. One could say to any one of these what Paul said to Elymas the sorcerer in Acts 13: 'You son of the Devil, swindler and rascal, enemy of all goodness, will you not stop falsifying the straight ways of the Lord?'

One such counsellor was that Haman, who took advantage of the guilelessness of that most noble prince Ahasuerus with his deceitful counsels and led the innocent mind of that noble king into an act of unspeakable cruelty. Hence our enemy, that worst foe of all, is said to be a Haman, for 'Haman' means 'unjust' and 'one who restricts men', or 'keeps them in confinement', or 'the cause of their confinement'. This meaning fits very well those evil counsellors who are unjust. Some of them deserve to be called not just 'Haman', but in our mother tongue 'nae man'. (c.5)

The Comyns seize Alexander III

The Comynite group of nobles who had since 1252 controlled the council that governed the country during the king's minority were in September 1255 removed from office by the Durwardite group. They regained power in October 1257 by seizing the person of the king (then aged 16). Bower offers puzzled reflections on the motives of those concerned, probably in the light of the behaviour of the counsellors whom he had known during the minority of James II in his own day. In fact by 1258 the king was beginning to reunite the country by asserting his own authority over both factions. The earl of Menteith died in October or November 1258, but there is no agreement in the sources over the cause of his death. Poisoning by his wife was probably a false rumour.

In [1256] Walter Comyn earl of Menteith and his accomplices were frequently cited before King Alexander and his counsellors to answer many serious complaints, but did not appear. But because they did not dare await trial according to the laws of the kingdom, they adopted a plan which, though agreed among themselves, was ill-conceived and rash. Laying sacrilegious hands on the anointed of the Lord, they seized the king at night as he lay asleep in bed at Kinross, and shamefully took him with them before dawn to Stirling on the morning after the feast of St Simon and St Jude in 1257. They also seized by force the king's great seal, which Master Robert [de] Stuteville dean of Dunkeld had in his custody while acting for the chancellor Bishop Richard.

Among the prime movers in that kidnapping [was] Walter Comyn earl of Menteith. In his case this is much to be wondered at, for he was so loyal to the king at the time of his coronation and ensured that his first counsellors should be removed because they were guiding the king and the kingdom badly. But no doubt the possessions and revenues of the king which came into the hands of his counsellors and of those who did not think that they would have to render an account to him for them caused them to stray from the path of truth and equity. This is why Augustine says that: 'Avarice, which in Greek is *philarguria*, is to be understood as subsisting not only in the sphere of money [*argentum*] from which it has clearly got its name, but in all things which are desired to excess and seized. In every case', he says, 'where someone wants altogether more than he needs, desire of this kind amounts to avarice. Desire is an excessive wish for something. Hence wanting something to excess is the cause of all evils.' And wherever the accumulation of wealth kindles a greater flame, there desire becomes more insistent...

Well then, the prime movers in this were Walter Comyn earl of Menteith, Alexander Comyn earl of Buchan, William earl of Mar (a man well versed in evildoing), John Comyn (one who was prone to pillage and unruly behaviour), Hugh de Abernethy, David de Lochore, Hugh de Berkeley, and several others the henchmen of evil men. This group, who did nothing in accordance with the law but everything in accordance with their own wishes, ruled the people regardless of right or wrong. As a result this latest deviation was worse than the first. From that time on there arose many acts of persecution and many tribulations among the magnates of Scotland. For these more recent counsellors of the king now tried to retaliate against the former counsellors for the losses and injuries they had suffered previously. So there ensued a worse grinding down of the poor and spoliation of churches than had been seen in Scotland in ancient times.

In that same year Walter Comyn earl of Menteith, now an old man, died suddenly, poisoned by his wife, or so it is said. He had been the ringleader of those who had kidnapped the king. As I said earlier these Comyns were in the lead among those who rose against the king: as a consequence their name is now, so to speak, obliterated in the land, despite the fact that at that time they were multiplied beyond number in the ranks of the magnates of the kingdom. Thus at that time there were reckoned to be thirty-two knights of this name who at one and the same time wore the belt of knighthood in the kingdom. Therefore knights and magnates ought to pay greater attention to the words of the apostle: 'Honour the king.' (c.10, ll.10-55; c.11, ll.29-39)

The battle of Largs

All the Western Isles of Scotland (including Bute and Arran) had acknowledged Norwegian authority following Viking settlements there from the eighth century onwards, as confirmed by the visit of King Magnus III in 1098. King Haakon IV in 1263 was the next Norwegian king to mount a major expedition to the Northern and Western Isles of Scotland in 1263 with the aim of re-establishing his authority there. The turning point was a skirmish at Largs on the Firth of Clyde, probably on 2 October, for on his way home afterwards he died in Orkney on 16 December. Bower includes only a few details of the so-called 'severe battle' at Largs, but embellishes his account with the story of a vision and a miraculous healing indicating the beneficent intervention on the Scottish side of St Margaret, along with her husband King Malcolm III and her three sons Kings Edgar, Alexander I and David I. (The castles of Arran and Bute were probably at Brodick and Rothesay. John Wemyss belonged to East Fife.) Bower is interestingly sceptical about possible treasonable correspondence between some Scottish magnates and King Haakon.

In 1263 around the time of the feast of St Peter in Chains King Haakon of Norway came to the new castle of Ayr with his pirate ships, 160 in number, containing twenty thousand fighting men. For he asserted that all the islands of Scotland which lie between Ireland and Scotland were his by right of inheritance. So with a strong force he besieged and took the castles of Arran and Bute, and cruelly plundered all the churches that lay close to the coast without fear of divine wrath. As a result he enjoyed success which was, however, of short duration, for on the feast of the Nativity of the Blessed Virgin he and his fleet put in to the coast of Cunninghame at a place called Largs.

At that time it chanced that a courageous knight, John Wemyss by name, who was completely worn out by the severity of fevers which recurred daily, had gladly abandoned his weary limbs to sleep, as the illness had in some small degree abated, when he was privileged to see the following vision. He appeared to be standing at the [north] doorway of the church at Dunfermline. A lady of radiant beauty and resplendent in full royal attire came quickly out of the aforesaid church. She was leading on her right arm a distinguished-looking knight, clad in gleaming armour, girded with the sword of a knight, and wearing a helmet with a crown on it. Three noble knights, brisk and cheerful in appearance, followed them at a stately pace and in due order, all gleaming in similar armour. The knight was not a little disturbed by the suddenness of this unexpected encounter, but took comfort from the beauty and benevolence of the lady who headed the group, and so addressed the sainted queen as follows: 'Glorious lady, please tell me who you are and where you and your noble companions are going.' She replied: 'I am Margaret, formerly queen of Scots. The knight who has my arm is the lord king Malcolm my husband, and these knights who are following us are our sons, the most renowned kings of this realm while they lived. In company with them I am hurrying to defend our country at Largs, and to win a victory over the usurper who is unjustly trying to make my kingdom subject to his rule. For you must know that I received this kingdom from God, granted in trust to me and to our heirs for ever.' When the queen finished speaking she quickly disappeared and the knight awoke.

He was afflicted with chronic illness more severely than one could believe possible. If you had chanced to see him then you would have said that he was like a man becoming a wraith, a man without strength wishing to walk and unable to do so. Yet this man, feeble as he was, struggled against his own constitution and against the advice of his men that if he set out on a journey he would die without getting anywhere, immediately as it seemed to them. But whatever the wishes of his servants, the knight did not abandon his design; but travelling in a carriage or on a litter he finished the journey he had undertaken and reached Dunfermline. On arrival there he summoned the prior of the monastery and told him about his dream. It was not the sort of dream by which we are often deluded, but one revealed by heaven, as the outcome showed. For as yet his illness was so severe that his servants' hands could hardly hold him up so that he could, with tearful devotion, kiss the whole area round the shrine in which the relics of the queen were kept. As he was hurrying over to the relics to kiss them and pray with tearful jerks of his head, he suddenly felt well and in good spirits; and the man who had come there a permanent invalid went cured, giving praises to God. At this point, suddenly a servant came in, the bringer of the good news of the victory just won at Largs.

So in the course of that severe battle fought at Largs in the year and on the day aforementioned, in which Alexander Steward of Dundonald great-grandson of Walter the first Steward was in command and conquered the Norwegians, there fell on our side the knight Peter Curry. Alexander was the grandfather of the noble Walter Steward who married the daughter of Robert de Bruce. The battle of Largs was fought in the sixteenth year [of the reign] of this Alexander, the third king of that name. Meanwhile by the will of God and through the merits of St Margaret the queen and protectress of the realm of Scotland, on the very day of the battle a most severe gale arose on the sea. It smashed the ships together, tore up anchors and hurled sails into the waves, and the separate bits of rigging were seen to be torn away completely from every joint in turn by the huge waves and the fury of the winds and smashed to bits. The ships being thus driven out of position relative to each other, hurtling about and being crushed together, and also smashed against the land and the rocks, and dashed into thousands of pieces, the sea rendered shapeless the bodies of the people who had been drowned close to the shore when thrown out [of the boats]. Those who reached the land unharmed engaged our men and soon were overwhelmed, cut down, put to flight and drowned. Among all the thousands of slain the Norwegian king lamented [especially] the death of one noble Norwegian, the nephew of King Haakon, a man of great strength and courage. The king himself only just escaped, and returned homewards all the way back to Orkney, grieving and lamenting and in considerable disarray. As he was spending the winter there awaiting the arrival of a stronger force to enable him to conquer the Scots, he died in Orkney. A certain Norwegian says this of him:

King Haakon the Great, bold yet gentle as a lamb,
rejoices at the sight of the just, but threatens the unjust with his sword.

His son Magnus succeeded him, a wise man and distinguished by the gift of learning. It is said of him:

I rule the realm of Norway. Magnus is my name.

[This motto was engraved on the royal sword-belt.]

They say that his father, the Lord Haakon, before his death sent a letter sealed with the seals of certain noblemen of Scotland to King Alexander. This told how those nobles had written to the aforesaid King Haakon [suggesting] that he should come to Scotland, and promising him that they would help him against their own king. This is not likely. But others give an account that is more convincing, namely that on Haakon's death the Norwegians wrote a letter, accredited by their king's seal, to say that the king of Scotland should beware of certain nobles of his kingdom. [It is likely that] they wrote this with the intention that the king take vengeance on his magnates as if they had committed crimes, so that they themselves might more easily subdue the kingdom of Scotland at a later date if they so wished. (c.15 - c.16, ll.1-47)

End of Norse rule in the Western Isles

King Haakon's death in Orkney was followed by a long-term agreement by the Treaty of Perth in 1266, whereby these islands (but not Orkney and Shetland) were effectively restored to the Scottish kingdom. (For Eochaid Rothay see above I, c.29, ll.1-13.)

In 1265 Magnus [IV] son of Haakon king of the Norwegians sent his chancellor and sir Gilbert bishop of Hamar to Alexander king of Scots at Perth. As regards Bute and Arran he offered Alexander the islands to be held in peaceful possession in perpetuity, but with the proviso that he [Magnus] should possess peaceably all the other islands to which his father Haakon had laid claim. The king of Scots completely scorned this proposal. After the bishop had received the king's reply relating to his mission, he returned to Norway and informed his king that his labours had been in vain, but advised him to come to an agreement with the Scots. So next year the king of Norway sent his aforesaid chancellor and other magnates back to Scotland. On the strength of their letters of authorization they granted the king of Scots all the islands which lie between Scotland and Ireland to which his father Haakon had laid claim. They also restored to the selfsame king of Scots every right and claim which King Magnus or any of his predecessors ever had in the aforesaid islands, provided that the same king of Scotland would pay 4,000 marks of silver to the said king of Norway within two years, and subsequently 100 marks each year to himself and his heirs. When this offer had been given mature consideration, it was eventually agreed, although the treaty had displeased several on the Scots side. The reason for this was that the Scots had inhabited the aforesaid islands for a very long time long before they had come to Britain when they were brought there by Eochaid Rothay, one of their leaders; and, undisturbed by any incursion, they had held them in uninterrupted possession right up to that ill-fated time of strife between the sons of Malcolm Canmore king of Scotland and Donald Ban, the uncle of the said sons. When the kingdom had been completely split by this, Magnus Olafsson king of the Norwegians had invaded the islands and made them subject to his rule by force. (c.19, ll.1-30)

Robin Hood and Little John

Bower copies here (probably from a source kept at St Andrews) the earliest known version of the Robin Hood legends, attaching them to the disturbed period of the baronial rebellion in England and the death of Simon de Montfort at the battle of Evesham in 1265, which had led to the outlawing of many of his followers. He wants to emphasize Robin's piety and respect for the services of the church.

At this time there arose from among the disinherited and outlaws and raised his head that most famous armed robber Robert Hood, along with Little John and their accomplices. The foolish common folk eagerly celebrate the deeds of these men with gawping enthusiasm in comedies and tragedies, and take pleasure in hearing jesters and bards singing [of them] more than in other romances. Yet some of his exploits thus recited are commendable, as is clear from what follows.

Once when he was in Barnsdale, avoiding the king's anger and the prince's rage, and was hearing mass most devoutly as was his habit—he was unwilling to interrupt the service no matter the pressure he was under—when he was thus hearing mass one day, he was tracked down to that secluded woodland spot where he was hearing it by a certain sheriff and king's officers who had often proved themselves his enemies in the past. Some of his men who spotted this came to him and advised him to make every effort to escape. But because of his reverence for the sacrament which at that moment he was most devoutly worshipping, he absolutely refused. While the rest of his men were trembling in fear of death, Robert having great trust in Him whom he was worshipping, with those very few who happened to be there with him fearlessly took on his enemies and easily beat them. Being much enriched with spoil and ransom money taken from them, from then onwards he always chose to hold the ministers of the church and masses in even greater veneration. For he paid heed to the common saying:

God listens to the man who hears mass often.
(c.20, ll.38-63)

The right regard of prelates for royal authority

Bower develops here his admiring comment on the way that Gamelin bishop of St Andrews (1255-71) had stood up with exceptional vigour against King Alexander III by annexing and adapting much of a scholastic discussion by the English theologian Robert Holkot (died 1349) in his commentary on the biblical Wisdom of Solomon regarding the qualities of a good prelate. This reflects the breadth of Bower's university training as a student at St Andrews from its foundation in 1410 onwards.

From that time the lord king held Bishop Gamelin in great reverence and [devotion and] love, knowing him to be a just and holy man; moreover afterwards he did many good things on his advice, and willingly listened to him, not like Herod when he heard John, but like a catholic king. Because of this what is written in Wisdom, Chapter 10 could apply to both of them: 'He defied formidable kings.'

Every good prelate ought to be ready to defy princes and tyrants for the right of the church and for the truth of sound doctrine, like the apostles and prophets, the martyrs and confessors, so that it can be said of him: 'He defied formidable kings.' In these words four qualities in a good prelate are commended, two subjective [i.e. exercised by him] and two objective [i.e. earned by him]. The subjective ones are: an upright conscience and strong powers of resistance; the objective ones are: a high degree of respect and a great amount of benevolence. By these means 'he defied formidable kings'.

Firstly, indeed, a prelate must have an upright conscience; thus the apostle urges: 'Stand firm. Fasten on the belt of truth; put on integrity as your coat of mail; let the shoes on your feet prepare the way for the gospel of peace.' It is a characteristic of the palm-tree that it is not impeded by any weight, but rather it always keeps its upright stature, no matter how great a weight may be placed on it when it is growing. And because it is found to be of such unconquerable virtue, it was used for the adornment of the victorious. Allegorically the [good] prelate, no matter how great a burden may be placed upon him, either by tyrannical persecution, or by unjust slander, must nevertheless always keep his upright stature in his conscience, so that that line from the Song of Songs [Chapter] 7 may be deservedly quoted to him: 'You are stately as a palm-tree.' For Aristotle says in the first book of his *Ethics* that a virtuous man must be a tetragon or cube, in which every part is equal.

Secondly a good prelate must display strong powers of resistance against evil men; and I say 'against', because he may not flee, lie or fawn—fleeing by abandoning his charge; lying by dissimulation; fawning by adulation. But he must make a stand by moving against, acting against, and speaking against [evil men]. So it can be said of good prelates what is said in the Psalms: 'Thou hast humbled us before our neighbours.'

Thirdly, on the objective side a high degree of respect is noted where Elijah set himself against Ahab, [and John against Herod,] and all the prophets set themselves against kings, as is clear from the examples scattered throughout [the books of Kings and] the first and second books of the Maccabees.

And as is found in the history of the Persians and Medes, the eastern peoples use elephants in their wars. For the elephant is an animal so strong that a wooden castle is built on its back, in which approximately thirty or forty men can fight. So when Alexander was about to fight against King Porus, he used a deceitful trick against those elephants. On one occasion he arranged that bronze statues full of hot burning coals be placed in the road where these elephants were expected to cross. Thinking that the statues were men, they tried to overturn them with their trunks; and at once their trunks were burnt by hot bronze and they fled, causing very great slaughter in the army of the Indians. On another occasion he caused a herd of pigs to be driven in front of his army, and ordered one of the piglets to be held and beaten. When the herd heard its squealing, they all started to grunt. Now the elephant is naturally afraid of the grunting of swine; so when those elephants heard this great din of grunting pigs, they took to flight and caused very great slaughter amongst their own army. Allegorically these elephants, which are very big, very strong and chaste animals, represent the major prelates of the church on account of the greatness of their dignity and the similarity of their chastity, as the elephant is a very chaste animal. Their duty is to lead the army of the church, and to frighten evil enemies by the trumpeting of their preaching. On them are placed wooden towers, because churches are put under their authority and the care of souls is entrusted to them. Such was Peter, to whom the Lord said: 'You are Peter, the Rock; and on this rock I will build my church.' Therefore the devil is afraid of them and prepares a twofold trick: for at first he places in front of them bronze statues filled with fire. These statues are wicked nobles, magnates and men of power who seem to be as generous as were their fathers, who endowed churches; but they are nothing but statues and masks, because they have the outward appearance of a man, but they do not have the life, nor the wisdom, nor the reason, nor the gentleness which nature has granted to man. They are just bronze statues, because of the clashing sound of pomp and worldly pride, filled inside with the fire of anger, and for that reason they belong to the household and following of the devil, about whom Job says: 'His breath sets burning coals ablaze.' These men stand against the elephants—that is the bishops—and burn their trunks so that they do not dare to seize or correct them. And our modern bishops are afraid not only of them, but even more of the noise of pigs. Pigs are slippery creatures; and allegorically the pig is a harlot, according to Proverbs [Chapter] 11: 'Like a gold ring in a pig's snout is a beautiful woman without good sense.'

Our Gamelin was not afraid as they are, but defied formidable kings, just as Moses did with signs and wonders. (c.23)

Gamelin and William Wischard bishops of St Andrews

Bower contrasts the meritorious Gamelin with his successor William Wischard (elected 1271), of whom he did not approve. Inchmurdo was an episcopal estate near St Andrews. Wischard's election was technically a conditional one (hence 'postulated') until he obtained papal cancellation of his earlier election to the see of Glasgow.

Gamelin of St Andrews died following a stroke at Inchmurdo and is buried in the church of St Andrews next to the high altar on the north side. He was a man of weighty counsel [and fair judgment], the defender of generosity and courtesy in the church while he was alive and well. In his place Master William Wischard, archdeacon of St Andrews and the king's chancellor, was postulated to St Andrews. He was at that time bishop-elect for the see of Glasgow. And it seemed an amazing thing to many people that a man of such high repute, who was, as already stated, bishop-elect of Glasgow, archdeacon of St Andrews, the lord king's chancellor, and rector or prebendary of twenty two [churches], was seized by such ambition that all these were not enough for him; but indeed, more out of pretence than out of piety, more out of fear of the king than out of selfishness, he took possession for himself of the bishopric of St Andrews. This man appears to be one of those of whom Juvenal writes:

Some people do not make fortunes for the sake of living,
but rather, blinded by vice, they live for the sake of their fortunes.

The love of gain grows as much as the amount of money itself grows. (c.28, ll.36-54)

Wischard and the canonical offence of pluralism

*Reflecting on the information given earlier about the many benefices held in plurality by William Wischard before he became a bishop, Bower refers to the church's canon law on such matters as confirmed at the Second General Council of Lyons in 1274, and then extracts from Thomas de Cantimpré's collection of moral tales (*On Bees*) five stories illustrating the consequences of the practice. Thomas came from Liège in Brabant (hence 'Brabantinus') now in Belgium. The quotations supposedly from St Augustine and St Jerome have not been found in modern editions.*

William Wischard the chancellor of the lord king, the bishop-elect of Glasgow who had been postulated to St Andrews, was accused before the lord pope on many charges, the main one being that he held so many benefices, as has been already mentioned; whether these were compatible or not is immaterial. And for this reason his business was delayed for a while; but in the following year at the council of Lyons this matter was aired in various ways, and lest anyone presume to retain many benefices contrary to the spirit of canon law, a conclusion was reached similar to what had been written down before in various councils and famous disputations.

Brabantinus insists strongly on that point in his book *On Bees*, in which he says:

> Whoever might read this may want to know that I was in Paris in the year 1238, where the venerable William bishop of Paris, who had previously taught as a master of theology, had summoned an assembly, and when the question was put concerning the holding of benefices in plurality, it was concluded after a clever and extremely long disputation conducted by all the masters that two benefices cannot be held with spiritual safety if one of them is worth fifteen Parisian pounds. This was the conclusion reached by the said bishop; it was also what Friar Hugh of the Dominican order (who later became a cardinal of the Roman court), Friar Guéric and Friar Geoffrey of the same order, and Friar John de La Rochelle of the Franciscan order, as well as many other eminent masters of theology concluded successively in their own schools. There had also been a very long and much more illustrious disputation three years before, in which it turned out that all the masters

of theology except two came to the same conclusion as mentioned above in all cases. One of the two was Master Philip chancellor of Paris, the other was Master Arnulf later bishop of Amiens.

But let us hear what happened to the said Philip. When the said William bishop of Paris visited him in his death throes out of fatherly concern, he asked him to give up his individual opinion regarding the holding of benefices in plurality and to resign into the church's hands all his benefices which he held in excess at that time with the exception of one, on the moderate condition that if he recovered from his illness, he [the bishop] would make good to him out of his own pocket what he had lost. The chancellor stubbornly refused, saying that he would want to be sure whether or not it was damnable to hold many benefices. The holy bishop was accordingly very exasperated. A few days after the death of the same Master Philip, when after saying matins he sought out a quiet place, as was his custom, to pour out his private prayers to the Lord, the thought at length entered his mind to pray for Philip. When he was lying prostrate on the ground and attentively interceding, he saw between himself and the light what looked like the most hideous ghost of a man. He therefore raised his hand to cross himself, and bade the apparition to speak if it was from God. The spirit replied to him: 'I am alienated from God, but I am nevertheless his wonderful creation.' 'Who are you?' the bishop said. 'I am that most wretched of men who was chancellor of Paris,' he replied. 'And how is it with you, being as you are so wretched?' the bishop asked, groaning deeply. 'It is bad, indeed it could not be worse, as I am damned to eternal death', he said. 'Alas, my dearest friend', said the bishop. 'What is the reason for your damnation?' 'There are three reasons why I am damned to perpetual death', he said. 'One is that I was cowardly enough to keep back from the poor my growing annual income. The second one is that I defended my own opinion that holding benefices in plurality was right against yours and that of very many men of orthodox views, and in this I have exposed myself to the danger of mortal sin. The third and most serious of all the reasons is that I have committed unspeakable unnatural and abominable sins of the flesh over a long period of time to the offence of many.'

I [Bower] have also discovered elsewhere that one reason was that whatever he had taught or preached or enjoined, he had done rather for the praise of men and for worldly glory than for the glory of God.

Still speaking to the bishop he added: 'Has the world come to an end?' 'I am amazed', he replied, 'that you, who were once a most learned man ask this question, since you see that I am still alive, and all those now living must die before the world ends at the coming of the Day of Judgment.' 'Do not be amazed,' he said, 'for I now do not know even the basic elements of all the knowledge that I possessed when I was alive, because the person who comes amongst the dead has neither knowledge nor skill nor reason.' And so saying the ghost disappeared from the sight of the amazed bishop. He, however, covering his holiness with the cloak of his humility, would always tell the story to all his clergy not in the first person, as if he himself had seen this thing, but in one of his sermons, as if it had happened to someone else.

In the same way, when a certain cleric of very great learning, who was on his death bed, sent for me and asked my advice since he was soon to pass away, I reminded him of that famous disputation in Paris and of its conclusion regarding the holding of benefices in plurality. He had been present then as a great doctor holding the excellent view with tearful and urgent pleading that a man who held two prebends against the interest of his soul should give up one of them, as one prebend could be enough to supply all that a cleric would need to live on. Then he turned his face away, and pretending not to hear me he replied only: 'Pray to the Lord that he inspire you.' And not long afterwards, when I had withdrawn and he was scarcely clinging to life with a very weak spirit, a certain cousin of his, who had been present at the time of my advice to him on this subject, and who loved him greatly, crying profusely pleaded with him to heed the same advice which I had given him. He was unable to speak but, signalling with his hand that he was not to suggest this, he died. And after his death a certain cleric, very much amazed, was thinking why such a great cleric should die in such a state if it was a mortal sin to hold many benefices, when soon afterwards the dead man appeared to him while he was awake and said: 'It is only because of the prebends that I am eternally damned, unhappy man that I am.'

On the same question, when James de Vitry of blessed memory [a canon regular], formerly bishop of Acre and afterwards a cardinal of the Roman court, asked the most excellent former master of theology Robert de Courson a cardinal-priest of Rome as he was dying before the first siege of Damietta, Robert replied: 'I who am about to leave this life say that it is a mortal and damnable sin to hold many benefices when one is enough.' Master Peter of blessed memory precentor of Paris said and wrote the same. Master Guiard bishop of Cambrai confirmed the same in these words: 'I would not wish to hold two benefices for a single night, not for all the gold of Arabia, and I would make sure that one of them was given to a suitable man first thing next morning; and this because of the hazards of this uncertain life.' Friar Bernard who was at one time a penitentiary of the lord pope tells the following story on this subject: when Pope Gregory IX of blessed memory was asked if he could out of the fullness of his power grant dispensation to those holding many benefices, he replied: 'Where one benefice is sufficient, I cannot grant a dispensation except only where there is hardship for the holders.'

Therefore is a man wise who deceives himself and deludes himself with the thought of some dispensation or other? It is true that many masters say this and many others are of the opposite opinion; but this alone is judged as mortal sin by Augustine, the greatest teacher of all, that the man who never commits himself to the risk of an action of ambiguous legitimacy also never runs the risk of mortal sin.

However, so that you may know that the holding of many benefices is not pleasing to God, hear what the said Brabantinus testifies, saying:

I grew up in a certain episcopal city for eleven years, where sixty-two canons served in the mother church holding very rich prebends worth almost two hundred Parisian pounds. Many of them were holders of [other] rich benefices. May the Holy Trinity one God be my witness and my judge that I have seen few of them die an ordinary death, but all of them died suddenly and ignominiously, so that one of them, when he heard one of his fellows had been in good health during the night but had been found dead in the morning, clapped his hands and said: 'So what do you want? As you see, he died according to usage and custom of the church.' I myself saw in the same church within a few years four archdeacons die in this way, so, reader, be amazed at the miracle! The first of them fell from his ornately harnessed horse and died of a broken neck. The second one was unexpectedly found dead one morning sitting in a chair. The third was standing in the choir at the elevation of the host during mass when he fell on his back and, having lost his speech and his senses, he died like a dumb animal on the third day without the sacraments of the church. The fourth died refusing confession of his sins and the sacraments, and was buried outside the cemetery in a dung-pit.

And it is no wonder if the holding of benefices in plurality is at variance with the canonical laws, since Jerome writes in a letter saying: 'If the cleric who can support himself from his property takes anything more which belongs to the poor, he indeed commits sacrilege, and by abusing such people he eats and drinks his own judgment. If you receive when you are in need, then you give rather than receive. However, if you are not in need and receive, then you are committing robbery, because you are unlawfully taking what should be distributed to those in need.' (cc.31-32)

The Bruces earls of Carrick

This romantic tale of the Bruce marriage to the heiress of the earldom of Carrick in Ayrshire is first found as related by John de Fordun in the 1360s. Marjorie was in fact the widow of Adam (earl of Carrick by right of marriage to her), not the daughter. Her second marriage to Robert de Bruce is probably datable 1272. Turnberry castle is on the coast south of Ayr. Tenants-in-chief were supposed not to marry without the king's permission. King Robert I, the eldest son of this marriage, was born on 11 July 1274.

Adam earl of Carrick, who was going on a pilgrimage for Christ in the Holy Land, died there, leaving an only daughter called [Marjorie] as his heir, who succeeded him in the earldom. One day, while she was proceeding to the place she had chosen for a hunt with her men-at-arms and ladies-in-waiting, she met a distinguished and very handsome young knight by the name of Robert de Bruce, son of Robert surnamed de Bruce the Noble lord of Annandale in Scotland and of Cleveland in England, riding across the same stretch of countryside. When greetings and kisses had been given on each side, as is the custom of courtiers, she begged him to stay for hunting and walking about; when he hesitated, she by force, so to speak, with her own hand pulled back his reins and brought the knight with her, unwilling though he was, to her castle of Turnberry. And while staying there along with his followers for the space of fifteen days or more, he secretly married the countess, the friends and well-wishers of both knowing nothing about it. They had in no way obtained the royal consent for this marriage, and because of this it was the common talk of the whole realm that she had all but carried off this young man into marriage by force. When news of this reached King Alexander, he took the castle of Turnberry and resumed possession of all her other lands and property, because she had had the presumption to marry Sir Robert de Bruce without having consulted his royal majesty. At length, following the entreaties of his friends and the payment of a certain agreed sum of money, this Robert found the king better-disposed and benevolent towards him, and even obtained the whole lordship. Through divine providence he had a son by [Marjorie] who was named Robert after his father. He was to become the stick which beat the English; indeed he was to become the saviour, the champion and the king of Scots, born as he was of royal stock. His father was this Robert who was earl of Carrick by right of his wife; his grandfather was Robert Bruce senior, whose father was the famous Robert who married Isabella the second daughter of David earl of Huntingdon. Thus fortunately Robert the future king was born in the third year afterwards. (c.29, ll.15-48)

Bagimond the papal collector, and stories about papal legates

The Second General Council of Lyons in September 1274 ordered the levy for six years of a tax amounting to a tenth of the assessed value of church goods and revenues to assist crusading expeditions to Palestine. The Italian Bohemond di Vezza (here 'Bagimond') was sent to Scotland as collector. When he met the clergy at Perth on 6 August 1275, they argued for a tax levied on an existing (presumably lesser) assessment for a longer period. This was refused, but records (exceptional in Scotland for their extent) survive to show how successful Bagimond was as a collector until his death in the early 1290s. He was not himself technically a papal legate; but mention of him as another kind of papal emissary was enough to divert Bower into telling four stories of unkown origin demonstrating generally the venality and unpopularity of papal agents.

Master Bagimond, sent by the lord pope, arrived in Scotland to levy and deposit for safe-keeping the tenth as aid for the Holy Land. All the beneficed clergy without exception paid a tenth of all their church property under the compulsion of an oath and the threat of excommunication. The Cistercian monks in final settlement paid the lord pope 50,000 marks of silver for their whole order. A council was convened on the subject at Perth this year on the day after the feast of St Oswald the King, after which at the request of the prelates and clergy, not without great expense and greater promises if he was successful, he returned to the Roman court to beg the lord pope on behalf of the clergy of Scotland to accept the old assessment of all their property, but for seven [years] rather than six. But he returned to Scotland having failed in this matter and after spending a great deal of money on it, because, as the common saying goes, legates do not want to be entertained unless it is in a luxurious fashion.

Concerning this we read that a certain legate was visiting an abbey, and hearing that the abbot had an excellent mule, started to question him with a view to inducing him to give him the mule. The abbot completely ignored this. The following day when he was escorting the legate and riding on his mule, which was trotting along beautifully, the legate brought up the subject of the mule once more; the abbot excused himself from handing it over on account of his age and physical infirmity. Indignantly the legate said to him: 'I order you to give it to me this instant by virtue of the obedience you owe me.' The abbot replied: 'I grant that you can force me to canonical obedience, but you cannot force me to mulish obedience.' Whereupon the legate went off more offended at the abbot's reply than indignant at the loss of the mule. [For indeed great prelates such as cardinals and legates] do not want to hear anything except suave words.

In this connection we read that a certain cardinal legate, on coming to a place where he had heard that a certain friar was much commended because wherever he was, he would have a sermon up his sleeve which deplored lust, greed and pride above all else, the legate wanted to try the friar out, so he bade him there and then preach some concise sermon in his presence on the subject of cardinals, thinking that he would flatter him in his sermon, as lots of different people are in the habit of doing. The friar obeyed him, saying: 'Lords indeed are the hinges of the earth, that is the cardinals, who are like hinges; for a hinge when it is not oiled always squeaks and makes a noise; but when it is oiled it closes and opens smoothly. So cardinals unless they are well-oiled by gifts and money, are always found to be recalcitrant. But when they have been oiled they softly close and open the door of their chamber to servants and all comers.' Then the legate said to him: 'That's enough, brother; you may go.'

Another legate was visiting abbeys within his jurisdiction when he urged the monks who were priests to have him commended in their commemoration prayers [during mass]. Moreover he urged the lay brothers to say a certain number of Paternosters for him every day. But a certain simple and devout lay brother, who was diligent and enthusiastic in his duty when serving both the healthy and the infirm, prayed for the legate as he went to and from the kitchen, because he was very busy at other times with other things. When he was asked what he was saying, he replied: 'I am paying the legate.' Afterwards this saying was turned into a proverb directed against those who carry out the recital of their canonical office less than well, namely: 'Il paie le legate.'

Another legate who was going to hold a visitation of a certain abbey was very threatening towards the abbot. The abbot, fearing his ferocity and eager to pacify him, eventually remembered that the legate was a heavy drinker. So he had him plied with spiced wine, which was strong and very sweet, until he became so drunk that he was speechless and senseless like a dead man. As such he was laid on a bier, and in the morning the abbot had obsequies and offices for the dead sung around him while he was still asleep.

And so on waking up and coming to the legate fled in confusion: thus the abbot escaped his clutches. (c.35, l.22 - c.36, l.22)

Second marriage and death of Alexander III

This king's first wife had died in 1275. For his second wife an embassy was sent to France rather than England, who brought back the noblewoman Yolanda de Dreux to be married to the king at the place now called Jedburgh in Roxburghshire on 14 October 1285 when he was 44. Six months later on 19 March 1286 (still 1285 by the old calendar) he was accidentally killed after crossing the Queensferry passage to Fife on his way to the royal manor of Kinghorn. Bower's dramatises his account with portents of disaster to come.

In 1285 Lord Alexander king of Scotland married Yolanda the daughter of the count of Dreux on the feast of St Callixtus pope and martyr. Very many nobles of France and Scotland along with an innumerable multitude of both sexes met for the ceremonial celebration of their wedding in royal fashion. After the wedding was over the French, gladdened by all sorts of gifts, returned home in good spirits, although a few remained behind with the queen.

I cannot recall having read of such a famous feast ever before in Scotland. But alas! an unusual feast of this kind a short time later brought forth for the Scots a fast, or that herald of sickness, an insatiable hunger. In order that the place might grace the feast and the feast might harmonise with the place, they deliberately chose to celebrate the royal wedding at Jedwood. The said place is called after the river, which is the Jed, and the forest, which is 'wood' in our native language.

> [Since] river and wood are truly two things which exist to give pleasure, you must call it praiseworthy to have a compound made up from each of them.

While everything was going on at the royal wedding according to due custom, a kind of show was put on in the form of a procession amongst the company who were reclining at table. At the head of this procession were skilled musicians with many sorts of pipe music including the wailing music of bagpipes, and behind them others splendidly performing a war-dance with intricate weaving in and out. Bringing up the rear was a figure regarding whom it was difficult to decide whether it was a man or an apparition. It seemed to glide like a ghost rather than walk on feet. When it looked as if he was disappearing from everyone's sight, the whole frenzied procession halted, the song died away, the music faded, and the dancing contingent froze suddenly and unexpectedly. Laughter is [always] mixed with grief, and mourning takes over from extremes of joy: after such splendour the kingdom lamented ingloriously, when a short time afterwards it lost itself and as a consequence its king. For in the same year on 19 March the king was delayed by the ferry at [South] Queensferry until dusk on a dark night. When advised by his companions not to go beyond Inverkeithing that night, he spurned their counsel, and with an escort of knights hurried by a precipitous track towards Kinghorn Regis. To the west of that place beside the shore his horse stumbled in the sand, and alas! the noble king, too negligently attended by his followers, broke his neck and expired. [There a stone cross stands as a monument to the occurrence, and can still be seen by passers-by at the side of the track.] And he was buried in the monastery of Dunfermline, as befits a king. The losses of the times which followed clearly show how sad and harmful his death was for the the kingdom of Scotland. Let no one [I beg you] be uncertain about the passage of such a great king to glory on account of the suddenness of his untimely death, because, as it is said, the person who lives well cannot die badly; hence the lines:

> The sudden death of a just man, when preceded by a good life,
> does not lessen his merits if he dies thus.
> (c.40, ll.1-50)

The merits of Alexander III: the prophecy of Thomas the Rhymer

Bower's panegyric on Alexander III has anachronistic echoes of the activities and legislation of James I in his own day. The English before 1286 were not generally regarded as enemies of the Scots; and the later-medieval expression 'the estates of the realm' is preferred to the more contemporary term 'parliament'. The emphasis on the regulation of trade to the kingdom's advantage is noteworthy, though the mention of Lombard merchants is again perhaps a projection back from his own time. Bower offers the first known version of a prophecy of Thomas de Earlston (the Rhymer) that came to be widely circulated, and then builds on this reflection on the transitory nature of human life. He is always the preacher at heart.

Every day in the life of this king the church of Christ flourished, its priests were honoured with due respect, vice withered away, deceit disappeared, injustice ceased, virtue thrived, truth grew strong, justice reigned. He was exceptional in appearance, physically well-built, thick-set and tall in stature, though he could not be called fat. He had a jovial face, a steadfast heart, a devout spirit. He was affable in his speech, likeable in appearance, gifted with wisdom, famed for his moderation, unshakeable in his inner strength and well-tried in his outward strength, unwavering in the severity of his justice, unremitting in his forbearance, strong in patience, gentle in humility, unstinting in his charity and fair in all things. Thus he could rightly be called a king on the merits of his integrity and his even-handed justice, because he ruled himself and his people rightly, granting each person his rights. So it is that according to Isidore 'kings' [*reges*] are so-called because they 'act rightly' [*recte agendo*]; thus the name of king is retained by doing right, and it is lost by sinning.Therefore those who know how to restrain both themselves and their subjects by ruling well are rightly called kings:

> The king exists so that there may be law. Where there is no law, there is no king either.

And if Alexander sometimes had rebels amongst his people, he repressed their madness with such harsh discipline that with a rope round their necks and ready to be hanged if that was his will, they were subjected to his authority. For this reason he was held equally in fear and love both near and far, not only by friends but also by enemies, especially the English. Thus at all times after the king had reached the age of discretion his subjects lived in constant tranquillity and peace, and in agreeable and secure freedom, in such a way that there could be applied to them what was written [in Isaiah]: 'Then my people lived in beautiful peace, at ease in their houses, and richly at rest.'

And so that he might put an end to all civil discord and insubordination everywhere within his realm, he had this habit of travelling all over his kingdom almost every year with a strong company of picked knights and nobles, and of staying in a quarter of its districts for a fixed proportion of the year. He had his justiciar with him to administer justice to anyone at all, so that all the circumstances might be taken into account and justice promptly meted out to everyone. Also whenever it happened that the king approached on horse-back from afar, it was customary for the sheriff of that shire, when warned of the king's approach, to go to meet him at the boundary of his sheriffdom with all the chosen knights of the shire. And this band of knights would bid farewell to the king as he left the sheriffdom, and then would return home. Meanwhile at the boundary of the [next] shire another band of knights would be ready and waiting for the king, to escort him likewise from one end of their district to the other at their own expense. So everywhere the king, attended by a stout troop, rejoiced in his people, and the people exulted in their king many times over.

Also the king did not easily allow any persons without possessions or skills to be idle; but it was enacted by statute that under threat of punishment every such person was to dig seven feet square every day, as he believed that idleness is the mother of foolishness and the [wicked] step-mother of the virtues. It plunges a strong man headlong into robbery, it destroys orderly government, it nurtures pride, it encourages conspiracy, and it paves the way to the loss of the kingdom. He also decreed that in the household of any prelate or magnate whatsoever there was to be a defined small number of mounts, because a large number of unnecessary horses destroyed the [food and] sustenance of the poor.

It was concluded as a result of the careful advice of the king that the kingdom had a shortage of merchandise [on offer], and that for this reason the kingdom would be too greatly impoverished by the loss of ships, whether at the hands of pirates, or as a result of break-up on rocks, or unexpected storms, or threats of unwarranted seizure in various parts and ports. Therefore it was decided that for the time being merchandise was to remain in the kingdom. This was done, though not without some difficulty. On account of this, before a year was out, there came to various parts of the country ships from various regions laden with many sorts of goods which were exchanged for things confined to the kingdom. And it was laid down that no-one except burgesses alone might be involved in this sort of business. As a result of this, within a few years the kingdom was enjoying an abundance of all goods—food-stuffs as well as money, farm animals and cattle, merchandise and manufactures [with political integrity]—so that many came from east and west and the ends of the earth to hear the justice, to view the orderly government, to size up the might of the kingdom and [to admire] the wisdom of the king. And when they had experienced these things and wondered at the glory of the kingdom, they could indeed agree with the queen of Sheba when she said to Solomon: 'The report which I heard in my own country [about you] is true, but I did not believe what they told me until I came and saw for myself. And I have proved that not a half of [your wisdom] was told to me, for I have seen greater deeds than I learned about from common talk. Blessed be your Lord and King, who has delighted in you, and who has set you on a throne and made you a king to maintain law and justice.'

Justice so flourished in his days everywhere in the kingdom that even some very rich Lombards arrived in great numbers and made an offer to the king that within a certain number of years they themselves would build cities for the king in various places provided for this purpose, such as the hill at Queensferry or Cramond Island, if they were granted certain special privileges on this account. But this offer did not please certain people amongst the estates of the realm, and so the requests were not put into effect. But the Lombards would have been amply satisfied in another way, had not the destiny that governs human life, unexpected death, fatal chance, trampled our king under foot, and had not the subtle pain of that death by taking payment in advance exacted its due ahead of time. How truly unhappy you were, Scotland, when bereft of such a great leader and pilot! And what is sadder, when he left no lawful offspring to succeed him. Thus you have a perpetual reason for mourning and sorrow in the death of one whose praiseworthy life conferred on you above all so many and such great improvements in your well-being.

Scotland, how sweet it is to remember your glory while your king was alive! But now:

> The countless race of Eve is frail and fleeting.
> Speak, my flute, raise, tragedy, a woeful lament.
> The servile nation is making for the depths by the left-hand path.
> All is woeful and frail beneath this sun.

For your lyre changed to playing a lament and your pipes became the voice of the mourners, when you learnt of the sudden death of your dearly beloved king, as bitter as it was unwelcome. But if you too had recognised how many evils were hurrying to surround you on all sides, your heart, foreseeing the news to come, would have trembled violently from fear, and once you had more fully understood what was to follow, grief would suddenly have overcome you to such an extent that you would have been drained of strength of mind, your eyes obscured by tears, and your tongue seized by mournful sobs as if you had appropriately lost your power of speech. Indeed if in the depths of your heart you knew, understood and foresaw the calamities that were to come, you would have said: 'If it was not contrary to divine will, would that the abyss had suddenly swallowed me up, before my eyes had been mocked by the dawn of that wretched day, that most frenzied of hours, that worst of days!'

Do you not remember what the country prophet Thomas de Earlston had said to the earl of March at Dunbar Castle when he obscurely prophesied concerning the king's end the night before the death of King Alexander? The earl had asked him, half-jesting as usual, what news the next day would bring. Thomas gave a sobbing sigh from the depths of his heart, and is said to have made this clear pronouncement to the earl in front of his retainers: 'Alas for tomorrow, a day of calamity and misery! because before the stroke of twelve a strong wind will be heard in Scotland the like of which has not been known since times long ago. Indeed its blast will dumbfound the nations and render senseless those who hear it; it will humble what is lofty and raze what is unbending to the ground.' Because of his grave words the earl and his retainers kept watch over the next day carefully observing the passing of the hours until noon. Seeing no clouds or signs of wind in the sky, they decided that Thomas was out of his mind and hurried off to dinner. The earl had scarcely sat down at the table and the hand of the clock was almost at midday when the earl's ears were smitten with the importunate knocking of someone who had arrived at the gate demanding to be admitted into his presence immediately. So the stranger was let in and asked for his news. 'News I have,' he said, 'but it is bad news which will reduce the whole realm of Scotland to tears—because alas! its noble king met the end of his life on earth at Kinghorn last night. And this is what I have come to tell you.' At this news the earl and all his household, as if awakened from a deep sleep, beat their breasts. They discovered by experience that the prophecies of the said Thomas had become all too credible. (c.41 - c.44, l.24)

Book XI

The Interregnum and Great Cause

For his story covering the period between the death of Alexander III in 1286 and the inauguration of King John Balliol in November 1292 Bower follows the narratives assembled by John of Fordun, while adding information from several other sources now not identifiable. He provides first an account of the agreement in 1290 over the marriage of the heiress Margaret, the late king's grandchild in Norway, to Edward of Caernarfon the heir of Edward I of England, and then, following her death in September 1290, an account of the famous 'Great Cause', when Edward was invited by the magnates of Scotland to preside over a legal solution to the problem of who should succeed to the Scottish throne. Bower's genealogical facts are not all accurate and his chronology is confused: in fact Edward sat in judgment for four sessions—at Norham (on the Northumberland bank of the river Tweed) 5-13 June 1291, and at Berwick (then in Scotland) 3-12 August 1291, 2 June-3 July 1292, and 14 October-17 November 1292. The ultimate candidates were Robert de Bruce and John de Balliol, with the latter being awarded the throne in 1292, though the grandson of the former was to seize it on a permanent basis in 1306. Bower wrote with full knowledge of later events, and certainly included some pro-Bruce fictions in his explanations, whilst displaying constant antipathy to King Edward for having cunningly taken advantage of the situation to increase his own authority. (There is a reference to the 'Pleading' of Baldred Bisset which Bower included later in his work at Book XI, cc.57-64. The prophecy attributed to the sixth-century writer Gildas was in fact apparently composed about the time of Edward's death in 1307.)

When indeed the great prince Alexander III was dead, and likewise all the children fathered by him and also all his lawful heirs and relatives descended in any way (either lineally or collaterally) from King William his grandfather, except for one very little girl called Margaret, the daughter of Margaret queen of Norway the late daughter of the said King Alexander, the kingdom of Scotland was vacant without a king as ruler for six years and nine months, just as someone had prophesied long before:

> The land will be desolate, bereft of its glorious prince
> for six years and nine months.

Nevertheless, it was governed by six guardians, namely sir William Fraser bishop of St Andrews, Duncan earl of Fife, and [Alexander] Comyn earl of Buchan from the region north of the Firth of Forth, and Robert bishop of Glasgow, Sir John Comyn and James the Steward of Scotland from the region to the south of the Forth. But Duncan of Fife died shortly afterwards…

During the above-mentioned period of years Edward Longshanks king of England, knowing that the aforesaid girl called Margaret (daughter of the king of Norway and also the grand-daughter of his own sister) was the true and lawful heir of the king of Scotland, and striving with all zeal and effort to join and unite that kingdom of Scotland to his kingdom, appointed and established in 1289 six special proctors and eminent envoys, namely the bishops of Durham and Carlisle, the earls of Lincoln and Warenne, William de Vesci knight, and Henry dean of York, to agree, arrange and negotiate between himself and the aforesaid guardians and the other estates of the kingdom about the contracting of a marriage between his son and heir Edward of Caernarfon and the aforesaid Margaret then heir to Scotland. When indeed the said envoys duly carried out this commission and negotiated with the aforesaid guardians and others whom the matter concerned, it was decided to agree to the requests of the envoys, in such a way, however, that the kingdom of Scotland would be as free and quit of all subjection of service as had satisfactorily and freely been the case with regard to customs and rights, both ecclesiastical and secular, in the time of the aforesaid King Alexander, according to what appears in a certain instrument contained in the 'Pleading' of Baldred Bisset. So also that if the marriage did not last, or one of the parties to the contract died without issue while the other survived, the kingdom was to be freely and absolutely restored and returned to the nearest heirs, without any subjection, saving to the king of England his right as far as it was competent from ancient times. And in order to bring the said business to the desired end, the nobles of Scotland formally despatched to the king of Norway two knights distinguished by their knowledge and character—Michael Wemyss and Michael Scot—to effect the marriage and bring the girl to the kingdom. But, alas, with the business incomplete, the said girl died in 1291. In this year the Jews were expelled from England. Upon her death, a dispute immediately broke out between John de Balliol and Robert de Bruce senior—for there were then three members of the Bruce family called Robert, namely this nobleman who was the senior, his son the earl of Carrick, and his grandson who was later king—over their right by inheritance to the kingdom of Scotland. This dispute was settled for the time being in the following way.

The nobles of the said kingdom with its above-named guardians kept discussing among themselves who should be made their king, but they did not presume to express what they felt about the right of succession, partly because it was a difficult and troublesome case, partly because different people felt differently about that right and vacillated repeatedly, partly because they were justifiably afraid of the power of the parties which was great and much to be feared, and partly because they had no superior who by the strength of his power could demand the execution of their decision or compel the parties to observe it. When they had carefully considered these matters, they finally decided unanimously among themselves to send a formal embassy to Edward king of England, so that he might become the supreme judge in this case and declare the rights of each party, and by his power might duly restrain the party against whom he pronounced his verdict in accordance with the requirements of the law. Therefore they sent the lord bishop of St Andrews with some others to see him, while he was seeing to his own affairs in distant parts. (However the reply of the Scots to his [later] false claims makes the opposite suggestion that he came without being invited…) Edward came on being asked, and fixed a day for all the nobles of the kingdom of Scotland, whatsoever their status or condition to assemble in his presence at Berwick, and he ordered that the parties in the controversy, together with all the others who claimed a right in the said kingdom, should be summoned, on the understanding, however, that such a summons or appearance should not arouse any prejudice to the kingdom of Scotland, and also that he should not acquire through this procedure any right of superior lordship, since he was called to act in this matter not as superior lord or judge by right, but as a friendly arbiter and respected neighbour to settle a disagreement by both his wisdom and his power after the manner of a friendly conciliator and as a favour that might be returned. And he expressly gave security for this in his letters patent before the appointed day when the court case began.

Therefore all the freeholders of the kingdom of Scotland who should and could be there met together before him at Berwick, and the parties swore an oath that they would faithfully obey his decision, when it was issued as a judgment offering a declaration on the right of royal succession. And all the bishops and others of the clergy together with the aforesaid guardians, earls, barons and the rest of the community (both burgesses and freeholders) undertook in an authentic instrument supported by the seals of all the abovementioned attached at the same time that each and all of them would obey as *de jure* and *de facto* king and supreme lord whichever of the two competitors he declared should reign. Accordingly, when this had been arranged, the often-mentioned king chose twenty-four men distinguished by their knowledge, age, character and loyalty and sensible men whatever their status or rank, of whom twelve were from England and twelve from Scotland. When they had taken a solemn oath to speak the truth, he ordered them to exclude all the others who claimed a right to the throne (for there were very many), and bearing in mind their sworn oath and the danger to their souls to decide after careful enquiry between the said John (namely de Balliol) and Robert de Bruce senior, and by their decision to show plainly which of them had the nearer or clearer right to the realm of Scotland so that he might succeed the aforesaid King Alexander by right of proximity according to the approved customs of the kingdom.

For let us make known the order of events more plainly. In 1286, fifteen days after Easter, a parliament was held at Scone where the six aforementioned guardians were appointed, one of whom, as certain books say, was the bishop of Dunkeld; others maintain that he was a substitute in place of Duncan of Fife after he had died... Nevertheless when the right of succession to the kingdom of Scotland was keenly contested by Robert Bruce senior (that is the grandfather of King Robert), and John de Balliol, John said that he himself had the stronger claim to the kingship because he was the son of Dervorguilla the elder sister of the daughter of [David] earl of Huntingdon [the younger brother of King William] and his mother was still living, namely the first sister. Robert de Bruce on the other hand replied that it should not be John but himself, because although he was the son of the second sister, he was nevertheless the first male and one degree nearer, for he was the grandson of the said Earl David, and someone in the female line ought not to succeed as long as a male is to be found, nor ought a great-grandson to be placed before a grandson. When very spirited allegations of this kind had been heard from both sides, a great division arose in the kingdom, among both the clergy and people, between the parties of Robert Bruce and John.

Some wished to raise up John de Balliol as king because he was born of the daughter of the first sister and supported by the law of primogeniture. Others rejected this entirely on the grounds that Robert de Bruce ought to succeed because he was a man and one degree nearer to the said Earl David, despite the fact he was descended from the second sister. On account of disputes of this kind and other aforementioned discussions, they committed themselves at length by unanimous agreement to Edward king of England in the manner and form aforesaid, deciding then among themselves that he should declare the rights of each party in this case and also should duly restrain the party against whom he pronounced his verdict in accordance with the requirements of the law. Thereupon the bishop of Brechin (although others say the bishop of St Andrews), the abbot of Jedburgh and Geoffrey de Mowbray were chosen in parliament to appeal for his advice and patronage over the state of the kingdom of Scotland and of the lands of Penrith. These envoys started their journey to Gascony in the same year on St Donatus' Day, and travelled continuously so that from Newcastle to St Jean-d'Angély they had just one day's break in London. When they had found the said king at Saintes and explained to him the reason for their journey, they returned to Scotland, and on St Catherine's day came to Clackmannan with the king of England's reply. On that day the guardians of the realm were gathered there because it was then being said that Queen Joleta or Yolanda was pregnant and they were waiting for the birth of her offspring which they wished to see. When this event failed to take place or there was a stillbirth, the said king of England returned in a happy mood to England. And as soon as he could, he summoned the prelates and nobles of his kingdom and told them that an envoy had been sent across by the Scots to seek his counsel and aid, saying that a suitable opportunity had presented itself for subjecting the kingdom of Scotland with its subjects wholly to his power, which in the event was afterwards shown to be very true. Therefore, with the counsel and approval of the nobles, he briefed the French experts inappropriately... when seeking their advice and a ruling on the succession to the said kingdom of Scotland. (cc.1 - 3)

When these deliberations and pronouncements of the legal experts of France had been brought together and conveyed very speedily to England, the king of England previously mentioned came to Norham in the month after Easter 1289 where he had the prelates, magnates and guardians assembled. He then exhorted them with sweet words to make peace among themselves and agree upon a king, not least because, as he put it, it would give him particular pleasure. 'Worthy as a nation that you have been hitherto,' he said, 'you will be reckoned shrewd if you prevent foreigners from taking a disproportionate share among you in the matter of your land. Our affairs are enough for us: may you be agreed in coping with yours! But if you are unable to come to a unanimous decision, return here on such a day and we shall proclaim God's will in the matter and administer justice.' False cunning, enchantress lark, counterfeit pretender, venomous flatterer who snares with innocent concealments the traps you prepare for the ingenuous! Your poisons festering with plague lie hidden, overlaid with honeyed words; and you are soothing for such a long time as a delightful player on the shepherd's pipe until you fradulently charm to sleep. Therefore bereaved Scotland, you pay no attention to what Seneca well knows: 'Recognize that an evil man who speaks in flattering terms is your snare; for smooth-tongued eloquence contains its poison.'

In the following year therefore and in the interval (if I am to be truthful) as a result of the sly suggestions and insinuations breathed by wicked angels from the air around the king of England, lamentable civil discord arose among the estates concerning the kingdom of Scotland which caused a great division among both clergy and people as supporters of Robert Bruce and John de Balliol, all the others claiming right and jurisdiction in the kingdom of Scotland having been excluded, as previously stated. Meanwhile histories, annals and chronicles of many kinds were examined in Scotland, Wales and Ireland, not only among subjects of Scotland but also by the council of the king of England, upon his right to the kingdom of Scotland.

Therefore in this year all the magnates of the kingdom of Scotland met together at Upsettlington and at the request of the aforesaid king with his safe-conduct crossed the border and assembled at the parish church of Norham. Here tentatively at first and not as if he were serious, the aforesaid king of England claimed direct lordship over Scotland in so far as his predecessors possessed it hitherto with reference to solemn proofs. To this Robert Wishart bishop of Glasgow briefly replied that from long ago the kingdom of Scotland was free to the extent that it owed tribute or homage to no-one save God alone and his agent on earth; and he added to the aforesaid these words which I will record: 'Your majesty, I have made extracts from the books of the English, namely [a prophecy of] Gildas, as follows:—

The kingdom of the Scots was once noble, strong and powerful
among the other kingdoms of the earth.
After repelling the Britons, Norwegians, Picts and Danes,
the Scots nobly upheld their rights.'

On hearing this the king passed over the bishop's reply with a deaf ear as if deeming it worthless, and planned to proceed further and insist with all his strength on a new regime in the kingdom. He refrained from further reference to his own claim, and after taking advice privately entreated the prelates, magnates and nobles of Scotland to come to Berwick and there (such was his offer) have their case decided in a trustworthy manner. But in this he was found wanting because little trustworthiness was found in him as became very clear in what follows.

As was mentioned before, from those coming to Berwick twenty-four distinguished men (forty according to some and eighty according to others, but, as I find, several books agree in the first opinion), of whom twelve were from England and the same number from Scotland, were chosen and sworn in to decide and determine faithfully which of the two contenders Robert and John had the better right to the kingdom. Now when these men had taken an oath and a jury of twenty-four had been set up as mentioned above, the king had everyone else removed from the church except just those sworn in as jurors, whom he decided to have closely guarded from the public eye in a secret location. The same king went in alone among these jury members with no-one accompanying him whenever and as often as he wished, and frequently inquired about the progress of the case. At length, weighing up a report from some perjurers that Robert Bruce had the preferable right of succession according to the laws and established customs, he strengthened the guard on the jury, withdrew to his own men, and drawing some members of his privy council on one side, told them about the decision of the jury and with their counsel deliberated on what was to be done about this matter.

The king's questions were answered by a certain Englishman named Anthony Bek who spoke as follows: 'If Robert Bruce becomes king of Scotland, where will Edward king of England stand? For this Robert is of the best stock of all England and is personally very powerful in the kingdom of Scotland, and in times gone by many troubles have been inflicted on the kings of England by the kings of Scotland.' To this the same king, shaking his head so to speak, replied in the French tongue saying: 'Per le sang de Dieu tu as bien chanté', that is to say 'By Christ's blood, you have sung well! The matter will proceed otherwise than I had previously arranged.' In like manner all of his privy council both secretly and openly suggested to him by all means that he should never give judgment without subjection, since a suitable time was then at hand when he could fulfil a desire he had harboured for a long time.

When these things had thus been considered, he summoned the elder Robert de Bruce and asked him if he would hold the aforesaid kingdom of him in chief, in which case he would make and constitute him king thereof. Robert answered him frankly and said: 'If I can obtain the aforesaid kingdom by way of law and a trustworthy jury, it is well indeed; but if not, I shall never in gaining it for myself reduce to servitude the aforesaid kingdom which all its kings with great toil and trouble have until now preserved and held without servitude in firmly-rooted freedom.' When he had heard this and cunningly had Robert removed, Edward summoned John de Balliol and put to him the same question as before. After quickly deliberating with his advisers (who had been quite corrupted), Balliol agreed to the aforesaid king's wish that he should hold the kingdom of him and do homage for the same. When this had been done, the parties were soon afterwards summoned into the presence of the nobles of Scotland and England, and Edward declared John de Balliol to be the lawful heir in succession to the kingdom and adjudged him to have the better right. After the judgment was given, however, the earl of Gloucester, holding Robert Bruce by the hand in the sight of all, spoke thus: 'Take heed, your majesty, of the kind of judgment you have given today, and remember that you must be judged at the Last Judgment.' And immediately this Robert withdrew at the same earl's bidding and never offered homage or fealty to John de Balliol. (c.9, l.43 - c.11, l.37)

On the last day of November 1292 John de Balliol was made king at Scone and raised up there on the royal throne as was the custom. On the following feast of St Stephen against the wishes of all but a few of the leading men of the kingdom he did homage at Newcastle to Edward king of the English for the kingdom of Scotland—which was never heard of before this—subjecting himself for ever to dependence on him, as he had previously promised in his ear. (c.14, ll.46-52)

The humiliation of John Balliol

A property dispute involving Macduff, the uncle (not the brother) of the late earl of Fife, was raised as early as King John's first parliament in February 1293. An appeal was made to the court of King Edward as superior lord of Scotland, and John found himself forced in terms of his homage and fealty to Edward to answer for his treatment of this case before the English king in his parliament in London. The issues raised by this case were one of the reasons which alerted the Scottish magnates to the subordinate position which their country was now suffering under the masterful Edward, so that in February or July 1295 they supported John's revocation of his homage, and sought an alliance with Edward's enemy King Philip IV of France instead. An act of renunciation sent to Edward by John led to summonses to answer in England for his behaviour (though not to an act of deposition at this stage). Bower shows no sympathy for the hapless King John; but at the same time reports that his Bruce rival (in fact the son of the competitor of 1291-2 at this stage) was a shamefully pliant ally of the English king. It is clear that the Scots were not united to face a vengeful Edward when he had time to deal with their challenge to his authority.

But a little before this and in the same year, certain men of Abernethy, seeking to deprive Macduff the brother of the recently killed Duncan earl of Fife of his lands and property at Kilconquhar, arraigned the same before the king in the aforesaid parliament. But because, as it seemed to the aforesaid Macduff, the same king showed too much favour to the other side, he appealed from his verdict and court for a hearing by the king of England, and pursuing his appeal as assiduously as he could, he succeeded in getting the aforesaid John king of Scotland summoned to the king of England's parliament held in London. He appeared there in person and decided after consultation with his council that he would reply to the objections raised by the king of England and the party in the case through proctors. When, therefore, the king was called and his proctors appeared in court, the oft-mentioned king of England, presiding judicially, was not willing to listen to the proctors of the king of Scotland until that king, who was then sitting beside the king of England, would rise from his place and standing in court before him commit his answers to his proctors with his own lips. John carried out these orders, and after suffering innumerable insults and slights from everyone against his kingly rank and dignity, he finally committed his answers to his proctors. And thus, after seeking permission, he returned home very greatly troubled. He immediately organized a parliament and summoned the leaders of both clergy and people. He set forth openly the injustices, insults, slights and shame which he had endured, and strove to the best of his manly ability for a remedy to be applied by all means against the wickedness of the aforesaid king. At length it was determined there that the same king John should utterly revoke the homage and fealty offered to the king of England because it had been wrung from him by force and fear; and that he could in no way obey him and his commands any longer to the detriment of his kingdom's liberty.

Subsequently...while envoys were being sent to the king of the French, it was decided in parliament that an envoy be sent to the king of the English. Therefore King John, on the advice of his parliament, sent letters patent authenticated with his seal retracting and revoking his homage and fealty, with Henry abbot of Arbroath, a wise, just and plain-speaking monk, to the aforesaid king of England, because it was not easy to find someone else to send. When the letters were presented, the king of England replied in the French tongue: 'A toi fou félon, telle folie tu fais;' and immediately added: 'Si on ne le voit pas venir à nous, nous viendrons à lui', which is to say: 'I tell you, foolish felon, you commit a great folly, because if the man who has sent you does not wish to come to us, we shall come to him.' When this answer had been given, the aforesaid abbot (who had been sent there out of spite because his bad qualities made him hateful to many of the nobles and others of his country) was unable to obtain letters of safe-conduct from the king of England, and because of the short time remaining before the expiry of his safe-conduct, he barely escaped alive.

Afterwards the king of England more than once summoned the king of Scotland to the marches and frontiers of the kingdoms and had him cited and called to appear before him to stand trial for his disobedience and rebellion. But when he refused to respond to peremptory summons, and because of his manifold contumacy as well as the offence of violating his oath of fealty and homage, he [Edward] pronounced a judgment against him of deprivation and deposition from his kingdom, and from all other lands and possessions which he held from him; and thus the man whom he promoted to the kingdom in disregard of the law, he stripped of the right he had acquired and all honour that had been bestowed, both by a judgment and in deed.

This King John, intruded through the guile and power of the king of

England, was king for less than four years, in very great servitude and bondage to the king of England; before this the kingdom was so to speak headless for seven years after the death of the peace-making King Alexander III, and abnormal in the time of this disastrous King John, and after his deposition severely shaken and torn apart by very great instability and destruction for ten years on end; and so it remained headless and continuously afflicted and oppressed for approximately twenty years.

Meanwhile the same king of England prepared himself for war, and summoning Robert de Bruce the grandfather acknowledged that he had given an unjust decision and, retracting the same, he promised faithfully and pledged himself to the aforesaid Robert to promote him to the kingdom because he had the stronger and better right, now that the other had been totally set aside and deprived for ever. By such a promise and with smooth words full of every kind of falsehood and overlaid with honeyed deception, he induced the aforesaid Robert to write letters to all his friends living in the kingdom of Scotland advising them to surrender and deliver to him all castles and fortresses, since the whole aim of the king of England was directed to this—that he might constitute and appoint him king. Therefore Robert wrote and did what the other suggested; but when [the king] had got what he wanted, he by no means kept his promises.

Indeed, on this account a lamentable division arose in the kingdom between the Bruces and the Comyns, who supported Balliol. Therefore this proves what the Lord says: 'Every kingdom divided in itself will be desolated.' Assuredly this Edward can be compared with the devil, whose whole intention is to make divisions between friends, and about whom it is written in Hosea [13]: 'He will make divisions among brothers.' (c.15, ll.25-55; c.18, ll.1-60)

The Siege of Berwick

The English attack on Berwick by sea and land took place at the turn of the year by the old calendar, i.e. late March 1295/6. Edward's pretended retreat and return under false colours are not reported by English chroniclers; it is a story with an imaginative literary flavour, which by the time of Fordun and Bower may have well been in circulation as a late explanation of the Scottish defeat. The sack of the town after its capture was a horror story in Scottish tradition.

In 1295 the unfortunate King John, on the advice of the magnates supporting him, marshalled and sent off all the nobles and freeholders as well as other sturdy men of the earldom of Fife (which was then without its head and lacking a proper helmsman) to guard and defend the town of Berwick, where increasingly great danger was then threatening. A large fleet of the king of England arrived there, laden with a great number of men. They launched a great assault from the seaward direction, and the garrison of the town, which was vigorous in arms, strong in power, and fierce in spirit drove them back by force and burnt eighteen ships laden with armed men, all of whom they killed.

In the following year therefore, strongly aroused for the reasons stated above, the king of England attacked Berwick in person with a large body of men, and because he could not take it by force, he planned cunningly and craftily to gain his end by deception. Therefore when he had been encamped round the town for some considerable time, he made as if he wished to withdraw, and removing the tents he pretended he was going very far away; but on 29 March (Good Friday that year) immediately after daybreak, after raising the standards and war-ensigns of the Scottish army which had been deceitfully counterfeited before-hand, he approached the gates of the town. When they saw this, the Scottish defenders of the town became thoroughly elated and delighted when it was reported to them that help from their king was at hand: being unhappily deceived by this promise, like loyal subjects and unaware of the whole deception, they confidently opened the gates. But as soon as the deception was revealed and the truth learnt, they endeavoured to resist, but were at once surrounded by enemies and, enduring attack on every side, they were wretchedly overwhelmed by sudden onslaughts. Moreover, when the town had been taken in this way and its citizens had submitted, the aforesaid king of England spared no one, whatever the age or sex, and for two days streams of blood flowed from the bodies of the slain, for in his tyrannous rage he ordered 7,500 souls of both sexes to be massacred. There the noble, high-spirited and vigorous fighting-men of Fife were utterly destroyed, so that mills could be turned round by the flow of their blood. (c.20, ll.1-37)

Battle of Dunbar; Balliol and Bruce; King John's abdication

Edward's defeat of King John's supporters at Dunbar in East Lothian, and Richard Siward's apparently unexpected surrender to him of the castle there, gave the English king the upper hand in Scotland. In Bower's eyes Siward was a traitor, though in fact the owner of the castle (the earl of Dunbar) had already done homage to Edward. (Most of the nobles captured were conditionally released quite soon.) The Bruces were also on Edward's side, and were supported by other Scottish nobles in their hope to succeed to the Scottish kingdom on the resignation of King John. But Edward decided to take the kingdom under his own direct rule. John was deserted even by his Comyn relatives, and in early July 1296 resigned the Scottish kingship at Montrose in Angus. After a ceremonial degrading he was sent with his son Edward to imprisonment in England. In 1299 he was to be allowed to stay on some old family lands at Bailleul in Somme department in France until his death in 1313. His son Edward was to return to Scotland much later as a pretender to the throne, and had some success for a time after winning the battle of Dupplin near Perth in 1332.

Then after the capture of the town of Berwick by the English and the piteous slaughter of the Scots from Fife became known, the Scots who were sent by King John to help the town of Berwick fought in the same year on 27 April with the English at Dunbar, where Patrick de Graham and many nobles fell wounded. And very many other knights and barons, on fleeing to the castle of Dunbar in the hope of saving their lives, were received there with ready welcome. But the custodian of the castle in question, Richard Siward by name, handed them all—to the number of seventy knights, besides renowned men-at-arms and other sturdy men, together with William earl of Ross and the earl of Menteith—to the king of England, like sheep offered for slaughter. Without pity, he handed them over to suffer immediately various kinds of death and hardship.

It should be noted that from the first occurrence of dissension between the noble men Bruce and Balliol over the right to succeed to the kingdom of Scotland, that kingdom was split in two. For all the Comyns with all their supporters stood by Balliol; but the earls of Mar and Atholl with all the force at their command adhered in a firm compact of affinity to the party of Bruce, who was assisted by Robert bishop of Glasgow with an indissoluble bond of affection. It was for this reason—love and support for the Bruce party—that, according to the common view, the aforesaid earls with their troops fled unharmed from the field on the day the aforesaid battle was fought, and thus a great disaster befell the opposing party, and the enemy of both gained such a welcome and pleasing victory. And, just as afterwards when King Robert Bruce was making war, all the supporters of Balliol were suspected of treason in his war, so also in this Balliol's war, the aforesaid bishop and earls with all the supporters of Bruce's party were generally considered traitors to the king and kingdom. But alas! through discord of this kind, the innocent masses were exposed to the frenzied bites of these wolves and lay lacerated throughout the length and breadth of the land. After victory had been achieved over the Scots at Dunbar, Robert de Bruce the elder approached the king of England and begged him to fulfil faithfully what he had previously promised him as regards his getting the kingdom. That old master of guile with no little indignation answered him thus in French: 'N'avons-nous pas autre choses à faire qu'à gagner vous royaumes?', that is to say: 'Have we nothing else to do than win kingdoms for you?' That noble man, discerning from such a response the treachery of the wily king, withdrew to his lands in England and put in no further appearance in Scotland.

Then after the castles of Dunbar, Edinburgh and Stirling had been handed over to him, King Edward marched on and followed King John of Scotland as far as Forfar castle. John Comyn lord of Strathbogie met him and accepted his protection. Immediately afterwards, according to certain reports, Comyn craftily brought back King John himself and Edward his son from Aberdeen to Montrose castle. When the king of England arrived at the aforesaid Montrose castle, the same King John, stripped of his royal accoutrements and holding a white wand in his hand (prompted by force and fear for his life…) gave up with stave and rod all right which he had or could claim in the kingdom of Scotland, and resigned it into the hand of the king of England.

Therefore after this unwarranted and unlawful resignation of the kingdom, Edward king of England a few days later had the said ex-king John taken with his son Edward by sea to London, and there had both of them strictly imprisoned for no little time. But in the course of time, though the son was kept in custody, the father was released after, however, taking a most solemn oath never to claim the right to rule in the said kingdom of Scotland. And so he was restored to his lands of Bailleul in France, and met his end long afterwards. His son Edward was allowed restoration to his patrimony in France after first taking the oath. And there he remained after his father's death until he prepared for his own war which was stirred up and begun at the battle of Dupplin. So ended the reign of King John de Balliol, who ruled for three years and a half. (c.24, ll.30-42; c.25, ll.1-29; c.26, ll.1-13; c.27, ll.1-13)

William Wallace

Bower's plans for his chapters 28-34 in his Book XI on William Wallace 1297-8 were never completely carried out: c.31 is comparatively brief, whilst cc.32-33 were never entered into his working manuscript or any subsequent copies. What he did compose owes something to John de Fordun, but apparently he had access also to traditional tales which had been handed down orally, some of which cannot be traced further back than here. It may well be that Bower was the first to write them down.

It is a measure of the divisions among the Scottish nobility that the non-noble Wallace came to be accepted, however briefly, as the acknowledged leader of the resistance to Edward's administration of the country that led to the victory at Stirling Bridge in September 1297. But Bower is not surprised that once his fellow-leader Andrew de Moray had died, Wallace was deserted at Falkirk in July 1298 by the envious Comyns. Bower is always the holy abbot, ready to point the moral when things go wrong. It is not always easy to distinguish in his account historical fact from comment and literary embellishment. The formal organisation of Wallace's army along classical lines is surely exaggerated; the confrontation at Stainmore in Westmorland probably never took place; and the story of the conversion of the young Robert de Bruce to his true calling is highly imaginative. Modern historians can no doubt get nearer the truth about what happened than was possible for Bower; but he does here help us to understand the continuing reputation of Scotland's hero-leader against the treacherous English some 150 years after his death. Errors about who led the English force at Stirling, or about how many castles were recaptured from the English, are minor flaws on so grand a canvas.

In [1297] the famous William Wallace, the hammer of the English, the son of the noble knight [Malcolm Wallace], raised his head. He was a tall man with the body of a giant, cheerful in appearance with agreeable features, broad-shouldered and big-boned, with belly in proportion and lengthy flanks, pleasing in appearance but with a wild look, broad in the hips, with strong arms and legs, a most spirited fighting-man, with all his limbs very strong and firm. Moreover the Most High had distinguished him and his changing features with a certain good humour, had so blessed his words and deeds with a certain heavenly gift, that by his appearance alone he won over to himself the grace and favour of the hearts of all loyal Scots. And this is not surprising, for he was most liberal in his gifts, very fair in his judgments, most compassionate in comforting the sad, a most skilful counsellor, very patient when suffering, a distinguished speaker, who above all hunted down falsehood and deceit and detested treachery; for this reason the Lord was with him, and with His help he was a man successful in everything; with veneration for the church and respect for the clergy, he helped the poor and widows, and worked for the restoration of wards and orphans bringing relief to the oppressed. He lay in wait for thieves and robbers, inflicting rigorous justice on them without any reward. Because God was very greatly pleased with works of justice of this kind, He in consequence guided all his activities.

When Wallace was a young knight, he killed the sheriff of Lanark, an

Englishman who was dexterous and powerful in the use of arms, in the town of Lanark. From that time therefore there gathered to his side [like a swarm of bees] all those who were bitter in their outlook and oppressed by the burden of servitude under the intolerable rule of English domination, and he was made their leader. For we understand that he was wonderfully brave and bold, with a handsome appearance and boundless generosity; he came from a distinguished family, with relatives who shone with knightly honour. His older brother called Andrew was a belted knight who held a patrimony in lands in keeping with his status, which he bequeathed to be held by his descendants. When William had been appointed guardian of the realm and was destroying the English on all sides and daily gaining ground, he in a short time subjected all the magnates of Scotland willy nilly to his authority, whether by force or the strength of his prowess. And if any of the magnates did not gladly obey his orders, Wallace got hold of him, put pressure on him, and held him in custody until he submitted entirely to his wishes. And so once everyone had been brought under his control, he applied himself in manly fashion to attacking the castles and fortified towns where the English were in control, skilfully intent on the liberation of his homeland and the overthrow of his enemies.

And because he did not get the upper hand through aggressive valour, he sought to achieve it with more discerning carefulness. For he encouraged his comrades in arms towards the achievement of whatever plan he had in hand always to approach battle for the liberty of their homeland with one mind. And as regards the whole multitude of his followers he decreed on pain of death that once the lesser men among the middling people (or in practice those who were less robust) had been assembled before him, one man was always to be chosen out of five from all the groups of five to be over the other four and called a quaternion; his commands were to be obeyed by them in all matters, and whoever did not obey was to be killed. In a similar manner also on moving up to the men who were more robust and effective there was always to be a tenth man [called a decurion] over each nine, and a twentieth over each nineteeen, and so on moving up to each thousand [called a chiliarch] and beyond to the top. At length he himself as pre-eminent over everyone else was regarded as commander or general, whom all were bound to obey to the death. With everyone harmoniously approving this law (or substitute for law), they chose him as their captain, and promised to keep the said statute until the succession of a legitimate king.

The fame of William Wallace therefore, which was spread around everywhere, at length reached the ears of the king of England with news of the harm done to his men. Intent as he was on many kinds of difficult business elsewhere, he sent his treasurer Hugh de Cressingham with a large force to curb the audacity of William himself and subdue the kingdom of Scotland to his rule. On hearing therefore of the arrival of such a man with an armed force, the said William (who was then taken up with besieging the English who occupied the castle of Dundee) at once committed the responsibility for and attention to the siege of the castle to the burgesses of the same town under pain of loss of life and limb, and advanced with all haste with his army towards Stirling to meet the same Hugh. And in the fierce battle which took place at Stirling Bridge on September 1297 the same Hugh de Cressingham was killed and all his army was put to flight. Some had their throats cut by swords, others were taken prisoner, others were drowned; and when with God's help they had all been overcome, the said William secured a blessed victory with no mean renown. On his side amongst the number of the nobles of Scotland only Andrew de Moray (father of the noble Andrew) was wounded and died. The following lines concern this battle:

For this reason the Scots adopted a stout heart at the instigation
of William Wallace, who taught them to fight,
so that those whom the English nation held as living captives
might be made renewed Scots in their own homeland,
so that they might besides help King John to reign
in his own kingdom, because if they wanted to serve
an alien king, they could lose their rights.
Hence in the year one thousand three hundred less
three times one the Scots are said to have vanquished
the savage English, whom they put into mourning for death,
as the bridge bears witness, where the great battle is recorded,
which lies beyond Stirling on the river Forth.
The third before the Ides of September was the day of this grace
offered as a celestial gift to the faithful Scots.

Therefore after this kind of triumphal victory the said William Wallace the guardian of Scotland made haste to continue the siege of the castle of Dundee. On his arrival there the English keepers, terrified by the turn of fortune at the victory at Stirling, persuaded themselves to surrender the castle unconditionally with a vast haul of arms and treasure. When this became known, fear and trembling overcame the enemy. Of the other castles and fortresses which the English had wrenched from the control of our people, some the guardian himself cast to the ground, some he entrusted to the steady keeping of Scots, not a few he left empty.

And so as the season of autumn approached there was a threat of a major dearth and shortage of food in the kingdom, since there was a shortage of grain resulting from inclement weather. On this account, once the crops had been brought in to the yards and barns, the guardian ordered the summons of all and sundry Scots who were capable of defending their homeland to invade the country of their enemies and find their substance there, and to spend the wintry part of the year there so as to spare their own very limited food supplies that had been gathered in their yards, as we have said. Therefore from every sheriffdom and shire, barony and lordship, town and village, and country estate he had special lists drawn up containing the names of the men between sixteen and sixty who were fit for warfare. So that not one man could be absent unnoticed from a stated time and place without his knowledge, he laid it down as a fundamental law that not only in every barony but also in every sizeable township a gallows was to be erected on which were to be hanged all those inventing excuses to avoid the army when summoned without reasonable cause. And this was done. For he himself, when organising an expedition with an enormous army and finding that some burgesses of Aberdeen had not come, appointed (as we have described) the quaternions, pentarchs, decurions, centurions and chiliarchs to command those placed under them in this way, and intended to make a quick journey towards England before the feast of All Saints; he then himself with a very few men turned his horse round with all haste, and at Aberdeen and in its neighbourhood punished with a hanging those who had stayed away from the army without excuse. He returned to the army more quickly then you would believe, and then crushed underfoot and laid waste the whole of Northumbria up to Newcastle, spending the winter from the feast of All Saints until the Purification of Our Lady, or at least (as some books chronicle it) he was with his army in England until Christmas. After burning the whole region of Allerdale and seizing booty, he returned home safe and sound with his Scots enriched by the spoils.

Hearing this, King Edward, ablaze with mad anger and unable to contain himself through sorrow, broke off the war which he had planned against the king of France, a move which certainly gave very great comfort to the French. For in the judgment of some, if the Scots had not then recalled him from France by their efforts in battle, the greater part of the lineage of France would have been at risk. So turning aside from France, King Edward made for his own territories, where, observing the slaughter and destruction inflicted on him and his people by the Scots, he wrote a threatening letter to William the guardian of Scotland, stating among other matters that if the king himself had remained in his kingdom, Wallace would not have dared to attempt such deeds; but if he dared to invade England again, he would at once realise that the avenging hands of the king himself were seeking retribution upon him and his men for their presumption. In short, when Wallace heard of the impudence and threatening boasting of the king, he sent a message back to him to say that he would revisit his kingdom once more before the celebration of Easter.

When therefore the armies of both kingdoms had gathered on either side near Stainmore, it looked like coming to a conflict. Then on the Scottish side the squires and [other] courageous young men of the army asked the guardian's permission to make a trial of the English in front of the battle line in order to gild their own spurs. So as not to allow this to happen anywhere at all, he commanded them all by the voice of a herald under pain of death to maintain the position previously given to them, and to advance with their accustomed seriousness and also with the deliberation expected of them. On the other side the king of England, resounding with his innumerable multitude and his pretentious clamour of trumpets, claimed that he would destroy the Scottish army as though this was not difficult. But when the king saw the Scots advancing sensibly with harmonious and resolute step not half a mile distant from a clash, on the advice of his fellow soldiers he turned around his men and gave way to the ill-luck of the hour. Seeing this, the Scots wanted as one man to pursue the fleeing king. But the guardian forbade this to be done on pain of death, saying that in the course of other struggles between the kingdoms it was the prepared plan for a splendid victory to wait until the arrogant king of England along with his royal forces and fearsome commanders turned tail before a few commons and patriots of Scotland on land which he claimed as his, although the sword had not yet been drawn on the other side. Once this speech from his eloquent lips had been heard by the entire Scottish army, dismounting and throwing themselves to the ground they glorified God and St Andrew and the holy confessor Cuthbert whose memorable passage from this world was being celebrated on this day, because through the energy and care of such a leader the valour and power of their enemies withered away, and both the Scots and Scotland won the distinction of a famous victory with everlasting renown. But the English say that their king was not present there in person, but that someone else resembling him gleamed in his suit of armour.

On these matters we have the following verses on the battle of Stirling Bridge:

Then the said man named Wallace gathers the Scots,
he gathers them like grains because he is called 'Valais' in French;
he pursues the English in order to continue the war,
and to renew the freedom of Scotland by war.
Then was the destruction of the English of such a kind and magnitude
as the northern regions have never experienced the like.
The whole of Northumbria perished as far as Newcastle.
Thus towards Stainmore the Scots achieve their aims.

In the aforesaid year of the Lord once more the English return
ready to fight for Berwick, I tell you,
on the feast of Cuthbert in the spring, steadfast.
The Scots looked on, they thought they were to fight on the battlefield
as the English had promised; but they did not keep
to what they had promised, but at once took to flight.
When the Scots saw this, they departed sorrowfully;
England bears backwards the disgrace of their king's shield.
The Scottish assembly, praising the latest gifts,
gave thanks in their need, even if the gifts were not complete.
Every house rises and exults and resounds with praise.
Then the king flees; hence England groans sorrowfully.

So while Scotland by the shrewdness of the guardian was making a surprising, in fact a successful recovery, since every man remained safely on his own property and cultivated the land in the usual way and very often triumphed over his enemies, the magnates and powerful men of the kingdom, intoxicated by a stream of envy, seditiously entered a secret plot against the guardian under the guise of expressions of virgin-innocence but with their tails tied together. Hence some who had been restored to their fortresses and domains by him after they had been completely excluded by the same English, muttered with proud hearts and rancorous minds, saying to one another: 'We do not want this man to reign over us.' But the ordinary folk and populace, along with more of the nobles whose attitude was sounder and leaned more towards the public interest, praised the Lord on account of the fact that they themselves, saved from the daring attacks of rivals with the help of such a champion, were able to have the comfort of their own homes. What stubborn folly of fools! Wallace did not force himself into rulership, but by the choice of the estates he was raised up to be ruler after the previously-nominated guardians had been removed. And when you, Scotland, had been headless and unable to defend yourself, Wallace had appeared as a mighty arm for you and a salvation in time of trouble. Why is covetous envy so much in control in Scotland? How sad that it is natural for Scots to detest not only the happiness of other people, but also the happiness of their own countrymen; and this out of respect for inferiors, in case they are made equal to themselves, and respect for their superiors, because they are not equal to them, and respect for their peers, who are made equal to them. In this there can be seen a likeness between Cain, who envied Abel his prosperity, and Rachel who envied Leah her fertility, and Saul who envied David his felicity, and, let me say it, a Scot who envied Wallace his magnanimity. Thus by envy was achieved the downfall of the clergy, the ruin of the people and the collapse of the kingdom.

In the year 1298 the said king of England, grieving at the losses and difficulties inflicted on him and his people by William Wallace in numerous ways, gathered a large army and entered the country of Scotland with hostile intent, having with him certain of the nobles of Scotland to help him. Meeting him, the said William with the rest of the magnates of the said kingdom engaged in an arduous battle near Falkirk in July on the feast of St Mary Magdalene, not without severe losses among both the leading men and those of the middle rank of the Scottish nation, and was put to flight. For on account of the malicious outlook which they had adopted, arising from the stream of jealousy which the Comyns directed towards the said William, they abandoned the field along with their accomplices and escaped uninjured. When their malice became known, the aforesaid William, desiring to save his men and himself, hurried to flee by another road.

Pursuing them from the other side, Robert de Bruce, when a steep and impassibly deep valley between the troops of the two armies came into view, is said to have called out loudly to William, asking him who it was that drove him to such arrogance as to seek so rashly to fight in opposition to the exalted power of the king of England and of the more powerful section of Scotland. It is said that William replied like this to him: 'Robert, Robert, it is your inactivity and womanish cowardice that spur me to the liberation of the native land that is legally yours. And indeed it is an effeminate man even now, ready as he is to advance from bed to battle, from the shadow into the sunlight, with a pampered body accustomed to a soft life feebly taking up the weight of battle for the liberation of his own country, the burden of the breastplate—it is he who has made me so presumptuous perhaps even foolish, and has compelled me to attempt or seize these tasks.' With these words William himself looked to a speedy flight, and with his men sought safety.

On account of all this Robert himself was like one awakening from a deep sleep; the power of Wallace's words so entered his heart that he no longer had any thought of favouring the views of the English. Hence, as he became every day braver than he had been, he kept all these words uttered by his faithful friend, considering them in his heart. In this the words written by Seneca prevailed: 'The finest characteristic of a noble mind is that it is easily urged towards honourable ends. Things that are worthless delight no man of lofty disposition. Happy is the man who has turned his mind to better things on the advice of another. He places himself outside the terms of chance, he will attempt what is favourable, he will crush what is unfavourable, and will despise other things which are held in admiration.'

When William Wallace and his men had slipped away from the battle, sadly as a result of the arrogance and blazing jealousy of both kingdoms, the noble community of Scotland lay miserably prostrate across mountains and hills, valleys and plains. Among the nobles the most valiant knight John Steward with his men of Bute, and Macduff earl of Fife with his men from there were utterly destroyed. It is commonly said that Robert de Bruce, who was later king of Scotland but at that time supported the king of England, by his energy provided the opportunity for this victory. For when the Scots stood fast in their ranks unconquered and could not be broken by force or craft, the same Robert, making a long detour round a mountain with a force commanded by Anthony de Bek, took the Scots in the rear from the opposite side; and thus the Scots, who at the earlier stage stood unbroken and unconquered, in the later stage were cleverly overcome. And it should be noted that we rarely if ever read that Scots were overcome by the English except as a result of jealousy among their leaders or by guile or deceit on the part of natives going over to the other side.

After the said victory, which had been granted to their enemies through the treachery of Scots, the same William understood from these and other plausible arguments the clear wickedness of the said Comyns and their supporters; and choosing rather to be of lowly position along with the common folk than to be in command when that involved their ruin and heavy loss to the people, he voluntarily gave up his office as guardian not long after the battle of Falkirk beside the river Forth. (c.28 - c.34, l.67)

Book XII

More on William Wallace

Though all the Scottish nobles (including John the Red Comyn the younger of Badenoch, the guardian) submitted to Edward I in the spring of 1304, so that the English could plan a permanent basis for their government of Scotland, Wallace refused to submit. Bower offers here an analysis of his motivation, again perhaps based on oral tradition, though now elaborated with a biblical parallel (from Maccabees). His infamous capture on 3 August 1305 was followed by his speedy trial and execution in London on 23 August (Bower's final reflection on his untimely death introduces rather feebly the same quotation that he had used for King Alexander's death in 1286.)

In [1304] also, after the whole community of Scotland had submitted to the king, John Comyn, then chief guardian, and all the magnates (except the noble William Wallace and his followers) one by one in succession submitted to him, handing over all their castles and towns except Stirling Castle and its keeper. For the noble William was afraid of the treachery of his countrymen. Some of them envied him for his uprightness, others were seduced by the promises of the English, and others with tortuous machinations and infinite care prepared traps for him, hoping thereby for the favour of the king of England. In addition persuasive arguments were offered to him by his immediate close friends that he like the others should obey the king of the English, so that they might thus obtain peace. Besides, others were sent by the king himself to persuade him to do this, promising him on the same king's behalf earldoms and wide possessions in England or in Scotland, to be chosen by himself and held by his successors for ever. He despised all these approaches, and speaking for the liberty of his people like a second Mattathias he is reported to have answered: 'Scotland, desolate as you are, you believe too much in false words and are too unwary of woes to come! If you think like me, you would not readily place your neck under a foreign yoke. When I was growing up', he said, 'I learned from a priest who was my uncle to set this one proverb above all worldly possessions, and I have carried it in my heart:

I tell you the truth, freedom is the finest of things;
never live under a servile yoke, my son.

And that is why I tell you briefly that [even] if all Scots obey the king of England so that each one abandons his liberty, I and my companions who wish to be associated with me in this matter shall stand up for the liberty of the kingdom. And (may God be favourable to us!) we others shall obey no one but the king [of Scots] or his lieutenant.'

In [1305] the noble William Wallace, suspecting no evil, was deceitfully and treacherously captured by Sir John de Menteith at Glasgow. He was handed over to the king of England and dismembered at London, and his limbs were hung up on towers in different places in England and Scotland to dishonour the Scots. By this that tyrant thought to destroy the fame of the noble William for ever, since in the eyes of the foolish his life seemed to be ended with such a contemptible death. But such a death does not count against him, for it has been written:

The sudden death of a just man after a good life
does not lessen his merits if he dies thus.
(c.3, ll.24-54; c.8, ll.1-11)

Stirrings of Bruce

Bower includes here Fordun's introduction of Robert de Bruce as the saviour of the Scottish nation from 1304 onwards. He uses the same biblical parallel as Bower himself was to use in relation to Wallace.

After the king's departure the English nation was dominant in every part of the kingdom of Scotland, and cruelly afflicted the Scots in a great many different ways under a dire yoke of bondage with insults, wounds and killings. God in his mercy took pity on the miseries and continuous complaints and griefs of the Scots, and in the usual manner of his fatherly kindness raised up for them a saviour and champion, that is one of their fellow-countrymen called Robert de Bruce, who saw them lying in a pool of misery and utterly lacking any hope of help or salvation. He was moved inwardly with heartfelt sorrow, and like a second Maccabeus adopting forceful measures in order to free his fellow-countrymen, he endured innumerable and unbearable burdens and toils of the heat of the day, cold and hunger by land and sea. He happily faced up to plots and weariness, hunger and dangers arising not only from enemies, but also from false fellow-countrymen. (c.4, ll.24-36)

Bruce and Comyn

Robert de Bruce had mde his peace with Edward I in 1302, and succeeded to his father's estates in Scotland and England in April 1304. John the Red Comyn inherited his father's estates in Badenoch and elsewhere c.1303, and was thereafter the head of the senior branch of the Comyn family. Both had in the past served as guardians of the Scottish kingdom for the exiled King John: both had now made their peace with the English king instead. Bower provides more than one version of the story of how these two men were at first allies, but then fell out to such an extent that Bruce found it necessary to kill Comyn in February 1306. In this version Comyn is the first to suggest rebellion against English rule to their mutual advantage, while Bruce is pictured as having moral claims with justice on his side. Comyn, however, supposedly let his fellow-plotter down by revealing the plot to Edward, so that Bruce was forced into killing him. Thus ran the propaganda in justification of Bruce's actions, which with varying details was inherited by Bower 150 years later. Much of what happened is in fact obscure. Edward certainly did not hold a parliament at the time stated here by Bower. Furthermore there is no evidence that he ever left Scotland to explain himself to the English king—so that his supposed flight back to Scotland on a horse that left reversed footmarks in the snow is a imaginative literary borrowing from classical sources. There is no doubt that Bruce killed Comyn (or had him killed); but the reasons for this drastic action that was widely condemned at the time, and the true story of how it came about, are now irrecoverable.

I have found elsewhere that John the Red Comyn was the first to persuade the said Robert Bruce to assume royal power, pitifully lamenting thus: 'See how these English kill our people without pretext and occupy our kingdom without reason! Take comfort therefore and be strong, consult your friends and take up arms, and when you have yielded your possessions to me, you will gain the crown with my help. Otherwise let all my lands be yours, exert yourself and rise up supporting me, so that I may rule, and you will be second to me in the kingdom, and everything will be done with your agreement.' Attracted by these hesitant words, the lord de Bruce decided to offer agreement to one or other of his proposals, and said to him: 'I thank you, kinsman, for your conciliatory offer, and so long as you match your actions to your words I shall do as you urge. The burden of ruling will be a help to me, since I know that I shall have justice [on my side] for this task, and, as they say, justice usually makes the weak strong. I shall reckon my justice to be the kind under which with the help of the grace of God nothing that belongs to someone else will be claimed, and each will be given his own, and I shall assuredly disregard my own interest in order to maintain fairness for all.' When these matters were agreed with the safeguard of oaths on either side, indentures were written the same night and guaranteed by the seals of each of them.

A few days later Sir John Comyn went and revealed the agreement to the king of England. As evidence he gave the indenture to the king. Very much disturbed by this, the king called a parliament to which Robert Bruce was summoned along with the other leading men, with no thought in his mind of Comyn's treachery. When Sir Robert Bruce appeared, the king handed him the indenture sealed with his seal, asking if he himself recognized the indenture and if he had attached his seal to it. Robert responded: 'I ask for a respite until tomorrow to allow me to consider this indenture. Tomorrow I will produce it intact at a full meeting of parliament, and in earnest of this I pledge all the lands which I hold from you.' The king believed himself to be safe in this matter, until on the following day he realized that he had been deceived. Then a cry was raised because the traitor had escaped in this way; and many were astonished when it was discovered that some tracks of horses in the snow led to the stable, but none led away from it.

As I have found it written, Sir Robert Bruce travelled with such haste that he reached Lochmaben on the seventh day after starting out from London. At Lochmaben he found his brother Edward, who was greatly surprised at his arrival, as sudden as it was secret. Robert told him how treacherously he had been accused before the king of England, and how in the Lord's name he escaped from his clutches.

On the same day before his arrival at Lochmaben, when the said Robert was approaching the neighbourhood of the Borders, he met a man on foot. Seeing him from a distance, he suspected both from his gait and from his dress that he was a Scot. Seizing this man as he turned away, he asked him where he was going to and where he was coming from. When he gave one excuse after another for his sins, Robert's own attendants on his orders investigated the secrets of this messenger whom they had come across. Missive letters were at once discovered with the seal of the said John the Red Comyn, addressed to the king of England, concerning the secure confinement or detention of Robert himself or his speedy execution in view of the very serious and dangerous circumstances. These letters were removed, the messenger beheaded, and God greatly praised for guiding this journey.

At that time Sir John the Red Comyn was staying at Dumfries. Bruce too hurried there to pay him back in a way that was fitting for his offence. Robert came upon John in the choir of the friars of Dumfries in front of the high altar. After an animated greeting and an exchange of remarks for a time on lesser topics, the missive letters of the same John were produced and the same John was attacked for his betrayal and breach of faith. But soon the reply was given: 'You lie!' A fatal blow was dealt in the same church on this slanderer; and on being wounded by the said Sir Robert, John was carried behind the altar by the friars. When this happened, Robert Bruce, like a man beyond endurance and beside himself, made for his horses at the entrance to the cemetery. His kinsman Sir James de Lindsay [and Sir Roger] de Kirkpatrick ran up to help him as had been arranged at Lochmaben; and as they attended Robert, faint and beside himself as it were, they asked him how it had gone with him. 'Badly,' he said, 'for I think I have killed John the Red Comyn.' 'Should so vital an assumption be left in doubt?' said James de Lindsay. And Lindsay himself, entering the vestry with Kirkpatrick, asked if Comyn might live. At once the reply came from Comyn himself: 'I can if I have a doctor.' A second wound was dealt [him] by these questioners, when the knight Sir Robert Comyn also fell wounded in the defence of his kinsman Sir John Comyn and along with him. And so on 10 February 1305 they were removed from this life, and Edward king of England, it is believed, was cheated of his desire both marvellously and wonderfully.

Next night when the corpse had been placed on a bier and the friars of the convent gathered on either side of the choir were repeating the psalter and prayers for the dead, the unreality of sleep had crept over all the friars shortly before daybreak except for a certain old retired father, more painstakingly vigilant than the rest, who as he devoutly recited the general absolution of souls suddenly heard a voice like that of a crying child shouting out in piercing tones: 'How long, Lord, will you put off your vengeance?' At once he heard the answer from another in a remarkable unknown voice: 'Wait patiently for what you seek, and on the fifty-second anniversary of this day you will achieve your aim.' (c.6, l.30 - c.7, l.56)

Bruce's inauguration and desperate deeds

Bruce secured a ceremony of inauguration as king of Scotland at Scone near Perth on 25 March 1306, six weeks after the murder of Comyn. (Bower is anachronistic to call it a 'coronation', which was not the term used at the time; and since King Edward had in 1296 removed the 'Stone of Scone' to England, it is unclear what 'royal seat' was used on this occasion.) Bower copies Fordun's anecdotal rather than chronological account of the king's hardships dating from the 1360s, and opts out of a detailed study of events in the following years because of the availability since the 1370s of John Barbour's vernacular poem on The Bruce, *which he assumes to be familiar to readers of his own day (i.e. the 1440s).*

1306. When a few days had passed after the death of Sir John the Red Comyn, the same Robert Bruce, then earl of Carrick, hastened to Scone, taking with him as many as he could, and on 27 March, sitting on the royal seat, he was crowned in the fashion in which the kings of Scotland were customarily distinguished. Hence:

> In the thirteen hundred and sixth year
> when Robert Bruce was discovered to be of royal stock
> he assumed at Scone the diadem of the kingdom of Scotland.
> This took place on the sixth day before the Kalends of April.

It was indeed a mighty undertaking that the king began, taking unbearable burdens upon his shoulders, for not only did he raise his hand against the mighty king of England and all his confederates and flatterers, but he also devoted himself to a struggle against one and all in the kingdom of Scotland, with the exception of a very few well-disposed to him, who in comparison with the multitude of the other side were like a drop of water reckoned against the waves of the sea, or a single grain of any seed against a great number of grains of the sand. No person now living can, I think, recall or is capable of relating his misfortunes, flights and dangers, afflictions and irritations, his hunger and thirst, the watches and fasts, scanty clothing and chills, ambushes and exiles, the captures, imprisonments, killings and ruinations affecting kinsmen and those even more dear to him, which he suffered everywhere when defeated and a fugitive at the beginning of his war.

Furthermore, amid so many adversities and innumerable difficulties which he endured with a cheerful and indomitable spirit, whoever has learned to recount his individual conflicts and particular triumphs—the victories and battles, in which with the help of the Lord, by his own strength and his energetic valour as a man, he forced his way through the ranks of the enemy without fear, now powerfully laying them low, now powerfully turning them aside as he avoided the penalty of death—he will find, I think, that he will judge none in the regions of the world to be his equals in his own times in the art of fighting and in physical strength. On that account I now defer writing about his individual deeds, because they would occupy no small number of pages, and because, although they are undoubtedly true, the places and dates where and when they happened and were accomplished are known to few nowadays, and also because Master John Barbour archdeacon of Aberdeen has made the case adequately in our mother tongue about his several deeds with eloquence and brilliance, and with elegance too. And so I would consider it a waste of time to commend his deeds of this kind to the leaders of the present day. (c.9, ll.1-42)

Reflections on Bruce's hardships

Bower tells the heroic tale of King Robert's hardships when things were not going well for him. Then comes the story of his gradual success. Christina of the Isles was a major heiress in the West Highlands, with whom he had family connections through marriage. He returned to his Ayrshire earldom of Carrick about February 1307, and then made progress in the north, where he attracted enough support to capture castles and confront Comyn forces at Slioch near Huntly in Aberdeenshire. Bower typically takes the chance to introduce scholastic reflections on the merits of Bruce's cautious approach (citing the pseudo-Seneca i.e. the sixth-century writer Martin of Braga).

Now it happened that soon after this the said king was separated from his men, suffered endless misfortunes, and was shattered by innumerable dangers. Sometimes with three companions, sometimes with two, but in most cases on his own, he remained deprived of all human aid. Once he spent a whole fortnight without the nourishment of any food apart from raw herbs and water; once he went barefoot, his shoes worn away by age. Once he was left alone in the islands; once he fled alone from his enemies; at another time, despised by his servants, he remained in utter desolation. He was driven out and deserted by his friends; and the English ordered an enquiry to be made about him through the churches as if he was some abandoned or stolen object. And thus to everyone both close to him and distant he became an object of contempt, of gossip and of derision.

That is why afterwards in the days of his prosperity he used to speak like this to those of his household:

> If I was not moved by [love for] the old freedom of the Scots,
> I would not suffer so many evils even to rule the world.

When the king had endured these adversities alone for about a year, finally at the inspiration of God, aided by the assistance and power of a certain woman of noble rank, Christina of the Isles, who was well-disposed to him, after many and various roundabout journeys and innumerable toils, pains and afflictions he returned to [his] earldom of Carrick. When he arrived there, he at once gained possession of one of his castles, killed the inhabitants, destroyed the castle and divided the arms and other spoils among his men. Delighted therefore at such beginnings, more satisfactory than he had been used to after his long-lasting misfortunes, he united his men who had been scattered far and wide, and crossing the mountains with their united forces he reached Inverness, stormed the castle there by main force, and after the garrison had been killed he razed it to the ground. In the same way throughout he dealt with all the castles and the rest of the small forts set up in the northern districts and with their inhabitants, until he reached Slioch with his army.

From this, reader, you will be able to form the view that the lord king showed foresight and wisdom in that he patiently waited for the time of his visitation. He could not be counted among those two kinds of men who are described as 'impaciens', namely the impetuous and the slothful. For it is not wisdom, but folly, that leads the headstrong, rash and impetuous. For Seneca says that there are two things most opposed to good counsel—haste, of course, and anger. And on that account the angry and impetuous will never give wise counsel to someone who needs it, for wisdom needs deliberation and calm. And so Seneca says in his *Four Virtues*: 'It is fitting for the prudent man to weigh up advice and not slide swiftly towards false counsels with easy credulity.' And so wisdom does not guide such men but will follow them eventually and too late. Secondly wisdom does not guide the slothful, since they are careless in foreseeing and foreordaining in advance, and so when the time comes, it will be too late. This is why the same writer says: 'If you desire to be prudent, turn your attention to the future, and put before your mind everything which can happen. Let nothing be unexpected to you, but look only at what lies before you, for the man who is prudent holds his tongue. I do not think this happens because he has doubts, but because he is waiting expectantly, not because he is suspicious, but because he is taking precautions.' The king foresaw this in his mind and carried it out in his actions. (c.11, ll.43-59; c.12, ll.22-60)

The ups and downs of worldly honour

Bower considers the death of King Edward I in 1307, whom he considers to have been cast down by the Lord when apparently riding high. He introduces two reflections on the falsity and fickleness of worldly honour. From James of Vitry comes a moral tale in which worldly honour is elaborately compared to a horse, which can be manipulated to the detriment of its rider; and from Boethius come thoughts about the cyclical ups and downs of the wheel of Fortune. So did battles between the English and the Scots bring alternating fortune (Dunbar 1296; Stirling Bridge 1297; Falkirk 1298; Roslin 1303).

When this King Edward was held in honour, he did not understand [his situation], for the grandeur of honour blinded him and led him on until he fell into a trap. For worldly honour is like a horse which raises a man up from the ground and carries him agreeably, because it is delightful for a man to be honoured by men's attentions, by their flatteries, bowings, genuflections and prostrations, and to be addressed as 'Rabbi', 'Master', and 'Sir'. But all men who enjoy honour should beware that this horse of theirs is very treacherous.

A tale is told of an actor who had a small horse on which he used to ride, and with which he would perform in front of men in the hall. And among other tricks which he had taught the horse, he trained it to obey him and bend down whenever he said to him 'Let us kneel', and to get up whenever he said 'Rise'. It happened that this entertainer, on coming to a feast given by a certain lord, put his horse in the stable along with the horses of other guests. Now when the men had eaten, the actor was busy in the hall with his performance. Meanwhile a certain man-at-arms came to the stable and, seeing the actor's sleek round horse, left his own lean mule there, mounted the entertainer's horse and departed. Soon afterwards the actor became aware of what had happened. Leaving everyone behind he ran and followed the man-at-arms, who, on realizing that the actor had almost reached him, tried to cross a river which a man on foot could not cross. When therefore the actor saw that he was in danger of losing his horse, he shouted out loudly to it in midstream, saying 'Let us kneel'. On hearing its master's voice the horse at once knelt and drowned the man-at-arms in the water, shook itself and returned to its master. Figuratively speaking this entertainer who plays and mocks and deceives men is the world. The horse which is his main plaything is temporal honour, hence the saying: 'A horse is a deceptive guide to salvation.' The man-at-arms who robbed him is anyone at all who is ambitious for honours, like King [Edward] who could not be content with England, Wales and Ireland, but had to go hunting for honour from Scotland as well. Such a man therefore should be on his guard, because whenever the world chooses (at the instigation of the Lord), it will say 'Let us kneel' to him who it thinks is on top of things and riding agreeably and quite safely, and will at once deprive him of the honour he has gained.

Hence Boethius speaking as Fortune to men who are impatient when they are deprived of honours and dignities, puts it like this in the second book of his *De Consolatione*, the [second] paragraph: 'This is our power, this is the game which we play. We turn the wheel with all speed, we take pleasure in changing the lowest for the highest and the highest for the lowest. Climb up if you want, but on condition that you do not think it an injury to climb down when the pattern of my game requires it.' For it is written: 'The Lord will destroy the thrones of proud princes.'

This king conquered the Welsh and subdued more or less all [of that country] by guile; but he never governed it peacefully. In his time dreadful battles took place, namely at Dunbar [which went] against the Scots, at

Stirling Bridge against the English, at Falkirk against the Scots, and at Roslin against the English. (c.15)

The capture of Perth

Bower dramatises the siege and capture of Perth by King Robert in January 1312 by introducing verses of unknown origin. They may have been influenced by literary parallels, but give the impression of containing sound information. William Olifard had been the defender of Stirling Castle for King John against Edward I 1300-1306; but after release from prison in England he had from 1311 been the commander of the English garrison in the town of Perth. Robert was still fighting a civil war.

[St] John's town for many years was given the name Berta.
It is [now] called Perth because it is ruined and conquered.
The excavated dampness of three moats surrounds it
on three sides; it fortifies its gates and strikes down those who attack the moats.
With them as a barrier and the arrow-barbs as a weapon, as long as they could
the bitter and very arrogant men of this city then rejected
the king's demands for money which he requested without the backing of law.
Then Fate which is easily moved and never stable gratuitously abandoned [them]
and showed favour to Robert, a man candid in his honesty,
whose piety as a king was the same whether in a lowly or an exalted position.
The king asked his followers to cut down some wood, to shape the logs,
to bring the shaped timber when it was ready; and he encouraged them as they brought it:
'Now let us choose the time of darkness and concealment,'
he said, 'and now make for the gateways of the town.'
On this advice from their confident prince, King Robert,
his people took ladders and portable bridges. And see! suddenly
they crossed over the deep waters and muddy ditches of the town.
The king and his followers soon brought the heavy timber,
lifted it up and crossed over to defeat the citizens.
One ladder fell down, at which the company rushed back full of the omen.

The king, exerting his sure strength anew, moved forward, if only to carry ladders;
his people again made for the gateways across the bridges.
Afterwards Robert broke the deadly door-bars
and the way was opened for the company by the brave prince.
The columns also passed over the streams by bridges;
then as they entered, they thundered on, raising their standards;
and they took prisoner those who were holding and guarding the gates.
Thus were overcome, plundered and utterly destroyed throughout the town
those who used to do the overcoming and plundering.
Now were overcome, now plundered throughout that town
those who rejected terms while they could [have accepted them].
Hence they deserved and received destruction.
The king asks for money, but the town refused [to pay]; he looks favourably on them, but they are swollen with arrogance;
he profits in silence, they lie prostrate, reduced to nothing.
After cockcrow William Olifard ineptly
lost his honour, his city, his estates during the night;
and on 8 January 1312
the over-confident and wicked citizens
lost a status which they liked to have, because they had ceased to value it.
(c.18, ll.48-97)

The Battle of Bannockburn

Bower offers more than one description of the advance of King Edward II into Scotland with his ambition to crush the Scots that led to his defeat at Bannockburn near Stirling on 23-24 June 1314. Here it is not known how he learned of Edward's lack of widespread consultation that probably explains why some of the English nobles stayed at home. The numbers on the English side have presumably been misunderstood somewhere along the way, though they appear here to go back to a statement by Bernard abbot of Arbroath, whose verses about the battle have the immediacy of the work of an eye-witness. He adopts the literary convention of inventing the speech of a leader before a battle as a device for explaining the motives and attitudes of those concerned. The St Thomas mentioned along with St Andrew is presumably St Thomas Becket of Canterbury, revered in Scotland as the martyred opponent of an overbearing English king, in whose name

Bernard's monastery at Arbroath was dedicated. The supposed remarks of Ingram de Umfraville are modelled on a passage in Herodotus describing the battle of Thermopylae.

So when the king of England was ready along with his forces, he summoned all the hereditary magnates and all his army commanders both from England and those from Scotland who supported the English, and held a private meeting of his council with them on what death that Bruce, the rebel against the king, should suffer, and on how to root out the Scots who opposed him and to remove their memory from the land. And he told them that his intention was to subject the entire Scottish land to his rule for ever. When this statement had been approved by everyone, he summoned his commanders and officers to reckon how many fit men he had for the expedition; and there were counted three hundred and forty thousand cavalry and about as many thousands of foot-soldiers, apart from the baggage train, as Bernard abbot of Arbroath put it into verse at that time:

There came also three hundred thousand cavalry
and about forty thousand foot-soldiers.

So the king of England advanced in pomp with his forces with an abundance of supplies for them. He arranged also for the collection of herds of cattle, and flocks of sheep and of pigs beyond number, corn and barley with portable mills for supplying the army, and wine in large jars and casks. Gold and silver, golden and silver vessels and every kind of precious furnishings he took from the king's treasury. He himself set out with his attendants, his vehicles and waggons, carts and horsemen, slingers and archers, crossbowmen and men-at-arms, with their ingenious pieces of equipment for besieging castles such as petraries and mattocks, trebuchets and mangonels, ladders and engines, pavilions and awnings, slings and cannons, and other engines of war, while trumpets and horns rang out so that every district which they reached became fearful with frightened dread. So like locusts they covered the surface of the entire land until they reached Bannockburn.

After the king of Scotland had had them reconnoitred, he caused pits to be made with sharp stakes fixed in them and covered over so that they would not be noticed; and he advised his men to make confession and hear masses devoutly, and that they should all take communion in the sacrament of the body of Christ, and put their trust in God alone. And as the said Abbot Bernard indicates when he goes on to say:

Then very early in the morning masses were celebrated in due fashion
as their king advised them, saying from the kindness of his heart:

'My lords, my people, who lay great weight on freedom,
for which the kings of Scotland have suffered many trials,
dying for the Lord,
now all of you take note of the many hardships we have undergone
while struggling now certainly for eight years
for our right to the kingdom, for honour and liberty.
We have lost brothers and friends and kinsmen.
Your relatives and friends are captives,
and now prelates are shut up in prison with [other] clergy,
and no order of Mother Church remains safe;
the nobles of the land have passed away in the bloodshed of war.
The armed magnates whom you all see before you
have already had the impudence to order the destruction of us, our kingdom and our people;
and they do not believe that we can offer resistance.
They glory in their waggons and horses; for us
the name of the Lord and victory in war is our hope.
Happy is this day! John the Baptist was born on it;
and St Andrew and Thomas who shed his blood
along with the saints of the Scottish fatherland will fight today
for the honour of the people, with Christ the Lord in the van.
Under this leader you will conquer and make an end to war.
If you weep from the heart for your sins,
our royal power pronounces that all offences
committed against us are remitted
for those who now defend their ancestral kingdom well.'
So he spoke, and the people, stirred up by the king's words,
promised to go into battle readily and wholeheartedly.

At these words, as the hammered horns resounded and the standards of war were spread out in the golden dawn, the venerable father sir Maurice abbot of Inchaffray [later the bishop of Dunblane], who heard the king's confession on that day and celebrated mass for the Scots on a prominent spot, put forward a short and effective statement on freedom and the defence of their right. After he had spoken zealously and with abundant feeling, the army resounded without words with such a joyful murmur that you would have thought they were filled with a sudden and incredible boldness. Bare-footed then and wearing his canonicals, the said abbot went before them bearing a crucifix like a commander, and before the battle was engaged he told them all to kneel and pray to God as suppliants. Seeing this, the English, buoyed up with a baseless light-heartedness, began to shout: 'Look! all those Scots have surrendered to us with trembling hearts.' An older English knight,

Ingram de Umfraville, formed a sounder understanding and replied to them saying: 'You are right that they are surrendering, but to God, not to you. I hope therefore that no greater spirit of enthusiasm is vainly aroused than consideration of the circumstances will require for action.' At this the Scots rose eagerly, attacked their enemies, and victory (as usually happens) fell gloriously to the Scots, who had endured wearisome struggles for the justice of their cause. On the English side two hundred knights were killed, besides the [earl] of Gloucester and innumerable others. On the Scottish side two knights fell, namely William de Vieuxpont and Walter de Ross. (c.22, ll.1-16, 35-110)

James de Douglas and William de Sinclair

King Robert's brother Edward de Bruce took advantage of King Edward's disgrace at Bannockburn to attempt from May 1315 onwards to obtain a kingdom for himself in Ireland. Robert followed to help him for a time in January 1317. Following the same unknown source which Barbour used for The Bruce, *Bower relates episodes of fighting in the Borders, when Sir James de Douglas was the hero who repulsed the invaders, and also reports in some detail on an English maritime expedition that landed at Donibristle in Fife very near his own monastery on Inchcolm. When the sheriff of Fife was too cautious to attack, the bishop of Dunkeld sallied forth in heroic fashion from his manor at Auchtertool near Kirkcaldy and sent the invaders packing. It is stirring stuff.*

Hearing that the king of Scotland had crossed over to Ireland, the king of England thought that he now had a convenient occasion for subjecting the kingdom of Scotland to himself very easily. He gathered various English forces, in command of which he placed strong leaders. Entering Scotland in separate divisions, they were repulsed with very great disgrace by Sir James de Douglas, then the warden of the Marches. When some companies of the English were put to flight and others successfully defeated (though not without a stiff fight), the warden so behaved and defended himself that in three fierce battles he killed with his own hands three noble English captains, namely the Gascon Edmund de Caillau, who was captain of Berwick, and Robert Neville, both of them knights, and another. And so, praise be to God, the kingdom sustained little damage throughout the land that year in the absence of the king of Scotland.

When therefore they heard reports of the worth of the lord of Douglas, the English, no longer thinking it safe to invade by land, gathered a fleet and took to the sea. Steering into the Firth of Forth, they made for land at Donibristle, where they began to cause cruel disturbance to the ordinary people along the coast. But the joy which they won there was very short-lived. The sheriff of Fife came upon them with a troop of five hundred armed men. But when he perceived that the English were raging freely among the country people, he turned the horses round and decided on flight, abandoning altogether those who had been attacked. At the same time William de Sinclair, then bishop of Dunkeld, who was staying at his manor of Auchtertool, heard that the English had landed at Donibristle. He armed himself as quickly as possible, and mounting a fine steed, hurried fearlessly with sixty of his men who were experienced in battle to the place mentioned. He met the sheriff and his force of five hundred right away, and said to him: 'Why do you turn back so hurriedly instead of facing our enemies?' 'Because', said the sheriff, 'the English outnumber us and are much stronger; and we decided that since we cannot fight them we should retreat from them.' 'It would certainly be proper', said the bishop, 'for the lord king to order your gilded spurs to be cut from your heels. Follow me, and we shall take revenge on them in the name of the Lord.' With these words, throwing away his [episcopal] staff, he seized a fearsome lance in his hand and spurred on his horse saying to the sheriff not 'Go in front', but 'Come on behind me'. So everyone followed him as he led the way so manfully; and when they closed with the enemy they quickly gained victory by the worthy words and blows of this renowned bishop. Five hundred and more of the English were killed on the field of battle, besides those who ran too hurriedly to the ships. These men put one of the ships into difficulties with their precipitate numbers, and on attracting other heavy men to join them, they were drowned when it sank. (c.25, ll.11-56)

Edward de Bruce; Celebrations at St Andrews

Bower reflects on the death of Edward de Bruce at Dundalk in Co. Louth in Ireland in October 1318, explaining it in terms of headstrong behaviour on Edward's part. The argument is backed up in typical fashion with biblical and philosophic quotations. 5 July 1318 had seen a national thanksgiving service for the victory at Bannockburn in St Andrews cathedral. This was also the occasion of the solemn dedication of the completed cathedral church, which had been under construction for 160 years; and in honour of the assistance in the battle which the Scots attributed to their national saint, St Andrew, the cathedral community's endowment was significantly increased by the traditional method of appropriating to them the excess revenues of a further four parish churches (Fordoun in Kincardineshire; Dairsie, Abercrombie and Kilgour in Fife).

In the same year on 14 October the battle of Dundalk took place in Ireland, where the noble king of Ireland, Edward brother of Sir Robert the renowned king of Scots, perished and many Scottish nobles along with him. The cause of this war was as follows: this Edward was a man of mighty ambition who was unable to live with his brother the king of Scotland as though that kingdom was not enough for the two of them. Another reason was that he was such a good fighting man and so fortunate in his encounters with the English that the kings and magnates of Ireland chose him to be their king to fight their battles and to drive their English enemies out of Ireland. This he would certainly have done, in men's judgment, if he had not been a little headstrong and impetuous. This was clear on the day of his death: his brother King Robert would have come to him with a great army if he had waited until the next day. In this the opinion of Solomon is proved true, which says that 'a man in a hurry misses the way'. And on that account Gregory says in his *Moralia*: 'Courage is destroyed unless it rests on good judgment, because the more valour sees what it can do, the worse it rushes headlong down if it is not controlled by reason.' In the same year on 5 July the great church of the apostle St Andrew in Scotland was dedicated by sir William de Lamberton, bishop of the same. At this dedication, in order to augment the resources for divine worship, Sir Robert the king, acting in person in the presence of seven bishops, fifteen abbots, and nearly all the nobles of the kingdom, both earls and barons, offered one hundred marks sterling to be paid annually from his treasury in commemoration of the signal victory given to the Scots at Bannockburn by the blessed Andrew, protector of the kingdom. Instead of these hundred marks he afterwards granted in perpetuity to the same church the patronage of the church of Fordoun in the Mearns with all its revenues. The said William bishop of St Andrews ratified this gift and confirmed the canons in full ownership in perpetuity. On the same day and for the same reason the same Bishop William conferred and granted the churches of Dairsie and Abercrombie to the same canons in full ownership. Similarly on the same day and for the same reason Duncan earl of Fife with the consent of the king and the confirmation of the bishop conferred the church of Kilgour on them in full ownership. (c.37, ll.5-42)

Book XIII

Tit for tat 1322

By 1322 the Scots under King Robert were in a position to mount two major raiding expeditions into Northern England in July and October, reaching as far as Stainmore (on the Westmorland/Yorkshire border) and mid-Lancashire on the first occasion, and York on the second. In between these incursions Edward II came in person on an expedition in August that reached Edinburgh, though he then had to retire swiftly because of lack of supplies. As a Haddington native Bower includes an anecdote from nearby Tranent, and the English destruction at the famous monasteries of Holyrood, Melrose and Dryburgh is emphasized. The Scottish victory against Edward on 14 October at Byland (near Rievaulx Abbey in North Yorkshire) confirmed their dominant superiority.

In 1322 King Robert entered England on 1 July with a powerful force, laying it waste for the greater part down to Stainmore along with the county of Lancaster. After his return Edward king of England on 12 August entered Scotland with a great army of cavalry and infantry and an ample fleet of ships, and came to the town of Edinburgh in search of a quarrel and fight with the said king of Scotland. But the king of Scotland sensibly avoided such an engagement for the time being, and cunningly moved away from the path of Edward's army all the cattle and other foodstuffs which they might have consumed. As starvation loomed after fifteen days, because bad weather made it impossible for the English to obtain what they needed from their ships, Edward returned home in confusion. On account of their transport difficulties they did not find more than one lame steer to eat, which could not be driven away along with the rest of the cattle, and in its acquisition they lost a knight and his men. In this regard a certain English knight (namely the earl of Warenne) said that the beef was too dear. Then at the Tranent coalmines it also happened that a certain lame serf coalminer with a hooked stick drew a knight towards him, who by paying a large ransom relieved the serf's poverty. Nevertheless as the English returned home the monasteries of Holyrood at Edinburgh and Melrose were despoiled and looted, reduced to the point of utter desolation. For in that monastery at Melrose sir William Peebles the prior of that monastery, and one monk who was infirm, and two blind lay brothers were killed by the same Englishmen in their dormitory, and many monks were fatally wounded. The Body of Christ was flung on to the high altar when the silver pyx in which it was kept was stolen. The monastery of Dryburgh was entirely destroyed by fire and reduced to ashes. And the fiery flame consumed very many other holy places as a result of the said king's violence, which with God as the avenger did not turn out auspiciously for them.

On 1 October of the same year King Robert entered England with hostile intent, and laid it utterly waste as far as York, after despoiling monasteries and putting very many towns and villages to the torch. When Edward II king of England met him at Byland with a large force, made up both of mercenaries brought at a price from France and many other places and of natives of that kingdom, he was routed at the aforesaid place in the middle of his kingdom, not without great slaughter among his men and amid considerable confusion. Among those of his army who fled to the monastery at Rievaulx John of Brittany, Henry de Sully and not a few other nobles were made prisoner there, and later ransomed for very large sums of money. And so the king of Scotland and his men returned home amid joy and honour, happy to have obtained a great victory. (c.4, ll.13-56)

Death of Robert I

In noting King Robert's death at Cardross (on the west bank of the river Leven opposite Dumbarton), Bower offers a summing up of this man's career with literary quotations (the second of which may have been taken from the Gesta Romanorum*). The mention of 'a pretended peace' looks forward to the renewed efforts of the English in the 1330s to displace the Bruce dynasty in Scotland by the Balliol dynasty again, fearful as they were of possible Scottish intervention in Wales as well as Ireland.*

On 7 June 1329 Robert de Bruce the wholly invincible king of Scots of pious memory died at Cardross in the twenty-fourth year of his reign. He was a prince who was outstanding in vigorous action of every sort, distinguished for the honesty of his dealings, who surpassed others of his subjects in boldness and shrewdness, and in defending his kingdom in manly fashion from the fear of enemies on every side, especially the English, whom in his time he made subject and subdued, driving them far from the borders of his kingdom. For this man vanquished the king and people of England with such courage and forcefulness that they established a pretended peace with him only out of fear for their other kingdoms. But as the poet suggests:

When the wolf was sick, he then wanted to be a monk;
but when he recovered, he wanted to be as before.

On the same theme:

While I was weary, I inclined towards love of religion;
now that I am free of weariness, I have no memory of this love.

The king was buried in the monastery at Dunfermline in the middle of the choir with due honour. (c.13, ll.45-64)

The Guardian Thomas Randolph

The following largely undatable stories about the vigorous rule of Thomas Randolph earl of Moray as guardian of the kingdom for the young King David II 1329-32 under arrangements made by King Robert in 1318 have perhaps been taken from a lost Life *of Randolph. Bower adds a parallel French case from the time of a bishop of Poitiers in France who was in office c.1235-57. An account of the guardian's justice at Eilean Donan in Wester Ross leads to general reflections on the inadequacies of justice in the Scotland of Bower's own day, backed up by quotations from the twelfth-century writer Peter of Blois and a traditional fable about a lion, an ass and a wolf. The story of Randolph's death on 20 July 1332 at Musselburgh near Edinburgh as a result of poisoning by an English friar at Wemyss in Fife may have some basis in fact, though it must be largely fanciful. King Edward III was certainly nowhere near Cockburnspath in Berwickshire in the summer of 1332. Barbour in* The Bruce *also believed the story about the nature of the guardian's mortal illness; but the tale of Randolph's bluff in the face of an English herald was probably borrowed from some unidentified literary parallel.*

As we have said already, once the magnificent King Robert was dead and buried, as had previously been arranged in a tailzie, the responsibility for the government of the kingdom fell on Sir Thomas Randolph earl of Moray, who was regarded as guardian of Scotland for this purpose; and he ruled the kingdom and executed justice so devotedly and even-handedly that we do not read of anyone surpassing him in this direction from the first establishment of the law. For he issued a law that [if] any rider on a journey has occasion to dismount and turn aside to an inn or elsewhere, or to perform any kind of task, he may attach his bridle to his saddle; and if it happens that the bridle is stolen, the sheriff of the shire is to pay the price to the rider, and at the next audit at the royal exchequer the sheriff is either to be given an allowance for this payment with priority over other items, or at any rate to be repaid. Similarly among other praiseworthy statutes which would benefit the country it was laid down that any husbandman or peasant might safely leave out the ploughshare with his plough; but if it happens to be stolen, the sheriff is to pay the price, and be repaid as above. On hearing this a certain country peasant who was greedy for gain stole his own ploughshare, which he hid in the nearest peat-bog, while bringing his complaint before the sheriff about the theft of his plough. The sheriff quickly paid two shillings to the peasant, then convened his court and conducted a very thorough enquiry into the theft. The sheriff soon learned the truth; the peasant was arrested for theft, and once he had been convicted and had confessed, he met his death by hanging. And so while he was thirsty for money, he obtained the noose.

Soon afterwards while he was on tour in Galloway as justiciar holding court in the town of Wigtown, a man came to Randolph reporting in a whisper that he was then a fugitive from a band of criminals whose lights were shining in a nearby wood, and who (as he indicated by certain signs) were lying in wait to kill him and others of the king's subjects on the road. Randolph at once quietly sent a strong detachment of armed man to make all those murderers captive while they were off their guard, and then to bring them to the guardian of Scotland for judgment. When they had been accused before an assize, they were all found guilty, and therefore condemned to death. Subsequently he continued his justiciar's tour to Inverness, where it was brought before the judge that in a case in a court of justice a man had been found to have recently returned from the Roman court, who had been arrested for killing a priest, and accused of spilling the blood of one of the king's subjects. Although it was sufficiently proved that he had been absolved for his sin, nevertheless he ought to be punished for his offence, and with all the heavier a penalty in that he had not been afraid to lay sacrilegious hands on one of the Lord's anointed. For this reason a priest-murderer is killed, and his blood is upon his own head, and the justice of a just judge is honoured on both sides.

And it is not surprising if a secular judge punishes the killing of a priest, since even an ecclesiastical judge seeks restitution for this offence. For we read that in the diocese of Poitiers a certain knight killed a priest, and then at once sought absolution from his ordinary, Bishop John de Melun. But knowing that a case of this kind was reserved to the Apostolic Lord, the bishop sent the man to the Roman court, where he sought absolution. On returning he brought to the bishop a letter notifying that he had been absolved, but that he was not at peace until the bishop had imposed a salutary penance on him. He allowed the man to die in prison, so bearing witness before God and men that he had imposed a salutary penance on the man for his action.

While on this journey he sent his official coroner on ahead to Eilean Donan with an armed force to arrest lawbreakers in accordance with enrolled indictments. This official pursued fifty of them; and because they resisted arrest, they were slaughtered by their pursuers; and the walls were adorned with their heads fixed to poles and sticks before the judge's arrival at Eilean Donan, which presented a grim spectacle for onlookers. By pressing on with similar acts of justice, this justiciar was not influenced by anyone's prayers, nor corrupted by gifts, nor even was he led astray by fear, hatred or affection to deviate from the truth. Nowadays modern judges do not act in this way, when they delay or overturn a judgment out of greed, and do not conclude business between parties that has come to trial until the purses of the litigants have been emptied. [Peter of] Blois speaks of this in a letter: 'The role of officials today is to upset the laws, to stir up lawsuits, to annul agreements, to devise delays, to suppress the truth, to encourage falsehood, to follow profit, to sell justice, to attend closely to exacting money, to practise cunning.' Thus without doubt is justice done today, just as it is visualized in poetry that a lion once held a court of the beasts, and everybody was bound to confess his faults before the lion. An ass spoke: 'Sir,' he said, 'I was following sometimes a waggon full of hay, and when a handful of hay had fallen from the waggon, I took it and ate it.' The lion said to him: 'You have gone badly astray, and acted against the law and loyalty. For you ought to have made restitution to the man who has had a loss; for anything which you have found and have not returned you have stolen.' Therefore by order of the lion the ass was beaten to death. A wolf approached and said: 'Sir, I have sometimes prowled round flocks of sheep and herds of cattle, and sometimes I have snatched a tender lamb by the throat, and sometimes a plump calf when I could reach it, sometimes a sheep, sometimes a kid.' Because the wolf had previously been in the habit of sending him presents from the fattest of these, the lion said to him: 'My dear kinsman, give up weighing such matters; you have too stringent a conscience; it is natural for you to act in this way, and no one who acts as nature dictates is a sinner.' Thus by a false judge the rapacious wolf was vindicated and the blameless ass was beaten. This is to say that Barabbas the robber was set free, while the innocent Christ was crucified.

While the said earl of Moray was alive as guardian of Scotland amid such tranquility and peace, he ruled the kingdom for four years both before and after the king's death, so that from then until now no one can recall it being governed more successfully. For he boosted the church and preserved its liberty, he delighted the nobles and pleased the common folk, and effectively humbled the insolent pride of the English. On this account, stirred by stings of jealousy, they arranged for a certain English friar to poison him as he was celebrating a feast in his hall at Wemyss. He lived for a little while after this, and died at Musselburgh on 13 August. This false friar, thinking that he had done a service that was pleasing to the king, gladly reported to him that the guardian of Scotland was waiting at the gateway of death because, he said, even if his belly had been made of iron or bronze, he would by necessity have had to break wind. Absolutely delighted, the enemy gathered an army together to invade the kingdom with a view to subjecting it to them in a short time. Once reports of this had grown, it came to the guardian's ears that the English were speeding up this expedition. Although the guardian was weak almost to death, and amazingly swollen by the poison, he did not for this reason lose the audacity which was based on his upright character; rather he collected some fighting men with all speed, and came to Cockburnspath, where he pitched camp, apparently oblivious of his illness, yet carried on a litter. When the enemy heard this they were astonished beyond belief; and a herald was sent by the king of England to make an assessment of the situation. When the guardian heard that he had arrived, he had himself placed at the door of his tent on an appropriate chair decked with golden coverings. Arrayed in festive garb himself, and surrounded by a shrewd crowd of brave men, he ordered the herald to be presented to his gaze. On bended knee he greeted the guardian, who was making a pretence of a cheerful face as best he could, flushed as he was from the strength of the poisoned drink. After a short conversation the guardian said to him: 'Without doubt we reckon that you have come to reconnoitre our army. All right; but you should return to the king your lord, who, we understand, is now nearby with a powerful force, and explain [to him] on our behalf that tomorrow we shall be ready to meet him somewhere between us, so that in this way at all events we may put an end to our old contest.' Saying this, he had the the herald removed, sending to him all the accoutrements with which he had been clothed as he sat on his chair. The herald gratefully accepted these precious doublets worth much gold; and at once hurried to his king saying: 'The guardian has said such and such; I do not recall ever having seen a more vigorous knight than him, nor in my judgment a more powerful one.' On hearing this the king was agitated, and immediately ordered that the friar be sought; but he from then on was never seen again. The king for his part turned back to England in disgrace. Meanwhile the guardian became extremely ill. Hearing that the king of England and his men had gone away back, he immediately had himself conveyed towards the royal town of Edinburgh; but after arriving at Musselburgh he received the sacraments of salvation, and was happy to die in the Lord on the date mentioned above. He left Scotland plunged into grief, and was buried at Dunfermline in 1332 [before the altar in the Lady Chapel]. (c.17 - c.18, l.37, and ll.62-114)

James de Douglas and King Robert's heart

Bower includes this romantic, but factual, tale of King Robert's commission to James de Douglas to take his heart for burial at Jerusalem. The Scottish party travelled via Spain, and Douglas died with the honoured status of a Crusader while helping the king of Castile to fight the Moslem Moors near Cordova—a death which Bower regards as fortunate. It was Barbour in The Bruce *who recorded the return of Bruce's heart to Scotland for burial at Melrose Abbey.*

Accordingly, as the renowned king was approaching his last, he arranged for the disposal of his property; and among other things he bequeathed his heart to be sent to Jerusalem and buried at the Holy Sepulchre. He chose James de Douglas to carry it, the most loyal champion in all his wars.

In 1330 on 26 August the king of Spain and the noble James de Douglas, who was carrying King Robert's heart, fought against a sultan and his countless Saracens, after armies from various parts of the world had gathered together to aid the Holy Land. At length they had the good fortune to defeat the Saracens and put them to flight; and after first killing many of them and distributing their spoils, the said king and his army returned from the battle unharmed. But alas! Sir James de Douglas kept with him very few men of his own force. And this was not unobserved by another sultan who was hiding in ambush. He came out of his hiding place with his men and offered the challenge of battle. Recognizing his force and standards from afar, the said James, fearless as he was, immediately and eagerly attacked them with his own [tiny] force. After many Saracens had been killed, James himself had the good fortune to end his last day with his men there as a martyr for Christ. With him the knights Sir William de Sinclair and Robert Logan, and many other nobles of Scottish birth laid down their lives. This noble James was in his day a powerful hammerman of the English, on whom the Lord conferred such grace during his life that he triumphed over the English everywhere. (c.19, ll.1-5; c.20, ll.1-19)

The perfidious English

Bower's vituperative denunciation of the double-dealing of Edward III and the generally deceitful character of the English pours out in his reflections on how they abandoned the guarantees of Scottish independence agreed by the treaty of Edinburgh of 1328 and were supporting Edward de Balliol as a pretender to the Scottish throne—albeit c.1332 he was not yet very successful. It is a fearsome indictment, seemingly as much a comment on his own day as on the previous century.

When Edward de Windsor king of England heard of the misfortune of Edward de Balliol who had approached him for help, entirely unconcerned with his own salvation, this breaker of oaths and violator of his own pledge disregarded the promise of eternal peace which had been confirmed by seals and letters, and promised speedy help. After breaking the bonds of peace and alliance, he assembled from all sides a very large army against his brother-in-law King David and his subjects, with the whole force of Wales, Gascony and England together with Scots who supported Edward de Balliol, of whom there were many. Thus very often it appears a great marvel to the Scots that this English nation, which is capable of quite angelic things when it is so inclined, knows how to arrange peace with them, pretend friendship, conceal wrongs, and continue the deception, that is as long as they expect not to be able to resist the will of the Scots. Indeed when they are being chastised for a while by the rod of righteousness, the rod [of the brave men] of the kingdom of Scotland, then in yielding they know very well how to pretend that they are friends, although in their hearts they are enemies; they have been reconciled with words on the outside, but they are raging with hatred on the inside. They know how to twist their faces away from their intentions, their words from their feelings, their language from their minds, and their discourse from their meaning. And often they mislead the Scots, whom on the outside they praise in a pleasing way, with contrasting scorn on the inside. In public they commend them with innocent faces, inside they jab with a scorpion's sting; in public they send down sweet showers of flattery, but inside they are devising storms of desolation. Hence the saying:

An Englishman is an angel whom no one can believe;
when he greets you, beware of him as of an enemy.

Just as if you want to hold an eel or a small murena close in your hands, the stronger you press, the more quickly it slips away, so is it with the English as it is with eels.

And is it surprising if more than all other peoples they are intent on treachery...when indeed their kings have never been interested in keeping faith with the Scots? Therefore more than all other peoples under Heaven they are more involved in treachery. To nobody do they keep a promise they have made. A solemn bond secured by an oath on the Bible or the Sacrament, which they wish [men] to observe regarding themselves, they are neither ashamed nor afraid to violate that oath daily when it is given by them to others. Hence even you, the Scottish people, though you exercise every precaution, though you are watchful in every way for your security and indemnity (as much for those firmly based on oaths and hostages as for those based on friendships) and for benefits granted in many ways, in these circumstances you must first of all defend your interests, because their malice is on the alert especially when they feel that in the light of your abundant security you are not on your guard. Then at last they return to their artful wickedness, and have recourse to their usual weapons of deceit, so that by taking the opportunity given by security they are able to cause harm quite unexpectedly. Therefore their cunning is much more to be feared than their warlike spirit, their poison more than their strength, their peace more than their firebrand, their sweetness more than their bile, their wickedness more than their fighting force, their treachery more than their campaign, and their counterfeit friendship more than their contemptible enmity. (c.25, ll.1-57)

Siege of Loch Leven castle

Bower's story of the siege of the castle on an island in Loch Leven in Kinross-shire (apparently in the spring of 1334 rather than 1335) by supporters of Edward de Balliol has little factual substance. Sir John de Strivelyn came from near Hexham in Northumberland, and was in 1334 serving Balliol and the English interest as sheriff of Perth. The water level of Loch Leven was then considerably lower than it is now, which makes it all the more unlikely that its level could imaginably be raised to surmount the castle walls without flooding a wide area of the countryside. There was another island in the loch on which stood a priory dedicated to St Serf.

In 1335 Sir John de Strivelyn, a knight of the king of England, with a great multitude of both English and Anglicised [Scots], among whom were the knights Michael de Arnot, Michael and David de Wemyss, and Richard de Melville, with many others who had accepted the authority of the king of England, all assembled together in the middle of Lent of the aforesaid year to besiege the castle of Loch Leven. Then after traversing the shores of the loch and viewing the strength of the castle, and [judging] that it could not be taken easily, they chose for themselves a place to stay near Kinross which was safer than the rest of the area, as a launching point for storming it more easily. Disregarding divine judgment they built the fortress of Fale along the boundaries of the consecrated cemetery there. In this way, shocking as it was, a church of Christ was despised by people that were Christians only in name, and wrongly converted into a den of robbers.

But at that time there were living in the aforesaid castle Alan de Vipont its keeper, James Lamby a citizen of St Andrews, and many other brave and hardy Scots. The English side, however, stayed on to carry through the work that had been begun, and toiled daily with engines of war with the aim of overthrowing the castle. The garrison on the other hand had enough foresight to be busy safeguarding themselves and their belongings securely; for while the English were pressing on with tricks and traps, the Scots fought to repel their crooked stratagems. At the outlet for the water of Loch Leven, indeed, where there was a hollow, the English laboured to obstruct the channel completely; with this in mind they forced the Scots from everywhere in the neighbourhood, both male and female, to construct a very strong wall out of turf and peat, so high and deep, and so firm and impacted with lumps of earth for the purpose, that the water, no longer having its accustomed outlet, would build up, and rising in time to the height of the castle walls would flow over them and drown the garrison without exception. But no plan can prevail against the Lord. For the adviser and protector of the islanders, the blessed Serf, when faced with the assaults of this invasion and construction by the English, inspired his own with stratagems of defence and, so to speak, of destruction.

Meanwhile the annual celebration of the blessed Margaret queen of Scots was drawing near, and the aforesaid John de Strivelyn, desiring to attend this celebration which is customarily held every year at Dunfermline [in June], made some of his people go with him; but he ordered many to stay and keep watch in the fortress and around the loch because of the siege of the castle. When the garrison, who were certainly suffering from scarcity of both food and other necessities, observed the departure of the said Sir John, they sent out four bold men at night to relieve their needy situation. These went out in a fast boat to where the water way was blocked, with tools provided for the purpose, and, unnoticed by the guards, laboriously dug through the wall from the eastern side. They worked nearly all night, but at length they despaired of their plan and decided to withdraw without having finished their project. But then it was suggested by one of them that they should stay at work for a little longer, and in the faith which he cherished towards St Serf, help was promised. When therefore they worked [again] on what they had begun, a little water, if only in drops, began to seep through. When they saw this, the clandestine diggers climbed into the boat in all haste, returned to the castle, and brought the very happy news to their companions, who were on this account filled with unexpected courage. For the water widened its channel more and more, and within the space of two hours flowed out with great force after building up in abundance for a month and more. It carried away the houses, tents, huts and shelters of the English, and the men lodging on the banks of the river with their horses and equipment, and conveyed them to the sea. And thus they were drowned in the violent waters. The force of their flow delighted the men on the island. There was indeed so great an inundation of flood-land that it cut its way through large areas while widening and destroying the river banks, so that they can still show traces to anyone who looks closely. Afterwards as the day advanced, when their men had been arrayed and had taken up their weapons of war, the disheartened [English] crossed over to the fortress.

When they saw this, the guards of the fortress were greatly stunned, and went quickly out to meet them. Thus when the fight began, many on both sides were wounded by archers. And at last with great difficulty the English were forced to flee. After they had been put to flight, the Scots happily entered the fortress, seized booty, took away provisions and spoils, and carried off with them everything inside of choice appearance. And so after securing victory they returned to their castle in good spirits. But when the aforesaid Sir John had been more fully informed about the outcome of the said battle by a report from some of his men as they fled, he speedily returned to the castle and bound himself by oath never to withdraw from the said besieged castle until he had demolished it completely, and destroyed and punished its inhabitants by sentence of death. But the providence of God, which sets all things in order and bestows all kinds of largess on those faithful to him, looked with an eye of pity upon the Scottish people, and for a little while relieved it from the English yoke of dreadful servitude by which they were wretchedly held in oppression; it increased the Scots' power and strengthened them, and weakened the bold fierceness and courage of the English until it made their position in the kingdom of Scotland utterly untenable.

The said Sir John de Strivelyn realised from this that it would not be advantageous to himself and his men if they stayed any longer, but rather disadvantageous, and he feared that his own person was under threat of harm. And so once some sort of treaty about peace and friendship had been fabricated between him and the men on the island, he retired dishonourably to his own accustomed strongholds, but not without the blemish of perjury. (c.29 - c.30, l.27)

Inchcolm and English raiders

In 1336 English forces were operating in Scotland in support of Edward de Balliol. It is at this time that Bower inserts a story about the activities of men whom he calls 'English pirates', who were raiding not far from Inchcolm and despoiling the parish church at Dollar in Clackmannanshire which was appropriated to Inchcolm Abbey. (This implied that the maintenance of the chancel of this church was the abbey's responsibility.) As Bower tells it in typical fashion, with a quotation from St Augustine and three biblical allusions, retribution overtook the raiders through the power of St Columba in his supposed active capacity as protector of a monastery that was dedicated to his name. It is a tale which the canons of Inchcolm would not want to forget.

At this time it happened that English pirates landed from their ships, and cruelly laid waste the whole coast on this side of the river Forth as far as the Ochil Hills without meeting any resistance. Before this time an outstanding abbot had presided over the monastery of St Columba of Inchcolm, who had taken a great interest in embellishing the house of God. He had extended a helping hand to transform not only his abbey, but also his commensal church at Dollar, which was then completely destroyed. Therefore he caused the whole framework of the choir to be constructed of great oak beams, which were carved with wonderful artistry, and cut into shape and fitted together in such a way that each beam was held together with the next one by means of dovetailing, which provided a pleasant sight to look at.

When therefore the pirates came to this church of Dollar, they remarked on how its choir had been constructed with such a fine wooden framework. And because they could easily and without damage to the work take every piece of wood out of its joints individually along with the trimmed boards, they put their fear of God aside, and admittedly led on by some blind greed—with regard to which it is true about these robbers what Augustine says; 'There is no difficulty in doing without, [except] where there is a passion for possession'—they clearly formed the desire and eventually decided to move all the wood of the choir to their ships, with the beams, ceiling panels and outer roofing dismantled in pieces, and to re-assemble the pieces as a precious jewel at some place in England, and that once it had been put together again the choir should be dedicated as a wonderful sanctuary as soon as possible. But no plan can prevail against the Lord. Thus when this construction of skilled craftsmanship had been placed on one splendid barge, the pirates happily and without delay hurried on their course for England with their sails set and with a light west wind, which had come in answer to their prayers. They were rejoicing overmuch, as victors rejoice when they divide their spoils among themselves when booty has been seized, and when they ceremonially march about, ringing their trumpets and sackbuts, resounding with the sound of trumpets, and singing amid loud applause. While they were thus proceeding—safely, as they believed—they were not heeding the word of the apostle who says: 'When they talk of peace and safety, then sudden destruction will come upon them, like the labour of a woman with child, and they will not escape.' For when on their voyage they moved from calm water to the south opposite the monastery of the canons of Inchcolm, their harp was turned into mourning and their joy to lament, because look! not just suddenly, but within the twinkling of an eye or the passing of a moment they sank into the deep like a stone, and their memory perished with their sound. When the ship sank, everything else sank with it and went down like lead in turbulent waters, so that not one piece of board was visible anywhere or floating on the surface. When their companions in the fleet beside them saw this, they were afraid, struck by extraordinary terror; and whether they wanted or not, glorified God in St Columba because of such unforeseen retribution. And from henceforth they swore not to inflict any violence upon him or his servants or their buildings. Because of this it has been made [into a proverb] in England that St Columba will thoroughly punish and take revenge on those who commit a crime against him. And so (to be open about it) whatever may be said about him, they commonly call a Saint Columba. (c.36, ll.23-77)

Black Agnes of Dunbar

The siege of Dunbar Castle in East Lothian by English forces January-June 1338 produced the famous story of its defender the Countess Agnes or Annot, described by Bower as 'Black' probably because of her appearance.

On 13 January 1337 the castle of Dunbar was besieged by Sir William de Montague earl of Salisbury, and by a certain other who was earl of Arundel, the commanders of the army of the king of England; and with huge engines and various bits of equipment for the conduct of war the siege was continued for twenty-two weeks. However, the countess, who was commonly called 'Black Agnes', defended this castle courageously. It is said that she was very active and cautious, showing manly feelings as she zealously incited her people to defend [the castle,] and even ridiculed the invaders wittily with gestures and words. For after an engine had thrown a missile which made the towers tremble, while the earl of Salisbury looked on, she arranged for a very pretty girl to be sent, adorned like a bride for her husband, who with a white piece of cloth or handkerchief held in her hand would wipe and gently rub the place of impact.

Meanwhile the said earl of Salisbury, angry about the damage which had been inflicted from both sides on the English, renewed the attack with vigour, and with a strong force of armed men and various pieces of equipment sent forward to the walls an enormous wooden screen conveyed on revolving wheels, which in the vernacular is called a 'sow'. At this the countess Black Annot shouted in a strong voice, saying: 'Montague, Montague, beware, for your sow will farrow!' With that, she caused an ingenious machine inside the castle to be drawn back for discharging a missile, and a large heavy stone, almost like a millstone, came down from a high trajectory, struck the sow fiercely like lightning, and dashed the heads of many inside to pieces. Those who barely escaped with their lives lost all their equipment in this way, although those inside the castle were very short of food. (c.39, ll.1-14, 34-46)

Robert Prenderguest and sanctuary at Holyrood

This story dates probably from the winter of 1337-8, after Andrew de Moray the Scottish guardian had given up his attempt to capture the Edinburgh castle site. As Bower tells it, the English occupation force is painted in a bad light. (Calder Muir is on the western boundary of Midlothian; Salisbury Park is adjacent to Holyrood Abbey; the Pentland Hills lie south-west of Edinburgh.) This tale is early evidence for a long tradition stretching forward to as late as the nineteenth century that the environs of Holyrood Abbey were a sanctuary where men fleeing from justice or retribution might stay—but not necessarily survive there for long!

Then, after the retreat of the said guardian, the English garrison of Edinburgh vented their fury overmuch on the poor common people. For among them a certain Scot called Robert Prenderguest, a strong and daring person, went out one day with the garrison, and following the instructions and the persuasion of this Robert they drove a great prey of beasts away from Calder Muir; but for supper in the castle they sat him at a table with the servants. Offended that he was reckoned among the lower people in the hall, Robert did not eat any of the food, although he had spent this whole day without eating. The marshal, called Thomas Knayton, thinking that he was unhappy, asked him for the reason, saying: 'Why, you Scot, do you not eat, seeing that there is plenty of food before you?' 'Because I thought', the other replied, 'that I had deserved better today than to obtain a seat among the pages.' 'You are being arrogant', said the marshal. 'You Scots ought to be humbled.' And with that he hit Robert's head with a baton which he was carrying in his hand, until the blood was splashed over the others sitting at the table.

Hiding his sense of injustice, Robert sought the town. He remained for the night in his lodging, until on the next day, waiting for his opportunity, he watched for the time when the marshal usually withdrew to the town for his recreation. When he, swollen with the pride of arrogance, was advancing down the middle of the street with a sizable train of English retainers, Robert rushed out of a side street, first greeted him light-heartedly with: 'Well now, you rabbit', and then with a dagger which he pulled out from under his cloak he pierced the marshal's heart and forced him to breathe out his life along with his guts. The followers of the dying man rushed upon the fleeing Robert, but were not able to do him any harm. Instead, as he fled he struck at them and wounded three of his pursuers mortally. Then he went through the door of a passage towards the north, fastened it with a hanging bolt as he had arranged beforehand, and mounted his horse which was waiting for him just by the loch. Melting away into the air, he reached unharmed the abbey church of Holyrood. Safe from his pursuers he escaped to sanctuary, ringing the bell (as is the custom) by pulling the bell [rope]. Because the chancel was not open to him for the time being, he entered the chapel of St Augustine and was found by the English kneeling by the altar, ready to pray. Out of reverence for God they ceased to follow him any further for the time being. However, they set up a watch over him and enclosed him there, preventing him from being provided with any food; and at night, whenever sleep overcame him, they pricked him with goads fixed to long wooden sticks, so that in this way he would from lack of food and sleep soon end his miserable life. In this manner indeed he spent twelve days, for in the middle of each night, while the brothers were concentrating attention on lauds and matins, the sacrist would secretly climb up to the vaults, tie some food to a piece of rope, and in this way lower it down without being noticed. Finally one night the sacrist took two fellow-canons with him and they let down a stronger rope which the captive tied around himself; then he was quickly pulled high up by the canons. They clothed him in a canon's habit without delay, and in the early morning—while it looked as if they were going for a walk from the monastery—they led him out with them to Salisbury Park and there allowed him to go free.

Given his liberty, he exulted as a giant to run along the road, and did not stop until he had found William de Douglas who was hiding in the Pentland Hills, watching with his men the English sentries. At the instigation of this Robert, William himself and his men moved down to Edinburgh the following night and slew about eighty of the English who were scattered in brothels. Because of this the English in protecting themselves more cautiously inflicted countless damages upon the Scots whenever they could. But these actions did not always turn out well for them, because very often the Scots by means of traps paid them back. (c.41)

Alan Steersman and Guardian Andrew de Moray

It is perhaps to the winter of 1337-8, while Cupar Castle in Fife was still in English hands, that the following story belongs. Relating as it does to a crossing of the Firth of Forth from Donibristle near Inchcolm on the northern shore of the Firth of Forth to the opposite shore, it was presumably remembered locally. Andrew de Moray was a magnate who held estates at Bothwell in Lanarkshire and at Avoch on the Black Isle in Ross. Rosemarkie parish contained the cathedral of Ross diocese. Bower does not omit to mention the devastation caused by the loyalist Scottish forces as they attacked the English and their supporters. Robert Steward is the later King Robert II (1371-90). The young David II was safely in France from 1334 to 1341.

For at the same time the garrison of Cupar numbering around sixty came to Donibristle, and from there sent their horses back to the castle. And in the middle of the night, when the moon was beginning to shine, they forcibly compelled a certain seaman called Alan Steersman who lived there along with his people to transport them across the Forth in his boat. Since he seemed to be resisting them a little, they gave him and his men a good beating. But he, with placid face but bitter in his mind, let them into his ship and steered them to a sandbank which, when the tide which is called the spring-tide is out, stretches from Cramond Island to Barnbougle and extends for a long way. On this sandbank he ordered them to alight as if it was dry ground, and with unfurled sails he bade them farewell for ever. They light-heartedly began to run; but when they saw a great lake between themselves and the land they shouted to be let on board the ship, and those who had refused to pay a fare before now promised fifty pounds as long as he took them on. Turning a deaf ear, Alan made sail with his people, and without using their hands they inflicted pains on the English as they shouted their commands to the sky that were more severe than the blows which the Scots had experienced themselves. For at once the onset of the flood-tide overwhelmed them, and in the midst of the waves not one of them remained alive.

In 1338 the noble Andrew de Moray, the guardian of Scotland, was struck by illness after the siege of Edinburgh castle. He went to his own lands beyond the mountains, and at Avoch he was fated to end this present life; he was then buried at Rosemarkie. He had been very useful for the liberty of the kingdom, a great commander, and very devoted to justice and works of mercy. For by assault he destroyed all the castles and fortresses on this side of the Forth that were occupied by the English, except Cupar and Perth. But he also reduced all the regions through which he passed during his expeditions to such desolation and scarcity that more perished through hunger and extreme poverty than the sword destroyed from the time of the outbreak of war. He served as guardian of Scotland for two years and a half. After his death the king's nephew, Robert Steward, was elected guardian. Although he was a youth in terms of years, he showed himself an old man in his deeds, especially against the English. He remained guardian until the arrival of the king from France. (c.42, ll.1-37)

William de Douglas and William Bullock

The capture of Edinburgh Castle by the Scots under William de Douglas of Liddesdale in April 1341 makes a good story that was no doubt often re-told. Inchkeith is an island in the Firth of Forth opposite the port of Leith. Bower is probably misleading to suggest that 'The Turnpike' was part of the castle buildings: it is more likely to have been a spiked barrier at the castle gate. William Bullock is an enigmatic character. As a talented administrator who first served Edward de Balliol and then by 1341 at latest changed his allegiance to the young David II (and compared here with Chusai, the faithful servant to the biblical King David), he earned distrust. (Lochindorb is an isolated loch in th hills of Moray with an island castle; 'Malmoran' is probably an unidentified place-name which Bower mistook for a personal name.)

In 1341 on 17 April Edinburgh castle was captured with a strong force by [Sir] William de Douglas [of Liddesdale, the priest] William Bullock, [and two men-at-arms] William Fraser and Walter Curry, in a way that was both lucky and subtle, after all the guards of the same castle had been disposed of in this manner: following the advice and foresight of sir William Bullock, who in his time surpassed all the others in intelligence, Sir William de Douglas, William Fraser and Joachim de Kinbuck met Walter Curry who had then a ship at Dundee. This ship they loaded, and with two hundred chosen men [they steered] it to Inchkeith. As he disembarked from it on to the land, the said Walter pretended to be an English merchant. Then at a late hour taking one servant with him he went to the captain of Edinburgh castle, saying that he had come from England with the best wine, grain and beer from Ely; and to prove what he had said he produced two skins which the servant had carried with him, and gave the captain some wine and beer to taste. He said that early the next day he would send the captain two casks of wine and beer and two baskets of biscuits highly spiced with cloves, and these he promised to give the captain for nothing as long as he had the captain's support for selling the rest to him or to others. The captain joyfully accepted this offer, assuring him that he would find the gates [of the castle] open in the [early] morning. On being informed of this arrangement, the said Sir William de Douglas hid himself nearby with his troop ready for the attack. And early the next morning the said Walter, accompanied by twelve chosen armed men whose armour was concealed by cloaks and by one man carrying a stake, went openly to the castle with two horses carrying baskets and casks that contained water. There they found the gatekeeper ready, and after the great gate had been opened, they entered the castle itself and immediately cut the throats of the janitor and his two assistants; and after they had placed under the portcullis the strong stake which had been prepared for this purpose by the said Walter, and had thrown the baskets and casks towards the entrance of the tower, William de Douglas and his men at a trumpet signal immediately rushed out from a nearby place called 'The Turnpike'. Roused by the noise, the garrison hurried to the gate, where a most violent fight was fought, in which the English were trampled down, wounded, killed, captured and driven out beyond the walls; the castle was taken by the Scots, the burgesses rejoiced and returned to their allegiance to the king. The said William de Douglas placed his elder illegitimate brother, [also] called William, as keeper in the castle, and after a few days went to Teviotdale, where he forcefully expelled from the realm all the remaining English that were found there. (c.46)

It was also at this time that sir William Bullock, the chaplain, stood out among all his contemporaries for his remarkable sagacity and the succinct eloquence of his speech. He was first chamberlain under Edward de Balliol and treasurer of the other English; then he was chamberlain of Scotland under King David, and the most important of his principal concillors. Because of the intelligence of his experienced counsel he was consequently regarded as most celebrated and praiseworthy, almost like another Chusai. But whereas he imagined that he could remain [favoured by the king and trusted by the kingdom], functioning in various different posts which were most necessary to the kingdom and the state, he came as a result of the envy of the magnates and many others to be denounced to the king for treason. On his orders Bullock was seized by [Sir] David Barclay, assigned with Molmoran and other treacherous men to Lochindorb, committed to prison there, and died of hunger [and cold]...After [his death] sad events replaced fortunate happenings in the kingdom. (c.49, ll.70-86)

A Bruce imposter and a Seton heiress

The two stories here probably belong to the years 1344-5. The apparent imposter claimed to be the illegitimate son of King Robert's brother Edward de Bruce, who is otherwise reported to have been killed at

Halidon in 1333. It is interesting that Bower suspects that he may have been judged unfairly. The romantic tale that follows concerns a couple whose families both had interests in lands at Winton in East Lothian.

In the meantime a man came from England who, pretending to be the son of a certain burgess of Aberdeen and concealing his own name, claimed to have been in prison for fourteen years. When a ransom had been fixed and pledges had been given for paying the money, he with the help of many tokens and clear evidence made many of the kingdom and especially the common people understand and firmly believe that he was in reality Alexander de Bruce. After various disturbances and a number of interviews with the king and certain magnates, fearing that he might be put to death, he said, by those who occupied his land, he secretly withdrew into the region of Carrick, where he was on the king's instructions captured and taken to Ayr as an impostor and fraudster. There, in the presence of Robert Steward, Malcolm Fleming and many others, he ended his life by hanging in the month of July, although, as some believe, proper judicial procedure had not in all points been observed. Because of this many still think that he was the real Alexander and condemned to an unjust death so that his lands could be retained [by others].

In this year [a certain man-at-arms,] Alan de Wynton, by a forcible abduction seized the lady of Seton, a young girl. He was in this deed abetted by William de Moray, the keeper of Edinburgh castle. Because of this such disagreement and discord arose in Lothian that for a year a hundred ploughlands, it is said, could not be cultivated. The parents of the abducted girl complained about the abduction to the lord king, and when the said Alan had been seized and the king was sitting in judgment, there were offered to the young girl a sword and a ring to choose between. She quickly took the ring and was awarded to Alan in marriage. By her he had a son named William and a daughter Margaret. However, because of the intrigues of the friends of [the relations of] his wife he went away to the Holy Land and died there a pilgrim in the Lord. (c.50, ll.25-54)

Book XIV

The battle of Neville's Cross

Details of the battle at Neville's Cross near Durham on 17 October 1346, when King David II was wounded and captured by the English forces led by the archbishop of York and others, have been found by Bower in a source now lost. David had one arrow-head extracted by English doctors soon after the battle; the other must have remained in his head for some twenty years, giving him headaches, until it worked its way out when, significantly for him, he was on pilgrimage to the chapel of St Monance on the Fife shore of the Firth of Forth. The power of saints to control events could be helpful or unhelpful. At the battle itself St Cuthbert was regarded as having protected the lands of Durham Cathedral, since it was dedicated to him.

Hence as the Scots were meanwhile preparing themselves for battle, the English approached the manor of Bearpark which lay just two miles from where they were then, and took up their position on the same moor at a certain place near Durham beside the cross which is called Neville's Cross just a short distance from the said Scots. They took up their stations for the fight by dividing their men into three sections.

In the meantime while the English were positioning themselves for a battle, the king of Scotland remained still in the park with his men, unaware of the English approach. In the morning he sent Sir William de Douglas to ravage the land of the church of Durham, and to collect booty to refresh his army. When he came upon the enemy unexpectedly, they met in a way that was sudden for both sides at a place which is called Ferryhill. But because the said Sir William de Douglas did not have the backing of a force adequate for confronting so large a multitude of adversaries, he began a withdrawal towards the king with his men, during which he lost five hundred sturdy Scottish troops at the place called Sunderland [Bridge]; but Douglas himself was fortunate to escape their hands. On hearing this the Scots were thrown into confusion to an extraordinary degree. They were divided into three sections with the king in command of one, the earl of Moray and Sir William de Douglas in command of the second, and the earl of Dunbar and the Steward of Scotland in command of the third. But as the formations approached the line of battle, Sir John Graham requested a hundred mounted lancers to break up the English archers, so that by this means the king might more easily attack the enemy; but to tell the truth, he could not obtain even one [for no one dared to commit himself to such a risk]. On this account Graham became angry and rode alone among the archers shaking his lance; he fiercely scattered them in turn, when his noble horse was killed by a flying arrow, and he only just escaped to the king scarcely with his life. At length everyone was in position and the sound of trumpets was heard. The line commanded by the earl of Moray was attacked and involved in a fearful fight between ditches and hedges; the earl was killed and his men overcome. Next a band of Englishmen which included ten thousand archers as well as armed men attacked King David, who was ensnared with his men between ditches, and captured by John Coupland, though not without a substantial fight and the lamentable slaughter of his men. First, however, Coupland had two of his teeth knocked out by a blow from the king, while the king for his part was seriously wounded by two arrows.

The tip of one of these could not be extracted by any doctor's skill until the king developed a devotion to St Monan and went there as a pilgrim; while he was standing absorbed in prayer before the saint's statue, the arrow-tip sprang forth a long way as if forcibly pulled out, an event that was not so much a wonder as a miracle. When this happened, the king built the saint's church in noble fashion, as can be seen today, so as not to seem ungrateful for such a benefit; and he endowed it in a kingly manner with very many possessions.

As the Scots therefore fled from the two whirlwind attacks so fiercely launched by the English, with the rest of them captured or killed, the Steward of Scotland (that is the king's nephew) and Earl Patrick followed wise advice and saved themselves with the help of an about turn, so returning home safely. Note how disastrously David king of Scotland was defeated and captured along with his army on account of his attack on the lands of the church of St Cuthbert! (c.2, l.53 - c.3, l.49)

The Black Death: first and second occurrences

Scotland in 1349 shared in the devastation of the plague known as the Black Death, though there is little detailed evidence about it. Bower reports here what happened in the St Andrews cathedral monastery. It has been thought that twenty-four Augustinian canons would have formed about two-thirds of the community. A second visitation of the plague followed probably throughout 1362.

In 1349 there was a great pestilence and mortality among men in the kingdom of Scotland, and it also ranged over a wide area during many earlier and later years throughout the whole world, such as had nowhere been heard of or written down in history books for the information of future generations from the beginning of the world until now. Such was the severity of that plague that nearly one-third of the whole human race was obliged to pay the debt of nature. The way in which this painful death happened by the divine will was strange and unusual; once the swollen inflammation of the flesh had taken hold, life in this world hardly lasted for a further two days. Wherever it happened, it affected for the most part the middling and lesser folk, and seldom the magnates. Everyone trembled at it with such fearful dread that children would not dare to visit their parents suffering in the last extremity; instead they fearfully shunned the contagion as they would flee from before a serpent. In this year it so pleased the Lord that twenty-four professed canons of the house of canons at St Andrews were called from the troubles of this present life, as is the way of all flesh, of whom all except three were priests. They were all men of ample education, circumspect in spiritual and in temporal matters, and upright and honourable in their way of life. These plagues occur from time to time because of the sins of mankind.

In 1361 a certain Franciscan friar called John, who was then at the Roman court, delivered a prophecy to our most sainted father Innocent [VI], who was then serving his turn in the apostolic office, regarding the many tribulations and afflictions which were going to befall the whole world continuously throughout the next nine years because of men's sins. On this account he was imprisoned until this period of years had passed, and the result and outcome of his prophecy was seen. For in the kingdom of Scotland it turned out as he foretold, because a second extremely severe mortality began on the feast of the Purification of Our Lady and lasted until the Christmas immediately following. It spread its strength and virulence as much among nobles and magnates as among common people and other persons of intermediate rank, to such an extent that it seemed to men at the time that nearly a third of the human race that remained after the first pestilence were forced to render their debt to nature. It took its course in the same way and with the same character among those who took ill as before. But King David, accompanied by many of the more wealthy and more noble men of the kingdom, withdrew to the northern parts of the same kingdom, partly because of the horrible sights and sounds of the multitude of ill and dead, partly because of fear and alarm at that pestilence which was then spreading in the southern parts of the kingdom, and which he planned to escape in good health. (c.7, ll.1-21; c.24, ll.1-23)

A papal appointment to Dunfermline Abbey

The story of John de Stramiglaw's papal appointment (on 22 June 1351) to the abbacy of Dunfermline is one of the earliest pieces of evidence for the introduction of the practice of 'papal provisions' to monastic headships in Scotland. Popes for a hundred years had been enlarging their control of church appointments in various categories, and by the fifteenth century were normally to control the more important monastic headships (taking a fee called 'services' for their trouble). This case arose under a particular heading of the canon law which permitted the pope to make an appointment when a prelate died while on a visit to the papal court (or Rome in this case, though at this period the pope ruled from Avignon). This story illustrates how new procedures came gradually to be accepted in Scotland; but Bower from his 1440s point of view takes the trouble to end with a statement of the normal (as it seemed to him) method of appointing an abbot, even if in practice this was outmoded by time he was writing.

In the same year Alexander Ber abbot of Dunfermline died when he was visiting the tomb of the blessed Peter in person to obtain the general indulgence. While he was returning from Rome, he died at the town of San Stefano in Lesser Lombardy, with the monk who was his companion and all the servants he had with him going like him to sleep in the Lord. He held his office for twenty-two years, ruling himself and his [monks] profitably. When they heard this, the convent of the said monastery elected as their abbot sir John Black, the terrar of the convent, as they were allowed to do by law and custom, by leave of their patron the lord king and with the advice of their diocesan bishop. When he had been confirmed and had returned home, he graciously ruled the house entrusted to him for as long as he held office.

But at the same time a certain monk of the same monastery called John de Stramiglaw, a student at Paris (fearing an impending loss to his monastery because of the general reservation which the supreme pontiff had made [of all presentations] to all the kinds of dignities held by those who died on a pilgrimage of this kind), lest that dignity should fall into the hands of a foreigner, went to the curia at Avignon and petitioned for appointment to the abbacy of Dunfermline by papal bulls. When the said sir John Black heard this, though advised by the clerical and lay lords not to resign his abbatial dignity nor defer in any way to this papal [appointee], concealed his intentions; but after studying the papal reservation and collation made in papal bulls addressed to himself, when the papal [appointee] entered the cemetery of the monastery with a few companions, the said abbot (on the advice of his brothers with a view to preserving the monastery's immunity) went to meet him dressed in his ecclesiastical vestments and mitre, with the convent following in procession, and placed that mitre on the papal [appointee's] head and the pastoral staff in his hand. Then along with the resonant singing of the 'Te Deum laudamus' he led him to the choir and altar, and after prayer humbly and cheerfully caused him to be installed, and was the first to offer manual obedience on bended knees, followed likewise by the rest. The said papal [appointee] in turn showed his gratitude to him by providing him with an honourable pension; and later he was elected prior of Urquhart. This sir John de Stramiglaw paid the papal chamber fifty marks sterling for the assessment made on his monastery in the papal court.

And it is to be noted that he received that dignity in this way by grace of the apostolic see, so that the right of election remained with the monastery in future as previously from the beginning, and the right of confirmation thus remained with the lord bishop, clear, unimpaired and entire, as it had from ancient times and the first foundation of the house, without diminution of its rights or any prejudice or exaction whatsoever. (c.8, ll.26-71)

The battle of the Thirty

This set-piece fight between an equal number of the pro-English and pro-French sides in a civil war in Brittany took place on 26 March 1351. No Scots were involved. The site was near Josselin in central Brittany (not in Normandy as here). Bower's account differs substantially from that found in French sources; it was probably based on oral tradition brought back by Scots returning from France sometime during the next hundred years. No record of this battle has been traced in English sources. Here it illustrates Bower's dominant interest in French affairs. There are a number of instances of this kind of combat in the later middle ages, with its most famous Scottish example at Perth in 1396 (see below).

At that time in Brittany it happened that quite a fierce fight was stirred up between the French and the English. Although the English were there in greater numbers, they nevertheless submitted to the French on the field of battle, where a certain brave French knight called John Beaumanoir captured a certain conceited knight from England in this fight; and although he had been put in confinement, he nonetheless impudently taunted the French to express his low opinion of them, saying that one Englishman could and should be the equal of two Frenchmen in a fight. This was despite the fact that for the time being the French were victors over the English. On hearing this man's angry words the Frenchman was in some way moved to say that a Frenchman could easily be found who would fight an Englishman over a just cause, and would play his part in manly fashion to the end. 'I agree', said the Englishman, 'that it could turn out that way if it is a case of single combat. But let us put five against five, ten against ten, twenty or thirty against the same number, and in this way there will be real proof of which nation is master.' In short, it was agreed that thirty should fight against thirty, and that the defeated side should pay a ransom to the winning side; and meantime the English knight was set free without having to pay any kind of ransom unless it turned out that he was captured afresh. A place in Normandy was selected, a day appointed for this purpose, and the battle was fought bravely on both sides. For at the first encounter victory appeared to go to the English; whereupon a certain Frenchman suddenly left the battle-line, and mounting a horse that was in armour like himself, while his companions believed that he was taking to flight, he led his horse away using his ankles as spurs, filled the air with a shout, and covered his breast with his shield. Brandishing a terrifying lance he unexpectedly attacked the English, confidently penetrated their formation which was crowded together like a hedgehog, split them up from each other, and violently struck some of them to the ground. By his spirited behaviour almost by himself he secured the revival of his scattered companions, and so stimulated them along with himself to secure a victory over their enemies. Nine of the English were killed, and the rest were taken prisoner, while only one of the French met with death. And so as a result of one man's pride the outcome was utter ruin for many; and the arrogance of one was humiliation for many. Thus it is said:

> Man, whoever you are, when showing your pride in actions and words,
> grasp this word: 'God shatters all trace of pride.'
> (c.11)

The Burnt Candlemas

Bower here from local knowledge adds to Fordun's account of Edward III's devastation at Haddington in East Lothian during his invasion of Scotland in February 1356. The church that was destroyed was not the present grand parish church that was built later, but the church of the Grayfriars that has since then disappeared. (Candlemas is celebrated on 2 February each year.)

Therefore while the said king stayed at Haddington and in its vicinity for ten days, and was waiting for his fleet bringing food supplies, a strong wind came from the uninhabited region, that is from the north, for 'evil is spread from the north'; it rushed against his fleet as it lay at anchor off North Berwick. And when they had altered sail towards safer ports, contrary winds arose against the fleet and in a short time scattered the whole force. The ships were therefore in danger, and for the most part were sunk beneath the waves; indeed those which escaped this great danger were carried here and there in different areas where the force of the wind drove them. The king therefore was deprived of his supplies, and soon was suffering very considerably along with his army from shortage of bread. After first burning the burgh and the whole monastery and famous church of the Friars Minor at Haddington—a building work that was undoubtedly costly and wonderfully beautiful, and the one source of comfort for the whole of the countryside (whose choir indeed was commonly called The Lamp of Lothian on account of its remarkable beauty and brightness of the light [within it])—he moved his camp and set off through Lothian, burning and laying waste everything round about, and as far as possible saving nothing, until he might come to the burgh of Edinburgh. Leaving there after burning everything that would burn (which is why the common folk call that time 'The Burnt Candlemas'), he dishonourably made his way home. (c.13, ll.1-23)

Sons of Lindsay and Kirkpatrick

This murder at Caerlaverock Castle near Dumfries must be dated 24 June 1358. Kirkpatrick and Lindsay are interesting for Bower's assertion that they were heirs of two men with the same names who had helped Robert Bruce to murder John Comyn in 1306 (see above). Bower finds an apposite passage in the writings of St Bridget of Sweden to fit the circumstances.

In the said year around the feast of the Nativity of the blessed John the Baptist, the noble man-at-arms Roger de Kirkpatrick was killed at the castle of Caerlaverock by the knight Sir James de Lindsay, who was staying with him that night. After dinner when the wine had been pleasurably drained and both men had said goodnight, Roger went to bed with no anticipation of evil and with the door of his bedroom closed. Led by some unknown impulse, the said knight knocked and entered the bedroom with lighted candles, and without more ado heartlessly cut Roger's throat on his bed. This James, who by committing that wrongful act had changed from a knight to a tyrant, decided that it would be better to flee and save himself. He left the said castle by night, and as a servant of the night fled on horseback through all that vilest of nights, hoping to cover a long distance without retribution;

but as the sun rose in the morning he was scarcely three miles away from the said castle. Without delay he was presented for King David's attention by friends of the dead man on behalf of the wife of the said dead Roger, and the execution of the law was enforced by the king. Immediately the king ordered the holding of an assize, by which James was found guilty of blood-feud, and punished with a capital sentence at Dumfries.

For this reason it should be noted that James and Roger were the first-born or heirs of those who were accomplices with Robert Bruce in the slaughter of John the Red Comyn in the church of the friars of Dumfries. And so here was fulfilled what the elderly friar heard from a spirit in the choir of the friars of Dumfries on the night following the killing of the same Sir John Comyn, when he heard a voice crying out for vengeance, to which the answer was made: 'Wait for a little while, for the matter is handed on to the heirs' (see above, Book XII, Chapter 7)...In matters of this kind you are not to be amazed that the judgment of God is a great bottomless pit; hear what is written in the *Liber Questionum* of the Lady Bridget, to whom the Lord states that:

> Many times it happens that sons copy the sins of their parents; and so some day the sins of the fathers are punished in the sons, not because the sins of the fathers will in themselves go unpunished, although the penalties for the sins are transferred for a time, but because everyone will die and be punished for his own sin. Also some day the sins [of the fathers] (as it is written) are visited in the fourth generation, because my justice is Divine, inasmuch as when sons do not seek to soften my anger, either for themselves or for their fathers, they are to be punished with their fathers whom they have followed against me. (c.20, ll.1-42)

Floods at Haddington

Bower here uses local tradition to paint a graphic picture of two aspects of a summer flood in his home town of Haddington in East Lothian on 7 September 1358. He is happy to introduce the miraculous into his tale.

In 1358 on the eve of the feast of Our Lady's Nativity flooding of rain and water suddenly burst out in parts of Lothian in such quantity and of such a kind as have not been seen from the days of Noah to the present. Its extent was such that the rising water overflowed channels, embankments and reservoirs, and spread into fields, villages, towns and monasteries. By its force it threw down from the foundations and demolished stone walls and the strongest bridges, as well as built-up areas and the most substantial of houses. Likewise the violent flow dragged tall oaks and strong trees sited near rivers, uprooted by the flood water, all the way to where the rivers joined the sea. It was also responsible for removing from human use from places near and far and destroying corn that had been cut and spread out where it had been cut for drying. It also came about in Haddington that rising water destroyed and by itself levelled practically all the Nungate quarter which lay well above its banks. There a man called John Birley, as the water entered his house and to a great extent took it over, climbed to the upper part of his roof, and was carried to the Nuns' Bridge at Haddington, securely resting on the top of his house, which had beams and panels of wood. As the man riding the house approached the bridge, he detached himself on to the top of it; and by holding firmly to the cross-beam, he saved himself along with a cat, a dog and a cockerell that were his inseparable companions, [while all the other living things in his house were drowned.] As the waters were going down, he was asked how he was, and made the following answer (which to this day is frequently used there as a proverb), namely: 'Now we row merrily,' said John Birley.'

But now that we have first set out something wonderful, listen to something miraculous which happened there. For as that violent storm over the sea was increasing and blowing past the bounds of the river, a certain nun with a degree of foolish simplicity, but with devout intention even if without understanding, when the water threatened to submerge the monastery, seized an image of the Virgin from the church, and ran speedily to plunge it into the water if Mary did not defend the abbey from the flood. When therefore the water reached the doors of the domestic quarters, and the nun was raising the image to throw it away, behold! in a moment the water fled from the image that was driving it away; and the wonder was that it never paused until it had flowed back to its [customary] limits. (c.21, ll.1-38)

A revolt against David II; plans for his succession

Bower here relates two developments in the wrong chronological order. First comes early in 1363 a revolt by some leading magnates (elsewhere named as including the earls of Douglas and Dunbar and Robert Steward), perhaps sparked off by rumours of King David's proposed second marriage to Margaret Logie. The leaders were pardoned on making submission and renewing their fealty on 14 May. Then a year later on 4 March 1364 (end of the year 1363 Old Style) comes the parliament at which the king proposed that a younger son of Edward III of England be adopted as David's heir. Bower suggests that he made this proposal only under pressure, and that he was not disappointed when it was rejected. (The rules for the succession to the Scottish crown had been set out in settlements—'tailzies'—made under King Robert I.)

In 1363 King David called a parliament at Scone, where he proposed to the three estates the suggestion that after his death they should adopt as king one of the sons of the king of England. In many various ways David recommended Lionel, a son of the said king. He subsequently argued that the kingdom might achieve permanent peace, since on the one hand Lionel would be free to protect the kingdom, and on the other his father the king of England would never by any title or pretext now and in future assert a right or claim to the kingdom for himself and his heirs. He was answered at once and without further discussion or hesitation by all of the three estates each together and all separately that they would never be willing to give consent for an Englishman to rule over them. They criticized the king's proposal as blinkered, since men of splendid character and standing were available as heirs apparent. The three estates were bound to stick faithfully to these heirs by virtue of tailzies which had been agreed with the most solemn of oaths. On this account the king, apparently convinced, turned to other matters.

It is not surprising that a proposal of this kind created among the lieges a seed-bed and kindling of a certain unfortunate antagonism towards the king, although he (it is presumed) never expected that an unprecedented action of this kind would be put into effect. For it may be that before he escaped from the hands of his English enemies, he had promised to set aside the tailzies, and as far as he could, he did what he had to do. Hence the king, in rendering to every individual his due, kept his promise to the English, and did not regret in his heart that his request had been refused.

But whether because of this or for other reasons a great seditious conspiracy was planned in the kingdom by the magnates. For the leading important men were agreed against their lord the king, and formed a plan among themselves either to persuade him to return to their point of view or to drive him out of the kingdom. And in case any of them backed out from this plan, indentures were formally drawn up, securely reinforced by seals added by all the parties. But as an immediate demonstration of the purpose they had planned (let me not call it treachery) in their actions, they arose cruelly in an armed band in serious numbers to achieve their aim by force and fear. Accordingly in whatever places supporters of the king were found, who had no wish to give approval to their misdeeds, the conspirators seized them and thrust them into prison as captives. They rushed into towns and burghs and around the whole country, dividing the loot taken from the people among themselves, and perpetrating other evils in damnable fashion, with this end in view that as often as the king was pricked with the sword of compassion with fellow-feeling for the distress of the people, he might more easily acquiesce in their prayers. But the king, recalling the superiority of his own power, sent a force in strength, wishing to oppose their boldness, and on his guard for the future lest on another occasion this sort of insolent behaviour should serve as a precedent to others if so serious an attack remained unpunished and so much destruction increased further and the condition of the state was seen to weaken. He assembled men loyal to him from the four regions of the land, spending a great deal of money on their wages, so that he might shatter the presumption [of the conspirators] and break up their plan. This was, however (in accordance with his usual leniency), after he had issued a public edict that [the leaders] and their supporters were to desist and abstain from folly of this kind. He pursued them, however, hardened in their obstinacy and defensive about their actions, for men of spirit who would rather die than see their people harmed and their land desolate take up their arms and in manly fashion go to meet their opponents. But his adversaries did not dare to clash openly with the king and his men, mindful of the saying of Solomon: 'A king's threat is like a lion's roar; whoever provokes him sins against his own soul.' When they realized that they did not have the power to complete what they had begun, they sent a deputation to the king, asking for peace, and submitting themselves and their property for disposal at his pleasure. But he, as the mildest of men, preferred to forgive them rather than take revenge; he accepted an oath of fealty from them lest they try to act in a similar fashion again, or the community suffer serious harm any more; and following wise advice on that occasion, he decided to be lenient with them etc. That disturbance then ceased. (c.25, ll.14-83)

Choice of a wife

As a comment on the unsuccessful marriage of King David and Margaret Logie, Bower offers a short scholastic exercise on the foundations of any successful marriage, with many biblical, early Christian and classical literary quotations. These two chapters form an introduction to an even longer and seemingly misogynistic discussion (not included here) of the characteristics of bad women. Bower is always the academically-trained Christian pastor.

With the aim therefore of providing for the succession to the kingdom from the fruit of her womb (if God granted it), King David chose a most beautiful lady, Margaret Logie, the widow of John Logie, perhaps not so much for the excellence of her character as a woman as for the pleasure he took in her desirable appearance. Yet marriage ought not to be entered into lightly for immediate advantage without first establishing previous mutual regard and serious forethought. And thus a man about to marry will get to know the following four matters which King David did not fully anticipate, namely: (1) in choosing a wife, she ought to be chosen prudently, so that it is done with prudent consideration; (2) in correcting a wife, she ought to be given gentle guidance, so that it is done with gentle control; (3) in guiding a wife, she ought to be corrected in private, so that it is done with private instruction; (4) in loving a wife, she ought to be loved to the full, so that it is done with full sharing.

Firstly therefore, a wife should be chosen prudently, and not married suddenly or hastily, for such passion in the beginning produces its penalty in the future. We have an example in Genesis, chapter 34, regarding Shechem son of Hamor, who on first seeing Dinah the daughter of Jacob raped her, and then wanted to die if he could not marry her. And he acted with such passion that for the sake of his love he promised that he and all his people would be circumcised. Because of the hasty nature of this deed, he and his people were killed by Dinah's brothers. In choosing a wife therefore, not all consideration should centre on the appearance or beauty of the woman, because 'many have been seduced by the beauty of a woman' (Ecclesiasticus, chapter 9), nor on her wealth or her parentage, but rather on her good character. For to marry well is to such an extent a matter of God's grace that, as Solomon says, it is strictly speaking regarded as a gift from God. Hence Solomon says: 'Home and wealth may be provided by parents; but a sensible wife is strictly speaking a gift from the Lord.'

But Aristotle in his *Ethics* says that there are three kinds of friendship, whether because it is useful, pleasurable or honourable. This last case is based on good character, and it alone is a perfect friendship. And whatever good there is in the first two kinds is all included in it. Hence it alone is friendship strictly speaking. In the case of useful friendship, which properly belongs to old merchants, the benefit of utility disappears when the utility comes to an end. Likewise with friendship based on pleasure, which properly belongs to young men; it speedily comes to an end when the pleasure goes away. And thus Aristotle says that the friendships of young men are easily changeable for two reasons: first because pleasure changes with age—for the same pleasure does not please the adolescent as pleases a boy; and second because they begin loving, not out of the mature judgment of reason, but out of passion. But passion quickly passes; and they speedily fall in love, and speedily fall out of love. But the third kind of friendship, which is the honourable one, has these qualities—that it is permanent and individual, because it is founded on good character, which always lasts in people of virtue. It is indeed individual, because few people are virtuous; and this kind of friendship requires a lengthy period of time, intimate association, and knowledge of character.

Since therefore a man's greatest friendship ought to be with his wife, it cannot be founded on the essence of beauty, for that quickly fades, as is said in Proverbs, chapter 31: 'Charm is deceptive and beauty fleeting; but the woman who fears the Lord is honoured.' Nor can it be founded on wealth, for this kind of friendship is based on utility; it is friendship [only] accidentally, because it is possessions that are loved, not a person. Hence Jerome writes that: 'When Marcia the younger daughter of Cato was asked why she did not marry again after losing her husband, she replied that she could not find a man who preferred her to her possessions. By saying this', says Jerome, 'she neatly called attention to her wealth rather than her modesty.' Certainly today it is not modesty nor respect for character that lead to marriage, but only regard for wealth or lust.

And therefore friendship does not last, nor are children produced, because if they are produced, they do not fit in well with such marriage partners, as is frequently the case. Hence Chrysostom in his *First Homily on Matthew*, commenting on Matthew, chapter 1, 'Salmon fathered Boaz by [Rahab]', says: 'Because he took a wife according to God's command, a wife who had been offered in marriage by God, he virtuously fathers sons who practise virtue among themselves; for Boaz means "strength". Those who take wives who have been offered by the Devil, either never produce children, or produce them as weaklings; they seem to produce sons who are neither healthy nor strong except in evil-doing, and as a punishment for the irregularity of the union, rather than to be a joy and consolation.' And later 'Boaz fathered Obed by Ruth'; Obed means 'subject'. 'For now they choose wealth and not character, beauty not honour. And', he says, 'they desire in their wives what is customarily found in mistresses. Besides they do not father sons obedient either to themselves or to God, but who defy both themselves and God, so that their sons are not the fruits of their legitimate union, but are the appropriate penalties of irregular behaviour.'

We find this exemplified specifically in Tobias, chapter 6, where we read that Sarah daughter of Raguel was given to seven husbands, each of whom a certain demon called Asmodeus strangled on their first night, leaving her still a virgin. And therefore when Raphael suggested to the younger Tobias that he marry her, and that she ought to be his wife, he said to the fearful Tobias:

> Listen, Tobias, and I shall show you who they are over whom a demon can prevail. For those who enter matrimony in such a way that they shut out God from themselves and their minds, and who give their

> time to their lust like the horse and the mule who have no powers of understanding—the demon will have power over them. But you, when you take her, go into the bedroom and avoid having sex with her for three days, devoting yourself only to prayers. When the third night has passed, take the young woman in fear of God, uniting with her more for the love of children than for lust, and you will have her as your wife, so that in the seed of Abraham you may acquire a blessing in children.

And it is noteworthy that this was the first occasion whereby the sons of Seth withdrew from God, and whereby the Flood spread over [the land] (Genesis, chapter 6): 'When men began to increase over the land, and sons were born to them, the sons of God saw that the daughters of men (that is the sons of Seth saw the daughters of Cain) were beautiful, and took as wives from all of them such as they chose.' So therefore a wife had to be chosen discreetly for the first man who wanted to marry. For example Abraham charged Eliazar not to take a wife for his son Isaac from the Canaan girls. Jacob also with mature deliberation provided himself with wives, serving fourteen years for them.

I said secondly that a wife should be guided gently, not with cruelty, severity and terror, with severity in words or blows, but with love not fear, sweetness not bitterness. Colossians, chapter 3: 'Husbands, love your wives, and do not be harsh with them.' In this way woman was fashioned, not from the head, nor from the feet, but from a rib from the side, as a sign that she ought not to be a mistress nor a maidservant, but a companion to her husband. For there are three things which the Holy Spirit says are pleasing to him (Ecclesiasticus, chapter 25): 'There are three sights which warm my spirit and are approved of by God and men—concord among brothers, amity among neighbours, and a man and his wife in agreement with each other.'

Thirdly, a wife should be corrected privately, not publicly in confusion and shame, or with contemptible accusations. As Varro says in one of his comedies: 'A wife's fault should be ignored or tolerated. Whoever ignores a fault, will make his wife more agreeable; whoever tolerates it, will make himself a better man.' And therefore the strictness of three husbands has rightly been shown to be severe by Valerius. The first was called Sulpicius Gallus; he publicly repudiated his wife because she had appeared in public with her head uncovered. The second was called Sempronius Sephus, who similarly repudiated his wife because she dared to watch public entertainments without his knowledge. The third was called Metenius; he killed his wife by striking her with a club, because she had been drinking wine. St Job did not condemn in this way, even if the wife was of the worst kind, but spoke privately and temperately: 'You have spoken like a foolish woman.' He did not say she was foolish, but that she was speaking like a foolish woman.

Fourthly a wife is to be loved to the full. The Apostle spells out the completeness of the love and friendship which there ought to be beween husband and wife under three headings. The first aspect arises from the love of God for the church, which was very great. Thus Ephesians, chapter 5: 'Husbands, love your wives as Christ loved the church; for he gave himself up for it.' The second aspect arises from a man's love for his own body. Thus in the same place: 'Men ought to love their wives as they love their own bodies.' The third aspect arises from a man's love for himself. Thus: 'Every man must love his wife as his very self.' But on hearing this a married man who has a viper for a wife may reply to me: 'How can I love her, when she is always hostile to what I do?' Varro has given the answer to this above: I refrain from inserting more to that answer.

But a man has every reason to be careful over his marriage, for no one doubts that wives cannot be easily mastered, because if a wife once strays into immorality, Scripture will be confirmed when it says: 'There is nothing so wicked as a wicked wife; the fate of the wicked will overtake her!' Thus a little earlier in the same chapter Wisdom compares her to three very harmful beasts, and says nevertheless that she surpasses them all in wickedness. Indeed a wife is compared with a serpent, a lion and a dragon. Regarding the serpent the text says: 'There is no head deadlier than the serpent's, and no anger deadlier than a woman's.' Regarding the lion and dragon it says: 'It will be more agreeable to stay with a lion and a dragon than to live with a wicked wife.' (cc.28-29)

Good wives

After relieving his feelings about bad women, Bower looks at the other side of the question and collects quotations about the characteristics of good wives from the Bible, the first-century Valerius Maximus, fifth-century St Jerome, and the twelfth-century Paris master Hugh of St Victor. He also relates an anecdote which possibly derives from the divinity classroom in St Andrews University, and which would have had all the students talking. As a celibate he displays little sympathy for the problems which may arise in marriage.

But because we have set out some aspects of the bad characteristics of women, there remains for us to insert a few [words] in praise of good women. For there are good wives who are pleasing to their husbands in many matters, namely in living together, in providing sympathy, and in staying together.

With regard to the first of these, Valerius tells about a certain queen, the wife of Mithridates, that she loved her husband to such an extent once the reins of affection had been loosened that she cut her hair, adopted male attire, and accustomed herself to horses and arms, so that she might follow her husband continuously across the country as he fled. He tells there of an excessive example of gratitude, of how a certain Roman seized two lambs, male and female; it was foretold by a soothsayer that he would lose one, or both married partners would perish, and that on the escape of the male, his wife would speedily die, and on the escape of the female he himself would die. He immediately ordered the female lamb to be let go, and endured that, while he looked on, he should himself be killed in the killing of the male one.

Second, they are pleasing in providing sympathy. For the above author tells that when the Spartans were captured by the Lacedaemonians, and had been kept in prison for beheading, their wives of distinguished lineage entered the prison as if to comfort the men who were about to perish, after asking the guards for entrance. After changing clothes the women veiled their heads in pretended grief, and the guards allowed them to leave; and thus both the men and the women were saved.

Third, they are pleasing in staying together. Jerome tells of this in his *Contra Jovinianum*, book 1: 'The Indians', he says, 'like nearly all barbarians, have many wives. Among them it is the law that the favourite wife is burned on funeral pyre along with her dead husband. These women therefore compete with each other for the man's love; and it is the highest ambtion of the rivals, and a testimony of fidelity, to be declared worthy of death; and so the victor lies next the corpse adorned in her finest clothes, embracing and kissing him, disregarding the flames of fires which have been lit underneath amid praise for her fidelity.' And if such praise is awarded to a pagan wife, what should be done for a Christian one? For Scripture says in Ecclesiasticus, chapter [26]: 'A good wife makes a happy husband.' I have heard it said that a certain young man, the son of a burgess, who as an adolescent when his father died, took a girl as his wife. She, by her biting abuse and shameless sexual appetite, daily annoyed her immature husband to the point of despair. Not daring to oppose her vindictive tongue, although pierced with grief inside, he nevertheless patiently put up with her until she died. After her death, with the deadly snare wiped out, as a freed man he laid down a rule for himself that he would never submit his neck to the yoke of the marriage bond; but also because he married just one young girl, he moved to the schools so that after subsequently becoming a priest he might devote himself to God more freely. There it happened that he along with his fellow-students each in turn had to comment on a passage in the Bible. At length his turn came to expound the text in Ecclesiasticus, chapter [26] 'A good wife makes a happy husband' he turned inward, or rather right out of himself, faltered, and as if in a trance stood in the rapture of a third heaven without the ability to utter a single word. His master said to him: 'Expound the text, my son.' In response to words of this kind often repeated, he replied haltingly: 'Master, I am thinking, I am thinking.' 'Wretch,' he said, 'what are you thinking? Expound the text.' In the end indeed he burst into tears, and cried out in a ringing voice, saying: 'By the Omnipotent God, sir, few husbands are happy.'

Lest therefore anyone inadvisedly enters marriage on account of the foregoing good aspects of marriage, the words of Hugh of St Victor should be noted in a litle book which he wrote to one of his circle who was wanting to marry, saying:

> A wise man should not take a wife, firstly because she gets in the way of philosophical studies, for no one can devote himself to books and a wife. Many things are needed for maintaining marriages, namely valuable clothes, gold, jewels, extravagant expenditure, maid-servants, various furnishings, then chattering discussions through the night. One wife goes out in public richly adorned; another is respected by everyone [when she says]: 'I am despised as a wretch among other women. Did you notice the woman next door? What did you say to the maid-servant? Coming as you are from the market, what have you brought me?' Her antipathy suspects his love for another.

And further on:

> The choice of a wife is non-existent, but whatever kind it is that comes along, that is the kind you will have—whether hot-tempered, or foolish, or ugly, or proud, or suspicious, or foul-smelling—whatever is the defect, we identify it after the marriage. A horse, an ass, an ox and the lowest of servants are examined beforehand, and then bought; only a wife is not put on display before her marriage lest she is not pleasing.

Hence someone says:

> We hardly have the power to know the shortcomings of a marriage-
>   partner or a son,
> and we are the last to know just by chance what is happening at home.
> When a marriage-partner, son, servant or foster-son does wrong,
> though these things are the subject of songs among neighbours, they
>   are hidden from us.
> (c.33)

Queen Margaret Logie

David and Margaret (daughter of Malcolm Drummond and widow of John Logie) were married sometime in 1363 at the bishop of St Andrews' house at Inchmurdo near St Andrews. He divorced her probably in February 1369. She then raised a case against him in the papal court at Avignon before the king's death in February 1371, and went there in person in the spring of 1372. It was a messy business, unprecedented for a Scottish queen.

King David married this Lady Margaret de Logie therefore at Inchmurdo, and exalted her in splendour as queen. He lived with her for a short time, [but following animosity that arose between them,] he divorced her about the beginning of Lent 1369. On this account she secretly boarded a ship in the Firth of Forth [well supplied with money] and made for the papal court. She arrived at Avignon where the pope was then to be found. By making an appeal she transferred her case there, and disturbed the whole kingdom by her legal action. And so once the king's proctors had travelled to the apostolic see, the case was bitterly disputed, and the pleading between the advocates of the contending parties was so prolonged that a book compiled from that source and certified by notarial marks is longer [in] wordage (in my judgment, for I who have written this have seen this pleading) than the contents of the text of four Psalters. For her case was many times committed for hearing by auditors and cardinals, so that if she had lived, she would have subjected the kingdom to an interdict; but she died on a pilgrimage to Rome. (c.34, ll.1-17)

Robert II and his family

In introducing Robert Steward as King Robert II (crowned at Scone on 26 March 1371) Bower balances admiration for his character with comment on the mixed merits of his thirteen known legitimate children and eight illegitimate ones. His quotations from the Bible and an (untraced) Aesop fable are not wholly apposite, for Robert's most notorious children, Alexander earl of Buchan and Walter earl of Atholl, were both legitimate.

So on the following feast of the Annunciation of Our Lady the said Sir Robert Stewart was crowned at Scone with due ceremony. He was humble and gentle, friendly in appearance, a cheerful man, an honourable king, witty in his responses, admirable in the way he carried himself, surpassing others in stature and the height of his body. Like another Abraham he was the father of many descendants, for he had plenty not only of children, but also of other living riches, so that this quotation from Deuteronomy [chapter] 30 could apply to him: 'The Lord your God will make you prosperous in all the works of your hands, in the offspring of your womb, in the fruit of your cattle, in the productivity of your land, and in abundance of everything.' All these things happened to him, for his times were made prosperous by way of great abundance of provisions, fruits and animals, and especially the tranquillity of peace.

But what am I to say about his children? Some were peace-loving and open-handed, some were arrogant and ill-disposed, because some people think that the saying in Isaiah [chapter] 59 is appropriate for his natural children, namely: 'What is nurtured from snakes' eggs will hatch into a viper.' That is to say that from a snake's eggs (as is characteristic of mothers) is hatched a viper, which is called the king of the most poisonous of beasts or serpents. Similarly from undisciplined mothers irregular offspring are born. Therefore it is not a matter for rejoicing on both sides if a king or prince fathers a son who is not the offspring of a marriage, but [merely] of pleasurable intercourse, just as Aesop writes in his *Apology* that when a son was born to a certain magnificent prince, all the courtiers danced for joy and indulged in entertainments, whilst a philosopher who was present wept. To those who asked why he was weeping he answered: 'Fools! Watch out for your rejoicing, for when the sun fathers a sun, every living thing begins to groan. Thus far we have had only one sun and no one has concealed himself from its scorching heat; but now the sun has been multiplied and will burn you all up and reduce you to nothing.' Certainly King Robert as a sun was kindly and an encouragement to his lieges; but to the extent that he has been multiplied in his sons, he is burning up the poor with scorching heat and is upsetting the kingdom. On the subject of bastards someone has this to say:

Lavish nature gives three rights to bastards:
they are either rich men, or thieves, or wastrels.
(c.36, ll.20-58)

The Peasants' Revolt in England

In this acount of the troubles in London in 1381 Bower displays fierce hostility to the peasant cause. His information about events in England is essentially muddled, for King Richard was never literally a captive of the rebels, and Jack Straw has been confused with Wat Tyler. No English source has been identified with the same errors: it is just possible that Bower was following an account written in the Low Countries. His own home base at Haddington would have provided facts about the visit there and at Holyrood of the duke of Lancaster. The earl of Carrick (the later King Robert III) had responsibilities as lieutenant of the Marches on the Scottish side of the Border to cope with Lancaster's request for asylum. Bower's reflections at the end leave the reader with a sour taste, even if the couplet of verse which he includes has respectable ancestry from the pen of the Roman poet Ovid.

In the same year, but a little before the embassy of the king of Scots was sent to France, in view of various troubles, losses and dangerous situations brought upon the English by the Scots, [the former] requested the arrangement of a truce with the Scots. For this purpose they sent the noble and distinguished prince Sir John of Gaunt duke of Lancaster to the Borders to negotiate a truce. He negotiated at the town of Berwick with representatives from Scotland a truce for three years. And while he was returning to the south of England, he learned from oral reports of how a mob of peasants had revolted at London against the new king Richard II, had arrested him forcibly with a formidable armed band, and had put him into custody among themselves. Furthermore on the day of his arrest they had cruelly murdered the archbishop of Canterbury and various renowned knights and barons; and they had torn the most celebrated palace or manor of Savoy belonging to the duke himself down to the ground, and bore hatred for him more than for all human beings. The leader and commander of these peasants was a brutish fellow, more spirited than the rest of the peasants, but also more crude in his manners, called Jack Straw, a man inclined to cunning and ready for all kinds of evil. On learning this news the duke of Lancaster was fearful when he heard that the peasants had plotted his death; he turned his horses back towards Scotland as quickly as he could, and humbly asked in a letter to the earl of Carrick, the prince [of the kingdom] and eldest son of the king of Scotland, for asylum and a welcome for him to remain in the kingdom of Scotland for the time being. The said prince responded favourably to his request, and sent Sir William earl of Douglas and Archibald de Douglas lord of Galloway with an honourable following to accompany him on his journey from the Borders to Scotland on a safe-conduct from the prince, after the king's permission had been requested and granted. They escorted him to the town of Haddington for his first night; and in the morning they lodged him honourably with his knights and servants at the monastery of Holyrood. And while he remained a guest in the kingdom, they treated him and his following there in a friendly manner; and various magnates and prelates, burgesses and others from all parts of the country sent to him not only provisions, but also royal gifts.

After some time had passed, Richard king of England sent a messenger to the duke of Lancaster, enjoining that he ought to return home speedily, because the forces of those peasants had been dispersed and overcome through the enterprise of a certain worthy knight who was then alderman or mayor of London, whom more than others the peasants were busy trying to bind to their side. He [agreed that] on a certain agreed day the peasants would bring the king face to face at a certain place in the city for a meeting with them, and if the king ordered the mayor himself to obey them, he would by no means hesitate to follow their wishes; but if this was not what the king did, he would advise a further period of truce. The peasants were buoyed up by this promise, and boldly decided to bring the king to meet the mayor, having no fears because of their heightened impudence and the vast extent of their numbers. Therefore at the pre-arranged place and time the king, surrounded by base-born villeins, was led by the hand by Jack Straw to the mayor of the city, and that officer was charged to give in to them; but on seeing his liege-lord the king, the mayor's heart began to swell with bitter anger, and, unable to contain himself under the pressure of this emotion, he quickly went up to Jack Straw, surrounded as he was in the middle of his many supporters, stabbed him with one blow of a dagger, knocked him to the ground, and once he was dead succeeded in disembowelling him. Once Straw had been struck down [and the king had been snatched from his followers] the alderman of the city exhorted his fellow-citizens, saying: 'Kill the gluttons, hang the robbers, run the traitors through, and clear this royal city of peasants.' At his call the nobles and citizens (who were very few compared with the peasants) unsheath their swords and daggers, and run the peasants through, angrily dashing out life along with their brains, and force the rest [whom they could not arrest] into flight. Thus in their thousands and hundreds they escape to wherever the force of the spirit led each man this way and that. So the courtiers secured victory over the peasants, making a most severe slaughter of them. They even surrounded some of those who had fled in narrow confined places, and in no way left from there until those who had been confined offered their necks either to be bound by the alderman with ropes, or to be bound by chains.

Rule by peasants is intolerable, because, as someone has said:

Nothing is more cruel than a poor man when he rises high.

And for that reason as soon as they have risen in revolt, they have to be subdued lest they get the upper hand, as Jerome says: 'Kill your enemy while he is young, so that his villainy is crushed as a seed.' The poet hints at this when he says:

> Resist beginnings. The medicine is prepared too late
> when the disease has gained strength by long delay.

For this reason you should never give your power to a peasant, since it is of a peasant, as of a dog, that it is said: 'Wash and comb your dog; he is a dog and remains the same.' But still [I dare say] a peasant is inferior to a dog, because in showing partiality for himself a dog is showing partiality. This is not the case with a peasant, for:

> A peasant stabs a man who anoints [him], and anoints the man who stabs him.
> (c.43 - c.44, l.15)

An English invasion 1384

Bower blends into one account three stories about an English raiding expedition in the Firth of Forth. The date was in fact 1384 (not 1385), when the young King Richard was just sixteen and did not come in person. His uncle the duke of Lancaster was mindful of the hospitality he had received in Scotland in 1381 (see above). The island monastery called here 'Emonia' that was attacked was Bower's own Inchcolm, and he emphasizes his belief in the active role of St Columba in protecting an institution dedicated to him. (Barnhill lies on the Fife shore opposite the island; North and South Queensferry are upstream; Dunipace is near Denny in Stirlingshire.)

With many and various unfortunate reverses of this kind affecting the English about the same time, the young Richard II king of England and all of his land were dismayed along with him, and they said among themselves: 'If we allow the Scots to rage amongst us in this way, they will remove from us our place and race; therefore we must resist and oppose them.' And because the said duke of Lancaster the king's uncle surpassed everyone else at that time in resources and capacity, the king called upon him with the support of his following as his choice for this task to invade Scotland, and to punish all of that land up to the Firth of Forth with fire and sword. In obedience to the king's order he entered Scotland with a large army in Holy Week 1385. But on account of the courtesy previously shown to him by the Scots, he imposed as little harm on them as he could.

Also at that time the duke's piratical fleet put in at Leith on the Forth bringing supplies for the army while he was staying at Edinburgh. When his men wanted to burn the town, he was firm in not allowing this to be done.

Admittedly the burgesses promised to pay a sum of money on this account to obtain favourable treatment, and once this had been paid they redeemed their town.

One special barge in the aforesaid fleet containing (it is said) one hundred and forty armed men landed at the island on which stands the monastery of St Columba of Emonia. All the ornaments of the church there and the furnishings of the place were looted by these men, and some sons of Belial, not content with that booty, turned their hands (which had already committed sacrilege) to burning the church of the monastery. A certain long lean-to outhouse was attached to it on the north side, whose ceiling or vaulted roof is generally called a tofall in the vernacular. It was roofed with dry heather, which with a whiff of fire was speedily reduced to ashes. The wooden roof of the church projected for a little over the top of this vaulted roof, for between the roof and wall of the choir some transparent material had been inserted to keep out the north wind and the winds from the north-east and north-west on either side, and spanning the wall was some well-packed and compressed dried heather. Due to the fierceness of the fire leaping up from the vaulted roof, and like food ready for it, [the church] clearly appeared to be scorched and blazing to those who were watching the outcome of the affair at some distance at [North Queens-] ferry and beyond the strait at Barnhill (who were all-but countless of both sexes, some being persons of noble birth and some of middle social standing), and as witnesses saw the church being utterly destroyed. Some of these began to decry the power of St Columba. But the more sensible of them held the same opinion as the man in Ovid's *Tristia*:

> Nothing is so lofty or reaches so far above perils
> that it is not beneath God and subject to him.

Prostrating themselves to the ground they earnestly prayed to the saint to save his church intact from the fire since this was within his power, so that his name might accordingly be honoured even more. The outcome was wonderful! No sooner had this prayer been uttered than the north wind, which had up till then helped to kindle the fire, now in an instant changed direction, so that people across the strait saw that the sparks that were vomiting fire, which had been ignited by means of bundles and faggots on the spears of the enemy, had, as it were, submitted to force and been hurled back. Thereupon voices and hands reached up to Heaven, glorifying God in his saint who had checked the strength of the fires so effectively that their church which had been put in urgent peril suffered no loss at all.

But note what follows: those same robbers made for their ship, loaded with bundles of loot, and right away landed at Queensferry in Lothian. And they soon took to raiding the coastline for beasts that were grazing there for food; others set fire to the town of [South Queens-]ferry. And as they were hurrying back to their ship with their spoils and loot, three noble Scottish knights suddenly came upon them unexpectedly. These were the two brothers Thomas and Nicholas Erskine and Alexander de Lindsay, who came up from the east with about fifty mounted troops, and Sir William Cunningham of Kilmaurs (as it is said), who came from the west with thirty mounted troops. They began to fight with the cattle-raiders. Some of those were killed then, others surrendered and were taken prisoner, others as well fled to their ship. Soon they paid the penalty for their greed and fire-raising; for more than forty of them (mainly those who had shown themselves hostile to St Columba) on fleeing to their ship sought help by seizing hold of the ship's rope attached to the anchor. As they crept along holding on to it for balance, they perished in the following manner. For the ship's captain, who was keeping watch on the ship with two or three others, and was exceedingly afraid of the savagery of the Scots who were pursuing his companions, grabbed an axe in his hands and violently cut the hawser attached to the prow. And so he was the means of the drowning and death of all his companions who were clinging to the hawser, and brought on their destruction.

And to add to that miracle it happened that the chief instigator of the attack of the church, the man who had raised sacrilegious fire in St Columba's shrine (as mentioned above), was taken prisoner in the following of the said Sir William de Cunningham. While Sir William was starting out with him, after building up a rage and becoming delirious, he at once began to strike some Scots with his fists, and to knock them from their horses to the ground in a frenzy, hissing through his teeth and crying out: 'St Columba! You are setting [me] on fire, and are imposing too severe a punishment on me.' As he raged excessively in this way, it was all that everyone could do to control him. But also when he was asked why he was behaving violently in this way, he replied: 'I deserve this suffering, for I have sinned against St Columba. It is I who have done it, who have acted wickedly, who have set the vaulted roof of his church on fire; and I would even have reduced his [whole] church to ashes if I had had the chance. For when I set fire to the heather blocking the space between the roof and the outhouse, the saint appeared in angry mood, enveloped in his abbot's chasuble, and sprinkled water and put out the blazing fire. And furthermore he has put his mark on my scorched beard and eye-lashes with a flying spark, as you can see.' With these words he let out a horrible roar, so that he caused those listening to and watching him to flinch and shudder; and furthermore he raged at three of the mounted troops with such confused speech that as he knocked one man down and then another he could not easily be restrained from his fury by all of them [together] until he was violently manhandled; and once he had been run through with swords, he was buried at a junction of two roads near the village of Dunipace.

The duke remained in Scotland as an enemy for ten days. (c.44, l.60 - c.45)

Invasion of Scotland by Richard II 1385

Bower reports on a short expedition to Scotland by the young English king Richard II in August 1385. The damage caused to famous churches leads him to include a sermon from the heart against the evil of burning monasteries (especially by a king), and against fire-raising in general. Richard supposedly had his punishment after his deposition in 1399, for Bower appears to believe in the legend that he did not die in prison in England, but came to live a clandestine life in Scotland (see also below XV, c.9, c.19 and c.31). (John of Gaunt duke of Lancaster had lodged at Holyrood when fleeing from the Peasants' Revolt in England in 1381.)

A little earlier in the same year about the feast of St Laurence Richard II king of England, sick at heart that the Scots and French were plundering his land so cruelly, and were attacking his fortresses and razing them to the ground, assembled a large army and entered Scotland at the age of 19. He advanced in the midst of an arrogant host, destroying everything on all sides and saving nothing. He burnt to ashes with consuming flames churches devoted to God and monastic sanctuaries (namely the monasteries at Dryburgh, Melrose and Newbattle), and the noble royal town of Edinburgh with its church of St Giles. And once he had carried through the maximum of destruction in Lothian, he returned home unharmed.

It is in a way surprising that such a Christian king had no difficulty in agreeing to the firing of any kind of lodgings used by Christians, much less the lodgings and sanctuaries of God himself, and this on various counts:

First, because it is a diabolical sin. For the Devil assaults souls in Hell with fire; so do fire-raisers in the World. And for that reason it is much to be feared that when such men are in practice likened to the Devil, they may be united with him in torment. It is a great decline in standards for a king to allow, or give orders for, such things to be done, because the more eminent a man, the more he is regarded as contemptible if he starts up fires. This is because since those who tend fires in the service of men are dishwashers and scullions, how can those who tend fires in the service of demons be other than contemptible persons? It was for this reason that it turned out that this same King Richard who previously in the prime of his majesty was surrounded by a crowd of knights and a host of retainers and was on a level with Solomon the Great in his expenditure, in the end escaped from the prisons [of his supplanter] to the Isles of Scotland, where he was recognized by a certain jester who had earlier been trained at his court, and found as a contemptible dish-washer in the kitchen of Donald lord of the Isles.

Second, that the sin [of fire-raising] is a great hindrance to the salvation of its perpetrator on account of the restoration of what has been burnt, which he ought to arrange, and on account of the curses which fall on him when a poor man who has suffered from a fire suffers some loss from the effect of the fire; naturally when he sees his children lamenting in some strange lodging, he curses the man who has burned his house. This curse brings the fire-raiser into the eternal fire, unless he is relieved by appropriate penitence and restoration as already stated, because we ought to believe Holy Scripture where it is said: 'The prayer of a man who curses you in bitterness of spirit will be heard; for his Creator will hear him.' And again in the thirty-fifth chapter: 'The Lord will hear the prayer of a man who has been wronged. He will not despise the prayers of an orphan, nor the widow when she pours out the words of her complaint. Do not a widow's tears run down her cheek, and do not they accuse him who causes them? For from the cheek they go right up to heaven, and the Lord who hears will not be pleased with them.'

King Richard would have burned the respected monastery of Holyrood as well, if he had not been dissuaded by his uncle the lord duke of Lancaster, who had previously found refuge there at his time of need when, as stated above, he was avoiding the savagery of the peasants. (c.47, ll.5-15, 19-60)

The prowess of William Douglas

Bower places this effusive account of Sir William Douglas of Nithsdale in the mid-1380s. His father was in 1388 to become the third earl of Douglas. William married a daughter of King Robert II.

At the same time the said Sir Archibald de Douglas had a natural son called William, who was young in years but surpassing others in prowess, and who was indefatigable in harrying the English by land and sea. He was a dark-skinned man, not very heavy but spare, gigantic in appearance, erect and tall, energetic and approachable, charming and amiable, generous and cheerful, reliable and clever. He checked the English so powerfully on all sides and made them so fearful that two thousand [of them] did not dare to fight with him as he frequently ravaged and destroyed their land, though he had scarcely five hundred men. This was because he was said to be so strong that whomsoever he had struck with a blow of his mace or sword or a thrust of his lance fell dead to the ground, or if protected by some kind of armour,

[fell] on his back scarcely half alive. For on one occasion when he had set fire to the suburbs of Carlisle with only a small force, and he was standing alone before the walls on a revolving drawbridge made of boards that was scarcely two feet wide, he killed a very strong champion from the town, and two splendidly armed men who were not inferior to himself he pounded and knocked down under his feet with a mace which he was carrying in his hand. And he ran unharmed to his men who were skirmishing with the townsmen some distance away, and brought speedy assistance and comfort to them, few as they were compared with the English who were violently attacking them. On another occasion with eight hundred men he defeated three thousand English in open battle, of whom two hundred were killed on the field, and he brought five hundred as prisoners with him to Scotland. (c.48, ll.27-52)

The battle of Otterburn

The Scots in 1388 mounted a two-pronged attack on northern England under the earl of Douglas in the east and the earl of Fife in the west respectively. Sir Henry Percy ('Hotspur') pursued the former's force and overtook it on the evening probably of 5 August at Otterburn in Redesdale. Bower shows considerable knowledge of the fight that brought about Douglas' death and Percy's capture; and goes on in his next chapter to insert a Latin poem of 343 lines recounting this famous bittersweet occasion (not included here).

But inside Newcastle all the armed levies of Northumbria from the city of York [northwards] were waiting under Sir Henry Percy the younger, the son of Henry earl of Northumberland (who was called Henry Hotspur in the vernacular), a very brave knight who was tested in battle. They were wanting to find ways of gaining advantage over the Scots. While therefore the earl of Douglas and his men were returning to their own country, the said Henry Percy reconnoitred the earl of Fife's force; but since it was large, he turned his attention to the said earl of Douglas's force, which was then encamped at Otterburn in Redesdale. Suspecting no harm from his enemies, the earl of Douglas himself, together with the two brothers the earls of March and Moray and a great many other knights and nobles, had disarmed, and on St Oswald's Day had dressed themselves in gowns and ankle-length robes, and were sitting down to supper. Then as they reclined at table, a certain Scot arrived riding a horse without any harness and frantically shouting for everyone to fly to arms, for, he said, 'the enemy are hurrying upon you'. On hearing his call everyone got up from supper, and as they rushed for the protection of their armour they were scarcely able to protect themselves with armour of a basic kind. The lord earl of Douglas indeed took himself off so hastily to arranging the battle-order that he omitted to fasten his own armour. On this account he was mortally wounded in the face and neck during the night by unknown hands, and in the morning, alas!, he was found dead. He left no legitimate heir behind him, and was succeeded in the earldom of Douglas by Sir Archibald lord of Galloway. Sir John de Dunbar earl of Moray also forgot his helmet because the fight had begun so suddenly [so that he fought in the field bareheaded.]

Sir Henry Percy accordingly, surrounded by ten thousand armed men, divided his army into two sections. He commanded one section along with his brother Sir Ralph; the other section he entrusted to the knights Sir [Matthew] de Redman and Sir Robert Ogle to destroy the pavilions and tents. For his part he hurried to the field of battle. When therefore as the din accompanying the arrival of the English increased, and most of the Scots took to flight, they were very eagerly pursued by Redman and Ogle. But as Percy with his section observed the Scots who were fleeing [to the baggage under a sudden attack by Redman and his men], and was exceedingly delighted at the sight of this rout, thinking that he was securing victory without opposition, the earl of Douglas and his men mounted their horses, and after hiding among shrubs and thorns as they hurried to the field of battle unseen for some time by the English, they finally burst out suddenly near the English line with twelve banners flying and glowing in the reflection of the sun's rays a little before it set. Dismounting from their horses they fearlessly sought out the English. But they on the other side, numbering three times more than the Scots, attacked them in return with lances, and strove to strike the other side.

When therefore they had begun to do battle, suddenly a certain especially doughty, vigorous and powerful knight, the Scot John Swinton, leapt out from the flank of the battle line, and as both sides were assailing each other with lances, he withdrew sideways a little from both sides, raised his terrible long lance energetically, struck the iron tips of many English lances from the side, and knocked them to the ground with each blow. As a result the Scots were the first to strike home on the English with their lances, and with powerful force compelled them willy-nilly to withdraw. So when the fighting had gone on for some time, the English soon turned to flee, whereupon through the whole of that night the Scots killed and pursued their enemies, and took prisoners. The English commander Henry Hotspur was captured along with his brother. As a result however many of those who did not take to flight were not killed, but were overcome by the Scots and led off as prisoners to Scotland in such quantity that there were more captives than captors. (c.50, l.13 - c.51, l.16)

Book XV

Aftermath of the coronation at Scone 1390

Robert III and his queen were crowned at the Augustinian abbey of Scone near Perth on 14-15 August 1390. Bower as a fellow Augustinian abbot relates with satisfaction a picturesque tale of how the abbey secured compensation for damages by those attending the ceremonies.

So great was the crowd from every part of the kingdom that gathered for the king's coronation that all the standing crops of the monastery of Scone nearby and in other places and granges round about were ruined by the horses. A certain canon who was granger of the monastery (Robert Logy by name) therefore approached the king seeking to bring to his notice the loss which the monastery had suffered at the king's hands through the destruction of its crops; but because the king was then engaged on more important matters, the canon was contemptuously turned away from the royal presence by the servants of the court. Because he had not obtained an answer from the king, the canon left a sad man. So very early the next morning, on the day when the king was due to leave the monastery, the same canon brought with him a crowd of men and women servants of its husbandmen and of women who worked on the land for its knights, each carrying a basin and a stick. He arranged also for a leader to go ahead of the others carrying a harvest corn-dolly (which the people call a rapegyrne) attached to the top of a pole, and for a sudden trumpet-sound to be raised outside the room as the king rose from his bed, to the extent that he and his attendants were as a result stupefied and astonished. Enquiry was therefore made into the cause of all this din, and the canon was brought to the king as the perpetrator of the offence, that is the man who the day before had been summarily refused access to the king's presence. He gave the king an explanation of his musical skill, saying: 'Do not wonder, most illustrious king, that we have serenaded you at dawn, for I must confess that every year we usually spend £30 or £40 as the cost of [gathering] our crops. But now, thanks to your royal highness, the summer is over, the crop has been cut, and there is no need to spend one shilling on bringing the crops to the barn, for your reapers have lightened our expenses and our labour. I have therefore come to tell you about it.' On hearing this the king's chamberlains and servants of the court who were standing by pronounced the canon worthy of severe punishment for his presumption in disturbing the king and alarming the court. But the king, on considering the matter (wise man that he was) and keeping God in mind, understood and explained the heart of the matter with greater understanding: he immediately had the damage to the crops assessed and compensation paid in full to the monastery. For ever afterwards he held the canon in highest esteem, commending him for his diligence. (c.1, ll.13-51)

Clan fight at Perth

Bower has litle sympathy with the highland clans (so-called for the first known time here), which he regards as made up of 'caterans' (i.e. marauders). The famous judicial duel between two representative groups before the king at Perth on 25 September 1396 had various precedents in England and France. By the time Bower came to write this account, details of what was said and done had lost nothing in the telling (a biblical reference included).

In 1396 a large part of the north of Scotland beyond the mountains was disturbed by two pestiferous caterans and their followers, namely Scheabeg and his blood-thirsty men who were called Clan Kay and Cristy Johnson and his men who were called Clan Qwhele. They could not be reconciled by any agreement or treaty, nor could they be subdued by any contrivance of the king or the governor until the noble and vigorous Sir David Lindsay de Crawford and Sir Thomas earl of Moray, bringing both persistence and strength to bear, arranged that the two sides should meet before the king on a certain day at Perth. Each side would choose from its following thirty persons against thirty of the other side who, armed only with swords and bows and arrows, without doublets or other armour, but with their axes, were to meet in battle in this way and put an end to the dispute. The country would then have peace. This arrangement was highly acceptable to each side. On the Monday before Michaelmas they appeared on the North Inch of Perth before the king [and the governor] and an innumerable multitude [of compatriots as well as distinguished Frenchmen and Englishmen] and engaged in a battle of great ferocity, in which out of the sixty all were killed except one from the Clan Kay side and eleven from the other. It also happened on that occasion that when all were ready for the fight, one of them, looking for a place of refuge, slipped away from among them all to the river and swam across the water of the Tay. He was followed by thousands, but never caught. The two sides therefore stood astonished and apparently not prepared to start the fight because of the defection of the man who had fled, for the side with the full complement of participants would not agree to the removal of one of their number, and the other side could not at any price induce anyone to act as a substitute for the man who had fled. Everyone therefore was confused and perplexed, complaining of the harm done by the fugitive. But when people were beginning to think that the whole affair would be abandoned, a strong peasant rushed out into the centre. A man of moderate height but savage appearance, he said: 'Here I am! Who will hire me to join these men involved in this theatre-like game? I shall take part in the game for half a mark, with the further condition that if I emerge alive from the contest, I shall receive my keep from all of you for the rest of my life, [and if I die, you will be good enough to pray for me]. If, as it is said, 'there is no greater love than this, that a man should lay down his life for his friends', what shall be my reward for putting my life at risk for the enemies of the common good and the kingdom?' His request was granted by the king and various magnates. Thereupon he stretched his bow and was the first to send an arrow into the opposing side, killing a man. At once arrows flew on either side, men swung their axes, brandished their swords and struggled with each other; like butchers killing cattle in a slaughter-house, they massacred each other fearlessly; there was not even one among so many who, whether from frenzy or fear, or by turning aside from a chance to attack another in the back, sought to excuse himself from all this slaughter. The man [who had started the fight off] nevertheless emerged unharmed in the end; and from then on for a long time the north remained quiet, and there was neither evil nor upset there as before. (c.3, ll.11-62)

The pseudo-Richard II

Bower returns to the story that King Richard II did not die in prison in England in February 1400, but survived with the connivance of the Scottish goverment as a semi-prisoner in Scotland, never allowed to meet people such as the earl of Northumberland who had known him in England. Apparently this pseudo-Richard lived until 13 December 1419.

In this way King Richard was deprived of his kingdom, and was speedily removed and condemned to perpetual imprisonment. [But] he was cleverly removed from there and taken to the islands of Scotland, where he was recognised and discovered in the kitchen of Donald lord of the Isles by a certain jester who had been trained at the court of King Richard while he was in power. He was sent by this lord of the Isles with the lord of Montgomery to King Robert III, in whose care he was treated with respect so long as the king of Scotland lived; and after the king's death he was presented to the duke of Albany, the governor of Scotland, in whose care he was given royal honours befitting his rank. At length he died at Stirling Castle and was buried in the church of the friars there at the north end of the altar.

At this time many fled from England from the presence of King Henry IV and came to King Richard in Scotland. At the time King Richard could not be persuaded by the governor or any others to have a private meeting with the earl of Northumberland.

In the same year Richard king of England died in the castle of Stirling on the feast of St Lucy [the Virgin, and was buried by the north end of the altar of the friars preacher of Stirling]. (c.9, ll.16-28; c.19, ll.50-51, 57-59; c.31, ll.57-59)

Death of the duke of Rothesay

The duke of Rothesay (when aged 20) was appointed by his father, the incapacitated King Robert III, to rule as his lieutenant on 27 January 1399 for three years. His mother Queen Annabel died in the autumn of 1401. Bower tells of Rothesay's fate almost approvingly. It seems to have been master-minded by Rothesay's uncle Robert duke of Albany and the earl of Douglas. The young man was arrested near St Andrews in Fife apparently in February 1402, and died for whatever reason as soon as 25/26 March in Albany's castle at Falkland in central Fife. Bower makes it all seem understandable, indeed almost justifiable (see below for his admiring epitaph on Albany).

A little earlier the lord king in council appointed certain councillors (powerful barons and knights) under oath to control and advise Sir David Stewart duke of Rothesay, earl of Carrick and prince of Scotland, because it appeared to the king and council that he engaged too often in unruly games and trivial sports, so that he too was bound by wiser counsel and swore to conform to the control and advice of these men. But on the death of the queen his noble mother, who used to curb him in many things, it was as if a noose had become worn: he hoped to free himself and, spurning his council of honourable men, gave himself up wholly once more to his previous frivolity. As a result the council of magnates assigned to him resigned to the king, observing that even if they wished, they could not divert him to a serious way of life. Thereupon the weak and decrepit king wrote to his brother the duke of Albany as governor that [the said duke of Rothesay should be arrested by him] and put into custody for a time until, after punishment by the rod of discipline, he should know himself better. A father after all does not dote on his son, but sometimes punishes him. But what the king proposed for the improvement of his son brought him to harm [in this case]; for it happened that each messenger with the king's letter to the governor turned out to be a fomenter and instigator that the king should ask for something that was not honourable for either party, as the experience of the outcome of the affair proved. Sir William Lindsay of Rossie and Sir John Ramornie knights, members of the king's household and his councillors, were the messengers and bearers of the king's letters to the duke [of Albany]. They are also said to have suggested earlier to the duke of Rothesay that following on the death of the bishop of St Andrews he should take over and hold the bishop's castle for the king's use until a new bishop was installed. They then arrested that duke between the township of Nydie and Strathtyrum as with no evil in mind he rode towards the castle of St Andrews in simple fashion and with a moderate following, and led the same duke by force to the castle of St Andrews which was ready to surrender to him. There they held him in custody until the duke of Albany and his council meeting at Culross decided what to do with him. The duke of Albany with the second Sir Archibald earl of Douglas forcibly moved him to the tower of Falkland mounted on a mule and dressed in a russet tunic, and there they condemned him to be kept in a certain decent small room, in which he was long guarded by John Selkirk and John Wright until after languishing with dysentery or (as some will have it) with hunger he died on [the evening of] the day before Easter (which fell on 26 March) or on the morning of Easter Day, and was buried at Lindores. The said John Ramornie was a counsellor both of the prince and the lord king, a man who was bold in spirit [though of low birth] and highly eloquent in speech, who acted as king's spokesman in difficult cases and was a most skilful advocate [in the courts of princes and magnates]. It is said that he previously suggested to the prince himself, the duke of Rothesay, that he arrest his uncle the duke of Albany and, taking advantage of some occasion or another, remove him forthwith from the scene; but this the prince firmly refused to do. This attendant knight, blinded by the soot of his spite, could not leave off from what had been begun, being caught in the disgrace of it, because as Chrysostom says: 'A spirit once vitiated by a crooked inclination cannot be in any way corrected.' And therefore turning around and switching his cloak to the other shoulder, he enjoined the duke of Albany to do the same kind of harm to his nephew the duke of Rothesay; otherwise, he asserted, the duke of Rothesay would without fail have made an end to him. The said Sir William Lindsay chanced to hold the same opinion as this John de Ramornie, because the said duke of Rothesay had betrothed himself to his sister Euphemia de Lindsay, but had repudiated her in his subsequent attempted marriages to other ladies, as for example the daughter of the earl of March. (c.12, ll.14-77)

The character of Robert III

Bower offers reflections in literary style on the character and conduct of King Robert III on his death in 1406, with a quotation from the twelfth-century Alan of Lille and biblical allusions. He may well have seen this king in person; but the supposed dialogue between Robert and his wife Queen Annabel must surely be a product of his imagination. It is none the less valuable for that, as a guide to contemporary thinking.

In this king's time there was an abundance of provisions in the kingdom, but a great deal of dissension, strife and brawling among the magnates and leading men, because the king, being bodily infirm, had no grip anywhere. Therefore in the absence of fear there was justification of the poet's saying:

> Under a slack shepherd the wolf fouls the wool, and the flock [is torn to pieces].

There were also very often raids in the Borders and worthless truces: indeed the predominant Borderers at that time were those who in manly fashion checked the daring deeds and ventures of the English. The said king was tall in stature though lame; he had a very handsome face with a luxuriant beard; he had the attractiveness of a snowy-white old age, with lively eyes which always spread good humour, and rather long and ruddy cheeks blooming with every mark of handsome amiability. Wherever he went, moreover, he took with him humility as attendant of the virtues, that is as his constant companion. This had made him so beloved by his men that all his subjects thought it agreeable to look on him, both for his gentle countenance and for the proof of his humility. If therefore humility is always welcome in a poor man, it will assuredly be a sign of grace in a prince. 'The greater you are,' says Scripture, 'the humbler you must be in all things, and you will find grace before God and men.' Let princes who are arrogant in the belief that pride has a place blush and be ashamed when they hear that humility is an ornament in heaven and on earth alike. One day when the noble Queen Annabel (the wife of this most gentle king in her lifetime) asked him why he was not making arrangements for an honourable monument like other kings who had been his predecessors, and what words of appreciation he had in mind to be written as his epitaph, the king replied to her thus: 'You have spoken like a worldly woman, for if I think carefully over what, who and of what kind I am—on what is my nature (because I am a stinking seed), on what is my personality (because I am food for worms), and on what is the nature of my life (because I am the most wretched of men)—I should as a result have no desire to erect a proud tomb. Therefore let these men who strive in this world for the pleasures of honour have shining monuments. I on the other hand should prefer to be buried at the bottom of a midden, so that my soul may be saved in the day of the Lord. Bury me therefore, I beg you, in a midden, and write for my epitaph: 'Here lies the worst of kings and the most wretched of men in the whole kingdom.' (c.19, ll.1-41)

Founding of the University of St Andrews

As a canon of the cathedral priory at St Andrews Bower must have been associated at first hand with the founding and development of the university there from its beginning. Bishop Wardlaw and Prior Biset were its founding fathers. Laurence de Lindores was the most distinguished of the first teachers, qualified to lecture on the basic theological text-book, the Sentences *of Peter Lombard. The celebrations on the arrival of the papal bulls of privileges in 1414 are graphically described here as by an eye-witness. But Bower's sense of disappointment when reflecting in the 1440s on the lack of serious intellectual interests among the students rings a bell of disillusionment. (Hugh of St Victor was a twelfth-century master at the university of Paris who composed his* Didascalicon *as an introduction to philosophy.)*

In the previous year (namely 1410) after Whitsunday an institution of higher learning of university standing made a start in the city of St Andrew of Kilrymont in Scotland when Henry de Wardlaw was the bishop of St Andrews and James Biset was the prior there. Master Laurence de Lindores (a great theologian and a man of respected life-style) was the first to begin lecturing there on the fourth book of the *Sentences*, Master Richard Cornell (a doctor of canon law and archdeacon of Lothian) on decrees, and sir John Litstar (a licentiate in decrees and canon of St Andrews) [a man of great knowledge of the religious life and of distinguished life-style] in the same faculty in the mornings. Subsequently Master John Scheves official of St Andrews and Master William Stephenson (who was later bishop of Dunblane) lectured in the same faculty, and Master John Gill, Master William Fowlis and Master William Croyser in philosophy and logic. They continued their lectures for two and a half years before the confirmation of the privileges [of the university]. At last on 3 February (that is the morrow of the Purification of Our Lady, a Saturday, dominical letter F) the bearer of the privileges, Henry de Ogilvie M.A., arrived in the city of St Andrews. On his happy arrival a peal of all the [bells of the] city's churches was sounded. The next day, that is the following Sunday, at the ninth hour there was a formal meeting of all the clergy in the refectory (which had been specially fitted up for the occasion) when the bulls of privileges were presented to the lord bishop as chancellor of this gracious university. When the bulls had been read out before everybody, the clergy and convent processed to the high altar singing the *Te Deum laudamus* in harmonious voice. When this had been sung and everyone was on bended knee, the bishop of Ross pronounced the versicle of the Holy Spirit and the collect *Deus qui corda*. They spent the rest of this day in boundless merry-making and kept large bonfires burning in the streets and open spaces of the city while drinking wine in celebration. It was decided moreover to hold a solemn procession on the following Tuesday so as to celebrate the feast of the arrival of the privileges along with the feast of the arrival of the relics. Who can easily give an account of the character of that procession, the sweet-sounding praise of the clergy, the rejoicings of the people, the pealing of bells, the sounds of organs? On that day the prior celebrated a high mass of the Holy Spirit, the bishop of Ross preached a sermon to the clergy, and the beadle counted four hundred clergy besides lesser clerks and young monks taking part in this procession for the glory of God and the praise and honour of the [new] university, together with an astonishing crowd of people.

But some people think that there is one thing in the university in recent times that is not only reprehensible but also needs changing, namely that when clerks begin to learn and obtain degrees in the schools, they soon leave the schools and thus demean the learning which ought to distinguish them. Hugh [of St Victor] denounces men of this kind in his *Didascalicon*; when writing to one who, after procuring a degree in the schools, intended to leave them, he says: 'If you had looked down on learning beyond the alphabet, you would not now have such a reputation among the grammar students. I know that there are some [like you] who want to dabble in philosophy right away, whose knowledge is very like that of an ass. Do not copy this behaviour for:

> After instruction in little things you will with safety attempt weighty matters.

Themistocles the wise man of Greece, when he realised that he was dying at the age of 107, is reported to have said that he was sorry to depart this life when he had just begun to be wise. Plato also died writing in his 81st year. Socrates filled his declining years with the task of teaching and writing. Homer also relates that utterance sweeter than honey flowed from the tongue of Nestor, although already old and nearly decrepit.' It is otherwise in the thinking of today's clerks who move in an undiscriminating manner to those schools from which they think they will share in some material gain. (c.22, ll.1-65)

Storks at St Giles in Edinburgh

At the year 1416 Bower reports a natural curiosity, which he makes interesting by reference to the writings of the third-century A.D. naturalist Solinus (rather than the first-century A.D. Pliny, who has little to say on storks).

In the same year a pair of birds called storks came to Scotland and nested on [the belfry of] the church of St Giles in Edinburgh. They stayed there for part of the year, but where they went afterwards is unknown. They give the greatest care to their offspring, as Pliny says, to the extent that while they are carefully looking after their nests, they continuously cast their soft feathers while lying down. But no less extraordinary devotion is shown by the chicks to their mothers, for however long the mothers have spent on the training of their young, they are supported by the chicks for as long. Hence the stork is called the affectionate bird. (c.24, ll.3-12)

Scottish forces in France

Robert duke of Albany was governor of Scotland 1406-20 during the imprisonment in England of the young King James I. Responding to an invitation from King Charles VI of France or his son the dauphin (King Charles VII from August 1422), he sent a Scottish force to France in October 1419 in a successful attempt to prevent the total occupation of France by the invading English king Henry V. The Scottish troops had one notable victory over the English at Baugé north of the river Loire on 22 March 1421, which led to the dauphin (rather than his father the king as stated here) entrusting their leader the earl of Buchan with command of his troops as constable of France. This was hardly a popular appointment.

The king of France wrote to Sir Robert duke of Albany governor of Scotland on the strength of the treaty between the kingdoms for the help of men at arms against King Henry V of England who was then troubling the kingdom of France. After calling together the three estates in council, he sent to France his second son, the famous knight John Stewart earl of Buchan and chamberlain of Scotland, with a vast crowd of nobles, knights and men-at-arms to the number of 7,000. This man bore himself most gloriously for the time he was there: the laudatory statements of the French [still] acclaim him to the full. He and his men were therefore received with honour by the king of France and he was appointed constable of France after the battle of Baugé.

From a combination of venerable maturity, admirable industry, careful shrewdness, graceful bearing, comely apparel, care for his manners, fluent way of speaking and handsome shape of face he so won the hearts of king and community that he seemed to have arisen like another Messiah among and with them. The magnates of the kingdom, though, were annoyed because of all this, since, as it is said:

The envious man pines away at the prosperity of another.

And the more he was honoured by the king, the more they were corrupted with envy. It was therefore decided that the constable should remain at the small town of Châtillon with its well-fortified castle in the duchy of Touraine. His comrade and partner was Archibald earl of Wigtown, son and heir of the second Archibald earl of Douglas [afterwards duke of Touraine] who fell in defence of the right of France in the battle of Verneuil [in] Perche with many thousands of his men. Therefore this future constable and Archibald de Douglas earl of Wigtown, keeping the valiant Scottish knights with them at Châtillon, chose captains to control the countryside with bands of fighting men; each was in charge of his own troops with his little banners and blazons at the ready, and kept watch on the frontiers against the English. It was not without grim fighting that some towns were captured and castles recovered from the English: strenuously they accomplished strenuous acts of war, each on his own. But because they did not drive the English out of the kingdom at once, the Scots were denounced to the king and called wine-bibbers and mutton-eating fools [by the French]. The king patiently swallowed these men's murmurs with ready ears, but deferred giving a word in answer to the accusers until after the fight at Baugé, where the English were captured and beaten. Then calling the complainers to him he said: 'What do you think [now] of the Scottish mutton-eaters and wine-bibbers?' As if struck on their foreheads by a hammer for very shame they had no answer for the king. (c.31, ll.12-54)

'Le qwhew'

In commenting on an unusual number of deaths in Scotland c.1420, Bower attributes them to a sickness called 'le qwhew', a word which is not found elsewhere. His description of the condition is borrowed in a general way from the writings of Hippocrates (fifth century B.C.) as transmitted by Galen (second century A.D.), which were still the basis of medical understanding in fifteenth-century Scotland.

This sickness by which not only magnates but also numberless men of the people were snuffed out was called 'le qwhew' by the common people. The physicians say that it was caused by an inequality or excess in the preceding winter, spring and summer, for the winter was very dry and northern, spring was rainy like autumn, and so it was inevitable that in summer fevers, eye-inflammations and dysenteries became acute, especially in damp places. In winter dry humours, checked by the cold, are whetted. But in spring waste matters are generated in conditions of excessive intemperate dampness and are dispersed by warmth. In summer to be sure when the warmth is not strong enough to consume them, it causes putrefaction and so generates acute fevers and brings on many other diseases. If indeed a winter has been warm and damp, but spring cold and dry, it is inevitable that in summer men will fall sick and pregnant women will have miscarriages for a trifling reason. Galen offers an explanation of this, saying: 'When the bodies of pregnant women are warm and damp in winter, they are delicate and thin. As a result the coldness of the spring air is harmful to the foetus when it suddenly penetrates to the inner parts [of the body]. For by coldness and dryness which are deadly conditions, the foetus is destroyed. As a result the destroyed foetus chafes at its bonds and severs them; and so of necessity the woman aborts.' But what are these extraneous matters to us that we discourse on physic? Let us therefore turn to our chronicles. (c.32, ll.23-46)

The battle of Verneuil

Bower's account of the disastrous defeat of the forces of Charles VII including Scottish reinforcements at Verneuil on 17 August 1424 appears to be well-informed. Buchan had been joined by the earl of Douglas (made also duke of Touraine by the French king in April 1424). Bower lays the main blame on Scottish arrogant recklessness, while explaining also how some Lombard mercenaries hired by Charles from Milan had first turned the tide of battle against the Scots and French, and then had themselves fled in panic unscathed.

In August of the following year the battle of Verneuil-Perche in Normandy was fought on the octave of St Laurence 1424, in which fell the earl of Buchan constable of France, the earl of Douglas lieutenant of France and James de Douglas his son, and the lord of Swinton the grandson of [Robert] duke of Albany, with many knights and worthy men both Scots and French. On the French side the count of Harcourt a close relative of the king of France was killed, along with the viscount of Narbonne and also the count of Tonnerre. The number of dead on all sides, English and the others, was 6,000, with as many English killed as were Scots and French. It is said that it was the vain arrogance and reckless haste of the Scots which was the reason for their fall and ruin. When they had four times the number of the English, they rushed against their enemies neglecting the principles of sensible military practice; then after some fighting the English archers were pierced by Scottish spears and as one man took to flight. On observing this the English lancers would for their part have surrendered had it not been that a little before the start of the battle they had learned for certain that the duke of Touraine had had it proclaimed that there would be certain penalties if anyone took Englishmen as prisoners, and that they were to be killed indiscriminately without any [hope of] ransom. It was another misfortune that when a large and fearsome band of Lombards (on armed Spanish warhorses, while they themselves were splendidly armed) observed the English archers fleeing from the fight, they quickly forced them to return to the field. These Englishmen, seeing that flight was now out of the question, took their lives in their own hands. They sent such a vast cloud of sharp spears and arrows against their enemies that those at the receiving end were both frightened and distressed. Hence the reluctant turn-around by the archers was an unfortunate turn for the party on the other side, an irreparable misfortune, a deadly destruction. And what was more crazy, the troop of Lombards who like an angelic host forced the archers to turn from flight, never themselves attacked on the field of battle nor dismounted from their horses, but in a state of panic beyond belief did not show their faces anywhere in France [again] after they had themselves taken to flight. (c.35, ll.14-49)

Joan of Arc

Bower relates the story of Joan of Arc from her appearance at the court of Charles VII in March 1429 to her death at Rouen in May 1431. (Sir William Glasdale was the English commander at the English siege of Orleans; the constable of France was now Arthur de Richemont. John Kirkmichael had been a student at the university of Orleans before becoming associated with the Scots who were helping King Charles, and becoming with his support the bishop of Orleans in 1426.) It is interesting that Bower has doubts about an angelic visitation to Charlemagne, and reports from an eye-witness account some behaviour on Joan's part which left him non-committal about the validity of the spiritual powers which Joan claimed. She did, after all, fail.

About the same time a certain young girl called Joan appeared from Lorraine, saying that she had been sent by the Most High to repel and weaken the plans of the English. Along with 2,000 men given to her by the king of France she approached Orleans with food supplies, sending a herald on ahead with a letter bidding the besiegers in the name of the Omnipotent Deity leave the city and France; otherwise she threatened them with miraculous penalties. But they spurned the messenger with a deaf ear and did not deign to send her any answer. Wearing a man's suit of armour everywhere, she sent supplies into the city by boats, took possession of the siege-towers, killed Glasdale himself and more than six hundred men, entered the city and brought most merciful comfort to the citizens. From there she returned to the king at Tours, and after collecting a larger army returned to Orleans along with the duke of Alençon and the constable of France and raised the siege. The English withdrew to the town of Meung-sur-Loire, and following behind she engaged them in a fight in open country. 3,000 Englishmen were killed there, but scarcely twenty among the French and Scots. Lord Talbot and Lord Scales were captured [and fear of the Maid much alarmed the English]. Next she proceeded to lay siege to the town of Jargeau and took it by storm, capturing there the earl of Suffolk and his two brothers. As a result and on the Maid's advice the king went to the city of Rheims in Champagne and there was crowned and anointed with the oil in the sacred vessel brought [as it is said] by an angel to Charlemagne.

At this time the bishop who ruled the church of Orleans was a Scot, Master John Kirkmichael.

Leaving a garrison at Rheims the king moved to the city of Senlis, which was handed over to him, and then to St Denis, which was also delivered to him. Leaving the king there, the Maid approached Paris with 10,000 men and attacked it [fearlessly]; many in the king's army fell wounded there from the shooting of missiles, crossbow-bolts, stones and arrows, and the Maid herself was pierced in both thighs by the impact of a bolt. When he heard of this, the king moved to Orleans and she was conveyed to 'Valeis'. After recovering there she was moved to Compiègne; after discovery there and capture by the English and Burgundians, she was sent to Rouen, where by judgment of Sir John the regent she was confined in a cask and burned. She conferred many benefits on France and struck terror among the English for the time being; but what spirit it was that gave her courage, only He that knows all knows. On the fore-finger of her left hand, to be sure, she wore a ring which she used to watch incessantly, as someone who saw this has told me. (c.36, ll.4-46)

Robert duke of Albany

Bower composes a sympathetic and admiring epitaph for Robert duke of Albany, who had until his death in 1420 played a central part in the government of Scotland during the reigns of Robert II and Robert III as well as that of the captive James I. He finds a quotation from the late-classical Claudian to illustrate the merits of the quiet approach to exercising authority. Was this the whole picture in fact?

In 1419 the illustrious prince Robert duke of Albany, earl of Fife and Menteith and governor of the kingdom died on 3 September. After the death of his brother King Robert III he ruled as governor in an honourable fashion for fifteen years. If it happened that some outrages were committed by powerful men in the kingdom, he patiently hid his feelings for the time being. He knew how to put things of this kind right wisely enough when the time came and to secure reparation as he wished, paying heed to the saying of a wise man:

> Quiet authority accomplishes what violence cannot.

He was the most patient of all men, gentle enough and kind, talkative and friendly, a daily attender at feasts, outstanding beside all his companions, a man who was a big spender and generous to strangers. He was also distinguished in appearance, tall and lofty in body, gray-haired in appearance and understanding, lovable in countenance, gifted with prudence and bravery, famous for his discretion, unremitting in his forbearance. And so in him wisdom provided the ornament of nearly all the virtues, so that his discourse whether delivered in the highest councils of the kingdom or elsewhere was always seasoned with charm and wit. He died in the Lord in Stirling Castle in grand old age as an octogenarian and more, after receiving the sacraments of the catholic church, while of sane mind and in Christian fashion, and he was buried with royal honours in the monastic church of Dunfermline between the choir and the Lady Chapel. (c.37, ll.1-24)

The merits of the mass

In introducing an analysis of the merits of the mass, Bower relates a particular experience from the year 1421 while he was himself abbot of Inchcolm. It makes a dramatic tale, with three passengers in a boat drowned and three saved. But Bower, preacher that he was, turns it into a moral tale, claiming that those who were saved had all celebrated or attended mass that day, while the other three had not. This he takes as an illustration of a simplistic assertion (wrongly supposed to be a saying of St Augustine) that attendance at mass will save you from sudden death that day. He then adds a whole chapter of similar popularized beliefs about the merits of the mass (omitted here), which contrasts strikingly with the scholastic reasoning derived from his university training which he often exhibits elsewhere in his work.

Something truly amazing which is believed to surpass the common run is discernible in the rare quality of the miracle which follows and in the weightiness of an unusual event illustrating the laudable merit of the mass. This is described now also out of reverence for the honour of St Columba. It happened in 1421 that the abbot of Inchcolm was staying with his monks on the mainland during summer and autumn. They did not dare at this time remain on the island for fear of the English, for there were not then such defences at the monastery as there are now. As stormy winter approached after the crops had been gathered in the granary, now that there was less fear of an attack by the English, the abbot landed on the island with his monastic brothers and household and their necessary goods on 25 October to make a stay there. On the next day, Sunday, he sent the cellarer with servants to fill up casks with the beer brewed at Barnhill along with other food supplies and requirements of the house. About three in the afternoon, while the boatmen were proceeding from the harbour and sailing over peaceful calm seas cheerfully and tipsy with winged oars, they had no thought for any obstacle that would hinder their passage. But not content with this situation, the boatmen said that they wished to spread sail. Though [firmly] forbidden [to do this] by the two canons [in the party], they prevailed and raised the sail up high. Then without warning the boat was struck by a sudden whirlwind, battered by wild waves and ceaselessly tossed by the raging of the storm. The waves struck down and drove the boat sideways, now lifting the prow they raised it in the air, now they pulled it down in an abrupt descent to the lowest parts of the sea. At length the sail tore into shreds from the blasts of the storm that were too strong for it. One boatman lost the tiller which was required for steering the boat; forsaken and without the comfort of a rudder, it reared up and plunged in pieces into the depths.

What more? Of the six people whom the boat contained, three, namely Alexander [Made] the canon cellarer and two boatmen, were drowned; the other three, namely sir Peter a canon, William Bulloch a chaplain and a stonemason, escaped death for the time being, saved as much by a wonder as by a miracle. Peter was supported with the assistance of a certain [wooden] vessel given to him by St Columba, who appeared in a vision (as he claimed) and whose help he was incessantly importuning. The two others clung to a bundle of straw, and floated for an hour and a half, confessing their sins to each other and remaining there until some Aberdour men brought help to them in a boat from Port Haven. It is an additional fact in this miraculous story that on that day it was the three who had been participants in holy mass who were rescued from near death. Sir Peter the canon on that Sunday desired to celebrate mass with greater eagerness than usual. There was then on the island by chance only one communion wafer kept for the celebration of high mass, and the prior of the place arrayed in alb and stole had consecrated the holy water. Peter approached him asking in God's name that he strip himself of his ecclesiastical [vestments] and grant Peter the opportunity to celebrate mass. When this was denied him, Peter humbly requested the abbot to speak to the prior, who in obedience yielded to Peter. The latter prepared to celebrate with a burning eagerness as never before. After humbly making confession of his sins, he celebrated mass; and after tasting a small quantity of food, he set out for the mainland to fetch his bedding. He boarded the little boat with those who were going to perish and the others, taking with him the said stonemason, who had attended mass that day. The chaplain also who was then in the boat had celebrated mass that day in the church of Dalgety; and these three were saved. The others indeed did not bother with mass on that same day, or could not attend because they were troubled in mind; they perished. Hence here is justification for what Augustine says on the merits of the mass: 'On a day when anyone [says or] hears mass devoutly he will not meet sudden death.' (c.38, ll.1-63)

Book XVI

Address to King James II

In his introduction to his chapters on the active reign of James I, 1424-37, Bower (writing probably in 1443 when James II was aged 13) laments the disorder in Scotland during the minority of the young king, whom he addresses with reminders of his duty as a lawmaker and law-enforcer. Not least is the need for him to suppress local acts of oppression such as he was witnessing in West Fife.

As I reflect on the precarious state of this realm, that is on the degree of opulent tranquillity and desirable rectitude in the days of Sir James our dead king of glorious memory, whose activities and vicissitudes I am now going to relate, and as I compare these deeds with the deceit of the present era, I should like to weep rather than unravel the web of more recent annals. But since we have no hope of attaining heavenly joy except through earthly sorrows, the hope of felicity which follows present wretchedness gives us strength to bear misfortunes more patiently, so that this very hope of lasting joy will alleviate the sadness of our transitory distress. Thus even if our king the law-giver and leader is dead, we should nevertheless not give way to grief over his death, for he has left someone like him as his heir, with indeed the same name. If only he can be no less fortunate until his dying day! So far this young man furnishes a lively reputation for himself, at least in the eyes of his unoffending subjects. God be praised that signs of virtue are being consolidated as he enters the early years of full age! But as the proverb has it: 'While the grass grows, the calf is weak.' We ponder, sire, on the long time which it will take for you to reach manly estate. Then you will have the power, when we are troubled by daily acts of tyranny or oppressed by robberies and pillaging, to relieve us from the distress which weighs us down, to draw up laws, to exercise justice, so that you may free the poor man from the powerful man, [when] the poor man has no helper among us other than God. And you will remember that you have responsibility for the law, so that you may restrain the thief and check the robber. If you fail in this, you cannot rule properly, you cannot be a lawmaker, but will confirm lawlessness. What can be better than men having confidence in good laws and having no fear of further misfortune? The laws of the state are most certainly a comfort to human life, a help to the weak, a restraint on tyrants. It is from them that security comes and conscience can enjoy freedom. But alas! because at present we suffer from lack of justice, we lament that the time has come of which Ovid wrote in his *Metamorphoses*:

> Men live on plunder; guest is not safe from host,
> nor father-in-law from son-in-law; even among brothers affection is rare;
> duty lies vanquished, etc…

In view of the groans of needy people and the misfortunes of the poor, whom even I who write this have seen and heard on this very same day being stripped of their clothes [and cattle] nearby in my neighbourhood and inhumanly despoiled of their necessities, I would agree with the man who said: 'I have seen [all] the acts of trickery that are done under the sun; I saw the tears of the innocent and that they had no comforter; I saw that they cannot resist the violence of their oppressors, devoid as they are of everyone's help. I praised the dead more than the living, and reckoned more fortunate than either the man who is not yet born and does not see [all] the evils that are done under the sun.' (Ecclesiastes 4). (c.1, ll.1-37, 69-79)

The marriage of Princess Margaret

The dependence of the French king Charles VII on Scottish help while until July 1429 he was still uncrowned is illustrated by his need in 1428 to seek a Scottish royal marriage for Louis his eldest son and heir. This was negotiated in Scotland in July 1428 and confirmed in France in October 1428, when Prince Louis was aged 5 and Princess Margaret aged 3. The girl was sent to France with an elaborate escort in 1436, and the marriage conducted at Tours on 25 June of that year. Bower writes of the whole arrangement with flattered satisfaction, though the money to pay for it was not raised as willingly as he suggests, as he well knew since he had been officially involved in its collection. He was here clearly writing in ignorance of Margaret's early death on 16 August 1445.

In 1425 following this battle Sir John Stewart of Darnley, the constable of the Scots in France, *comes Ebroicensis* that is count of Evreux, lord of Concressault and Aubigny, along with the archbishop of Rheims and a splendid escort came to renew the pacts, alliances and old friendships between the kingdoms of France and of the Scots which stretched back to the time of Charlemagne, and also to ask for the hand in marriage of the said Lady Margaret the king's eldest child for the most noble Prince Louis, duke of

Vienne and heir of the king of France. This turned out to be a most honourable proposal for Scotland if the circumstances of the arrangements that were made are considered. First, in respect of the man who was seeking a wife, this was no nondescript fellow, but the eldest child of the Most Christian king, who (as is believed and had been written) was destined for this position from birth, a man who was to be a prince among his fellows, the prop of his nation and support of his people, of whom the said lady (although under age and just a young girl) could say in admiration: 'Why is this happening to me, that the throne of France is falling to me?' Second, considering that the most worthy go-between and envoy for so advantageous a marriage was so reverend a bride's attendant as the archbishop-duke of Rheims, first of his peers among the dukes, a leading personage both in spirituals and temporals, and primate under the king in the whole kingdom of France. The king [of Scots] was pleased to respond favourably to so distinguished an embassy, and forthwith sent as a solemn embassy to the king of France with a specific brief and commission the venerable men sir Henry Lychton bishop of Aberdeen, sir Edward Lauder archdeacon of Lothian, and Sir Patrick Ogilvie knight (the sheriff of Angus and justiciar of Scotland). Whereupon there was an agreement on both sides; and five years later, when each was of marriageable age, there came as envoys from the king of France La Hire the king's *maître d'hôtel* along with the distinguished cleric Master Aymer; and in terms of their commission they arranged the betrothal of the said eldest daughter of the king. The girl was sent to France by her father a little later, namely [1435-6], surrounded by a distinguished following of attendants, and in the following year she was married.

The English sent one hundred and eighty ships to sea against her with a view to capturing her. As they awaited her arrival opposite the Breton Race at St Matthew of the Havens, a fleet of Flemings suddenly came up near them, bound for Flanders with a cargo of wine from La Rochelle. The English captured them without a struggle; but it brought them little joy, for the next day a fleet from Spain unexpectedly rescued the Flemings and their ships, leaving the English empty-handed. While this was going on, the dauphiness luckily made her escape and landed at La Rochelle. She rested at Nieul Priory which is two leagues from La Rochelle without notice being taken of her until such time as the [arch-] bishop of Rheims, with the bishops of Poitiers and Saintes and the worthy sires de Graville, Gaucourt and 'Pontissey' welcomed her and lodged her honourably in a splendid place for more than two months until the marriage was celebrated at Tours in Touraine. This was performed there by the archbishop of Rheims with the greatest possible ceremony, in the presence of the king and queen and also of the queen of Sicily (the mother of the queen of France). Once the wedding had been formally celebrated, the Scots (except the few who remained with the dauphiness) were much gratified with various presents and after a safe voyage arrived home.

To pay the expenses of sending this lady to France, the king [of Scots] decided against imposing taxes on the kingdom. Instead he sought the money courteously from individuals among the leading men of each estate and the [better off among the] beneficed clergy. These people gave contributions cheerfully and happily according to their means, without the need for any compulsion. (c.11, ll.10-45; c.12, ll.20-46)

Reflections on taxation

Bower had experience of the problems which arose when either the king or any superior lord tried to levy a tax for some non-traditional purpose. Here he offers his thoughts on financial levies in general, with the backing of quotations from St Augustine and the Bible. His examples of what he considered to be permissible traditional levies on the one hand, and of improper levies designed to finance a lord's sumptuous living on the other, provide a useful view of aspects of contemporary society in Scotland.

Although the king was disposed to acquiring possessions, he nevertheless knew well from the stirring of his conscience that unjust exactions and savage extortions (such as are usual when lords tallage those under them) are highly displeasing to God. For the sword is given to a prince when he is anointed and to a knight when he is invested for the defence of the church and its members, not for their destruction. This is why the Apostle says: 'It is not for nothing that he holds the power of the sword; for he is God's agent for the wrathful punishment of the evil doer.' It follows that greedy princes become matricides if they brandish their swords against the church and the poor. But all who take the sword in this way will perish by the sword, because when no one asks and no one gives consent, men are arrayed against innocent blood, as Augustine writes in his *Contra* [*Faustum Manichaeum*]. In the matter of taxes and tallages and similar exactions you should fully understand that a king or any lord should seek from their subjects only what their predecessors have received honestly, without deception or compulsion. They should not follow any bad custom, [I say,] but rather that praiseworthy contract made between the first lords and their serfs in written documents and before witnesses, which spell out in due form an annual payment and other services and agreements. It is within these limits that everything which has been properly defined from the beginning should be rendered to lords, provided that it is not contrary to the will of God and not tainted money, because everyone in rendering what belongs to him can make such arrangements as he likes. In these circumstances no deception is perpetrated on someone who knows the law and acts willingly. Likewise princes and lords can ask for some levies, after taking into consideration their need, the common benefit and the resources of their subjects, provided they are raised without harsh measures.

There are however cases where a prince or lord can ask for and receive a levy over and above the [annual] payment and due service, namely for the defence of the homeland, and especially his city, castle or village. All are bound in this, not only to take a share in the affairs which they have in common, but also to undertake physical labour, such as keeping watch etc.

Also, if a lord wishes to go on an expedition called by the church or a prince against heretics or pagans, and he does not have the means without serious loss but lacks the wherewithal for the cost, he can ask for moderate help from those under him.

Also, if he is taken prisoner in a just war or a fight that is just on his side, and if he does not have the resources to ransom himself without serious loss, those under him are bound to offer suitable help.

Also, if a lord wishes to approach his prince for some privilege that will be useful and honourable for himself and those under him, and he does not have the resources for the cost without serious loss, he can ask [for help]. So too in other cases which arise, [provided that] those under him have no grievance [and that it is done] out of affection and not under threat of force. Some people add also the case where a lord is reduced to poverty as the result of fire or thieves or reasonable generosity.

You should understand always the reasonable cause which gives them power to ask for help [lawfully]. It always follows that whatever a lord takes without justification, he ought to restore, as for instance the seizures which they make forcibly without due cause for horses surplus to requirements, the building of elaborate manor-houses, over-sumptuous garments, [the consequences of] dice and games of chance, or luxurious dinner-parties and the like; these they are bound to make good.

It is worthy of note that a knight on a chessboard moves two places in one direction and a third sideways; and so knights on their domains can in two cases justly accept payment from someone under them, that is a due annual payment and reasonable compensation for wrong-doing. Anything more which they receive (except in the circumstances noted above) is plunder. It is for this reason that the Baptist taught that knights should be content with their pay, saying: 'No bullying; no false accusations; make do with your pay!' In this authoritative source they are debarred first from two of the sins whereby powerful men usually extort money from poor men, namely threats and chicanery—the first where it is said: 'No bullying!'; the second at 'No false accusations!' Then it shows them that they ought to be content with their pay i.e. their estates and knight's fees. If then they accept payment beyond these limits, they are traitors, for they despoil the sons of God who are entrusted to their care, unless they are acting within the aforesaid limits which are allowed. The Lord elsewhere complains of this matter, saying: 'Oppressors have stripped my people bare.' (c.13)

Reflections on legislation

Bower reports that James I was active in issuing new laws at his parliament of March and May 1426, but then laments how by the 1440s at any rate laws both old and new were not being enforced. He reflects with the help of quotations from an unidentified commentary on Aristotle's Politics *and from the writings of the first century A.D. Valerius Maximus on the desirability of maintaining old laws to the letter, as had been the practice of the Jews and the early Romans.*

In the following Lent the king held his parliament at Perth; then he prorogued it because of the approach of Easter and continued the session at Edinburgh, beginning on 12 May. There he issued various different statutes, some of which would have served the kingdom well enough for the future if they had been kept; but as it is written in the canon law: 'It is not enough to establish laws if there is no one to see to their enforcement.' Now (as I remark with regret) there is no one who keeps even the old laws, while the new ones are ignored, although as Aristotle says: 'Old laws should possess great stability and respect, and it should not be easy to add new ones.' In this connection he says that it is extraordinarily harmful for the public good [to allow] the easy establishment of new laws and the easy changing of old ones, because this involves accustoming people to the annulment of laws and to a belittling of the obligation of law. Thus it is better to leave some moderate and slight defects untouched rather than annul old laws, because those who change laws often do more harm than good, for they accustom people to non-observance of the statutes and precepts of princes. Therefore Aristotle holds that those who lightly change the law weaken the efficacy of the law. Yet if there are some old laws which contain obvious seeds of ruin for the public good, they ought to be repealed after mature consideration. Thus Valerius remarks to the point when discussing the customs of the people of Marseilles that 'in their city from its foundation a certain sword was preserved until his day by which criminals had their throats cut, though it was eaten with rust and hardly adequate for its purpose. But a judge who is a stickler for matters of tiny detail would take the view that all old matters of custom should be preserved once attention had been drawn to them.' As a symbol of these matters the Mosaic law was written down on stone tablets. The laws of the Romans were also written on twelve tablets of ivory as a sign of stability and a perpetual reminder to future generations of their imperishable character. (c.14, ll.25-56)

Reflections on a battle in Strathnaver

This clan battle in Strathnaver in Sutherland with large numbers on each side took place in September 1431. Bower as usual describes such participants as 'caterans' (i.e. marauders). Angus Dubh was chief of Clan Mackay; Angus de Moray has been identified (albeit improbably) as lord of Culbin in Moray. Bower has little sympathy for the participants, and falls back on the geographically distant physiological obervations of the fourth-century A.D. Roman writer Vegetius for his explanation of such behaviour by people living in the north.

In the same month there was a bitter battle in Strathnaver between Angus Dubh and Angus de Moray, who a little earlier had left the king's prisons on being released. On either side were 1400 caterans, all of whom on the one day set upon each other. Scarcely nine individuals escaped alive out of this large number. It was a matter of astonishment to many that they attacked each other with such spirit that no one protected himself with the help of flight so as to save his life. This is explained by the fact that our fellow-Scots across the mountains, living as they do on the border or boundary of the world, experience little of the scorching summer heat or the sun's blaze by which the blood as a friend of nature might be dried up: it is for this reason that, compared with the other nations of the world, they have been found to be naturally more stout-hearted. Vegetius in his *De Re Militari* Book I, Chapter 3 writes right to the point when he says: 'It is an established fact that everywhere some men are born faint-hearted and some energetic; yet one nation surpasses another in war, and it is the open expanse of sky which contributes most often to robustness of spirit as well as of body, for it is said that all nations which are close to the sun, being dried up with excessive heat, have greater mental awareness, but less blood, and in consequence do not have the self-possession and confidence for fighting, because those who know that they have very little blood are afraid of being wounded. On the other hand northern peoples who are far from the fires of the sun, are indeed more headstrong, yet with an overflowing and lavish supply of blood are eager for fights. New recruits (i.e. fighting men) therefore should be selected from the more temperate regions; such men have a good supply of blood available so that they treat wounds and death with contempt, and they cannot lack the practical good sense which both maintains discipline on active service and is of great service when it comes to advice in battle.' (c.17, ll.11-41)

The burning of Paul Kravar

Paul Kravar was a Czech rather than a German. An M.A. of the university of Paris and B.Med. of the university of Montpellier, he had been associated with the university of Prague since 1416. There he mixed with the Hussite academics who maintained Wycliffite doctrines that had been officially condemned by the General Council of Constance. It is not known what brought Kravar to Scotland; but once he was there the leading theologian at the university of St Andrews, Laurence de Lindores, using inquisitional powers, saw to his condemnation on 23 July 1433 and his subsequent execution. Bower goes on to demonstrate quite considerable knowledge of, but little sympathy for, Hussite doctrines. He clearly regarded such treatment of heretics as right and proper.

In the following year the German Paul Kravar was accused at St Andrews on 23 July. On being found an obstinate heretic, he was convicted, condemned, put to the fire and burned to ashes. This man is said to have been sent from Bohemia by the heretics of Prague, who were then very influential in their wicked ways. His purpose was to corrupt the kingdom of the Scots, and he came with letters of recommendation from them as an outstanding practitioner of the art of medicine. He was found to be fluent and skilled in divinity and in biblical argument, but he displayed his stupidity by stubbornly maintaining nearly all the erroneous articles associated with Prague and Wyclif. However he was silenced by that venerable man Master Laurence de Lindores, the inquisitor of heretical deviation, who gave heretics or Lollards no peace anywhere in the kingdom. (c.20, ll.6-18)

A debate over foreign policy

In his report of a debate in a general council of the Scottish kingdom in October 1433 regarding the response that should be made to English peace proposals (which King James was probably inclined to accept) at the expense of the long-standing Franco-Scottish alliance, Bower is recounting a political discussion in which he was with his fellow Augustinian abbot of Scone personally involved. He comments with satisfaction on the rejection of the pro-English arguments of John Fogo abbot of Melrose. It is interesting that Laurence de Lindores as inquisitor was brought in to discipline Abbot Fogo on a matter of secular politics, a procedure which Bower relates with satisfaction.

About the same time a certain knight called [ ] Scrope arrived from England, sent with instructions and a commission from the king and council of England to our lord king. Thereupon the king was moved [by him] to call a general council at Perth in October, where the topic of concluding peace with the English was raised. In particular they for their part would make a *de facto* restoration of Roxburgh and Berwick and everything else which they had wrongly taken from the kingdom of Scotland within a stated period of time, and by this act of restoration they would hope for a lasting peace. In the presence of the king, who sat in front of the high altar in the choir of the friars preachers of Perth, a clear reply was given by the prelates of the greater churches and by the magnates of the realm to the effect that they were united in aspiring after peace with liberty. Then the abbots of Scone and Inchcolm were given the task of seeking and eliciting everyone's views on this matter under discussion, and the agreed reply was that the king of Scotland was not free to negotiate on the subject of peace with the king of England on account of his alliance with the king of France, which they asserted had been scrutinised by the university of Paris and confirmed by the supreme pontiff. (The same king of Scotland had recently sworn a solemn oath to maintain this alliance.) Various other suggestions were made on all sides which tended to support this negative conclusion. Because they could not on that day agree on one and the same opinion, and since the day was ending with the coming of night, the question of a peace was taken up again the next day; and while the lords of the council debated both sides of the question as before and tended towards accepting peace with liberty, the matter remained undecided. But the venerable father in Christ sir John Fogo, master of theology and most worthy abbot of Melrose, argued against those who supported a negative conclusion. He claimed to be advancing the basic well-spring and foundation [of the thinking] of all for whom he was speaking, namely that fulfilment of the divine intention cannot properly, and ought not, depend on the wishes and consent of any created being other than the person responsible. From this he drew the inference that no king could properly bind himself by an oath to some other king never to make peace with a third except with the agreement of the king to whom he had thus bound himself. Then he enunciated the proposition that the king of France could not properly bind himself by an oath to the king of Scotland never to make peace with the king of England without the agreement of the king of Scotland, and vice versa. Following on this argument he again asserted that both by itself and in terms of what was claimed by the aforesaid abbots of the Order of St Augustine (namely that the king of Scotland could not properly make peace with the king of England except with the agreement and consent of the king of France) the suggestion (i.e. the negative conclusion) was untenable in its literal expression, and that as regards the grammatical sense which it immediately conveyed to the minds of its hearers it sounded faulty and was inherently erroneous. Following his brief speech along these lines there was such a wrangle that support for breaking the treaty dwindled away; instead it was finally agreed that the English were trying in this matter to stir up division in our kingdom, since it was very clear that they were not really proposing to restore to us what belonged to us.

These English indeed behaved like the artful wolf. The fable tells that when a great dispute arose between some shepherds and wolves and no agreed way of ending the quarrel could be found, the wolves eventually sent a deputation to the shepherds saying: 'We very much want to be at peace with you; since it is only your dogs which are behind our disagreement, we suggest that you call off the dogs and we shall not touch the sheep. By this means we shall achieve lasting peace.' On hearing this, the shepherds banished their dogs, and the wolves tore at the throats of the sheep without restraint. So did the deluded shepherds lose both dogs and sheep. [Take note therefore.]

When Master Laurence de Lindores (that most worthy licentiate in theology who was then also inquisitor of heretical deviation) heard the propositions and arguments of the abbot of Melrose and found them less than pleasing to his ears, they sounded off an alarm. Therefore he wrote to the abbot refuting the fundamentals and ultimate source of his thesis; and the abbot in his turn wrote back to him letters that were highly critical. On this account he was solemnly warned and cited by the inquisitor to recant his harmful sayings and writings, or to defend them in due form. He made his appearance at St Andrews on a certain day and gave in to the inquisitor. Thenceforth the said kings (both of France and Scotland), their fears allayed by a calm state of mutual regard, were agreed on continuing their accustomed alliance. (c.23 - c.24, l.23)

The assassination of James I

Bower composed this account of the murder of King James in February 1437 within six or seven years of the event. It appears that he was still then dependent on rumours rather than on proof about the part played by th earl of Atholl, whom he here links with the death of Rothesay in 1402 and the execution of three of the Albany family in 1425, though he does not mention any such part when recounting these events above. Furthermore in a later revision of this text Bower withdrew his assertion here that Atholl confessed. Even to a figure like Bower therefore, who was quite centrally placed in the royal administration, the facts about the king's assassination were not at all certain. It was for him a shattering event.

This fateful year then smote this famous kingdom and greatly shook it. It was my plan to put off my account of the manner and way of it, because it is not something that I want to write about. But now [after more mature thought] two considerations rouse me to write. On the one hand the exceptional nature of his [i.e. the king's] virtues of natural endowment and character compels me to speak: and on the other hand I am reduced to tears by the harm which the community has suffered. Now therefore I am forced to unfold a gloomy account although it is much against my inclination. But because the human condition must pay its debts to death, but bitter death does not spare that human condition, encompassing the classes of individuals and the single examples of classes which live in the flesh under its law, see how his mortal fate brought our king to the end of his reign, and, anticipating before its allotted time the date when this slight payment was due, if God had bestowed anything on him, how the web of fate was cut short while it was just beginning, and removed that which was due! I think therefore that there is truth in the sentiment of the saying: 'Suddenly when it is not expected, misfortune occurs, disaster intrudes, illness strikes, death which no one escapes cuts life short.'

It is said that this unlucky death for the king was brought about by his paternal uncle the earl of Atholl, a man grown old in a life of evil-doing, who is said to have had secret ambitions of attaining supreme office in the kingdom. On this account (as it afterwards came to be known) he was the author, instigator and principal adviser of the killing of the duke of Rothesay [the king's brother] as well as of Murdoch duke of Albany and his two sons [Walter and Alexander]. These men would have been preferred by law to the kingship over the earl himself if fate had given support and they had remained alive. According to his confession it was he who ordered his grandson Robert Stewart, Robert Graham and a few other accomplices to kill the king by assassination so that by this means he might imperceptibly take over the government of the kingdom by managing the affairs of the son of the king (who was then seven years old) as he thought fit, though not in a legitimate way, so that at the least he might be regarded as a colleague of the future king. But as the poet Lucan writes:

There will be no trust between partners in governing, and complete power
will resent a colleague. Have no faith in a colleague.
The first walls [of Rome] were sodden with a brother's blood.

Therefore the said Robert Stewart, grandson of the earl of Atholl, as an intimate attendant, kinsman and member of the king's household (who proves the saying: 'There is no worse a plague than a hostile servant'), along with the said Robert Graham and seven others, pernicious traitors that they were, cruelly and treacherously killed first the king's young page Walter Straiton, whom the king had sent out of the room to the cellar for some wine, and then the king himself. The queen also was seriously wounded [by them in the shoulder]. It happened at night during the holy season of Lent, on 21 February, in the thirty-first year of his reign and the forty-fourth year of his life, within the monastery of the friars preacher of Perth. There was no one in the king's entourage who gave him any help or who set about avenging his death at the time except the knight Sir David de Dunbar, a brother of Sir George earl of March, who, on hearing the disturbance, hurried from the town and entered the apartment of the king as he lay dead immersed in his own blood. Outraged by the crime which [the traitors] had perpetrated, he followed them with drawn sword; but once they had cut off some of the fingers of his left hand, he retired from the scene gravely wounded. (c.27)

The merits of James I

Bower devoted eleven chapters to reflections on King James, his attitudes and achievements. He was writing here from immediate personal knowledge, for he must have known the king well; but his account dates from the early 1440s during the troubled years of the minority of James II, when he was feeling keenly the loss of firm central control, and tended therefore to idealize the merits of the dead king rather than attempt a rounded assessment of what had gone well and what not so well. There were, after all, those who thought it right to kill him. James had been a prisoner in England and France 1406-24 between the ages of 12 and 29. It was from England that in 1413 he supported the moves at home to secure the papal bulls needed to found an internationally recognized university at St Andrews.

For this man was very prudent and diligent, excellently worthy and naturally gifted. In proclaiming his integrity and worth we would not direct attention to separate examples of general traits, but rather briefly to general examples of separate traits. He was of medium height, a little on the short side, with a well-proportioned body and large bones, strong-limbed and unbelievably active, so that he on his part would challenge any one of the magnates [of any size] to wrestle with him, fearing greatly however lest in such a contest he would be feared. He was the best of archers and a knowledgeable jouster; he could sling a stone and throw a hammer further than the usual standard of men; he was a very fast runner as if with wings on his feet, a most energetic rider and [untiring] traveller.

This man indeed [was a distinguished] musician, not only in singing but also in a high standard of performance on the drum, for example, and the fiddle, on the psaltery and organ, the flute and lyre, the trumpet and pipe, certainly not [just] as an enthusiastic amateur, but attaining the highest degree of mastery. Mother Nature (who is a kind of force and power grafted on to human kind by divine agency) gave him distinction of a lively kind beyond all human capacity for judgment, especially in handling the lyre, as if she had pre-eminently endowed with those gifts another Orpheus, the first and foremost of all lyrists who play delightfully and sweetly on their lyres. In this he clearly displayed the innate talent of the Scot, in surpassing wonderfully even the Irish themselves in performances on the lyre.

And not only was he found devoting himself to the art of music in this way from time to time [when he was at leisure from serious affairs] (in line with the character of the times and in harmony with the mores of those who aspired to be of his company as intimates), he applied himself with eagerness sometimes to the art of literary composition and writing, sometimes to drawing and painting, sometimes to herb-gardens and to the planting and grafting of fruit trees, sometimes to respectable games and recreations to refresh the spirits of his followers, without any suggestion of idleness on his part. The effort of learning the skills connected with all the mechanical arts which are appropriate for men of rank did not deter his royal majesty, nor did the areas of knowledge which gentlemen find vexatious when under the pressure of necessity. But the king appointed himself, as it were, to be schoolmaster and goad for himself, out of his desire for humility and knowledge, contrary to custom [and] without the forceful pressure of someone else. He loved knowledge of the Scriptures with incredible zeal. He loved also the exercise of varied laborious practical skills. Even if after being taken to England (like another Joseph led into Egypt) it was a tongue which he knew that he heard, he learned and mastered mechanical skills and philosophies which he did not know. Clearly the Lord was with him, and with His help he was the kind of man who was successful at everything he undertook. This is supported by his wonderful resourcefulness in foreign parts, where at one time it had been assumed that he would never be freed to return to his own country, especially since [King] Henry V tried to subject both him and the kingdom of Scotland to his dictation in perpetual servitude.

When [James] had for his support not much (indeed little or nothing) from his own revenue while living in foreign parts away from his native soil, this was in fact a step towards knowledge because of his love of learning; it provided a chance for study. Indeed he was not only skilled as a consequence of natural talent, but also gifted in moral philosophy, taught by many men famous for their knowledge. He strove to introduce philosophy and the other liberal arts into his kingdom to the extent that, after many requests had been made to him and various letters for his signature had been cancelled and signed, while indeed he was still kept in captivity he wrote to the Supreme Pontiff regarding privileges for setting up a university in his kingdom and obtained them.

Now besides these works of the cardinal virtues (that is prudence and justice, fortitude and temperance and the like) which demonstrate the effectiveness of an upright disposition, he was outstanding also (as we have already said) in his expenditure of physical energy. For with an eye to supplying and husbanding the needs of the regular clergy and of other subjects and lieges on both sides of his kingdom wherever there was need he often visited their habitations and monasteries in person; and [only] after he had re-established peace there did he turn to other matters which were threatening the harmony and utility of the state. He was seen to cherish and favour equally all churches and religious orders in proportion to the quality of their life, praising highly men of religion and their way of life as he heard of it. And if he found anything less than praiseworthy among them, he discussed it charitably without pretending to be embarrassed, quietly persisting until by some convenient way they might be turned back to a more correct way of life.

He established firm peace within the kingdom, and he did not allow magnates or freeholders who were quarrelling among themselves to vent their wrath in open disturbances in their usual way. But wherever he heard that disorder had arisen, even in distant parts of the kingdom, it was immediately quelled by a short letter sent under his signet, for his subjects were so fearful of offending him that no one was ever so high-spirited and masterful as to dare to flout or defy the king's written order or even his oral message. If anyone did oppose him, he immediately paid the penalty.

I have indeed known (which is why I speak) a certain great nobleman, a near relative of the king, who was on some occasion which I cannot now recall staying at the royal court. Because he slapped another man in the king's hall [at which the man who had been struck complained to the king], the king ordered the same hand as had struck the blow to be stretched out on the dining table, and handing a little knife to the young man who had been slapped, ordered him under pain of death to strike the hand that was pinioned in this way and pierce the palm. On hearing this the queen with her ladies and the prelates with their clerics prostrated themselves on the floor. They had difficulty for an hour in securing pardon for the culprit, and then only on the basis that the man who had struck the blow was forbidden the court and the king's presence for a time. Perhaps a saying of Seneca in his book *De Moribus* had come into the king's mind: 'The man who forgives crimes in his own day transmits failings to future generations. The man who is merciful to the evil does damage to the good.' (c.28, ll.27-50; c.30, ll.1-27, 102-13; c.31, ll.1-16; c.33, ll.14-22, 52-68)

A poetic epitaph on King James I

From the manuscript evidence it appears likely that these verses were the work of Bower himself. (Some figures at the end are misleading: the king died in 1437 [New Style]; he was then aged 42; he had reigned for nearly 31 years.) James was buried at the Charterhouse monastery in Perth which he had founded in 1429. (See other verse epitaphs in Volume 9, pp.128-33.)

Here honour is buried [i.e. James], scion of a distinguished stock,
an ornament made gracious, shining with virtues,
radiant with his noble character, illustrious, charming,
and rich with merits, cheerful with his upright character.
This man was a patron of peace, and a most weighty deviser of laws,
one who washed away feelings of envy, an energetic foster-father of peace.
The law was available to all while he was alive, with crime buried,
theft then lay low, dishonour did not remain unpunished.
This man was spirited in his thinking, witty in word and deed,
cheerful in appearance; generous, he delighted in company.
Sumptuous nature rained on this man with such adornment
that he shone with honour in a way that can hardly be described.
One who nurtured the church, protector of all who were needy,
prop of the unfortunate, helper of the deceived,
when alive he shone in so many ways that one cannot mention them all;
famous from the age of childhood, he is mourned by Scotland.
Who could not speak of the king's many qualities
nor say how many great virtues this king possessed?
But, Fortune, you have been too unfriendly to him,
after pledging at first that you would always be sunny towards him.
How quickly you have turned round, turning things upside down

as you suddenly sent the pain of death to him!
What a pity that that manly king had been deceived!
What a shame that the noble lordly stock had been misled!
See how the wearied king, overcome by a throng of traitors,
fell down, suffered, and, sad to say, was struck down as an act of vengeance!
Sadly a king lay dead who was a tower, a lion, a light,
a flower, a jewel, and truly a pillar, and a leader.
The tower is thrown down, the lion loses his strength, the light grows faint,
and the radiant jewel withers, the pillar collapses, the leader dies.
When the king is dying, see how law becomes diseased and is disfigured,
and the people are scattered, the dregs of society arrive and show their true colours.
Sadly the illustrious King James (always first of that name)
is now the lowest slime, though formerly a king and prosperous ruler.
No one stays long at the summit, but quickly moves on;
any kind of glory in the world is short and insubstantial.
In the year one thousand four hundred and the third decade
and six he made his way from his bodily prison to Christ himself.
The king lived forty plus twice two years;
he lies buried within the Charterhouse in the lowest depths.
This man reigned as king for thirty and two years;
and after his death at Perth Scotland mourned him sadly.
(c.38)

Epilogue

Here Bower returns to the themes of his Prologue, explaining his reluctance to include information from years more recent than 1437. His recommendation for the regular compilation of an official national history reign by reign was not followed: he was wrong in thinking that this was done in England (and excised this suggestion from a later version of his work), but there may have been a model of this kind in France. He repeats his hope that his work will be studied by the young James II, for he had written it with this purpose in mind. He ends by acknowledging again his debt to John de Fordun for five books of the work out of the total of sixteen.

I am resolved to bring this laborious work to a halt here, requesting any courteous reader not to blame me for any matters in which I have overstepped the mark when following written sources by citing a possibly inaccurate text, or where I have transgressed in establishing the exact order of events when following oral accounts, but to correct and change any errors without ill-will in accordance with fuller knowledge of his own. I shall not be able to deny that several things may possibly occur to the mind of the reader in a better and even clearer form, and these ought deservedly to be corrected. But because nothing is found to be perfect in human devisings, the good nature of the merciful reader will kindly tolerate my imperfection. Even if he does not go so far as to decide to excuse me completely, I hope that at least he may not condemn me to excessive blame. On this account the reader of this little work should first read and understand rather than criticise; he should first make inquiries among those with knowledge rather than condemn. He should bear in mind that I did not undertake unfamiliar work of this kind very willingly for my own reasons, but I took it on for the good of the public interest, as a comfort for the king and kingdom, and at the pressing request of the man [Sir David Stewart of Rosyth, knight] who inspired me to a task which, thanks to the God Omnipotent, I have brought to an end. I know that if I continued further with writing chronicles, someone would certainly say that I want to agree with those around me, and praise what is pleasing to those in high places. For in praise of a living person there is an opportunity for hollow glorification of the man who is praised, and a special reputation for flattery is attached to the man doing the praising. Lest therefore I provide such people with material for censure, I am bringing this work to an end here, knowing that it is written: 'Do not praise a man in his lifetime', as if to say: 'Give praise after life is over; extol a man after he has met his end.' This is what everyone does who shrinks from being a flatterer. In this connection Jerome wrote in his book *De Viris Illustribus*: 'Ambrose bishop of Milan is still writing at the present time. Because he is alive, I shall withhold my judgment on him, lest I be criticised for flattery or the truth on the one side or the other.'

For that reason it has been suitably laid down in very many countries (including England, I have heard) that each monastery founded by kings should have its scribe or writer appointed from among the community, who should make a dated record of all noteworthy things during a king's reign which affect the kingdom and neighbourhood at any rate as seems to be the truth of the matter; and at the first [parliament or] general council after a king's death all the annalists should meet and produce openly their sworn statements or writings. The council should choose wise men who are skilled and expert in such matters to examine the writings, make a careful collation of them, extract a summary of what has been brought together, and compile a chronicle. And they should store away the writings of the copyists [of this work] in monastic archives as authenticated chronicles which can be trusted, lest by the passing of time memories of happenings in the kingdom perish. I would advise our king to make arrangements along these lines, lest, if the present work be lost (God forbid!) along with those things which should be written up in the annual record as described above, memory of the high qualities of earlier kings and bishops, magnates and famous men (insofar as they are a stimulus to virtue and a warning of wrongs) may be carelessly lost through negligence. For as Jerome writes to Demetriades: 'Interest in the Scriptures is not at all extinguished by their age; on the contrary', he says, 'if I may make use of the opinion of a pagan writer: "Interest is all the more aroused by the passage of time."' May at least our present king, I ask the Almighty, be aroused by reading this book, and then proceed to rule by good deeds of a temporal kind so that he may hope for eternal rewards. In addition I pray to Christ by the gift of his mercy to bring the king up as the kind of man who will give us something worthy of eternal memory (just as we have from the outstanding kings his ancestors), which we may transmit to posterity with the help of writings about him.

Be silent, breeze, my ship has reached the shore. Gladly I abandon the seas
and come to a halt, praise and glory to Christ.
Here this work comes to an end and the author ceases to write
the book which he is rightly accustomed to call the *Scotichronicon*.
This book covers the acts and awesome deeds
of kings, bishops, and likewise of the leading men of the people.
Fordun has produced five books and the author eleven,
which it will be clear to you make sixteen in all.
So, reader, in return for their prayers we ask you [to pray that]
both authors may be dwellers in the realm of the sky.

Christ! He is not a Scot who is not pleased with this book.

(c.39)

Index

Fuller index entries with additional identifications of persons (including offices held) and of places (including locations) are to be found in each of the volumes of the full edition, especially Volume 9. References to Biblical characters and to most persons mentioned in literary quotations are omitted here.

Aachen, Germany, 28
churches in, 27
Abercrombie, church of, 209
Aberdeen, 133, 185, 189
burgesses of, 189
bishop of. *See* Lamley, Radulf de; Lychton, Henry
Aberdour, men from, 272
Abernethy, church and bishopric of, 37
Pictish royal capital, 37
chronicle of quoted, 37
men of, 180
Abernethy, Hugh de, 151
Aboyne, castle, 141-2
Achaia, Greece, 17
Adam, abbot of Melrose, bishop of Caithness, 122, 136-7
Adam, earl of Carrick, 164
Adiabeni, the, 14
Adomnan, St, 7; quoted, 22, 36
Adrian, St, 7
Adrian IV, pope, 100-1
Aed, king of Scots, 13
Aedan, son of Gabran, king of Scots, 23, 45
Aedinburgh. *See* Edinburgh
Aelius, son of Hadrian, Roman emperor, 45
Aesop, fable quoted, 134, 247
Agned, city of the Britons. *See* Edinburgh
Agnes, countess of Dunbar, 222-3
Aigolandus, 27
Ailred, abbot of Rievaulx, quoted, 72
Ailsa Craig, island, 7
Alan, lord of Galloway, 139
Albany (Scotland), 6, 15, 34, 147
duke of. *See* Steward, Robert
Albion, island, 7, 9, 10, 11, 19, 20, 21, 33
Alemania, 27
Alençon, duke of, 269
Alexander the Great, king of Macedon, 158
Alexander III, pope, 108, 110
Alexander I, king of Scots, 63, 64, 65
Alexander II, king of Scots, 124, 126-8, 132-3, 136, 139, 141-5, 147
Alexander III, king of Scots, 145-9, 151, 154-5, 157, 164, 167-73, 182
Alfonso XI, king of Castile (Spain), 216
Allerdale, 189
Almond, river, 124
Alnwick, 106
Alpin, king of Scots, 35
Aluclud/Aldclide. *See* Dumbarton
Ambrose, St, quoted, 47
Andrew, St, apostle, 17, 20, 38-39, 190, 206, 209
Anglicised Scots, supporters of Edward de Balliol, 218
Angus, earl of. *See* Malcolm
Angus, mormaer of. *See* Cruchne
Angus, brother of Fergus II king of Scots, 21
Angus Dubh (or Mackay), a cateran, 279
Anjou, men from, 19
Annabel, Queen, wife of King Robert III, 260, 262
Anthony, St, opinion of, 129

Appleby, 106
Aquitania, 9,
Arabs, the, 14
Arbroath ('Bayeux'), monastery, 129
abbot of. *See* Bernard; Henry
Arcadius, Roman emperor, 21
Argyll, 79, 144
see erected, 79
bishop of. *See* Harold
Aristotle, quoted, 46, 49, 131, 157, 240, 278
Arnot, Michael de, knight, 218
Arran, island, 155. *See also* Brodick
Arras, bishop of. *See* Robert
Arrouaisian order, 66
Arundel, earl of. *See* FitzAlan, Richard
Athelstan, son of King Æthelstan of Wessex, 38-39
Athelstaneford, battle at, 38, 39
Athens, kings of, 147
Atholl, earl of. *See* Galloway, Thomas of; Hastings, David de; Patrick; Strathbogie, John de
Aubigny, France, lord of. *See* Stewart, John
Auchtertool, manor, 208
Augustine of Canterbury, St, 23, 24
Augustine of Hippo, St, quoted, 46, 82, 102-3, 151, 221, 272, 276
Avicenna, quoted, 149
Avignon, France, papal court at, 232, 246
Avoch, 225
Aymer, Master, French envoy, 275
Ayr, castle, 152

Bagimond, papal collector, 165
Bailleul, France, 185
Balliol, Edward de, king of Scots, son of King John, 185, 217
Balliol, John. *See* John Balliol, king of Scots
Bamburgh, 123
Bannockburn, battle of, 204-7, 209
Barbason. *See* Cantimpré, Thomas of
Barbour, John, archdeacon of Aberdeen, author, 199
Barclay, David de, 227
Barnbougle, 225
Barnhill, 251, 271
Barnsdale, 156
Bas, island, 7
Baugé, France, battle of, 265-6
Bearpark, manor near Durham, 229
Beaumanoir, John, French knight, 233
Beauvais, order of, 66
Beauvais, Vincent of, specifically quoted, 45
Bede, quoted, 15, 31, 109
Bek, Anthony, bishop of Durham, 174, 179, 193
Benedict XIII, pope, 286
Ber, Alexander, abbot of Dunfermline, 232
Berkeley, Hugh de, 151
Bernard of Clairvaux, St, quoted, 104; cf. 103
Bernard, abbot of Arbroath, quoted, 205-6
Bernham, David de, bishop of St Andrews, 145, 146
'Bertha'. *See* Perth
Berwick, 133, 175, 178, 182-4, 191, 248, 281
captain of. *See* Caillau, Edmund de
abbey of nuns near, 66
Bethoc, daughter of Malcolm III, 48-49
Bethsaida, Galilee, 17
Béziers, France, church in, 27
Bicchieri, Guala, papal legate, 132-4
Birley, John, 237
Biset, James, prior of St Andrews, 83-86, 263
Biset, Thomas, prior of St Andrews, 83
Bisset, Baldred, envoy to Roman court, 174
Bisset, John, 143
Bisset, Walter, 141-3
Bisset, William, 143
Black, John, abbot of Dunfermline, prior of Urquhart, 232-3
'Black Agnes'. *See* Agnes, countess of Dunbar
Blaise, St, 7
Blois, Peter of, quoted, 46, 214
Boar's Chase, near St Andrews, 64
Boethius, quoted, 202
Bois, William del, chancellor, 128

Borders, men of the, 262
Bower, Walter, abbot of Inchcolm, author, 1-4, 85, 271, 281-2
Brabant, fighting men of, 122
Brabantinus. *See* Cantimpré, Thomas de
Braga, Martin of (pseudo-Seneca), quoted, 130, 201
Bray, France, 113
Brechin, bishop of. *See* Comyn (or Kilconcath), William
Brendan, St, 6
Bridget of Ireland, St, 37
Bridget of Sweden, St, quoted, 29-31, 236
Brigantia, Spain, 6
Britain, 6-8, 12, 14, 15, 21
Brittany, France, fight in, 233-4
Brittany, John of, earl of Richmond, 211
Brodick, Arran, castle, 152
Brough-under-Stainmore, 106
Bruce, Alexander de, son of Edward de Bruce, 228
Bruce, Edward de, earl of Carrick, king of Ireland, 197, 209
Bruce, Robert de (d.1237), 165
Bruce, Robert de, lord of Annandale and Cleveland (d.1295), 164-5, 174, 176-9, 182?, 184
Bruce, Robert de, earl of Carrick (d.1304), 164-5, 174, 182?, 184-5
Bruce, Robert de, earl of Carrick, later King Robert I, q.v., 164-5, 174, 192-3, 195-8, 236
Bruces, the, 182, 184
Brude, son of Maelchon, king of Picts, 22, 37
Bruno of Wartburg, elder and younger, 24, 25
Brutus, consul of the Romans, 51
Buchan, earl of. *See* Comyn, Alexander; Comyn, William; Stewart, John
Bulloch, William, chaplain of Inchcolm, 271-2
Bullock, John, bishop of Ross, 85
Bullock, William, 226-7
Bury St Edmunds, abbey, 106
Bute, island, 7, 155
 men of, 195
 castle on, 7. *See also* Rothesay
Byland, battle at, 211

Caerlaverock, castle, 235
Caesar, Julius, 46
Caesarius, provost of abbey of St Denis, France, 113-14
Caillau, Edmund de, captain of Berwick, 207
Caithness, 120, 136
 men of, 120
 bishop of. *See* Adam; Gilbert; John
 earl of. *See* Harald; John
Calder Muir, 223
Cambrai, bishop of. *See* Robert
Cambuskenneth, abbey, 66
Canterbury, monks from, 66
 archbishop of. *See* Dover, Richard de; Lanfranc; Sudbury, Simon; Thomas Becket
Cantimpré, Thomas of (Barbason, Brabantinus), quoted, 24, 73-75, 96-97, 160-3
Cardross, 211
Carlisle, 13, 65, 99, 105-6, 124, 132, 133, 255
 nunnery near, 66
 bishop of. *See* Ireton, Ralph de
Carrick, 228
 earldom of, 200
 earl of. *See* Adam; Bruce, Edward de; Bruce, Robert de; Marjorie; Stewart, David
Carron (Scrimgeour), Alexander, chamberlain, 63
Caspian Sea, 17
Cassiodorus, quoted, 107, 139
Castile, Spain, king of. *See* Alfonso XI
Chalon-sur-Saône, bishop of, 95-96.
Champagne, France, countess of. *See* Mary
Charlemagne, emperor, 26-28, 269, 274
Charles III the Fat, emperor, 89-92
Charles VII, king of France (dauphin until 1429), 265, 269, 275, 278, 281
Charterhouse, Perth, 288
Chartres, France, 102
Chartres, Reginald de, archbishop of Rheims, 274-5
Châtillon, Touraine, France, castle, 266

Chencres, pharaoh, father of Scota, 5, 147
Chester, 99
Christina of the Isles, 200
Chubaculus, companion of St Regulus, 19
Cicero, quoted, 129, 149
Cistercian order, 66, 96, 134, 165
Cîteaux, France, monastery, 96
abbot of. *See* Molesme, Robert de
Clackmannan, 177
Clan Kay, 258,
Clan Qwele, 258
Clare, Gilbert I de, earl of Gloucester, 179
Clare, Gilbert II de, earl of Gloucester, 207
Claudian, quoted, 270
Claudius, Roman emperor, 12
Clodius Albinus, emperor of the Gauls, 14
Cluniac order, 66
Cockburnspath, 215
Cologne, Germany, archbishopric of, 27
Cologne, Henry of, O.P., 140
Colosia, Phrygia, 19
Columba, St, 7, 22, 23, 45, 222, 252, 271
shrine of. *See* Inchcolm
Comborel, Hugh de, bishop of Poitiers, 275
Commodus, Roman emperor, 14
Compiègne, France, 269
Compostela, Santiago de, Spain, church of St James, 27
Scottish monk dies at, 98
Comyn (or de Kilconcath), William, bishop of Brechin, 176
Comyn, Alexander, earl of Buchan, 142-3, 149, 151, 174
Comyn, William , earl of Buchan, justiciar, 122, 124, 125-6, 128
Comyn, Walter, earl of Menteith, 146, 149, 151-2
Comyn, John II the Red, 142-3, 151, 174, 185
Comyn, John III the Red, 194, 196-8, 199, 236
Comyn, Robert, knight, 198
Comyns, the, 152, 182, 184, 192, 193
Conall, king of Scots, 31
Concressault, France, lord of. *See* Stewart, John
Conrad II, emperor, 49, 52
Constantine III the Bald, king of Scots, 40-41
Constantinople, 17, 18
Constantius, Roman emperor, 17, 18
Cornell, Richard, archdeacon of Lothian, 263
Coupland, John, 230
Cowie. *See* Cullen
Crambeth, Matthew de, bishop of Dunkeld, 176
Cramond, island, 170, 225
Crannach (or Aberdeen), Adam de, abbot of Scone, 85
Crawford, earl of. *See* Lindsay, David
Cressingham, Hugh de, treasurer of Scotland, 187-8
Crete, 19
Crinan, abthane of Dull, 48
Croyser, William, 263
Cruchne, mormaer of Angus, 41
Cullen, 39
Culross, 26
Cumberland/Cumbria, 49, 52, 99, 105, 106
Cumbrae, Great and Little, islands, 7
Cumbrians, king of the, 56
Cunchar, possible father of Finuele, 41
Cunningham, William, of Kilmaurs, 252
Cunninghame coast, 153
Cupar, castle, 225
Curry, Peter, knight, 154
Curry, Walter, man-at-arms, 226-7
Cuthbert, St, 190
lands of. *See* Durham

Dairsie, church, 209
Dalgety, church, 272
Damian, St, companion of St Regulus, 19
Danes, the, 36, 39
David I, king of Scots, 65, 66-68, 70, 147
David II, king of Scots, 217, 227, 229-31, 236, 238-40, 246
David, grandson of King David I, earl of

Huntingdon, 65, 106, 111, 121-2, 124, 128, 176
Dax, Gascony, France, church, 27
Dervorguilla, daughter of David earl of Huntingdon, 176
Diocletian, Roman emperor, 16
Dollar, church, 22
Dominican friars (Preachers), 144
Donald, earl of Mar, 184
Donald, lord of the Isles, 254, 259
Donald *Ban*, king of Scots, 45, 49, 52, 156
Donald *Ban*. *See* MacWilliam
Donibristle, 208, 225
Dorset, 23
Douglas, earl of. *See* Douglas, Archibald I and II de; Douglas, James de; Douglas, William de
Douglas, Archibald I de, the Grim, lord of Galloway, earl of Douglas, 248, 254, 256
Douglas, Archibald II, earl of Douglas, duke of Touraine, 261, 266-8
  his son James, 267
Douglas, James de, earl of Douglas, 255-6
Douglas, William de, earl of Douglas, 248
Douglas, Archibald de, earl of Wigtown, 266
Douglas, James de, warden of the Marches, 207, 216
Douglas, William de, lord of Liddesdale, 221, 226-7, 229
  his illegitimate brother William, 227
Douglas, William, of Nithsdale, 254-5
Dover, Richard de, archbishop of Canterbury, 108
Drumalban, 21, 36
Dryburgh, abbey, 211, 253
Dryhthelm, monk at Old Melrose, 87-89
Dumbarton, 13
Dumfries, 197, 236
  Franciscan church, 197, 236
Dunbar, battle at, 184, 202
  castle, 171, 184-5, 222-3
  countess of. *See* Agnes
  earl of. *See* Patrick II, III and V; *see also* March, earl of
Dunbar, George I de, earl of March, 255
Dunbar, John de, earl of Moray, 255-6
Dunbar, Thomas I de, earl of Moray, 258
Dunbar, David de, knight, 284
Dunblane, bishop of. *See* Maurice; Stephenson, William
Duncan I, king of Scots, 45, 48, 49, 52
Duncan II, king of Scots, 111
  his son William, 111
Duncan I, earl of Fife, 65
Duncan III, earl of Fife, 174, 176, 180
Duncan IV, earl of Fife, 209
Dundalk, Ireland, battle at, 209
Dundee, 226
  castle, 188
Dundrennan, abbey, 66
Dunfermline, abbey, 64-66, 153, 168, 212, 215, 219, 270
  abbot of. *See* Ber, Alexander; Black, John; St Andrews, William de; Stramiglaw, John de
  prior of. *See* Mongal, Richard
Dungal, son of Selbach, king of Scots, 31
Dunipace, 253
Dunkeld, church, 73
  bishopric, 79
  bishop of. *See* Crambeth, Matthew de; Inverkeithing, Richard de; Liberatione, Geoffrey de; Sinclair, William de
  dean of. *See* Stuteville, Robert de
Dunsinane, 41
Dunskeath, castle, 111
Dupplin, battle at, 185
Durham, bishop of. *See* Bek, Anthony; Marsh, Richard; Ranulf Flambard
  prior of, 132, 133
  lands of St Cuthbert at, 230
Durward, Alan, justiciar, 143, 145
Dutch, the, 19

Earlston, Thomas de, prophet, 171-2
Ebro, river, Spain, 6
Edgar, king of Scots, 63
Edgar the Ætheling, 57, 58, 60-62
Edinburgh, 8, 13, 122, 143, 210, 215, 224, 235, 250-1, 253, 278,
  castle, 139, 185, 223, 225-7

keeper of. *See* Douglas, William de; Moray, William de
church of St Giles, 253, 265
Edward the Confessor, king of England, 52, 53, 55, 56
Edward I, king of England, 174-80, 180-5, 187, 189-90, 192, 195, 197-9, 201-2
Edward II, king of England, 174, 205, 207, 210-11, 215
Edward III, king of England, 217, 222, 234-5
Egypt, 5, 6, 8, 14, 21
Egyptians, the, 5
Eilean Donan, 214
Eildon, grange of Melrose abbey, 76
Elgin, 50
Elrisenius, companion of St Regulus, 19
Ely, 226
Emerea, St, with St Regulus, 19
Emonia, monastery of St Columba. *See* Inchcolm
Ennodius, bishop of Pavia, quoted, 3
Eochaid, king of Scots, 21
Eochaid Buide, king of Scots, 45
Eochaid Rothay, 155
Eric II, king of Norway, 174
Ermengarde, queen of Scots, wife of William I, 128
Erskine, Nicholas, knight, 252
Erskine, Thomas, knight, 252
Esk, river, 15
Etherdouer, castle, 111
Ethiopian, an, 135
Eugenius, hermit with St Regulus, 19
Evreux, France, count of. *See* Stewart, John

Fabricius, Roman general, 47
Falaise, Normandy, castle, 106
Falkirk, battle at, 192, 193, 203
Felix, hermit with St Regulus, 19
Fergus, son of Feradach (or Ferard), 11
Fergus II, son of Erc, king of Scots, 21
Fergus, son of Aed Find, king of Scots, 26
Fergus, lord of Galloway, 100
Ferracutus, 27
Ferryhill, near Durham, 229
Ferteth, earl of Strathearn, 100
Fettercairn, 41
Fife, nobles and freeholders of at Berwick, 182-3
thane of. *See* MacDuff
Earl of. *See* Duncan, I, III and IV; Malcolm; Steward, Robert
sheriff of, 208
Findlaech, father of Macbeth, 50
Finuele, 41-42
FitzAlan, Richard, earl of Arundel, 222
Flanders, troops from, 105
merchant fleet from, 275
Fleming, Malcolm, 228
Flemings, the, 19
Fogo, John, abbot of Melrose, 281-2
Fordun, John de, chaplain of Aberdeen, author, 1, 2
Forfar, 122, 136, 142
castle, 185
Forteviot, 34
Forth, Firth of, 7, 21, 39, 208, 221-2, 225, 246, 250
Fowlis, William, 263
France, constable of, 269
Francia, 28
Franks, the, 19
Fraser, William, bishop of St Andrews, 174-6
Fraser, William, man-at-arms, 226
Fulgentius, consul or duke of Britons of Albany, 14-15

Gaels, descendants of Gaythelos, 6
Galen, quoted, 267
Galicia, Spain, 27
Galloway, 100, 106, 117, 139, 213
men of, 105, 106, 139
bishop of. *See* Gilbert
lord of. *See* Alan; Fergus; Gilbert; Roland; Uthred; cf. Gillecolm
Galloway, Thomas of, earl of Atholl, 125, 128, 139
Gamelin, bishop of St Andrews, 157, 159
Garnard, son of Domnach, king of Picts, 37
Gascony, France, men from, 217
Gattonside, grange of Melrose abbey, 76
Gaucourt, France, sire de, 275

Gaul, 28
Gaythelos Glas, first king of Scots, 5, 6, 8, 147
Gelasius, companion of St Regulus, 19
Gigha, island, 7
Gilbert, bishop of Galloway, 139
Gilbert, bishop of Hamar, 155
Gilbert, earl of Strathearn, 128
Gilbert, son of Fergus, lord of Galloway, 117
Gilbert, a Scottish cleric, 108-10
'Gildas', prophecy of, 178
Gill, John, 263
Gillecolm, lord of part of Galloway, a rebel, 117
Gilpatrick, a rebel, 117
Gilroth, 139
Glasdale, William, 269
Glasgow, 23
  citizens of, 139
  bishop of. *See* Kentigern, St; St Albans, Walter of; Wischard, William; Wishart, Robert
Glenluce, abbey, monk of, 139
Gloucester, earl of. *See* Clare, Gilbert I and II de
Godwine, knight from Winchester, 60-62
Gobard, son of Charlemagne, 28
Godric, St, quoted, 102
Gowrie, earl of, 63
Graham, John, earl of Menteith, 229-30
Graham, Patrick de, 184
Graham, Robert, regicide, 283-4
Graville, France, sire de, 275
Gray, Walter, archbishop of York, 132
Greeks, the, 5, 51, 147
Gregory the Great, pope, quoted, 109, 209
Grim, son of Kenneth, king of Scots, 40-41, 44
Guala, papal legate. *See* Bicchieri, Guala
Guisborough, prior of, 132

Haakon IV, king of Norway 152-5
Haddington, 38, 127, 141, 234, 237, 248
  Franciscan church, 235
  nunnery 237
  Nungate and Nuns' Bridge, 237
Hæmgisl, a monk at Old Melrose and in Ireland, 89
Haldenston, James de, prior of St Andrews, 85
Halkirk, 136
Hamar, Norway, bishop of. *See* Gilbert
Harald, earl of Orkney and Caithness, 120
  his wife Hvarflod, 120
Harcarres, Adam de, abbot of Melrose, 139
Harcourt, John de, 267
Harold, first bishop of Argyll, 79
Haselrig, William de, sheriff of Lanark, 186
Hastings, David de, earl of Atholl, 141
Heisterbach, Caesarius of, quoted, 113-15
Henry, abbot of Arbroath, 181
Henry III/II, emperor, 52
Henry IV, emperor, 93
Henry I Beauclerc, king of England, 99
Henry II, king of England, 99-100, 106-7, 108
  his son Henry, the 'Young King', 105, 107
Henry III, king of England, 123, 132-3, 141, 143
Henry IV, king of England, 260
Henry V, king of England, 265, 285-6
Henry VI, king of England, 281
Henry, son of King David I, 65, 147
Hiber, son of Gaythelos, 6, 147
Hibernians, 6
Holkot, Robert, quoted, 157-9
Holm Cultram, abbey, 66
Holy Land (Palestine), 143, 165, 216, 228
Holyrood, abbey, 66, 100, 210, 248, 254
  sanctuary at, 224
Honorius, Roman emperor, 21
Honorius III, pope, 132
Hood, Robert, outlaw, 156
Horace, quoted, 134, 266
Humber, river, 105
Hungus, king of Picts, 20, 38, 39
Huntingdon, earldom of, 99
  earl of. *See* David; Senlis, Simon I and II de
Hurgust, son of Fergoso, king of Picts, 20

Inchaffray abbot of. *See* Maurice
Inchcolm, island, 8
abbey, 8, 64, 221-2, 251-2
abbot of. *See* Bower, Walter
Inchgarvie, island, 39
Inchkeith, island, 7, 226
Inchmarnock, island, 7
Inchmurdo, manor, 159, 246
Indians, king of the, 49. *See also* Porus
Indulf, king of Scots, 39-40
Innocent VI, pope, 231
Invergowrie, 63
Inverkeithing, 8, 168
Inverkeithing, John de, abbot of Scone, 281-2
Inverkeithing, Richard de, bishop of Dunkeld, chancellor 151
Inverness, 111, 213
battle near castle, 120
Iona (I, I Colmekill), island, 22, 48, 50
Ireland, island, 8, 9, 12, 22, 126, 139, 202, 207
king and magnates of, 209
king of. *See* Bruce, Edward de
Ireton, Ralph de, bishop of Carlisle, 174
Irish, the, 12, 21, 139, 285
Isabella, daughter of King William I, 123-4
Isabella, daughter of David earl of Huntingdon, wife of Robert de Bruce, 165
Isidore, St, quoted, 169
Islay, island, 7
Isles, lord of the. *See* Christina; Donald

James I, king of Scots, 273, 275, 276, 281, 283-8
James II, king of Scots, 273, 283, 290
Jargeau, France, 269
Jed, river, 167
Jedburgh, 136
abbey, 66
abbot of. *See* Morel, John
Jedwood, 167. *See also* Jedburgh
Jerome, St, quoted, 2, 46, 163-4, 241, 244, 249, 289, ?290
Jerusalem, Holy Sepulchre in, 216
Jews, 14, 51,174
in France, 112-13, 140
Joan (of Arc) from Lorraine, 269
Joan, Queen, wife of King James I, 284, 287
John Chrysostom, St, quoted, 214, 161
John, bishop of Caithness, 120
John, king of England, 121-4, 126-7, 132
John Balliol, king of Scots, 174, 176-82, 184-5, 188
John of Gaunt, duke of Lancaster, 248-9, 250-1, 254
John, earl of Caithness, 136-7
John de Fordun. *See* Fordun, John de
John, Franciscan friar at Avignon, 231
Johnson, Cristy, a cateran, 258
Joleta de Dreux, Queen. *See* Yolanda de Dreux
Jura, island, 7
Juvenal, quoted, 159

Kelso, abbey, 66
Kennedy, Henry, a rebel, 117
Kenneth I, son of Alpin, king of Scots, 34-36
Kenneth II, king of Scots, 40-42
Kennoway, castle, 53
Kentigern, St, bishop of Glasgow, 23
his *Life* quoted, 23
Kerrera, island, 144
Kilconcath (or Comyn), William de, bishop of Brechin, 176
Kilconquhar, 180
Kilgour, church, 209
Kilrymont (St Andrews), 19, 20, 263
monastery, 7, 20, 64
Kinbuck, Joachim de, 226
Kincardine, 126
Kinghorn Regis, 168
Kinloss, abbey, 66
abbot of. *See* Radulf
Kinross, 151, 218
Kirkmichael, John, bishop of Orleans, 269
Kirkpatrick, Roger I de, knight, 198, 236
Kirkpatrick, Roger II de, man-at-arms, 235-6
Knayton, Thomas, English marshal in Edinburgh castle, 223-4
Kravar, Paul, Bohemian heretic, 280
Lacy, Henry de, earl of Lincoln, 174

La Hire 'Bussak', French envoy, 275
Lamberton, William de, bishop of St Andrews, 209
Lamby, James, citizen of St Andrews, 219
Lamley, Radulf de, bishop of Aberdeen, 142
Lanark, 187
sheriff of. *See* Haselrig, William de
Lancaster, county of, 210
duke of. *See* John of Gaunt
Lanfranc, archbishop of Canterbury, 93, 146
Largs, 153-4
La Rochelle, France, 275
Lauder, Edward, archdeacon of Lothian, 275
Laundells, William de, bishop of St Andrews, 80
Leicester, 106
earl of. *See* Robert
Leith, 250
Le Mans, France, bishop of. *See* Maurice
Lennox, earl of. *See* Menteith, John de
Lewis, island, 7
Liberatione, Geoffrey de, bishop of Dunkeld, 145
Liff, 63
Limekilns, 98
Lincoln, earl of. *See* Lacy, Henry de
Lindores, abbey, 261
Lindores, Laurence de, 263, 280, 282
Lindsay, David, later earl of Crawford, 258
Lindsay, Alexander de, knight, 252
Lindsay, James I de, knight, 198, 236
Lindsay, James II de, knight, 235-6
Lindsay, William, of Rossie, knight, 261
his sister Euphemia de 261
Lionel, son of King Edward III, 238
Litstar, John, canon of St Andrews, 263
Little John, outlaw, 156
Loarn, brother of Fergus II king of Scots, 21
Lochindorb, castle, 227
Loch Leven, 218
castle, 218-20
keeper of. *See* Vipont, Alan de
prior of. *See* Montrose, Robert de
Lochmaben, 197, 198
Lochore, David de, 151
Logan, Robert, knight, 216
Logie, John, first husband of Queen Margaret, 239
Logie, Margaret. *See* Margaret, Queen, 239
Logy, Robert, canon of Scone, 257
Lollards, 280
Lombards, merchants in Scotland, 170-1
mercenaries in France, 268
London, 177, 180, 185, 195, 248-9
mayor of. *See* Walworth, William
Lothair I, emperor, 91, 92
Lothair, son of Charlemagne, 28
Lothian, 117, 122, 126, 228, 235, 236, 253
Louis I the Pious, emperor, 28, 31
Louis II, emperor, 91 92
Louis III the Blind, emperor, 92
Louis the German, king of East Francia, 91
Louis VII, king of France, 99, 107
Louis IX, king of France, 140
Louis, son of King Philip II of France, 132
Louis, dauphin, later King Louis XI of France, 274-5
Lucan, quoted, 146, 283-4
Lucerna, Valverde, Spain, 27
Lucius, king of the Britons, 14
Luke, hermit with St Regulus, 19
Lulach, king of Scots, 45
Lumphanan, 56
Lundie, Thomas de, doorward of King William I, 125
Lychton, Henry, bishop of Aberdeen, 275
Lycurgus, 51
Lyons, France, 14
schools at, 95
Second General Council at, 160

Macbeth, king of Scots, 45, 50, 52, 53, 55, 56
Macduff, thane of Fife, 53-55
Macduff, brother of Colban earl of Fife, 180, 193
Macedonia, 17

Machabeus, companion of St Regulus, 19
MacTaggart (Farquhar), earl of Ross, 139
MacWilliam *alias* Donald *Ban*, 111
MacWilliam, Guthred, 125-6
Made, Alexander, canon of Inchcolm, 271-2
Madianus, hermit with St Regulus, 19
Magnus III Olafsson, king of Norway, 156
Magnus IV, king of Norway, 154, 155
Mahomet, 51
Mainz, Germany, archbishopric of, 27
Malcolm II, son of Kenneth, king of Scots, 33, 34, 40, 44, 47, 48
Malcolm III Canmore, king of Scots, 7, 49, 52, 53, 55-60, 64, 65, 148
  vision of, 153
Malcolm IV, king of Scots, 65, 99-100, 101-2
Malcolm, earl of Angus, 128
Malcolm, earl of Fife, 125-6
Malmesbury, William of, quoted, 56
Malveisin, William, bishop of St Andrews, 122-3, 128, 133
'Mam Garvia', battle at, 111
Man, Isle of, 7
  castle, 7
  monastery, 7
Mar, army of, 142
  earl of. *See* Donald; William
March, earl of. *See* Dunbar, George I de. *See also* Dunbar, earl of
Margaret, St, Queen, wife of King Malcolm III, 7, 57-60, 64, 65, 148
Margaret, daughter of King Alexander III, queen of Norway, 173
  her daughter Margaret, 173-4
Margaret, Queen, widow of John Logie, wife of King David II, 239, 246
Margaret, daughter of King William I, 123-4
Margaret, daughter of King James I, dauphiness of France, 274-6
Margaret, lady of Seton 228
  her son William, 228
  her daughter Margaret, 228
Marsh, Richard, bishop of Durham, 132
Marjorie, countess of Carrick, 164
Martin, St, body of, 92-93
Mary de Coucy, Queen as second wife of King Alexander II, 141, 148
Mary, countess of Champagne, 113
Mateus, hermit with St Regulus, 19
Matilda, queen of England, sister of King David I, wife of Henry I, 99
Matilda, Queen, wife of King David I, 70
Maurice, archdeacon of Troyes in France, bishop of Le Mans, 73-75
Maurice, abbot of Inchaffray, bishop of Dunblane, 206
Maurice, earl of Menteith, 128
Mauricius, hermit with St Regulus, 19
Maximus, tyrant of Britain, 21
May, island, 7
  priory, 7
Mearns, 63
Medes, the, 158
Mediterranean Sea, 6, 19
Melrose, abbey, 66, 75-76, 123, 144, 210, 253
  abbot of. *See* Adam; Fogo, John; Harcarres, Adam de
  prior of. *See* Peebles, William
  cellarer of. *See* Thomas the Good
  granges of, 76
Melrose, Old, abbey, 87
  monks at. *See* Dryhthelm; Hæmgisl
Melun, John de, bishop of Poitiers, 213-14
Melville, Richard de, knight, 218
Menteith, earl of. *See* Comyn, Walter; Graham, John; Maurice; Steward, Alexander; Steward, Robert
Menteith, John de, earl of Lennox, 195
Mercians, the, 24
Merniacus, brother of St Damian, companion of St Regulus, 19
Meung-sur-Loire, France, 269
Milo, king of Scots, 8
Mirenus, companion of St Regulus, 19
Molesme, Robert de, abbot of Cîteaux, 96
'Molmoran', a traitor, 227
Mongal, Richard, prior of Dunfermline, 98
Monmouth, Geoffrey of, quoted, 15

Montague, William de, earl of Salisbury, 222-3
Montgomery, John, of that Ilk, 259
Montrose, castle, 185
Montrose, Robert de, prior of Loch Leven, prior of St Andrews, official of St Andrews, 81-83
Monymusk, priors of, 85
Monzievaird. *See* Plain of Bards
Moravia, Andrew de, bishop of Moray, 143
Moray, 63, 111, 120, 125-6, 141
  bishop of. *See* Moravia, Andrew de
  earl of. *See* Dunbar, Thomas I de; Randolph, John; Randolph, Thomas I
Moray, Andrew I de, 188
Moray, Andrew II de, guardian, 188, 225-6
Moray, Angus de, a cateran, 279
Moray, William de, keeper of Edinburgh castle, 228
Morel, John, abbot of Jedburgh, 176
Morgrund, Malcolm, 125
Mortimer, Roger de, sheriff of Perth, 122
Mowbray, Geoffrey de, 176
'Mucross' (St Andrews), 19, 20
Muglington, 24
Musselburgh, 215

Narbonne, William, viscount of, 267
Neolus, king of Greece, 5, 147
Nerius, companion of St Regulus, 19
Neville, Robert, English knight, 207
Neville's Cross, near Durham, battle at, 229
Newark, Henry de, dean of York, 174
Newbattle, abbey, 66, 127, 253
Newcastle, 65, 121, 180, 189, 255
  monastery of Black monks, 66
  Premonstratensian canons of, 66
  nunnery, 66
Nieul, France, priory, 275
Norham, 121, 123, 127, 177, 178
Normandy, France, 96-97, 106
Normans, the, 19
Northallerton, 133
Northampton, 108
North Berwick, 235
North Queensferry, 251
Northumberland, 99, 105, 106
  earl of. *See* Percy, Henry
Northumbria, 87, 189-90
  earl of. *See* Siward
Northumbrians, the, 38, 65, 106, 255
Norwegians, the, 21, 39, 154
Nostell, monastery of St Oswald, 64
Nydie, near St Andrews, 261

Ocean, 6-8, 19
Ochil Hills, 221
Ogilvie, Henry de, 263
Ogilvie, Patrick, knight, sheriff of Angus, justiciar, 275
Ogle, Robert, English knight, 256
Olifard, William, commander of English at Perth, 204
Orgar, English knight, 60-62
Orkney, islands, 36, 120, 154
Orleans, France, siege of, 269
  bishop of. *See* Kirkmichael, John
Oronsay, island, 7
  monastery, 7
Otterburn in Redesdale, battle at, 255
Ovid, quoted, 146, 250, 251, 274
Oykell, river, 120

Pamplona, Spain, 27
Paris, France, 137-8, 140, 269
  churches, 27
  bishop of. *See* Sully, Maurice de
  university, 281
    student at. *See* Stramiglaw, John de
  a provost of, 118
  Jews in, 112
Parthians, the, 14
Patras, Greece, 17
Patrick, St, 37
Patrick, earl of Atholl, 141-2
Patrick II, earl of Dunbar (d.1248), 139
Patrick III, earl of Dunbar (d.1289), 171-2
Patrick V, earl of Dunbar (d.1368), 229-30
Peebles, William, prior of Melrose, 210
Penrith, lands of, 176
Pentland Hills, 224
Percy, Henry, earl of Northumberland, 255, 260

Percy, Henry, the younger (Hotspur), 255-6
Percy, Ralph, 256
Persians, the, 158
Perth (Bertha), 100, 120, 124-5, 128, 142, 155, 165, 203-4, 225, 258, 278, 281, 288
  Blackfriars monastery, 281, 284
  sheriff of. *See* Mortimer, Roger de
Pescennius Niger, Roman imperial claimant, 14
Peter, St, apostle, 17, 18, 91, 101
Peter, canon of Inchcolm, 271-2
Pharaoh. *See* Chencres
Phenius, grandfather of Gaythelos, 6
Philip II Augustus, king of France, 112-14, 118, 129, 131, 137-8
Philip IV, king of France, 181, 189
Philip, hermit with St Regulus, 19
Phroneus, 51
Pictavia, kings of, 7
  kingdom of, 19, 21
Picts, nation of, 9-12, 14-17, 21, 22, 31-36
  kingdom of, 31, 32, 34-36
Pitgaveny, 50
Pladda, island, 7
Plain of Bards (Monzievaird), 44
Platar, Thomas, canon of St Andrews, 82-83
Pliny, quoted, 265
Plutarch, perhaps quoted, 51, 150
Poitiers, France, 213
  bishop of. *See* Comborel, Hugh de; Melun, John de
Poitou, men of, 19
Pole, William de la, earl of Suffolk, 269
  his two brothers, 269
Polyphemus, 105
'Pontissey', France, sire de, 275
Porchester, castle, 106
Port Haven, 272
Porus, Indian king, 158
Potencia, St, with St Regulus, 19
Prague, Bohemia, heretics of, 280
Premonstratensian order, 66
Prenderguest, Robert, 223-4
Pyrrhus, king of Epirus, 47

Quincy, Saer de, earl of Winchester, 122

Radulf, abbot of Kinloss, 134
Ramornie, John, knight, 26
Randolph, John, earl of Moray, 229-30
Randolph, Thomas I, earl of Moray, 212-15
Ranulf Flambard, bishop of Durham, 93
Redman, Matthew de, English knight, 256
Regulus, St, abbot, 17-20
Remigius, St, 91
Rey Cross, 23
Rheims, Champagne, France, 269
  archbishop of. *See* Chartres, Reginald de
Rhine, river, 20
Rhone, river, 20
Richard I, king of England, 117-18
Richard II, king of England, 248-50, 253-4, 259-60
Richard, son of John king of England, 123
Richmond, 106
  earl of. *See* Brittany, John de
Rievaulx, abbey, 211
Ripon, church of St Wilfrid, 23
Robert, bishop of Ross, 128
Robert, provost of Aire, bishop of Arras and Cambrai, France, 102
Robert I, king of Scots 199-201, 203-7, 209-12, 216
Robert II, king of Scots, 246-8
Robert III, king of Scots, 257-63
Robert, earl of Leicester, 105-6
  his wife, 105
Rochechouart, Guy, bishop of Saintes, France, 275
Rochester, 24
Roderic, a rebel, 120
Roger, archbishop of York, 108, 110
Roger (of Leicester), bishop of St Andrews, 120
Roland, son of Uthred, lord of Galloway, 117
Romans, Humbert de, quoted, 115
Romans, the, 12, 14, 15, 21, 45, 47, 150
Rome, 12, 101, 232, 246
  citizens of, 101
  papal court of, 133, 165, 213
Romulus, founder of Rome, 101, 150

Roncesvalles, Spain, battle of, 27, 28
Ros, Robert de, 122, 149
Rosemarkie, 225
Roslin, battle at, 203
Ross, bishop of. *See* Bullock, John; Robert; Waghorn, Alexander de
Ross, 120, 125-6
  thanes of, 126
  earldom of, 111
  earl of. *See* MacTaggart, Thomas; William
Ross, Walter de, knight, 207
Rothesay, castle, 152
  duke of. *See* Stewart, David
Rouen, France, 269
Roxburgh, 121, 281
  castle, 120
Rymont. *See* Kilrymont

St Albans, Walter of, bishop of Glasgow, 122, 128
St Andrews (Kilrymont), 280, 282
  castle, 81, 261
  church, 64, 81, 84-85, 159, 209
    canons of, 231
  bishop of. *See* Bernham, David de; Fraser, William; Gamelin; Lamberton, William de; Laundells, William de; Malveisin, William; Roger (de Leicester); Trayl, Walter; Turgot; Wardlaw, Henry de; Wischard, William
  priors of. *See* Biset, James; Biset, Thomas; Haldenston, James de; Montrose, Robert de; Roger
  University, 85, 263-4
  archdeacon of. *See* Wischard, William
  official of. *See* Montrose, Robert de; Scheves, John
St Andrews, William de, abbot of Dunfermline, 98
St Denis, near Paris, France, 28, 113, 269
  abbey, tomb of the saint, 28
    abbot. *See* William
    provost. *See* Caesarius
St Germain-en-Laye, 113
St Jean-d'Angély, Gascony, France, 176
St John's Town. *See* Perth
St Margaret's Bay, 57
St Matthew of the Havens, at Breton Race, France, 275
St Kilda, island, 7
St Monance, church, 230
St Victor, Hugh of, quoted, 245, 264
Saintes, France, 177
  bishop of. *See* Rochechouart, Guy
Sajanus, hermit with St Regulus, 19
Salisbury, earl of. *See* Montague, William de
Salisbury Park, near Edinburgh, 224
Salzburg, Austria, archbishopric of, 27
Samuel, a rebel
San Stefano, Italy, 232
Saracens, 27-29, 51, 216
Saxons, the, 20, 35
Scales, Thomas Lord, 269
Scheabeg, a cateran, 258
Scheves, John official of St Andrews, 263
Scone, 47, 64, 128, 145, 176, 199, 238, 246, 257
  abbey, 63, 64
  abbot of. *See* Crannach, Adam de; Inverkeithing, John de
Scot, Michael, 174
Scota, wife of Gaythelos, 5, 147
  the Scots her descendants, 6, 7
Scotia (Ireland), 6
Scotia (Scotland), 6, 7, 8, 15, 17, 22, 55
Scotland, prince of. *See* Stewart, David
Scots, nation of, 5, 9-12, 14-16, 21, 31-35, 39, 50, 56, 72, 100
  kingdom of, 21, 34, 72
Scrope, [ ], English knight, 281
Scythia, 17
Seine, river, France, 138
Selkirk, John, 261
Seneca, quoted, 51, 102, 109, 177, 192, 287. *See also* Braga, Martin of
Senlis, France, 269
Senlis, Simon I de, earl of Huntingdon, 69
Senlis, Simon II de, earl of Huntingdon, 69
Serf (Servanus), St, 7, 219
Serlo, a monk, 136
Servanus. *See* Serf

Seton, lady of. *See* Margaret
Severus, Roman emperor, 12, 14, 15
Silvius, companion of St Regulus, 19
Simon Brecc, 8
Sinclair, William, bishop of Dunkeld, 208
Sinclair, William de, knight, 216
Siward, earl of Northumbria, 49, 52, 55, 56
Siward, Richard, 184
Skye, island, 7
Slioch, battle at, 201
South Queensferry, 168, 170, 251-2
Spain, 6, 8, 27, 275
  king of. *See* Castile
Spartans, the, 51
Spey, river, 63
Stainmore, 23, 190, 210
Steersman, Alan, a seaman, 225
Stephen, king of England, 69
Stephenson, William, bishop of Dunblane, 263
Steward, Alexander, earl of Menteith, 184
Steward, Alexander, of Dundonald, 154
Stewart, David, duke of Rothesay, earl of Carrick, prince of Scotland, 260-1, 283
Stewart, David, of Rosyth, 1, 289
Steward, James, guardian, 174
Steward, John, brother of James Steward, 193
Stewart, John, earl of Carrick, later King Robert III, q.v., 248
Stewart, John, earl of Buchan, chamberlain of Scotland, constable of France, 265-7
Stewart, John, of Darnley, count of Evreux, lord of Concressault and Aubigny, constable of Scots in France, 274
Steward, Robert, later King Robert II, q.v., 226, 228, 229-30
Steward, Robert, earl of Fife and Menteith, duke of Albany, 255, 259-61, 265, 270
  his son Murdoch and grandsons
    Walter and Alexander, 283
Stewart, Robert, grandson of Walter Stewart earl of Atholl, regicide, 283-4
Steward, Walter son of Alan I (d.1177), 154
Steward, Walter, husband of Marjorie Bruce, 154
Stewart, Walter, earl of Atholl, 283-4
Stirling, 122, 128-9, 151
  castle, 185, 194, 260, 270
  church of Blackfriars, 260
Stirling Bridge, battle at, 188, 203
Straiton, Walter, royal page, 284
Stramiglaw, John de, abbot of Dunfermline, 232-3
Strathbogie, John de, earl of Atholl, 184
Strathearn, earl of. *See* Ferteth; Gilbert
Strathnaver, battle in, 279
Strathtyrum, near St Andrews, 261
Straw, Jack, English peasant leader, 248-9
Strivelyn, John de, English knight, 218-20
Stuteville, Robert de, dean of Dunkeld, acting chancellor of Scotland, 151
Sudbury, Simon, archbishop of Canterbury, 248
Suetonius, quoted, 46
Suffolk, earl of. *See* Pole, William de la, 269
Sully, Henry de, 211
Sully, Maurice de, bishop of Paris, 119
Sunderland Bridge, near Durham, 229
Surrey, earl of. *See* Warenne, John de
Sutherland, 120
Swinton, John, knight, 256
Swinton, John, lord of that Ilk, 267
Syria, 14

Talbot, John Lord, 269
Tamworth, 24
Tara, Ireland, 8
Tay, river, 124, 258
Tarquin, king of Rome, 51
Templar (unidentified), almoner to KingWilliam I, 122
Teutons, the, 19
Teviotdale, 227
Thames, river, 109
Thomas Aquinas, St, quoted, 131
Thomas Becket, St, archbishop of

Canterbury, 24, 102, 106, 107, 110
Thomas the Good, cellarer of Melrose Abbey, 75-76
Thorfinn Haraldsson, 120
Thracians, the, 45
Thule, 7
Tiber, river, 20
Tiree, island, 7
Tironensian order, 66
Tongland abbey, prior and sacrist of, 139
Tonnerre, Louis count of 267-8
Toulouse, France, 99-100
church in, 27
Tours, France, 100, 269, 275
body of St Martin at, 92-93
Trajan, Roman emperor, 67
Tranent, coalminers of, 210
Traquair, 123
Trayl, Walter, bishop of St Andrews, 80-83
Triduana, St, with St Regulus 19
Trier, Germany, archbishopric of, 27
Troyes, France, archdeacon of. *See* Maurice
Turgot, bishop of St Andrews, 64
his *Life of Margaret*, quoted, 58, 59
Turnberry, castle, 164
Tweed, river, 87, 121
Tweedmouth, castle, 121, 123, 132
Tyne, river, East Lothian, 33
Tyne, river, Northumberland, 15, 36
Tynemouth, prior of, 132

Umfraville, Ingram de, English knight, 206-7
Upsettlington, 178
Urquhart, prior of. *See* Black, John
Uthred, son of Fergus lord of Galloway, 100, 117

Valerius Maximus, quoted, 51, 101, 242-4, 278
Valognes, Philip de, chamberlain to King William I, 122
Varro, ? quoted, 242-3
Vegetius Renatus, quoted, 279
Vendeuvre-sur-Barse, France, cleric from, 95
Venice, Italy, doge of, 45
Verneuil in Perche, France, battle of, 266-8
Vesci, William de, knight, 174
Vescy, Eustace de, son-in-law of King William I, 127
Vespasian, Roman emperor, 12
Vezza, Bohemond di. *See* Bagimond
Vieuxpont, Robert de, English knight, 124
Vieuxpont, William de, Scottish knight, 207
Vincennes, France, 140
Vipont, Alan de, keeper of Loch Leven castle, 219
Virgil, quoted, 51
Vitry, James de, quoted, 28

Waghorn, Alexander de, bishop of Ross, 264
Wales, 122, 127, 202, 217
Wallace, Andrew, knight, brother of William Wallace, 187
Wallace, Malcolm, knight, father of William Wallace, 186
Wallace, William, guardian, 186-93, 194-5
Waltheof, St, son of Simon de Senlis I earl of Huntingdon, 69-71, 75-76
Walworth, William, mayor of London, 249
Warenne, earl of. *See* Warenne, John de
Warenne, John I de, earl of Warenne/Surrey, 174
Warenne, John II de, earl of Warenne/Surrey, 210
Wark, castle, 105
Wartburg, Germany, 24
Wemyss, 215
Wemyss, David de, knight, 218
Wemyss, John, knight, 153-4
Wemyss, Michael I de, knight, 174
Wemyss, Michael II de, 218
Western Isles, 52, 254, 259
Westmorland, 106
West Saxons, 23
Whithorn, bishop of. *See* Galloway
Wigtown, 213
earl of. *See* Douglas, Archibald de
William I, king of England, 93

William II, king of England, 60, 93-95, 146
William I, king of Scots, 65, 105-8, 110-11, 117-18, 120-8, 147, 173
William, abbot of St Denis, France, 113
William, earl of Mar, 149, 151
William, earl of Ross, 184
Winchester, earl of. *See* Quincy, Saer de
Wisbech, Walter de, archdeacon of York (East Riding), 132-3
Wischard, William, archdeacon and bishop of St Andrews, king's chancellor, bishop-elect of Glasgow, 159-60
Wishart, Robert, bishop of Glasgow, 174, 178, 184
Wright, John, 261
Wyclif, John, errors of, 280
Wynton, Alan de, man-at-arms, 228

Yolanda (or Joleta) de Dreux, Queen, second wife of King Alexander III, 167, 177
York, 15, 143, 211, 255
  archbishop of. *See* Gray, Walter de; Roger
  archdeacon of (East Riding). *See* Wisbech, Walter de
  dean of. *See* Newark, Henry de